P9-ECR-122

HUMANISTIC PSYCHOLOGY

Concepts and Criticisms

PATH IN PSYCHOLOGY
Published in Cooperation with Publications for the Advancement of Theory and History in Psychology (PATH)

Series Editors:
David Bakan, *York University*
John Broughton, *Teachers College, Columbia University*
Miriam Lewin, *Manhattanville College*
Robert Rieber, *John Jay College, CUNY, and Columbia University*
Howard Gruber, *Rutgers University*

WILHELM WUNDT AND THE MAKING OF A SCIENTIFIC PSYCHOLOGY
Edited by R. W. Rieber

HUMANISTIC PSYCHOLOGY: Concepts and Criticisms
Edited by Joseph R. Royce and Leendert P. Mos

HUMANISTIC PSYCHOLOGY

Concepts and Criticisms

Edited by

Joseph R. Royce
and
Leendert P. Mos

University of Alberta
Edmonton, Alberta, Canada

Plenum Press • New York and London

Library of Congress Cataloging in Publication Data

Main entry under title:

Humanistic psychology.

Includes bibliographies and indexes.
1. Humanistic psychology. I. Royce, Joseph R. II. Mos, Leendert P. (date) [DNLM: 1. Psychology—Collected works. BF 204 H919]

BF204.H868 150 81-2521
ISBN 0-306-40596-2 AACR2

A Division of Plenum Publishing Corporation
233 Spring Street, New York, N.Y. 10013

Printed in the United States of America

CONTRIBUTORS

Daniel E. Berlyne, Late of the Department of Psychology, University of Toronto, Toronto, Ontario, Canada

John Charles Cooper, Dean of Academic Affairs, Winebrenner Theological Seminary, Findlay, Ohio

Harold G. Coward, Department of Religious Studies, University of Calgary, Calgary, Alberta, Canada

Harry Garfinkle, Department of Educational Foundations and Theoretical Psychology Center, University of Alberta, Edmonton, Alberta, Canada

Amedeo P. Giorgi, Department of Psychology, Duquesne University, Pittsburgh, Pennsylvania

Carl F. Graumann, Psychologisches Institut der Universität Heidelberg, Heidelberg, Federal Republic of Germany

Richard Jung, Department of Sociology and Theoretical Psychology Center, University of Alberta, Edmonton, Alberta, Canada

Donald Kuiken, Department of Psychology, University of Alberta, Edmonton, Alberta, Canada

Joseph Lyons, Department of Psychology, University of California at Davis, Davis, California

Floyd W. Matson, Department of American Studies, University of Hawaii at Manoa, Honolulu, Hawaii

Harold G. McCurdy, Department of Psychology, University of North Carolina at Chapel Hill, Chapel Hill, North Carolina

Leendert P. Mos, Theoretical Psychology Center, University of Alberta, Edmonton, Alberta, Canada

Carl Rogers, Center for Studies of the Person, La Jolla, California

Joseph R. Royce, Theoretical Psychology Center, University of Alberta, Edmonton, Alberta, Canada

Herman Tennessen, Deparment of Philosophy and Theoretical Psychology Center, University of Alberta, Edmonton, Alberta, Canada

Thaddeus E. Weckowicz, Department of Psychiatry and Theoretical Psychology Center, University of Alberta, Edmonton, Alberta, Canada

FOREWORD

THE FORMATIVE TENDENCY

I have often pointed out that in my work with individuals in therapy, and in my experience in encounter groups, I have been led to the conviction that human nature is essentially constructive. When, in a therapeutic climate (which can be objectively defined) a person becomes sharply aware of more of his or her internal experiencing and of the stimuli and demands from the external world, thus acquiring a full range of options, the person tends to move in the direction of becoming a socially constructive organism.

But many are critical of this point of view. Why should such a positive direction be observed only in humans? Isn't this just pure optimism?

So quite hesitantly, because I have to draw on the work and thinking of others rather than on my own experience, I should like to try to set this directional tendency in a much broader context. I shall draw on my general reading in the field of science, but I should like to mention a special indebtedness to the work of Lancelot Whyte in *The Universe of Experience* (Harper and Row, 1974), the last book he wrote before his death. Though the book has flaws, in my judgment this historian has some thought-provoking themes to advance. I have learned from many others as well.

My main thesis is this. There appears to be a formative tendency

This paper constitutes the opening comments by the author at the Association of Humanistic Psychology Theory Conference, April 5, 1975. Reprinted by permission of the author and the *Journal of Humanistic Psychology*, where it appeared in 1978, Vol. 18, No. 1.

at work in the universe which can be observed at every level. This tendency has received much less attention than it deserves.

Physical scientists up to now have focused primarily on entropy, the tendency toward deterioration. They know a great deal about this tendency toward disorder. Studying closed systems they can give this tendency a clear, mathematical description. They know that order or organization tends to deteriorate into randomness, each stage less organized than the last.

We are also very familiar with deterioration in organic life. The system—whether plant, animal, or human—eventually deteriorates into a lower degree of functioning organization, into a lesser and lesser degree of order, until decay reaches stasis. In one sense this is what a part of medicine is all about—a concern with the malfunctioning or the deterioration of an organ, or the organism as a whole. The complex process of the death of the physical organism is increasingly well understood.

So a great deal is known of the universal tendency of systems at all levels to deteriorate in the direction of less and less orderliness, more and more randomness. When it operates, it is a one-way street.

But there is far less recognition of, or emphasis on, the even more important formative tendency which can be equally well observed at every level of the universe. After all, every form which we see or know emerged from a simpler, less complex, form. This is a phenomenon which stands as being at least as significant as entropy. Examples could be given from every form of inorganic or organic life. Let me illustrate just a few.

It appears that every galaxy, every star, every planet, including our own, was formed from a less organized whirling storm of particles. Many of these stellar objects are themselves formative. In the atmosphere of our sun, hydrogen nuclei collide to form molecules of helium, more complex in nature. It is hypothesized that in other stars even heavier molecules are formed by such interactions.

I understand that when the simple materials of the earth's atmosphere which were present before life began (e.g., water and ammonia) are infused by electric charges or by radiation, heavier molecules begin to form and are converted into amino acids. We seem only a step away from the formation of viruses and more complex living organisms. It is a creative, not a disintegrative, process at work.

Another fascinating example is the formation of crystals. In every case, from less ordered and less symmetrical fluid matter, there emerges the startlingly unique, ordered, symmetrical and often beautiful crystalline form. All of us have marvelled at the perfection and complexity of the snowflake.

When we consider the single living cell, we discover that it often forms more complex colonies, as in the coral reef. Even more order enters the picture as the cell emerges into an organism of many cells with specialized functions.

I don't need to picture the whole gradual process of organic evolution. We are familiar with the steadily increasing complexity of organisms. They are not always successful in their ability to cope with the changing environment, but the trend toward complexity is always evident.

Perhaps for most of us the process of organic evolution is best recognized as we consider the development of the single fertilized human ovum through the simplest stages—the aquatic gill stage, and on to the vastly complex, highly organized human infant. As Jonas Salk has said, there is a manifest and increasing order in evolution.

Thus, without ignoring the tendency toward deterioration, we need to recognize fully what Whyte (1974) calls the "morphic tendency," the ever operating trend toward increased order and interrelated complexity evident at the inorganic, the organic, and the human level. The universe is always building and creating as well as deteriorating.

Jonas Salk points out that consciousness has a very small part in all this. I would agree. A number of years ago I used the metaphor of the human organism as a pyramid of organic functioning, partly suffused by an unconscious knowing, with only the tip of the pyramid being fleetingly illuminated by the flickering light of fully conscious awareness. We are thus much wiser (organismically speaking) than our intellects, than our consciousness. It seems, however, that the human organism has been moving toward the more complete development of awareness, perhaps the highest of the human functions.

Some of my colleagues have said that organismic choice—the nonverbal, subconscious choice of being—is guided by the evolutionary flow. I would agree and go one step further. I would point out that in psychotherapy we have learned something about the psychological conditions which are most conducive to self-awareness. With greater self-awareness a more informed choice is possible, a choice freer from introjects, a conscious choice which is even more in tune with the evolutionary flow. There is (to use Claudio Naranjo's term) an organismic convergence with that directional evolutionary process.

I would like to use Gregory Bateson's statement as an example. He says that he has never made a choice in his life, that he floats like a cork on the interrelated network of ongoing ideas both inside and outside his skin. I would be so bold as to suggest that the more Gregory's cork is *aware,* not only of the *ideas* inside and outside his skin, but of the ongoing flow of feelings and emotions and physiological reactions which he senses in himself and in others, the more surely he will float in a direction consonant with the directional evolutionary flow. Thus, consciousness can participate in this creative, formative tendency.

But then Stan Grof and Joan Halifax (and others) have taken us beyond the ordinary level of consciousness. Their studies appear to reveal that in altered states of consciousness persons feel they are in touch with, and grasp the meaning of, this evolutionary flow, and that it tends toward a transcending experience of unity. The individual self seems dissolved in a whole area of higher values, especially beauty and harmony.

Thus, overall, I would like to state a hypothesis, very tentative in nature, but which for the sake of clarity I will state in definite terms.

It is hypothesized that there is a formative directional tendency in the universe, which can be traced and observed in stellar space, in crystals, in microorganisms, in organic life, in human beings. This is an evolutionary tendency toward greater order, greater interrelatedness, greater complexity. In humankind it extends from a single-cell origin to complex organic functioning, to an awareness and sensing below the level of consciousness, to a conscious awareness of the organism and the external world, to a transcendent awareness of the unity of the cosmic system including people.

It seems to me just possible that this hypothesis could be a base upon which we could begin to build a theory for humanistic psychology.

CARL ROGERS

Reference

Whyte, L. *The universe of experience.* New York: Harper & Row, 1974.

CONTENTS

INTRODUCTION

Humanistic psychology is a peculiarly North American phenomenon. As an academic movement, it arose in protest to Anglo-American scientific psychology—opposed to the excesses and limitations of positivistic science—and flourished, somewhat parasitically, on various strains of European philosophy, notably the existentialist and phenomenological traditions. Its initial impact in the late 1940s and early 1950s came by way of the personality theorists and practitioners of psychology who rejected the reductionism of both behaviorism and psychoanalytic theory. In the social-political climate of the 1960s, humanistic psychology was identified with the human-potential movement, thereby affecting not only the academic community (Koch, 1974) but also society at large (Roszak, 1969).

Not surprisingly, the psychoanalytic movement was not disturbed by these developments. After all, its practitioners had always considered themselves humanists. Moreover, its theoretical progress during the 1930s and 1940s, which remained relatively immune to the influences of academic behavioristic psychology, was explicitly antireductionistic. Furthermore, the humanists of the counterculture (e.g., N. O. Brown and H. Marcuse) were themselves proponents of and contributors to psychoanalytic thought. Indeed, it has become quite apparent that the clinical writings of Sigmund Freud and the neo-Freudians must be counted as an integral part of the intellectual ancestry of current humanistic perspectives on psychotherapy (Burton, 1967).

The influence of humanistic psychology on behaviorism during this same period is somewhat more problematic. Thus, while behaviorists notably moved on to study more complex human phenomena (they staunchly maintained that nothing in their methodology ever prevented them from doing so) it is perhaps curious that they were willing to identify themselves as engaged in a humanistic enterprise (e.g., MacCorquodale, 1969). Of course, the substantive work of such humanistic psychologists as G. W. Allport, C. Buhler, K. Goldstein, G. A. Kelly, A. H. Maslow, G. Murphy, H. A. Murray, C. R. Rogers, and others, as well as the considerable body of research initiated by their students, was dealt with routinely in psychology courses; yet, perhaps, most of that research was well within the methodological scope of a behavioral if not a behavioristic psychology. In any case, behaviorists can find support for their claim to be engaged in humanistic science in Abraham Maslow's vision of the emergence of a comprehensive psychology—a humanistic psychology—which includes the psychology of behaviorism and psychoanalysis (Maslow, 1968).

This is not to deny that there were and still are matters of profound disagreement between behaviorism and humanistic psychology—matters pertaining to man and method, society and science, and values and vocabulary (see, e.g., Rogers & Skinner, 1956). But there has also been rapprochement (Wandersman, Poppen, & Ricks, 1976) and, in the words of one observer, "a blunting rather than sharpening of the contrasts between behaviorism and phenomenology" (Wann, 1964, p. vii). Whatever may be the eventual outcome of communication (pertaining largely to methodology) between the behaviorists and the humanists of the phenomenological tradition, such communication is seemingly impossible between humanistic psychology in the existentialist tradition and behaviorism. In fact, the phenomenological and existentialist influences within humanistic psychology have remained quite distinct (Misiak & Sexton, 1973). The influence of the former has been rather more systematic and is more widely evident within the discipline of psychology. No doubt this is partly due to an established Gestalt research tradition and a respected European history of phenomenology in psychiatry (e.g., Karl Jaspers) and psychology (e.g., J. H. van den Berg, M. Merleau-Ponty, and E. Straus). Phenomenology was given prominence in the Rice symposium (Wann, 1964), and it received extensive theoretical exposition by Giorgi (1970) and substantive research support by the Duquesne group (Giorgi, Faber, & Eckartsberg, 1971; Giorgi, Fisher, & Murray, 1975). The existentialist perspective, which is particularly identified with the practice of psychiatry and psychotherapy (e.g., L. Binswanger, M. Boss, V. Frankl, E. Fromm, R. May, and also R. D. Laing and F. Perls), attained a place within humanistic psychology under the existential-humanistic label (van Kaam, 1966). Existential-humanistic psychology, which usually adheres to a phenomenological method and may count psychoanalysis as a strong substantive influence, has been especially influential in exploring the application of existential views of man in clinical and literary domains (Greening, 1971; Valle & King, 1978). In general, existential themes serve to uniquely qualify much of the historical development of humanistic psychology, whereas phenomenology as research methodology is probably common to all proponents of the movement. Thus, while some humanistic psychologists within the phenomenological tradition might reject certain existentialist views, the hyphenated existential-phenomenological label is probably acceptable to most adherents of "third-force" psychology.

The more eclectic writings of humanistic psychologists (e.g., Bugental, 1967; Goble, 1970; Jourard, 1968; Severin, 1965; Sutich & Vich, 1969; Wilson, 1972) have been largely exploratory and polemical with regard to new images of man—including not only existentialist and phenomenological views but also those of Marxist humanism (e.g., Fromm, 1965), Christianity (e.g., Hammes, 1971), and a host of other religious prescriptions (e.g., Watts, 1961) and ideologies—and only programmatic regarding formal theory and research methods. Since the proponents of all these rather diverse views can identify themselves with the term "humanistic," it is not surprising that its meaning has become rather problematic as it pertains to distinctive theory and method. Indeed, the last decade has seen a renewed focus on the terms "human" and "man" as these circumscribe prescriptions for the study of psychology (e.g., Kinget, 1975; Severin, 1973). What this suggests is that the initial revolutionary goal of the "third force" has been largely acknowledged by the academic community and that its proponents have settled down to the more modest but necessary task of formulating the specific problems and seeking the systematic answers of a human psychology.

The fourteen chapters included in this volume are intended to provide a selective and critical examination of some of humanistic psychology's contributions to date. They do so by concentrating on the conceptual presuppositions and theoretical formulations of the movement. What new concepts has humanistic psychology provided? In what sense is psychology both humanistic and scientific? What is the appropriate methodology for a humanistic psychology? What is its epistemology? What is its impact on other disciplines? This volume provides a historical, critical, and constructive forum for these foundational questions; it is not a rallying point for apologists of humanistic psychology or any of its ideologies. While therapeutic applications of humanistic psychology are not emphasized, the relevant conceptual issues are not excluded.

The majority of the contributors to this volume are psychologists. Nevertheless, the following chapters constitute a broadly evolving orientation whose diverse academic roots include philosophy, psychiatry, anthropology, sociology, and religion. Often the chapters have little or no apparent commonality, yet the authors all share the belief that a human psychology can develop only with due cognizance of a historical perspective, a philosophy, an anthropology, a theoretical program, and a methodology arising from the content of experience. Not unexpectedly, therefore, the range of content of these chapters is very broad indeed. While third-force psychology as an academic movement probably has little more coherence now than it did 20 years ago, its influence has not diminished. The movement has changed and has effected change—and the present volume attests to this state of affairs.

The chapters in Part I, The Historical Context, are focused on the philosophical and historical influences on humanistic psychology. Graumann provides an analysis of the historical roots of humanism both within and outside the discipline of psychology. Humanism outside psychology includes classical humanism (the shaping of the personality ideal by Greek and Roman classics during the Renaissance), socialist humanism (the freeing of the oppressed classes by revolution), and critical humanism (post–World War II impact of phenomenology, existentialism, and structuralism). American humanistic psychology is viewed as conceptually based on classical individualistic rather than critical humanism. As such, it emerges as an approach which is focused on the individual at the cost of the social context. Graumann recommends a dialectical analysis of the individual-situated-in-society as a corrective for unbridled individualism. He also recommends a human rather than a humanistic or naturalistic psychology and the key to this human psychology involves a phenomenological analysis of the "situated person." (Floyd Matson, in his Epilogue to this volume, provides an essential elaboration of the roots of American individualistic humanism as exemplified in humanistic psychology.) Giorgi argues that the discipline of psychology needs a conceptual framework which can accommodate its two cultures. Thus, he wants to maintain a scientific methodology, but not at the cost of studying what is uniquely human.

According to Giorgi, the key to the dilemma is the recognition that psychology does not have an adequate theory of man on the one hand, while maintaining a commitment to a natural-science methodology on the other hand. His answer is cast in terms of what he calls a "human science," founded on the problems of lived experience and guided by a scientific methodology emerging out of the nature of the phenomena themselves. Finally, Weckowicz examines the extent to which phenomenological and existential philosophies have affected our conceptions of man—in terms of the meaning of the individual's personal life and the understanding of the individual's world—and the manner in which these perspectives add new dimensions to the therapeutic encounter.

The next three chapters, comprising Part II, Experiencing and Epistemology, are concerned with the nature of experience and questions of epistemology for a humanistic psychology. Lyons focuses on the discontinuity of experience and the impossibility of communicating the ineffable. He wants to "speak whereof he can only be silent," for he is involved in a game of peekaboo with reality in an ultimate sense. For Lyons, however, body-based awareness serves as the ground for all knowing, and its systematic use constitutes a humanistic perspective on theory and method. Cooper, a theologian, develops the theme that human beings are meaning-oriented creatures and that this search for meaning is the key issue in epistemology and science. He argues that values are foundational to all meanings and, hence, that they determine the significance of facts. He takes the stance that there is no value-free science and argues for the epistemological priority of values over facts. Coward and Royce develop the theme that scientific and humanistic psychology are complementary specialties based on different epistemologies. Science is viewed as being dependent on rational-empirical epistemology whereas the epistemology of the humanities—including humanistic psychology—is metaphoric in nature. Metaphorism as an epistemology involves multiple meanings and the unmasking of existential realities.

In Part III, Paradigm and Method, we have two essays concerned with developing a methodology for humanistic psychology. McCurdy draws our attention to the two directions of mind which give rise to a duality of experience: the mathematical and the poetic. He argues that both modes of experience must be part of a psychology which aspires to humanistic completeness. He goes on to make a plea for the extension of quantitative analysis of poetic content, which he richly exemplifies by his ingenious analysis of Shakespearean and other literary works. Kuiken suggests that while humanistic psychologists have encouraged alternative moral imperatives and images of man, they have unfortunately not developed methods appropriate to their analysis of human experience. He proposes systematic descriptive procedures as a basis for evolving an "empirical phenomenology."

In Part IV, Interdisciplinary Perspectives, two authors take an interdisciplinary approach in their proposals for a humanistic study of human beings and their world. Garfinkle, an anthropologist, interprets human biological and cultural evolution as the basis for understanding the process of humanization. In his novel paradigmatic analysis of psychology, he argues that a humane psychology must be embedded in an axiological perspective of "jeshuralization" (universal justice or righteousness). The sociologist Jung explores the formal requirements for a humanistic science and, with reference to his general theory of action, proposes cybernetic phenomenology as a general methodology for human science.

Finally, in Part V, Critical Analysis, a psychologist and a philosopher present rather different critiques of the humanistic endeavor. The philosopher Tennessen addresses the metatheoretic issues which underlie scientific and humanistic psychology. He maintains that this division is the result of our conception of science as an autonomous machine which produces facts. The chasm between humanistic and scientific psychology adheres to an outmoded view of science, and when properly understood, science is not dehumanizing; rather it is a very human and humane enterprise. Berlyne begins with the most obvious characteristic of third-force psychology, namely, that it became established as a protest movement against the prevailing scientific zeitgeist. His essay focuses on five humanistic dissents: (1) the application of the scientific method to human behavior; (2) the prevailing conception of science; (3) the domination of behaviorism; (4) the failure to study uniquely human characteristics; and (5) the inadequacy of research effort devoted to problems having human relevance. Berlyne maintains that the first three protests "have no merit whatsoever, and the last two have some basis but are overstated."

Despite the range of content of these chapters, they obviously do not span the full spectrum of philosophical and theoretical issues pertinent to an analysis of what is both an academic and a social movement. Furthermore, as with most complex problems, genuine communication with respect to the issues of humanistic psychology is riddled with difficulties. Not only do these authors have different viewpoints, they use different languages and frequently refer to different phenomena. Nevertheless, the contributors to this volume have taken humanistic psychology very seriously; they have attended to the demand that their first allegiance be to the "family of mankind," and within that framework, they are engaged in understanding the psychology of man. As Carl Rogers suggests in his provocative Foreword to this volume, it is the "evolutionary tendency toward greater order, greater interrelatedness, greater complexity"—the formative tendency—which leads to an emerging awareness of the "unity of the cosmic system."

Nevertheless, many within the third-force movement have failed to develop their ideas with disciplined scholarship. They have accepted the validity of their goal and simply rested their case. This stance is neither adequate for the scientist as a member of the human family nor will it do as humanistic *psychology*—that is, it will not do if we are to achieve a disciplined psychology. What is required is both theoretical sophistication and methodological relevance for studying human reality, whether it be called science or scholarship, scientific psychology or humanistic psychology. A human psychology will be achieved only if disciplined inquiry is brought to bear on its problems. This volume is intended to continue with renewed vigor such serious inquiry. For, although we view the contributions to this volume as examples of such endeavor, with at least a concern for rigor if not always rigorous, we are also aware that the questions raised by the demand for a human psychology are foundational and, therefore, not likely to succumb to immediate or final solution. However, by posing the big questions, inquiring humanity may at least be able to put its limited knowledge into perspective. It is in the spirit of reaching for a larger perspective that the endeavor for a humanistic psychology makes sense, and it is in this context that this volume is put forward.

We gratefully acknowledge the Canada Council and the University of Alberta for its financial support in preparation of this volume and thank Mrs. Frances Rowe who typed the manuscript in its entirety.

LEENDERT P. MOS
JOSEPH R. ROYCE

University of Alberta
Edmonton, Canada

References

Bugental, J. F. T. (Ed.). *Challenges of humanistic psychology*. New York: McGraw-Hill, 1967.

Burton, A. *Modern humanistic psychotherapy*. San Francisco: Jossey-Bass, 1967.

Fromm, E. (Ed.). *Socialist humanism*. New York: Doubleday, 1965.

Giorgi, A. *Psychology as a human science*. New York: Harper & Row, 1970.

Giorgi, A., Faber, W. F., & Eckartsberg, R. (Eds.). *Duquesne studies in phenomenological psychology* (Vol. 1). Pittsburgh: Duquesne University Press, 1971.

Giorgi, A., Fisher, C. T., & Murray, E. L. (Eds.). *Duquesne studies in phenomenological psychology* (Vol. 2). Pittsburgh: Duquesne University Press, 1975.

Goble, F. G. *The third force*. New York: Grossman, 1970.

Greening, T. C. (Ed.). *Existential humanistic psychology*. Belmont, Calif.: Brooks/Cole, 1971.

Hammes, J. A. *Humanistic psychology: A Christiam interpretation*. New York: Grune & Stratton, 1971.

Jourard, S. M. *Disclosing man to himself*. New York: Van Nostrand, 1968.

Kinget, G. M. *On being human: A systematic view*. New York: Harcourt Brace Jovanovich, 1975.

Koch, S. Psychology as science. In S. C. Brown (Ed.), *Philosophy of psychology*. London: Macmillan, 1974.

MacCorquodale, K. B. F. Skinner's "Verbal Behavior": A retrospective appreciation. *Journal of the Experimental Analysis of Behavior*, 1969, *12*, 831–841.

Maslow, A. H. *Toward a psychology of being*. Princeton, N.J.: Van Nostrand, 1968.

Misiak, H., & Sexton, V. S. *Phenomenological, existential, and humanistic psychologies: A historical survey*. New York: Grune & Stratton, 1973.

Rogers, C. R., & Skinner, B. F. Some issues concerning the control of human behavior. *Science*, 1956, *124*, 1057–1066.

Roszak, T. *The making of a counter culture*. New York: Doubleday, 1969.

Severin, F. T. *Humanistic viewpoints in psychology*. New York: McGraw-Hill, 1965.

Severin, F. T. *Discovering man in psychology*. New York: McGraw-Hill, 1973.

Sutich, A., & Vich, M. (Eds.). *Readings in humanistic psychology*. New York: Free Press, 1969.

Valle, R. S., & King, M. *Existential-phenomenological alternatives for psychology*. New York: Oxford, 1978.

van Kaam, A. *Existential foundations of psychology*. Pittsburgh: Duquesne University Press, 1966.

Wandersman, A., Poppen, P., & Ricks, D. *Humanism and behaviorism: Dialogue and growth*. New York: Pergamon, 1976.

Wann, T. W. (Ed.). *Behaviorism and phenomenology*. Chicago: University of Chicago Press, 1964.

Watts, A. W. *Psychotherapy east and west*. New York: Ballantine, 1961.

Wilson, C. *New pathways in psychology: Maslow and the post-Freudian revolution*. New York: Taplinger, 1972.

I

THE HISTORICAL CONTEXT

1

Carl F. Graumann

PSYCHOLOGY

HUMANISTIC OR HUMAN?

> *The psychologist is committed to a belief in the worth of the individual human being.*
>
> —APA: Ethical Standards of Psychologists

On Humanism

American Humanistic Psychology

"Humanistic psychology" has become a label for a movement of which some of us do not yet know whether it is going to become part and parcel of, or a secession from, mainstream psychology. That is, we do not know whether it is going to enrich psychology by making up for some ignored and repressed topics of research or whether it is a countercurrent, incompatible with so-called established academic psychology. What we do know in the second decade of "humanistic psychology" is that after a largely programmatic initial phase it has established itself. The indicators of this are a journal of its own, an association of its own, a recorded history of its own (Misiak & Sexton, 1973), and (as a social psychologist I have to add) a subculture of its own.

What is humanistic about this movement? What is peculiar at all? Before I consider what the protagonists of this movement claim to be

---

Carl F. Graumann • Psychologisches Institut der Universität Heidelberg, Hauptstrasse 47–51, 69 Heidelberg 1, Federal Republic of Germany.

humanistic, I would like to underline that for a psychologist from Europe "humanistic psychology" is a predominantly American phenomenon. Not that the epithet "humanistic" has never been used to characterize psychology in Europe. In 1949 H. von Bracken, a German psychologist, translated the first edition of G. W. Allport's *Personality* (1937) and introduced it as the embodiment of "what one may call the 'humanistic turn' in American psychology" (Allport, 1937/1949, p. vi). Allport himself, in a special preface to the German edition, reported on a "revolution of American psychological thinking" (Allport, 1937/1949, p. xx), referring to Kurt Goldstein, Karen Horney, Kurt Lewin, and Carl Rogers. In 1957, the British psychologist John Cohen published *Humanistic Psychology*, which was translated into German under the title *Psychologie, psychologisch betrachtet* (psychology psychologically seen); this book, however, does not have much in common with Maslowian humanistic psychology. Finally, in 1970 and 1971, when the first two International Conferences on Humanistic Psychology were held in the Netherlands and in Germany, Europeans became aware of the existence of a new movement in psychology.

Surprisingly, this movement has not had any noticeable impact on psychology in Europe, although humanism has monumentally shaped European thinking. Could it be that what American psychologists call humanistic is so different from the humanism that has been and still is being discussed in Europe? In order to understand both the recent American ("third-force") humanism in psychology and the fact of its nonreception by psychologists in Europe, I will briefly try to discuss a few basic conceptions of humanism. They have in common *an endeavor to return to, or recover, what is considered to be essentially human.* Where (a) "return" or "recover" implies that there is an awareness that an original conception of humanity has been distorted, spoiled, largely forgotten, or repressed, 'b) "endeavor" implies that an earnest attempt remains an effort, (c) "considered" means that what is essentially human is, of course, a function of extant beliefs, and (d) the whole implies that humanism is bound to be critical of prevailing human doctrines. Beyond this commonality the various historical manifestations of humanism differ.

Classical Humanism

While almost all humanism can be characterized by its educational intention, the historically first manifestations of European humanism refer to a special form of education, namely, the formation of personality by a comprehensive study of Greek and Roman antiquity. At the time of the Renaissance, this humanism was one way of emancipation from medieval dogmatism. It was mainly scholars and artists who depicted the ideal of the New Man: *il uomo universale,* fully grown and evolved in all potentialities, shaped after the Greek ideal of *paideia,* trying to attain (or emulate) the synthesis of Roman *virtus* and *doctrina.* In spite of the fact that this humanism was largely developed by "men of the church" as an attempt to revive a truly Christian way of life that would be influential for both Reformation and Counter-Reformation, its imitation of Greek and Roman forms of life naturally involved pagan features. The glorification of Man, liberated from the old bondage and centered on the uniqueness (singularity) of the "*uomo unico*" ("*uomo singolare*"), was the discovery of man as the individual. The individual's highest manifestation of unrestricted (today we would say) self-realization "beyond good and evil" became the ideal of an elitist culture and philosophy, reflected still in Nietzsche's philosophical figure of superman.

No doubt, this first figure of European humanism was elitist, reserved for those who had access to the *humaniora* (i.e., higher education) and not suitable to promote the humanity of all humankind. What remained, though not for a great many, was "humanistic education," that is, the study of Greek and Latin.

Classical antiquity was again rediscovered, this time mainly in Germany, in the late eighteenth and early nineteenth centuries, when the philosophy of German idealism and the writings of Herder, Goethe, Schiller, and von Humboldt centered on the freedom and dignity of man. Again, education as the most powerful emancipatory force and humanity as the state of perfected desirable human qualities were seen as belonging together. And once more the humanities were considered to be the proper means to attain such humanity. Although this neohumanism was mainly the philosophy of education for the *Bürgertum* (middle class) it was, through the influence of the French Revolution, less elitist in its perspective. If we consult Herder's famous "Letters on the Promotion of Humanity" (Herder, 1793–1797) we find an unmistakable plea for more equality in the education of personality, which should be open to everybody. A society which impedes or blocks general education must be called inhuman.

This neoclassical humanism also aimed at the formation (*Bildung*) of individuality, which was believed to be the final goal or *telos* of the history of mankind. The image of man, though different from that of the Renaissance, was held to be expressible in universal terms, that is, for mankind.

Socialist Humanism

Among the major criticisms of idealistic humanism, Marxism deserves special mention. For according to Marx and his followers, it is no longer the individual as such who is thought to be capable of emancipation. True humanity can only be attained by the revolutionary effort of the working class. It is the historical mission of the proletariat "to overturn all circumstances under which man is a humiliated, enslaved, deserted, contemptuous being" [my translation] (Marx & Engels, 1958, Vol. 1, p. 385) in order to establish a society in which man, no longer exploited by others, is enabled to realize his own human essence, working in the ongoing historical society (cf. Paci, 1972, p. 379 f.).

For Marxists, humanism as upheld and proclaimed in the capitalist society is only a complement of inhuman conditions. As long as there exists private ownership of the means of production, man is alienated. In Marx's conception of "human nature," this alienation means a fundamental cleavage. Ollman (1971, pp. 133–134 f.), who interprets Marx's theory of alienation, speaks of a threefold separation:

1. Man is separated from his work, powerless to decide what to do and how to do it.
2. Man is separated from his products, without control over them as they become isolated (i.e., "abstract") commodities.
3. Man is separated from his fellow men, because "competition and class hostility have rendered most forms of cooperation impossible" (Ollman, 1971, p. 134).

Thus, man in capitalist society, isolated from nature, society, and himself, is a mere "abstraction." It is up to socialism and communism to reconstitute man into his "human, i.e., social mode of existence" (Marx, 1959, p. 103). History is the inevitable preparation of man to attain full humanity—the state in which the conflict between individual and society is resolved (Marx, 1959, p. 107). To reach this state of humanity, all social humanism must be militant. In the words of Adam Schaff, one of the leading Marxist philosophers of Eastern Europe:

> The aim of militant humanism is the development of the individual and the creation of the best possible conditions for his happiness . . . . To be a hu-

> manist today, when the realisation of humanist ideals is no longer a utopia, is to be a fighter. And he who fights well must hate well. It is hence possible and necessary in the name of love of one's neighbor to hate those who oppress him. (Schaff, 1968, pp. 109–110)

The issue implied in the dialectic of freedom and its limitation (Schaff, 1968) has been discussed mainly by Merleau-Ponty (1947/1969) as the relationship between humanism and terror.

For a more detailed discussion of socialist humanism up to the present, see Fromm (1965); for divergent views on the relationship between Marxism and humanism, see Sève (1972), who bases his theory of personality on Marxist anthropology.

Critical Humanism

Humanism again became a topic widely discussed in Europe after the second world war. The experience of freedom endangered, even stifled, by the ideologies and powers of inhuman totalitarian regimes, the awareness of the powerlessness of the individual, and the resulting feeling of frustration and meaninglessness were, perhaps, nowhere as intense as in Europe during the 1940s and 1950s. The humanity of man had been questioned in a very radical way.

The challenge of this situation was answered by a group of mainly French and German philosophers who tried to redefine humanism within the contexts of phenomenology, existentialism, and structuralism. This new conception of humanism evolved in opposition to and explicit negation of all preceding humanisms insofar as the concept of a given "essence of man" (*Wesen des Menschen*) and its derivative "image of man" were considered to be untenable. Nor were there universal moral qualities, which men would have to realize to attain "full humanity." Man is neither purpose nor telos of a history understood as development: "il est toujours à faire" (Sartre, 1946, p. 92); that is, there is no ideal state of humanity to be recovered, as in classical humanism, nor a final stage to be attained, as is postulated in socialist humanism. Unlike hominization, humanization is no evolutionary process; at all times it remains the risky enterprise of individuals or a society.

Since life as such has no *a priori* meaning, it is only through human choice and commitment (*engagement*) that life becomes meaningful. Thus, the "human condition" (rather than "human nature") is characterized by the necessity for human beings to project themselves into a future of more humanity. Man is conceived of as a being "qui ne se contente pas de coïncider avec soi" (Merleau-Ponty, 1960, p. 285).

Since Camus, Merleau-Ponty, and Sartre, "humanism" no longer designates a philosophical current or a school of thought but has become a constituent of, and challenge for, human thinking: to define the humanity of man and to posit it as something to be practically achieved. Practically, however, this means that the *practice of humanization* must be fully incorporated into what we today call humanism. We must give up the dichotomies of traditional humanisms where the "values" (of truth, beauty, goodness) stood against a "reality" (less true, beautiful, and good), where there was the "spirit" and also the body, where there was an inner life, potentially rich, and an outer world inhibiting or deforming those inner riches. Those of us today, concludes Merleau-Ponty, who take up the word humanism can no longer maintain *l'humanisme sans vergogne* of our predecessors.

> Le propre de notre temps est peut-être de dissocier l'humanisme et l'idée d'une humanité de plein droit, et non seulement de concilier, mais de tenir pour inséparables la conscience des valeurs humaines et celle des infrastructures qui les portent dans l'existence. (Merleau-Ponty, 1960, p. 287)

The inseparability of our awareness of human values, the decision (*choix*) to realize them, and the "infrastructure" of such a realization become central problems for "revolutionary humanism." For Merleau-Ponty (1947), the problem of humanism and terror is ethically solved if force used against people is truly revolutionary, which exclusively means that it helps to bring about more humanity in interhuman relations. Humanity here is used in the double sense of (a) something to be achieved and (b) the criteria of its realization. As compared with the certainty of Marxist humanists that full humanity will be reached (in the era of Communism), for Merleau-Ponty the realization of humanity, in principle, bears the risk of failure.

Merleau-Ponty's negation of the traditional dichotomies which, in a sense, halved former humanisms is fully understood only when we consider his phenomenological conception of the *human dialectic*. Since this important concept was developed within Merleau-Ponty's analyses of the structure of behavior (1967) and of perception (1962) and, thus, has a direct bearing on psychology, I shall reserve its presentation and discussion for a later paragraph.

First, however, I will try to summarize and evaluate this brief review of the basic conceptions of humanism. It has to be called brief since for all three types of humanism many positions and authors had to be ignored. Mainly with respect to socialist and critical humanisms, the controversies between different Marxists, neomarxists, existentialists, and structuralists have been set aside. I still hope that this simplification for brevity's sake enables us to compare, as is the major purpose of this chapter, the concepts of humanism in European philosophy and contemporary American psychology.

Humanisms in Comparison

Although classical and socialist humanism differ in that the former is retrospective and, in the strict sense of the word, conservative, the latter is prospective and, in a secular sense of the word, eschatological, they have in common a basic (and literal) educational intention—even zeal. They differ considerably, however, as to the means of education (as pedagogues would). Classical humanists were convinced that the *studia humanitatis,* that is, classical or "humanistic" education, as such would promote humanity; Marx and his followers believed that full actualization of human potentialities and "happiness" for everybody within a fully cooperative society could not be attained as long as there existed exploitation and suppression, alienation and objectification of human by human, that is, inhuman relationships which, in capitalist society, have become fixed givens or "second nature" to the majority of working people. According to the Marxist philosophy of history, these structures, which determine human consciousness and behavior, can be overcome not by educational evolution but only by political and economic revolution. That is why, for Marxists, true humanism in our time must be revolutionary, which inevitably implies both the use of force and education. Conversely, bourgeois talk of humanity, humanism, humanitarianism, and, worst of all, "human relations," is but a veil or camouflage of the inhumanity of the capitalist system of inequality and exploitation. Concretely, to appeal to the freedom, the dignity, the worth, the creativity of the individual, to refer to the equality of rights and chances for all, to understanding and peace between groups, classes, and nations, is interpreted as deceptively attributing to individuals the characteristics which an inhuman society and its infrastructures do not and cannot permit. Whether one shares this perspective or not, it would be difficult to contradict Merleau-Ponty's insistence that the awareness of (and belief in) values and the infrastructures for the implementation of these values cannot be separated. This understanding legitimizes the question of whether we live in a society in which the ambition to help people "to grow and evolve more fully in realization of their potential" (Bugental, 1967, p. 8) is a *sincere* aspiration. I will return to this question.

In spite of this radical difference between socialist and classical humanism, both adhere to an *essentialism;* that is, they feel able to define man in terms of essential characteristics. It is true that they differ considerably in what they see as the essence (*das Wesen*) of man. Classical humanism is (largely) individualistic, bestowing allegedly universal characteristics (traits, needs) on each individual and partly, though not always, disregarding the environmental (mainly social) context in which the individual is bound to exist. Social humanism, on the other hand, states that "the human essence is no abstraction inherent in each individual. In its reality it is the ensemble of the social relations" [my translation] (Marx, *Theses on Feuerbach,* in Marx & Engels, 1958, Vol. 3, p. 6); thus, according to Marx, man is essentially the product of social life.

Compared with these kinds of essentialism, which understand man as determined either by internal or external structures, the radical dialectic of the internal and the external "condemns" man to be free (Sartre, 1946); at the least, man is "condamné au sens" (Merleau-Ponty, 1960). Liberty (and truth) can only be achieved in a dialectic movement, with the everlasting risk of being lost.

> It is the essence of liberty to exist only in the practice of liberty, in the inevitably imperfect movement which joins us to others, to the things of the world, to our jobs, mixed with the hazards of our situation. (Merleau-Ponty, 1947/1969, p. xxiv)

In this perspective, it would be wrong to speak of human "nature" or "essence"; the adequate concept is the human "condition."

The Human Condition in Psychology

Psychology and Its Discontents

Whether Allport was right in his expectation of a "revolution of American psychological thinking" (Allport, 1949, p. xx) may seem doubtful after 25 years, although we know that scientific revolutions tend to remain invisible for a long time (Kuhn, 1962, Chapter 9). Yet Allport was definitely one of the leading spokesmen of a growing number of psychologists who voiced discontent with mainstream psychology. Since I can refer to such different scholars as Bakan (1967), Braginsky & Braginsky (1974), Chein (1972), Giorgi (1970), Kelman (1968), Koch (1959, 1961, 1964), Rosenthal (1971), and Sanford (1965), none of whom I would regard as a humanistic psychologist à la Maslow, I need not repeat the various criticisms leveled at behaviorism and psychoanalysis. Moreover, Giorgi (1970, p. 79–87) has listed the major current critiques of psychology. I need only emphasize that most critiques imply the reproach that psychology, in its imitation of the natural sciences, has largely disregarded the concrete person in a concrete environment. This critique does not deny that we have had many, perhaps too many, theories of personality nor that there is a potent environmentalism in psychology. It does deny, however, and here I fully agree, that the uniquely human relationship of person and environment, that is, the dialectic of the human condition, has been accounted for.

Instead of reiterating the inquiry into the reasons for this neglect I will concentrate on the question of alternatives: Which kind of psychology has the potency to become an authentic "human science"?[1] More precisely, which psychological theory is equal to the task of accounting for the human character of what psychologists have, sometimes loosely, called "experience" and "behavior"?[2]

Leaving aside that contemporary psychology, internationally seen, has roots both in natural science and the humanities (*Geisteswissenschaften*) (cf. Giorgi, 1970) we can state that the present situation is charac-

[1] "Human science" is used here in the sense in which *science humaine* and *Humanwissenschaft* are now being used in Europe, where the term *science* (*Wissenschaft*) was never restricted to natural science (for a comprehensive and detailed system of the human sciences, see Ananyev, 1974). Science qua *Wissenschaft* is a superordinate term encompassing the branches of natural and human sciences, so there is no need to withhold the attribute of science from a psychology which is not conceived as a natural science. This problem seems to be restricted to Anglo-American usage, which contrasts science and humanities. (For a systematic discussion of some epistemological issues involved in this dichotomous conception of *Wissenschaft*, see Royce, 1970.)

[2] Again, I am fully aware of a semantic problem. *Erleben* and *Verhalten* are not fully matched by their traditional near equivalents, "(immediate) experience" and "behavior." "Behavior" has, through the behaviorist usage, been removed considerably and almost alienated from the German *Verhalten* and the French *comportement*. In the following, I shall use the term behavior not in its impoverished S-R theoretical usage but, as will be described later, in the more comprehensive meaning of human activity as expounded, for example, in Merleau-Ponty's (1967) *Structure of Behavior*. Experience, then, is a constitutive element of human behavior.

terized by a predominance of natural-scientific psychology. Its topic of research is the animal or human organism insofar as it responds to, or is reinforced by, an environment which is basically conceived in terms of stimuli. The hidden anthropology of this quasi organism has been worked out appropriately by Holzkamp (1972, p. 35–73), a leading spokesman of (self-dubbed) critical emancipatory psychology (cf. Graumann, 1970, p. 53–56); the severely reduced humanity of "psychological man" is evident.

The most vehement and vociferous opposition to this reduced humanness of man comes from the (again self-dubbed) "third force" of humanistic psychology, from the "humanistic revolution." What is behind the "challenges of humanistic psychology" (Bugental, 1967) that could help to "rehumanize" psychology? The answer must be looked for in the conception of humanism. A second alternative which I would like to discuss is not so much a force or a movement, and still less a revolution, as a basic theoretical framework for human science evolving directly from critical humanism.

Psychology as a Humanistic Movement

In an article in the charter issue of the *Journal of Humanistic Psychology,* entitled "Eupsychia, the Good Society," Maslow (1961) described a state of affairs to be attained by the combined effort of men and women who were willing and prepared to be interested in, and promote, such human capacities and potentialities as were hitherto disregarded or underrated by mainstream psychology and psychoanalysis:

> e.g., creativity, love, self, growth, organism, basic need gratification, self-actualization, higher values, ego-transcendence, objectivity, autonomy, identity, responsibility, psychological health, etc. (Maslow, 1961, p. 1)

For the uninitiated reader, it is difficult to discover a cognitive order in this list, nor do the above words seem to be on one and the same conceptual level, nor is their commonality self-evident. However, the initiated reader, who would have failed to find these words in the average indexes of psychological textbooks, recognizes the sources from which they originate: the writings of Allport, Fromm, Goldstein, Horney, Maslow, and Rogers, a group of psychologists who, according to Hall & Lindzey (1970), are to be considered as personality theorists of a holistic and, partly, clinical orientation. In fact, the wholeness and unity of the person, the favorite topic of the late *Ganzheitspsychologie* and characterology, has been resurrected as a *leitmotif* of humanistic psychology. "The whole is greater than the part" (Severin, 1965, p. 3). The late Albert Wellek, the last German spokesman of the *Ganzheit* school, recognized by Misiak & Sexton (1973, p. 111–112) as a forerunner of humanistic psychology, stated as the "basic beliefs" of his school, which had its most influential period in the 1930s and 1940s, (1) holism, (2) emotionalism (irrationalism), (3) social evolutionism, and (4) substantialism (Wellek, 1954, p. 3). Is it lineage or only a striking degree of similarity that one discovers like elements in humanistic psychology? The parallels deserve a careful investigation, which cannot be given here. But at least those who witnessed, or are mindful of, the decline of German psychology after 1933 should think twice before they accept the tenets of holism and irrationalism as promises of a more human psychology.

The emphatic focus on the individual personality, together with the special "concern to man's subjective experience" and only secondarily his actions (Bugental, 1967, p. 9), and I must add a still lesser concern for the human environment,[3] threatens to isolate the individual. It reminds one of the emphasis on the individual which characterized and impaired classical humanism. But there are more similarities, which are more than superficial, between "third-force" psychology and classical humanism. There is the special interest in the vigorous, the healthy, the mature, the autonomous, the self-actualizing, the unique (as the "more fully human") individual (Maslow). The humanistic psychologist "is concerned with the individual, the exceptional, and the unpredicted rather than seeking only to study the regular, the universal, and the conforming" (Bugental, 1967, p. 9). He or she is interested in values worth living for and dying for, those "being-values" for which Maslow (1967) developed his theory of metamotivation.

No doubt, humanistic psychologists, deploring that behaviorists had lowered human beings to the status of organisms, lifted them to a level which seems to be above what one might call the everyday person, just as Renaissance humanists were guided by an image of man which only the more privileged of their contemporaries were able to live up to. For others, there was an intensified feeling of discrepancy be-

[3] The term *environment* is not even listed in the indexes of such humanistic standard texts as Bugental (1967), Bühler & Allen (1972), and Severin (1965)—a countermeasure against behavioristic standard texts?

tween what is and what ought to be. The danger is that in our time such humanism becomes inhuman insofar as the majority of "less evolved" people are treated as "less human" because their situation, by which I mean their economic, social, and ethnic circumstances, never gives them a chance to evoke those "human capacities and potentialities" which are the major concern of humanistic psychology (cf. Braginsky & Braginsky, 1974).

Humanists in the Renaissance were sometimes close counselors of the mighty and may have hoped to be influential in regard to the promotion of humanity through improving education. Today, we have learned that education alone cannot remove the inequality which is the basis of factual inhumanity. Do psychologists believe that they are of such importance as to be able to overcome the scourges of our time? Is it psychological hubris or political naiveté when the inaugurator of the "third force" confesses:

> I believe that psychologists occupy the most centrally important position in the world today. I say this because all the important problems of mankind—war and peace, exploitation and brotherhood, hatred and love, sickness and health, misunderstanding and understanding, happiness and unhappiness—will yield only to a better understanding of human nature, and to this *psychology alone* wholly applies itself. (Maslow, 1965, p. 17; italics mine)

Yet "human nature"—and this I think is the core of the conceptual confusion of "humanistic psychology"—does not reside in the interior of an individualistically conceived personality ready to be "actualized" or "evolved" in encounters with humanists but must be looked for in the dialectical interactions between people and their concrete social environments.

Behaviorists ignore human subjectivity in favor of the external variables of organism and environment. Humanistic psychologists tend to ignore human activities in concrete meaningful situations in favor of inner experiences and individual capacities. Though differing (and even antagonistic) in approach, both psychologies fail to account for the *humanum* of experience and behavior. This means that behaviorism is not really a systematic and comprehensive study of behavior and that humanistic psychology, in spite of its good intentions, is not truly humanistic.[4] It may be a movement though.

[4] As with "behaviorism," I have used "humanistic psychology" in the singular. I realize that there is considerable heterogeneity in both camps, but must leave differentiation to another time.

Psychology as a Human Discipline

"Psychology is the scientific study of the situated person." This statement of the late Dutch psychologist Linschoten (1953, p. 246) serves well to introduce the phenomenological perspective in psychology.[5] Whereas in America phenomenological psychology is very often subsumed under the so-called "third-force" or even confused with humanistic psychology, a separate treatment is required, and the main argument can be taken from Linschoten's definition-like statement. All psychology, whether behaviorist or humanist, is the study of experience and/or behavior and as such is individual centered, treating of personalities and making use of the word "situation." The phenomenological conception of the situated person conveys a different theoretical emphasis, namely, the *person–world (or person–environment) relationship.* In phenomenological psychology, the focus is not on individuals or even organisms but on the intentional relationship between man and the world. *Intentionality* here means that any human activity (consciousness, experience, behavior) refers to something which, by this very activity, is meant (intended) to exist independently of its being intended. Since we intend persons, things, events, signs to "be there" (or question or negate their existence), intentionality has rightly been named the "objectivating function" of consciousness (Gurwitsch, 1966). Only as objectivations of intentional human activity are the things and events in the environment, in a strict sense, human things and events of the world. Thus, they have meanings, valences, and values; that is, they have reference to actual and potential behavior. We encounter the things and events of our environment as "situated," that is, in actual or potential relationship to ourselves—not as mere *data,* (i.e., sensory givens) but as *agenda* (i.e., something to be dealt with, something which motivates us.) "Situation et motivation ne font qu'un" (Sartre, 1947, p. 568).

Conversely, if we characterize experience and behavior phenomenologically, we must include the world of things which we experience and with respect to which we behave (Graumann, 1974). I am always "with respect to" somebody or something actual or potential. This "être au monde" is the basic notion of being situated (Merleau-Ponty, 1962).

In other words, to analyze the person–world relationship phenomenologically (i.e., in terms of its intentionality) makes explicit what

[5] The following is partly based on the section "Psychology in Phenomenological Perspective" in Graumann (1975).

Merleau-Ponty (1967, p. 176) called the "human dialectic." This dialectic, which for Merleau-Ponty is the significant feature of the "human order," is essentially brought about by human work:

> For, between man and the physico-chemical stimuli, it projects "use-objects" . . . —clothing, tables, gardens—and "cultural objects"—books, musical instruments, language—which constitute the proper milieu of man and bring about the emergence of new cycles of behavior. (Merleau-Ponty, 1967, p. 162)

Human dialectic, then, means that human activity, essentially characterized as work from Hegel to Schütz, brings forth the "proper milieu of man" which, in turn, motivates new modes of activity in which man accepts, modifies, rejects, or surpasses the structures brought forth—structures which may help man to transcend his present situation, but in which he may also find himself imprisoned (Merleau-Ponty, 1967, p. 176). This *ambiguity* of being situated, which we experience from the moment of our birth and try to overcome by our activities, is thus an essential feature of the human condition. Humanity, far from being the ensemble of an individual's desirable characteristics, is the very quality of man's being situated.

For psychology, these may be only metatheoretical reflections. But the phenomenological conception of the situation, and its dialectic, has been offered as a possible alternative to the one-sided behaviorist concern with the controlling power of the environment and the equally one-sided humanistic concern with the potentialities of the individual. Perhaps the major problem and the central conceptual issue of a human psychology will be to overcome the person–environment dichotomy to which we have been conditioned from the beginning of scientific psychology.

What psychologists with a sincere concern for practical humanity should work at and need is less a humanistic movement than a theoretically and conceptually restructured human psychology.

References

Allport, G. W. *Personality: A psychological interpretation*. New York: Holt, 1937. (German translation by H. von Bracken, Stuttgart: Klett, 1949.)

Ananyev (Ananjew), B. G. *Der Mensch als Gegenstand der Erkenntnis* [*Man as object to knowledge*]. Berlin: Deutscher Verlag der Wissenschaften, 1974.

Bakan, D. *On method: Toward a reconstruction of psychological investigation*. San Francisco: Jossey-Bass, 1967.

Braginsky, B. M., & Braginsky, D. D. *Mainstream psychology: A critique*. New York: Holt, Rinehart, & Winston, 1974.

Bugental, J. F. T. (Ed.). *Challenges of humanistic psychology*. New York: McGraw-Hill, 1967.

Buhler, Ch., & Allen, M. *Introduction to humanistic psychology*. New York: McGraw-Hill, 1967.

Chein, I. *The science of behavior and the image of man*. New York: Basic Books, 1972.

Cohen, J. *Humanistic psychology*. London: Allen & Unwin, 1957.

Fromm, E. (Ed.). *Socialist humanism*. Garden City, N. Y.: Doubleday, 1965.

Giorgi, A. *Psychology as a human science*. New York: Harper & Row, 1970.

Graumann, C. F. Conflicting and convergent trends in psychological theory. *Journal of Phenomenological Psychology*, 1970, *1*, 51–56.

Graumann, C. F. Psychology and the world of things. *Journal of Phenomenological Psychology*, 1974, *4*, 389–404.

Graumann, C. F. *Phenomenological psychology as a metatheory of psychological ecology*. Paper presented at the 3rd Biennial Conference for the Study of Behavioural Development, Guilford, England, 1975.

Gurwitsch, A. On the intentionality of consciousness. In *Studies in phenomenology and psychology*. Evanston, Ill.: Northwestern University Press, 1966.

Hall, C. S., & Lindzey, G. *Theories of personality* (2nd ed.). New York: Wiley, 1970.

Herder, J. G. Briefe zur Beförderung der Humanität [Letters on the promotion of humanity] 1793–1797. In Werke in 5 Bänden (Vol. 5). Berlin: Aufbau-Verlag, 1969.

Holzkamp, K. *Kritische Psychologie* [*Critical psychology*]. Frankfurt: Fischer, 1972.

Kelman, H. C. *A time to speak: On human values and social research*. San Francisco: Jossey-Bass, 1968.

Koch, S. Epilogue. In S. Koch (Ed.), *Psychology, a study of a science* (Vol. 3). New York: McGraw-Hill, 1959.

Koch, S. Psychological science versus the science-humanism antinomy: Intimations of a significant science of man. *American Psychologist*, 1961, *16*, 629–639.

Koch, S. Psychology and emerging conceptions of knowledge as unitary. In T. W. Wann (Ed.), *Behaviorism and pehnomenology*. Chicago: University of Chicago Press, 1964.

Kuhn, T. S. *The structure of scientific revolutions*. Chicago: University of Chicago Press, 1962.

Linschoten, J. N. In J. H. van den Berg & J. Linschoten (Eds.), *Persoon en wereld*. Utrecht: Bijleveld, 1953.

Marx, K. *Economic and philosophic manuscripts of 1944* (M. Milligan, trans.). Moscow: 1959.

Marx, K. H., & Engels, F. *Werke*. 39 Vols. Berlin: Dietz, 1958.

Maslow, A. H. Eupsychia, the good society. *Journal of Humanistic Psychology*, 1961, *1*, 1–11.

Maslow, A. H. A philosophy of psychology: The need for a mature science of human nature. In F. T. Severin (Ed.), *Humanistic viewpoints in psychology*. New York: McGraw-Hill, 1965.

Maslow, A. H. A theory of metamotivation: The biological rooting of the value life. *Journal of Humanistic Psychology*, 1967, *7*, 93–127.

Merleau-Ponty, M. *Humanisme et terreur*. Paris: Gallimard, 1947. (English trans. Boston: Beacon Press, 1969).

Merleau-Ponty, M. *Signes*. Paris: Gallimard, 1960.

Merleau-Ponty, M. *The phenomenology of perception*. New York: Humanities Press, 1962.

Merleau-Ponty, M. *The structure of behavior*. (A. L. Fisher, trans.). Boston: Beacon Press, 1967.

Misiak, H., & Sexton, V. S. *Phenomenological, existential, and humanistic psychologies: A historical survey*. New York: Grune & Stratton, 1973.

Ollman, B. *Alienation: Marx's conception of man in capitalist society*. Cambridge, Eng.: Cambridge University Press, 1971.

Paci, E. *The function of the sciences and the meaning of man*. Evanston: Northwestern University Press, 1972.

Rosenthal, B. G. *The images of man*. New York: Basic Books, 1971.

Royce, J. R. The present situation in theoretical psychology. In J. R. Royce (Ed.), *Toward unification in psychology*. Toronto: University of Toronto Press, 1970.

Sanford, N. Will psychologists study human problems? *American Psychologist*, 1965, *20*, 192–202.

Sartre, J. P. *L'existentialisme est un humanisme*. Paris: Nagel, 1946.

Sartre, J. P. *L'être et le neant*. Paris: Gallimard, 1947.

Schaff, A. *A philosophy of man*. New York: Dell, 1968.

Sève, L. *Marxisme et théorie de la personalité*. Paris: Editions Sociales, 1972.

Severin, F. T. (Ed.). *Humanistic viewpoints in psychology*. New York: McGraw-Hill, 1965.

Wellek, A. *Die genetische Ganzheitspsychologie*. München: Beck, 1954.

2

Amedeo P. Giorgi

HUMANISTIC PSYCHOLOGY AND METAPSYCHOLOGY

Introduction

The purpose of this paper is to show that both humanistic psychology and traditional psychology have essentially the same problem, namely, that of coming up with a sound metapsychology within which psychology proper can thrive and grow. In my own harsh terms, psychology has not as yet come up with an indigenous adequate paradigm and is still in an essentially preparadigmatic state of development with respect to an authentic paradigm. My motivation for insisting on this state of affairs is not to scold psychology for being so slow—historically I do not believe that it could be otherwise, since all sciences follow the same route, and the other human sciences are in the same boat—but rather to bring to awareness that the problem of the precise meaning of psychology is still before us so that the interests, behavior, and research programs of psychologists can be guided accordingly. In contrast, consider the attitude that the basic paradigmatic problems of psychology are settled and that the main issue before us is simply to collect more data rather than think through new approaches to problems. Some behaviorists, for example, believe the problem to be one of merely applying a completely known and articulated paradigm to successive hu-

Amedeo P. Giorgi • Department of Psychology, Duquesne University, Pittsburgh, Pennsylvania 15219.

man problem areas (e.g., education, therapy, linguistic expression, etc.). In opposition to these latter viewpoints, the position of this paper is that the discovery and articulation of the paradigm is part of the problem.

At first glance, it would seem that humanistic psychology, because of its emphasis, is close to an adequate psychological understanding of man whereas traditional psychology is not. But a deeper analysis would show that the situation is more complicated than that. In actuality, the development of traditional psychology and humanistic psychology are intertwined. Humanistic psychology developed in opposition to traditional psychology, and traditional psychology in turn began to take on as thematic problems the issues raised by humanistic psychology in order to show how they could be handled (e.g., Hebb, 1974). Ultimately, traditional academic psychology is psychology in the service of science, understood as the approach of the natural sciences applied to man, and humanistic psychology is psychology in the service of an adequate image of man defined outside the context of science. But the reason that psychology is still preparadigmatic is revealed in the tensions that the two types of psychology manifest: traditional psychology, in being faithful to science, has difficulty in meeting the everyday needs of man, which is why humanistic psychology developed; humanistic psychology, however, while certainly centering on man, has difficulty in expressing itself scientifically, and when it does, it often looks no different from traditional psychology. Thus, the problem is one of how adequacy to man as a person and adequacy to science can be reconciled, and the reconciliation of this problem will also mark the beginning of psychology's authentic paradigm. However, for me, the resolution of the problem involves metapsychological issues which both movements must refer to, though in different ways.

Historical Development of Humanistic Psychology

Humanistic psychology, as a movement, is an amorphous amalgam of viewpoints, opinions, attitudes, and beliefs that is difficult to evaluate as a whole. It contains some brilliant insights along with some platitudes, some statements that are genuinely inspirational and much that is merely sentimental; it has elements of the courage that all founding movements require, and it contains much that is compromising with respect to the very values it claims to overthrow. If one were sufficiently selective, one could choose a series of statements from representatives of the movement that no psychologist could disagree with, or one could choose a series of statements that would have most of us up in arms. Hence, humanistic psychology is difficult to describe accurately as a movement. It seems to display more the coherence of a style than a unity of substance, and the coherence of style is defined as much in terms of what it is against as what it is for. It could even be shown that despite its protests against traditional psychology, humanistic psychology shares some of the former's endemic weaknesses, including a lack of unity, a philosophical naiveté, and a lack of genuine communication among its members. One could easily overlook many of these faults—for many important movements in history began equally amorphously—if one had confidence that other than superficial progress were being made or if one could seriously cling to the hope that the genuinely critical issues were being dealt with in other than a merely verbal way. Unfortunately, I, for one, do not perceive this kind of progress, mostly because the humanistic movement does not seem to encourage thinking and conceptualization (let alone philosophically based radical thinking) sufficiently for long-term breakthroughs to be made. Exceptions exist, of course, but they seem to be as few as in traditional psychology. I have the impression that once the generation of the founders of humanistic psychology has passed, so too will the movement. I would be happy to be proven wrong on this conjecture, but it would be dishonest of me to speak otherwise. Again, the reason I have this perception of the movement is that I do not feel that the intrinsic intellectual or theoretical breakthroughs necessary to sustain interest over generations are being made, and thus, younger thinkers of high caliber are not being attracted to the movement. My position is that, in this respect, humanistic psychology is no better than traditional psychology, and therefore both require the same remedy—a wholly new metapsychology. In part, this is because humanistic psychology developed merely in opposition to traditional psychology rather than in a genuinely dialectical way. In-depth dialectical thinking on the part of humanistic psychologists could have produced more lasting transformations or have led to a more significantly altered praxis. In this section I hope to show how, in its development, humanistic psychology depended on traditional psychology.

As a movement, humanistic psychology is exceedingly young.

While there are traces of it in the middle and late 1950s, it did not really begin in earnest until the founding of the *Journal of Humanistic Psychology* and the American Association of Humanistic Psychology (later the Association for Humanistic Psychology) in the early 1960s. Misiak and Sexton (1973) recorded the development of this movement thoroughly and were not able to come up with a comprehensive definition of humanistic psychology except to say that the movement is both "a protest and a new program" (Misiak & Sexton, 1973, p. 115). The only way they could articulate positive aspects of the movement was by selecting adequate expressions from the founders and other representative spokesmen.

Ultimately, we will have to use the same procedure. Our major interest here is to see why humanistic psychology developed in the first place and how it handled the objections with which it began as a separate movement. First of all, we should recall that the situation of psychology in the mid-1950s was certainly such that sufficient motivation for the founding of a humanistic psychology was warranted. Research in those days was dominated by sensory experiments, animal-learning studies, and delimited human-performance tasks related to military aims (the government was supporting much of the research). We will first outline the ideals and program of humanistic psychology and then see what kinds of praxis flowed from it. In 1957, Maslow presented a set of prescriptions for humanistic psychology, some of which are as follows:

> (1) Psychology should be more . . . concerned with the problems of humanity and less with the problems of the guild. . . . (2) American psychology should be bolder and more creative . . . not only cautious and careful in avoiding mistakes. . . . (3) Psychology should be more problem-centered and less absorbed with means or methods. . . . (4) Psychology should be more positive and less negative. . . . (5) Psychology should study the depths of human nature as well as the surface behavior, the unconscious as well as the conscious. . . . (6) Psychology should study the human being not just as passive clay, helplessly determined by outside forces. Man is, or should be, an active autonomous, self-governing mover, chooser and center of his own life. . . . (7) Psychologists should devote more time to the intensive study of the single unique person, to balance their preoccupation with the generalized man and with generalized and abstracted capacities. (Maslow, 1965, pp. 20–33)

First of all, we can note that all of Maslow's statements are prescriptions for what psychology *ought* to be, and he acknowledges that their actual existence is lacking. Secondly, all of his statements relate to certain weaknesses that he perceives in traditional psychology. The problems of traditional psychology which should be avoided are careerism, means centeredness, excessive caution, an attitude of negativity, superficiality, a passive image of human beings, abstractness, and a predominant concern for generalized man. A more humanistic psychology would be defined by a listing of the opposite characteristics. Thirdly, Maslow states in this same article that one difficulty is that a mature science of psychology is lacking. To some extent, therefore, Maslow is pointing to the status of psychological science as one of the problems with psychology. Otherwise, Maslow's approach is a shotgun one, lacking integration and merely pointing to inadequacies in the field with a general exhortation to change. One could not expect much more from a statement initiating a radical movement.

The founding of the American Association for Humanistic Psychology in 1962 led to another statement of the aims of humanistic psychology. The main parts of this statement are as follows:

> (1) A centering of attention on the experiencing *person* and thus a focus on experience as the primary phenomenon in the study of man. . . . (2) An emphasis on such distinctively human qualities as choice, creativity, valuation and self-realization.. . . (3) An allegiance to meaningfulness in the selection of problems for study and of research procedures, and an opposition to a primary emphasis on objectivity at the expense of significance. (4) An ultimate concern with and valuing of the dignity and worth of man and an interest in the development of the potential inherent in every person. Central in this view is the person as he discovers his own being and relates to other persons and to social groups. (cited by Misiak & Sexton, 1973, p. 116)

These aims here are somewhat more general and systematic than those presented by Maslow, but they are still defined primarily in opposition to traditional psychology (i.e., against theoretical explanations and overt behavior, against mechanistic and reductionistic terms, against objectivity, and against the determination of the individual by outside forces). Unfortunately, nowhere are the positive aspects clarified or made more precise (e.g., how does one select a meaningful problem?).

In 1965, Rollo May could still write "Humanistic psychology, as I see the definition, is the overall term which includes many different approaches" (May, 1965, p. 4). As if to emphasize the fact, Severin in the same year came out with a collection entitled *Humanistic Viewpoints in Psychology* (1965). This book included the Maslow article quoted above as well as an important article by Gordon Allport (1965) in which he wrote that personalistic thought meant that the individual person as a patterned entity must serve as the center of gravity for psychology. Bugental (1965) also had an article that was as scattered in approach as Maslow's and just as dependent on traditional psychology. However,

Bugental was more explicit about what he criticized and simply avowed that humanistic psychology could make a radical breakthrough without a full delineation of just how this was to happen. Essentially, Bugental criticized traditional psychology for its image of man, its extensive imitative practices (physics, medicine), its training, and some of its uncritically accepted criteria of clinical practice. In the same collection, Rogers (1965a) pointed out that one of the main stumbling blocks of psychology had been its description of science. Somehow it was always understood as something "out there," says Rogers, whereas it should be realized that science only exists in people. He went on to show that ultimately science is a way of preventing one from being deceived by his or her own subjective hunches. Thus, science itself is a human creation and should be understood in that light rather than as a huge, impersonal institution that determines man. About the same time, Matson (1964) called for a humane science of psychology, one that would break psychology's reliance on metaphors derived from classical mechanics which had given us a "broken" image of man.

Although these expressions are varied, a certain clustering was taking place: the humanistic psychologists were concerned about the image of human beings pursued or created by psychology, they criticized psychology's praxis as being too imitative, and they were critical of the understanding of science maintained by psychology.

In 1971, Frank Severin came out with a supplement to Morgan and King's introductory psychology text that explained humanistic psychology (Severin, 1971). The exposition is coherent and comprehensive, and while the themes have sharpened, they are not essentially different from earlier expressions. In delineating what humanistic psychology is all about, Severin's points clustered about the same two themes: the image of man and the conception of science. With respect to the image of man, Severin says that humanistic psychology wants "to present a more accurate picture of mankind—one that does not conflict with the way we experience ourselves and others. The image currently projected by psychology is at variance in certain respects with what we ourselves learned about mankind by being human" (Severin, 1971, p. 2). What is missing in current psychology, he explained, is sufficient emphasis on the unity of the person, human autonomy, explicitly human goals and values, and sufficient emphasis on the uniqueness of humanity. Severin then shifted his focus to science and described the need for a human science which would avoid reductionism and include more than objective methodology. Severin then outlined the aims of humanistic psychology in nine points that generally overlapped earlier presentations. The aims deal with the image of human beings (self-determining, holistic, primacy of experience), the limits of science (outmoded methodology, not value-free, we must go beyond prediction and control), and the need for psychology to study relevant problems (no topic should be eliminated, psychologists should be more interested in problems like education, human growth, and social crises). Severin (1971, p. 11) summarized by stating that humanistic psychology is not a new school of thought but rather "an *orientation* to psychology—a way of thinking about man and the whole scientific enterprise that modifies our image of human beings and frees psychology from several artificial restrictions placed upon it by theories that now appear outmoded" (italics in original).

There are many other statements concerning the aims of humanistic psychology, but they do not differ substantially from the ones presented. For example, there is a relatively extensive statement from Harman (1974, pp. 1–2) which indicates that humanistic psychology is interested in "systematization of subjective experience" and a "unified view of human experiences . . . and . . . of the processes of personal change." Systematization and unification are two characteristics of science, which shows that humanistic psychology is interested in scientific pursuits as well as those dealing with "helping relations."

This sampling of expressions concerning the founding and development of humanistic psychology, as a whole, is fairly consistent. It varies in emphasis from time to time and the expressions sharpen over time, but the main point never really varies: psychology needs a better image of human beings if it is to be of service to human beings. But the very fact that it called itself a "third force" in opposition to behaviorism and psychoanalysis, and insofar as it emphasized the image of human beings as opposed to the emphasis on science in traditional psychology, shows how much its development was in contrast to the emphases of traditional psychology.

The Meaning of Humanistic Psychology

The previous section indicated that, in very general terms, humanistic psychology is seeking a psychology that will lead to a more faithful image of man. If that is true, how could I state earlier that it was an amorphous movement, or how could Royce (1972) claim that there is conceptual confusion in humanistic psychology? I would claim that both assertions are true once the next step is taken—that is, if one pursues what is meant by a better image of man or if one tries to see how one can be faithful to both a better image of man and the criteria for science. This section, then, deals with the difficulties surrounding the term "humanistic psychology."

Precisely what is meant by "human" in the expression "humanistic psychology" has not been clarified in a way that is acceptable to all of its proponents. As far as I can determine, at least five meanings of the term "human" are in use. Human is used (1) in the sense of "humane," (2) in the sense of the philosophy of humanism, (3) in the sense of the humanities, (4) in an operational sense (i.e., whatever humans do), and (5) in the sense of specifying those human characteristics that differentiate people from other living creatures. Obviously, some members of the movement support some of the definitions, but not others. We will examine each of these in turn, but I would like to note in passing that the question of resolving the meaning of "human" is a metapsychological issue.

Human in the Sense of Humane

This interpretation of "humanistic" psychology has been spoken for by Matson (1964, 1974), Bugental (1964), and Rogers (1965b), among others. Yet it would seem that humanistic in the sense of humane would not be the best interpretation of humanistic psychology since, as a goal, this would not necessarily differentiate it from other psychologies. For example, I'm sure that Watson would claim that he had "humane" intentions when he exclaimed "Give me the baby!" Skinner would claim to be working in the interests of humankind when he claims that we must go "beyond freedom and dignity." Freud would claim that he was being humane when he encouraged people to see through the illusion of religion. On the other side of the fence, Koch (1969) has criticized the humanistic-psychology movement, especially its encounter movement aspects, precisely of being inhumane. Moreover, since only people bring evil into the world, would one really want to leave murder, rape, aggression, war, and so forth outside the scope of psychological investigation, even though hardly any psychologist would condone them? Certainly, psychologists want to be humane, but it is clear from the above examples that the intention to be humane is not sufficient. One would have to look at what one meant by the term—that is, exactly what one intended do—and then all the hoary difficulties of value enter in. But here we are interested in the best meaning of "human" for humanistic psychology, and we see that humane is not sufficiently discriminating. In the sense that one would want to retain it—that is, in the sense that one would want to evoke good qualities in people and promote human welfare—it does not necessarily discriminate among psychologies, since all would make that claim. This, of course, does not mean that all systems of psychology are equal with respect to the manner in which the intentions of humaneness are carried out, but this question cannot be answered in the concrete without referring to values, the intentions of the psychologist, and the effects of his or her actions, and each of these categories can produce honest disagreements. In other words, while the manner in which humane is understood can vary widely, the intention to be humane is common to all psychologies and thus is not a good way to differentiate humanistic psychology.

Human in the Sense of the Philosophy of Humanism

This second sense of "humanistic" also has a basis in fact (e.g., Richards & Richards, 1973). Deriving from the philosophy of humanism, it would mean in this sense the study of human beings, their achievements and interests, as opposed to the study of theologically tinged problems or problems posed abstractly or in general. Insofar as it has a philosophical precommitment to limit itself exclusively to human achievements and interests and insofar as many psychologists interested in humanistic psychology are interested in transcendent experiences, parapsychic phenomena, religious experiences, and so forth, this also seems not to be the best meaning of humanistic psychology. Those humanistic psychologists who do align themselves with this interpretation do so mostly because they dislike the abstractions of traditional psychology, but a return to the concrete does not necessarily imply a commitment to the philosophy of humanism. Moreover, it seems to confuse the reality of the human being with the phenomena that humans can experience. A strict humanistic philosophy, in this sense, would be no more interested in physical nature than it would be in God, since physical nature (earth, stars, oceans) is no more human than God is.

However, all would admit that nature is experienced by human beings, and a humanistic psychology that would remain open to the possibility of nonhuman or extrahuman realities could not adopt a strict philosophy of humanism. What humanistic psychology should demand is simply that whatever may be nonhuman be given in human experience. Thus, because of the specific interpretation of humanistic philosophy, this sense of humanism would not be the best for humanistic psychology.

Humanistic in the Sense of the Humanities

The third sense of "humanistic" psychology is that of the humanities in the classical sense of the term. This sense refers to the group of studies generally considered to be part of classical learning, such as art, literature, history of civilization, and so on. Some humanistic psychologists support this interpretation (e.g., Cantril & Bumstead, 1965; Harman, 1965), and indeed an interesting dialogue is possible, but the very fact of the possibility of a dialogue presupposes an essential difference. Undoubtedly, the humanities reveal profound insights into the nature of man, and psychologists can make fruitful use of these insights, just as they do with insights borrowed from biology, physics, or chemistry. But that does not make them psychological. Humanistic psychology may overlap the phenomena (or content) of the humanities, but the way of approaching, investigating, and making use of knowledge gained from these phenomena differs. To say that humanistic psychology is humanistic in this sense is not sufficient because the humanities present insights about human beings without speaking to the issue of methodology or to the context in which these insights are presented. If anything, there would be only one dimension of the humanities that would genuinely come close to what humanistic psychology should try to achieve, and that would be criticism, to which the humanities relegate the role of clarifying the achievements of artists. Criticism is the methodological wing of the humanities, but the critics do not proceed in the same way that the "humanists" of "the humanities" do. And humanistic psychologists who use the term in this sense speak of the achievers, the artists, not the critics. For this reason, humanistic in the third sense does not seem to be the best interpretation for humanistic psychology.

Human in the Sense of Activities of Man

The fourth sense of "humanistic" is simply that it is a descriptive term referring to anything done by human beings. In this sense, "humanistic" is used in the same way as one uses "animal" in "animal psychology". No precommitment is understood in the latter except that one is dealing with animals and all that implies. In the same vein, humanistic psychology deals with the experience and behavior of humans and all that that implies. Although this interpretation has the advantage of comprehensiveness, it is not penetrating enough, and it also includes too much. Is an eyeblink a human response? Are the memories obtained by Penfield through brain stimulation human responses? Is the adolescent who uncritically lives out the wishes of overweening parents behaving humanly? These are indeed difficult questions, but they must be answered if humanistic psychology is to advance. The operational definition of "human" is based purely on the fact of a human organism, defined physically, behaving or experiencing. It is a definition that desperately needs elaboration and clarification. At least, however, it forces us to make a distinction between the sheer content of the phenomenon we are observing and the quality, level, or type of phenomenon. In other words, we have to distinguish between phenomena that happen to, or within, a human organism—that is, those events that take place with respect to a person minimally (physically) defined—and genuinely human phenomena, those events with respect to a person that involve the latter's full participation. This leads us to the last meaning of human.

Human in the Sense of Uniquely Human

As stated above, this orientation tries to specify in a positive way what is meant by "human." For example, Sutich (1961) has written that humanistic psychology was founded by a group of psychologists and other professionals

> who are interested in those human capacities and potentialities that have no systematic place either in positivistic or behavioristic theory or in classical psychoanalytic theory, e.g., creativity, love, self, growth, organism, basic-need gratification, self-actualization, higher values, ego transcendence, objectivity, autonomy, identity, responsibility, psychological health, etc. . . . [Pursuing these interests] should greatly speed up the emergence of a more adequate—a more scientific—picture of the full possibilities inherent in the nature of man. (Sutich, 1961, p. viii)

The search for the meaning of the uniquely or genuinely human is necessary, but again, I do not think it can be done on the basis of content alone. It is true that the kinds of phenomena Sutich enumerates have been relatively neglected in psychology and that they should be investigated, but it is also true that many traditional phenomena—such as learning perception, motivation, emotion, and so on—could also stand thorough investigation from a specifically or uniquely human standpoint. In other words, it is not just the neglected areas that a genuinely humanistic psychology has to investigate; it should also reinvestigate many thoroughly investigated areas, this time from a strictly human viewpoint. This implies, once again, that it is not content alone that determines the meaning of "human."

I will present my understanding of "human" below, but just now I want to review where we are. Of the five possible meanings of "human," I would prefer the last, that is, trying to state in a positive vein what is meant by uniquely human. "Human" in the sense of humane and in the operational sense are too broad; the former is really more a value that all systems of psychology can share, and the latter is not sufficiently discriminating with respect to genuinely human acts. "Human" in the senses of classical humanism and the humanities are not inclusive enough; both omit certain kinds of experiences that psychologists would want to deal with. Thus, that which is genuinely human would seem to be the best understanding of "human" for humanistic psychology, with the understanding that it is to be distinguished from the merely "mankind-centered" in the physical and content sense. We will elaborate this further below, but first I would like to turn to certain other important distinctions.

Critical Evaluation of Humanistic Psychology

In this section I will try to evaluate humanistic psychology in terms of a number of distinctions. Earlier, I stated that the best description of humanistic psychology that Misiak and Sexton (1973) could find was to call it "a protest movement and a new program." It seems that humanistic psychology has been more successful as a protest movement than as a new program, perhaps because as a protest it is more unified, whereas as a new program the many differences among its members are also revealed. Misiak and Sexton (1973, p. 135) summarized the desiderata expressed in contemporary literature concerning humanistic psychology:

1. Avoidance of disunity and striving for a larger perspective, encompassing many viewpoints

2. Less protestation and rhetoric, more solid research and positive productivity
3. Continuous dialogue with other psychological orientations and systems
4. Generation of testable hypotheses and reliable working methods of investigation
5. Overcoming the often critized provincialism and ethnocentrism of American psychology

In my opinion, the above listing is a fair summary of what is being said about humanistic psychology from both within and without the movement. The list boils down to three essential points: humanistic psychology should be more unified, it should have a broader base and be in dialogue with other viewpoints, and it should be more productive in a positive sense. Again, as general aims, these comments cannot be faulted. However, when one attempts to achieve the general aims, all sorts of difficulties arise. How is unity to be achieved? What is meant by "positive productivity"? In what sense is humanistic psychology narrow? In this section, I will discuss some of the difficulties likely to be encountered by humanistic psychology if the next level of analysis is to be pursued. I am interested in discussing the critiques that I think are true whether they have come from within or without the humanistic movement.

Humanistic Psychology Needs Clarification of Key Concepts

The distinctions presented in the previous section were introduced in order to help resolve the problems involved in this critique. Key terms such as "human," "science," "growth," "authenticity," "encounter," "man," and "person" need theoretical clarification. No one expects psychologists to be philosophers and spend all their time trying to define complex and intricate human phenomena. On the other hand, evasive procedures or repeated attempts to ignore the issue are equally unsatisfactory. What is called for is a thoughtful reflection on psychological phenomena in context and a careful description of what actually takes place in research or therapy. The reflections of the researcher or therapist can then be a part of a dialogue with the general community of psychologists and others who are interested in the same phenomena. Improved theoretical articulation of key humanistic-psychology terms, as so many have pointed out, is definitely in order. But we should also be reminded that traditional psychology is not much better in this respect.

Humanistic versus Human Scientific Psychology

I think it would be useful here, in the process of clarifying, to introduce another distinction. When we were trying to determine the meaning of humanistic psychology above, we were concerned with the kind of phenomena to be dealt with. In trying to determine whether we are dealing with humanistic or human scientific psychology, we are concerned more with the attitude and interests of the psychologist. Much of humanistic psychology began with clinicians, therapists, and others interested in the "helping" aspects of psychology. Thus, when they perceived that the requirements of science were a serious stumbling block to the development of a humanistic psychology, they simply avoided any reference to science whatsoever. Those psychologists who were interested in research, however, were more concerned with the standards of science and thus sought a human scientific psychology.

The two demands are not mutually exclusive, but their relationship has to be understood. Historically, humanistic psychology has referred to any aspect of the phenomenon of man that functions at a human level. Human scientific psychology, on the other hand, emerged in the context of the research and systematic interests of humanistic psychology. In other words, the practical difference between humanistic psychology and human scientific psychology is the difference between clinical and research interests. However, a theoretical relationship could be established if the community of psychologists could agree that psychology ought to be a human science where human phenomena are concerned. In this way, theoretical unity would be achieved, and both clinical practice and research activity would simply be applications of psychology conceived as a human science.

Hopefully, the word "science" in this context will not cause difficulties. Here science simply means methodical or systematic knowledge. But this must be understood structurally and not in simply content (learning is scientific, therapy is not) or situational (labs are scientific, psychoanalytic couches are not) terms. When Freud reflected on his case histories in order to arrive at a theory of neurosis, he was considering his data methodically or systematically. When Robert Jay Lifton reflected on his experiences in helping victims of disasters in order to understand the psychological effects of extreme disasters on the human psyche, he changed his attitude toward all the experiences he had and considered them as a set of data to be worked with so that a fuller meaning of the entire situation could be disclosed. When he was a helper to the victims of disaster, his presence to them was different. Hence, the attitude required for good clinical work and for good research certainly differs, but at least they can both draw on a unified set of concepts and principles.

Overall, humanistic psychology has not developed very far in terms of research despite numerous expressions of the need to do so. The most consistent attempt thus far is the work by Child (1973), but his approach to research is not sufficiently radical. He sees objectivity, precision, and the verifiability of knowledge as being the virtues of the research tradition; he then goes on to admit that often the objectivity and precision of the research tradition is illusory rather than real, but he is not motivated to question how that can be so. His analysis stops just when it becomes interesting. The virtues of humanistic psychology for Child are its relevance to present social values, its regard for individual responsibility, its concern for personal fulfillment, and its openness. Child covers certain selected topics, such as moral development and the psychology of art, where he feels that psychology is breaking out of its narrow perspective. Unfortunately, Child still leaves the impression that the virtues of the two traditions are difficult to reconcile, and his approach is to use certain *de facto* examples of possible breakthrough rather than a theoretical justification or integration.

Unfortunately, there are other psychologists in addition to Child who are troubled by the idea of a "human science," believing the two terms to be inherently contradictory (e.g., Hebb, 1974; Royce, 1972). I have tried to show a number of times that this is not so (Giorgi, 1970a, 1970b, 1975a), and I will briefly indicate the reasons here. Science is methodical and/or systematic knowledge, but the methods developed by science to gain a more precise knowledge than that obtained in everyday life should not be viewed as contextless. There is no method that precedes all content, although there are methods that are highly general and can be used for a number of contents. What determines rigor—which is why methods are invented—is the relationship between the phenomenon to be studied and the adequacy of the method employed. In other words, one must first be sure that fidelity to the phenomenon is observed. To use coarse examples, one does not eat soup with a fork or use a screwdriver for writing. To use psychological examples, one does not use tbe method of constant stimuli for verbal material, nor does one use the method of free association when investigating sensory thresholds. The reason that psychologists do not do this is that there is a certain precomprehension of the phenomenon to be investigated that guides the selection of method so that relevancy of the method for the phenomenon is assured. In the same way, there are certain precomprehensions guiding our understanding of what it means to be human and what it means to be scientific. the difficulty for psychology in general, and humanistic psychology in particular, is that the understanding of human has thus far remained merely a precomprehension—there is no commonly accepted agreement among psychologists of what we mean by human—and humanistic psychology will remain ambiguous until a clearer understanding of what it means to be human is achieved. As a matter of fact, it seems that as broad a range of interpretations of "human" as is possible exists among psychologists, from those who see man as simply a more complicated type of nature (e.g., Kantor, 1924) to the humanistic psychologists who see him as unique. Obviously, what is sorely needed is a solid philosophical anthropology from which psychologists could draw an adequate image of man, but unfortunately, that field does not seem to be much more advanced than our own.

On the other hand, the precomprehension of "science" among psychologists is strongly biased by the factual development and explicit theoretical statements of the natural sciences. Rather than seeing the natural sciences as an intentional human achievement, they are imitated in terms of their factual history. In the former type of analysis, one reawakens the context within which the natural sciences developed and sees the actual procedures and methods employed as examples of general intentions rather than as norms to be followed. In other words, the norms should be the aims of the natural scientist rather than the specific procedures or solutions adopted.

Thus, we can describe the tension in psychology as follows: on the one hand, there is largely a void—no explicit meaning of "human"—and on the other hand, there is a highly developed and elaborated theory and praxis of what "science" means based on a history of man–nature relationships. The result is that the scientific framework rushes in and fills the void. The correction for this situation is to make explicit the meaning of human and then modify scientific praxis according to a more explicit comprehension of that meaning. In such a way is a human science entirely possible. In brief, scientific (i.e., methodical) rigor can be established only by understanding the dialectical relationship between a phenomenon and its method, not by submitting the phenomenon to the criteria of a generalized method in an *a priori* way. In order to do this precisely, one must also be cognizant of one's own approach, for the relationship between method and phenomenon can only be understood by standing somewhere (i.e., within one's own approach); there will probably never be one approach to encompass all phenomena. In closing this section, I merely want to state again that the meaning of "human," the meaning of "science," and the choice of approach are all metapsychological issues.

Humanistic-Psychology Aims versus Praxis

The aims and exhortations of humanistic psychology call for a redefinition of psychology and a total renewal of all aspects of the discipline. However, we find in actuality that it has been long on prescriptions and short on unequivocal transformations. Again, I say this not as a point of criticism from the outside but as a critique from the inside. One cannot expect a movement that is only about 15 years old to be fully developed, so the mere facts that praxis has not kept up with intentions, that some experimental forms of praxis have gone too far, or that hybrid combinations of the new and the old appear should not be in the least surprising. Still, one should point out the shortcomings of these flawed attempts if only to learn from them and point to a better way of practicing psychology.

The strength of the humanistic-psychology movement is clearly in the "helping" domain of psychology, whether it is helping ordinary people to "grow" or helping pathological persons to overcome their difficulties. Critics have pointed out many of the shortcomings of these ventures, and I will not repeat them here. Overall, what concerns me about the "helping" side of humanistic psychology is that its concentration, with very few exceptions, is on techniques rather than ideas and hence the breakthroughs are never radical enough. The longevity of ideas is much greater than that of techniques. I have the impression that humanistic psychologists are just as technical as their traditional colleagues; their technical expertise is simply camouflaged by the language of the body and experiential categories. In other words, the attitude within which this language is couched is technical, and it is often used in ways that are just as manipulative as, say, that of psychologists dealing with artificial intelligence. For example, in an article dealing with catharsis and human potential, Heider (1974) speaks about "spiritual technologies" (p. 27), "catharsis . . . [that] can be produced pretty much at will" (p. 45), and using tachistoscopes and negative-ion generators as training devices "for discovering paths of growth for contemporary people" (p. 46). Is it merely semantic quibbling to note that one speaks of spiritual "techniques" rather than, say, spiritual "exercises"? Is not the fact that one can "produce catharsis at will" simply another way of manipulating human experiences? Again I'm sure that the intentions of the author are different from my interpretations of them, but does his praxis measure up to his intentions?

Another way that I find humanistic praxis lagging behind its aims and exhortations is in the area of research. In terms of content or phenomena selected for research, humanistic psychology has certainly introduced a change. In fact, one could even argue that it has gone too far in that it often seems to seek esoteric phenomena as a way of proving that it is different from traditional psychology. However, when it comes to the actual practice of research, it often uses the same general methodological tools that are used by traditional psychologists. Obviously there are exceptions (e.g., Kolton, 1973), but the majority of self-conscious research efforts fall in line with the critique. For example, Jourard (1971) found it necessary to use analyses of variance with his research on self-disclosure and Reed (1973) devised a dream recall rating scale. Hendrickson (1973), in dealing with high-school morale, found traditional definitions lacking and hence turned to humanistic-psychology literature for more relevant statements but then proceeded to construct a scale to measure morale by following Thurstone's technique. And Bayne (1974) spoke of measures of authenticity or self-disclosure. Can one imagine Freud trying to devise a rating scale in order to understand the world of dreams or a scale to see if his client is authentic? In other words, while there is a shift to either more uniquely human phenomena, or at least to explicitly human phenomena, there is not a corresponding shift in methods for approaching these phenomena. It seems that methodological breakthroughs are needed just as much as those of content. This, in turn, implies the necessity of a different approach to phenomena such that a different methodology can ensue. Here humanistic psychology has not been so successful, and here is where the greatest need exists—in terms of theory and metapsychology.

Individual versus Historical and Social Emphasis

Humanistic psychology has spent a great deal of energy asserting the rights and dignity of the individual and the importance of experience. It reflects largely on the sad state of development of psychology when the mere affirmation of the individual as a creative self-fulfilling autonomous creature has to be argued for, debated, and demonstrated. But because humanistic psychology has had to fulfill this role, it has not elaborated the full dimensionality of humanness in terms of historicity and sociality. However, the role humanistic psychology was forced to play seems not to be the only reason for this. In Europe, for example, there has also been a critique of traditional academic psychology, but the correction of the critique is in terms of social relevance. Long ago Roback (1952) pointed out that American psychology seemed to express the characteristics of American society, especially rugged individualism and an ahistorical way of tackling problems, just as we had no history when we conquered the West and romanticized that expansion in terms of a lone cowboy or explorer against nature. It is disappointing to see that humanistic psychology is not different in this respect. While humanistic psychology has emphasized experience over overt behavior and a more proper image of man over a mechanomorphic image, it is still the individual's self-actualization, self-growth, or consciousness expansion that is being sought. I am not saying that there are not implications for the social-political realm or that one could not move more easily to historical understanding of man from a humanistic perspective, but only that it has not made very extensive moves in this direction thus far. Again, this criticism comes from both within and without the humanistic-psychology movement. Ansbacher (1971), for example, has expressed this point eloquently.

Antiintellectualistic Tendencies

Objections to these tendencies have been voiced as much, if not more, by those sympathetic to the movement (e.g., Kelly, 1969; May, 1965) as by outsiders (e.g., Koch, 1964). Nevertheless, despite these protestations, the tendencies persist. This seems to be encouraged in part by general openness of the Association of Humanistic Psychology (AHP) to whomever is interested in the cause, despite background, in part by the fact that many members seem to be practitioners interested in immediate results rather than long-range issues, and in part by the image created by ads that invite people to join AHP because there are "conferences such as Psychic Healing, Humanistic Politics, Biofeedback, Frontiers of the Mind, Eastern and Western Psychologies, Humanistic Education and Death and Dying" ("Why Join the Association for Humanistic Psychology," 1974). One cannot help but feel that a smorgasbord of "in" topics is being served to one and all and that the only requirement is interest in the topic. Rather than differentiating itself from traditional psychology in the simplest possible way (i.e., by content) humanistic psychology should try to encourage dialogue with traditional psychology by trying to understand the latter's problems better than it does and therefore achieving better solutions because of its better understanding. However, this too would entail metapsychological issues like a better theory of human nature and a better self-understanding of science, and both of these would initially involve not new techniques but newer and better conceptualizations which, of course, goes against the very antiintellectualistic tendencies displayed by many members of the movement.

Implicit Appeal to Life-World

This point is not so much a critique as the making explicit of a position. Whenever humanistic psychologists complain about scientific restrictions, the argument is always that the scientific image implied by traditional psychology is not the image of man in everyday life. In the conflict between the scientific image and everyday experience, most humanistic psychologists choose everyday experience. This is an implicit appeal to the priority of the life-world, a theme made explicit by Husserl (1970) and other phenomenologists, which should perhaps be more explicitly acknowledged. The point is not that the life-world is superior to science, but merely that it is prior in the sense that even science derives from it. The appeal is simply that humanistic psychology would prefer to turn to the life-world for the formulations of its problems rather than to science. It is recognized that the life-world expressions would have to be elaborated further, but differently from the way traditional science would elaborate them. My point is that strong theoretical justification for this step exists, but humanistic psychology never seems to make use of these arguments.

All the critiques of this section imply a groping with metapsychological issues in order to find a solution. Psychology, sooner or later, will have to confront this fact.

The Literature of Science

Humanistic psychology has tried to correct psychology by appealing to our everyday experience of man, to the literature of humanism, and to the need to change the image of man. I simply want to note that the literature of science is itself changing in order to bring its self-understanding in line with its praxis. Thus, there is more awareness within traditional psychology of the social relevance and historial character of science as well as more awareness concerning the human role in constituting science and an increasing emphasis on the actual humane value of science for humankind. There is also, finally, an admission of the fact that there are different ways to be scientific and different styles of science. Radnitzky (1970) has summarized most of these points in an enlightening way. My point, therefore, is that the literatures of science, the philosophy of science, and metascience show signs of moving in ways that should converge with the aims of humanistic psychology. However, even within this literature there is a need for a more fully developed metapsychology. Thus, it seems to me that a developed and articulated metapsychology is precisely what both literatures need in order to move forward. We will now turn to that problem.

A Metapsychology for Humanistic Psychology

As I see it, the metapsychology for humanistic or human scientific psychology requires that our understanding of "human" be compatible with our understanding of "science." Of the two, it seems that clarification of the meaning of human should precede the clarification of the meaning of science, since humanness is the content and science is the framework. While it is true that the two are dialectically related, it is really up to science to accommodate itself to the nature of humanness rather than the other way around.

I will not pretend to solve all of the problems surrounding the meaning of human. I simply want to show in this section how one must approach the problem of humanness, what some characteristics of human being are, and then to demonstrate that science, correctly understood, is not incompatible—indeed can flourish—with genuinely human phenomena.

Approach to Human Phenomena

It seems to me that we have to approach human phenomena not substantially but structurally; I use the term structure in the sense of Merleau-Ponty (1963). For Merleau-Ponty, a structure is a network of relationships that are sometimes lived and known and at other times merely lived, but these relationship always exist in relation to consciousness that knows them or lives them. By using of this term, Merleau-Ponty hoped to overcome the many dualisms inherited from philosophy that have plagued psychology—body–mind, subject–object, inner–outer, public–private, and so on. Merleau-Ponty would admit that there are tensions between such terms within human beings, but these are understood as intrastructural tensions that are dialectically related rather than substances that are causally related. In other words, there are dualities in human beings, a certain tension between exclusive directions or achievements, but they are *not dualisms*. In terms of images, we must think of these distinctions as branches emerging from a single trunk that eventually differentiates into leaves, fruits, and blossoms rather than as billiard balls that simply lie side by side or bang against each other. Thus, in order to understand the relationship between a specific leaf and a fruit from the same tree, we would have to understand the whole tree and its relationship to its environment. In the same way, to understand the relationship between "body" and "soul" or "subject" and "object," we would have to understand the entire structure of relationships that the person maintains. There are ways in which man belongs to the world, or the soul belongs to the body, or the public is related to the private, that the analytic style of thinking cannot capture because it presupposes the cutting off of these belonging relationships, then posits no relationship between the remainders, and then begins to study the relationships between the two remainders as though they were separate entities with no prior history. Modes of thinking and analysis will have to be found that do not require the initial severing of these important relationships.

The first major impact of this kind of thinking is that contexts become as important as themes. Spatial and temporal horizons, memories and expectations, relationships with significant others, and affective nuances all originally belong to whatever human phenomenon is under investigation. They are not variables that are originally independent and then become influential as a consequence of some kind of manipulation.

When one is confronted by such complexities, the only way to begin is to use the natural syntheses that everyday meanings provide and that are available to all of us through description. Both the researcher's description of a situation and the subject's description of the same situation are necessary points of departure. What for me is a simple nonsense syllable experiment may be for a subject proof of ability to succeed in college, and thus, that subject might perform in a very tense manner. It would be important for the researcher to know this when the time comes to evaluate the performance data. Thus, the meanings expressed in language help organize what would otherwise be a seemingly hopeless array of aspects of the dimensions of situations. These meanings can be deepened or developed, depending on the intentions of the researcher, until the appropriate level of psychological understanding is achieved.

In brief, then, it seems that the approach to human phenomena would have to be structural and at least initially descriptive in order to capture the phenomenon as human. Of course, much more is implied by these terms than I have elaborated here, but the major purpose of this section is not to fully elaborate on the approach so much as to show the compatibility of this approach to science. From our point of view, there is no difficulty with structure and description with respect to science since the natural sciences already employ both perspectives. The difficulty, if any, for most traditional psychologists is that structure and description are not sufficient for a mature science. Ultimately, we would also agree that a deeper analysis (if understood in the correct sense) is necessary, but the prescriptions regarding the type of analysis would still have to be determined by the nature of the phenomenon and not according to a certain preconception of science. If one understands science as an intentional human achievement, then one merely has to understand that man, as scientist, intends to gain systematic and methodical knowledge about fellow humans. The problem then becomes one of inventing the appropriate means of doing so. This is a different problem from presupposing that the aim of science is to measure phenomena quantitatively and then wondering how one can measure concious experiences in such a fashion. The difference between the two approaches is that the former has a minimum of dictates concerning the nature of the phenomenon to be investigated and thus can lead to more original ways of gaining knowledge whereas the latter is more specific, flowing from presuppositions concerning the nature of science, and though original ways of measuring can be devised, there is not the same guarantee that the kind of knowledge to be gained is equally fruitful. I will try to be more specific in the next section.

Concerning the Meaning of Human

Again, without in any way being exhaustive, I will describe three features that I feel set man apart from other living creatures: (1) the ability of man to overturn any given structure in which he finds himself, (2) his symbolic power, and (3) his power to reflect on his own lived experience. Obviously, these are not mutually exclusive but simply indicate different ways humanness is expressed.

The definition of "human" as man's ability to overturn any given structure is Merleau-Ponty's (1963). He prefers that description to the notation of the fact that man creates an order beyond nature, be it economic, social, religious, or whatever. In this way, we see once again the value of a structural approach where one is tied not to a specific content but rather to a certain way of relating to the world.

To say that man participates in symbolic activity is essentially to say that man can create worlds for himself. Pollio (1974), following von Bertalanffy, uses three criteria all of which must be present to identify symbols: (1) representation, (2) free creation, (3) transmission by culture. Cassirer (1973) emphasizes that the symbolic function is not restricted to particular cases as signals can be but that it is a principle of universal applicability which encompasses a whole field of human thought. Merleau-Ponty (1963) describes it as a relation between relations, or an intention or structure of the second power, or again, as a level of original conduct in which the "thing-structure" becomes possible so that one can recognize the same thing despite variations of perspective. Symbolic activity implies multiplicity of perspective and the possibility of varied expressions of the same theme.

Lastly, to say that man can reflect on his own lived experiences (or those of others) essentially means that he can transform the meaning of his own life or that of others. It is the difference between the fact of living through something and determining the meaning of what it is one has lived through. In this manner, one is able to change lived meanings, to be responsible for one's own life, and to be able to guide and direct it accordingly. Reflection does not merely take note of our prereflective life; it also transforms that life.

I think I have been conservative in delineating human characteristics, and I make no claim for originality. All three characteristics mentioned above have been mentioned before. What I want to show is that these characteristics do not rule out a scientific approach to human phenomena. To say that man can overturn any given structure, that he has symbolic power, or that he has the power to reflect on what he has lived through does not preclude gaining methodical knowledge about these activities. The ultimate irony, of course, is that human beings have used all three of these activities to create science. The ability to overturn any given structure is the way scientific paradigms are transcended (such as the move from the Ptolemeian to the Copernican system); symbolic activity is used to describe physical nature mathematically; and man's power of reflection is used in designing experiments, since any researcher has to interrogate his or her own past experiences in order to formulate researchable questions about any phenomenon. Indeed, the question is more one of how psychology could have denied or assumed away these very powers in regard to its human subjects.

For research, the ability of a subject to transform any given situation in which he or she is placed does imply that there is never, *a priori*, any guarantee that a subject will interpret a research situation the way an experimenter intends. Indeed, that is one of the implications of the work of Rosenthal (1966) and his colleagues, and it has not prevented him from conducting research, although in my opinion, he does not pursue the implications of his research to their radical conclusion. In any event, all this would mean is that an experimenter would have to interrogate subjects in order to see just how they perceived the situation. The researcher then has a number of options: to include only those who spontaneously perceived the situation the intended way, to find the different types of perceptions that were included and relate them to performance, and so forth. Philips (1969) has demonstrated the feasibility of this type of research. What is required is simply the removal of the assumption of an identical perspective—that is, that all subjects should view a situation identically. Research could also be conducted with the assumption of multiperspectivity, which would make it even more empirical and more faithful to the actual research situation because one would ascertain the facts about the subject's perspectives rather than merely assuming identity of perception and then trying to deal with the variation statistically. In other words, nothing has to change except certain assumptions about science.

The fact that man uses symbolic activity is likewise not a deterrence to research. We saw that symbolic activity means that man can create worlds for himself and that in the history of psychology research has been conducted concerning the "world of dreams" or the "world of the neurotic" or the "world of work," and so on. We also saw that it means that man can respond to the "thing-structure" and retain the thing's identity when the perspectives on it are changed. Köhler's apes could not do this; when the box was a container, the ape could not use it as a step ladder to get a banana hanging from the ceiling. On the other hand, Duncker's (1935/1945) breakthroughs in studies on functional fixedness depended entirely on the subject's symbolic ability; without it, no successes could have been achieved. Many other examples of studies on language could also be cited. As in the previous case, symbolic activity may appear to be a difficulty for science, but only because of certain assumptions that a certain conception of science carries with it.

Finally, the ability to reflect on one's experience to ascertain its meaning is also not an obstacle. Almost all therapy presupposes this ability. All description presupposes it. Moreover, there are ways of analyzing descriptions qualitatively that can yield intersubjective results (Giorgi, 1975b). Thus, it is even possible to avoid unnecessary quantification if one so chooses.

The difficulty in traditional psychology with respect to these issues is that it has only backed into acknowledging the legitimacy of the genuinely human characteristics (or used them surreptiously) rather than embracing them as valuable aids for research. The difficulty in humanistic psychology with respect to these issues is that while they have been acknowledged, their implications have not been pursued to the level of praxis in a rigorous and systematic way. Ultimately, only when we have a radically clarified metapsychology based on a solid philosophical anthropology can we begin to solve these issues in an adequate way.

Psychology as a Human Science

It seems to me that there have been, and still are, two essential critiques directed against psychology, both of which can be summarized by that recently much abused word—relevance. The two separate critiques are (1) lack of relevance of the approach or method utilized by psychology for the phenomena it wants to study, which can be corrected by being more attentive to the criterion of fidelity to the phenomenon as it is lived and appears, and (2) lack of relevance of psychology to society as a whole, which can be corrected by refocusing psychology's interests in the direction of the social-political-cultural problems of our age. The stumbling block for the facile correction of both critiques is the self-understanding of science that psychology has adopted. Insofar as commitments to the natural-science conception of science are sustained on the part of psychology, then genuinely human phenomena will always appear to be too complex or too elusive for the concepts, methods, and procedures, and the pressing social, political, and cultural problems of the day will always be perceived as technical problems that have to be dealt with in terms of knowledge gained in "pure" settings rather than genuine problems for academic psychologists. But if we let the ways in which human problems are lived and experienced guide the ways we approach and research them, then we might discover that the social, historical, and cultural contexts are indeed genuine aspects of the problems humans live. Then, if we allow ourselves the freedom to conceive of science more broadly and if we admit that it is theoretically possible to gain methodical and systematic knowledge about humans, then I am confident that an articulate expression of a human scientific praxis will emerge and will actually enrich our understanding of science in general. Authors have frequently pointed out how man is often a victim of his own ideas. Royce (1964) has spoken of this fact in terms of encapsulated man and Kelly (1963) in terms of personal constructs. My interpretation of the key problem is that traditional psychology is hampered by its self-understanding of science and that humanistic psychology, while it has moved a step beyond in the sense that it legitimately locates the problem within the context of science, has not developed the praxis of a new psychology because equal emphasis was not placed on conceptual and theoretical efforts. Thus, in both cases, an improved self-understanding of the meaning of psychology and science, which involves metapsychological issues, is the beginning of the correction psychology needs.

I am painfully aware that this chapter falls into the category of "exhortation" rather than achievement, but the enormous nature of the task makes it inevitable. I would only want to add that, in my opinion, recognizing the need for a more adequate metapsychology and increased effort in this direction on the part of psychologists would hasten the day that all of us can cease to be apologetic about psychology.

References

Allport, G. The person in psychology. In F. Severin (Ed.), *Humanistic viewpoints in psychology: A book of readings*. New York: McGraw-Hill, 1965.

Ansbacher, H. Alfred Adler and humanistic psychology. *Journal of Humanistic Psychology*, 1971, *11*, 53–63.

Bayne, R. Does the JSDQ measure authenticity? *Journal of Humanistic Psychology*, 1971, *14*, 79–86.

Bugental, J. F. T. The third force in psychology. *Journal of Humanistic Psychology*, 1964, *4*, 19–26.

Bugental, J. F. T. Humanistic psychology: A new breakthrough. In F. Severin (Ed.), *Humanistic viewpoints in psychology: A book of readings*. New York: McGraw-Hill, 1965.

Cantril, H., & Bumstead, C. Science, humanism and man. In F. Severin (Ed.), *Humanistic viewpoints in psychology: A book of readings*. New York: McGraw-Hill, 1965.

Cassirer, E. An essay on man. In F. Severin (Ed.), *Discovering man in psychology*. New York: McGraw-Hill, 1973.

Child, I. *Humanistic psychology and the research tradition*. New York: Wiley, 1973.

Duncker, K. [On problem-solving] (L. S. Lees, trans.). *Psychological Monographs* 1945, *58* (270), (Originally published, 1935.)

Giorgi, A. *Psychology as a human science*. New York: Harper & Row, 1970(a).

Giorgi, A. Toward phenomenologically based research in psychology. *Journal of Phenomenological Psychology*, 1970, *1*, 75–98. (b)

Giorgi, A. Phenomenology and the foundations of psychology. In W. Arnold & J. K. Cole (Eds.), *Nebraska Symposium on Motivation* (Vol. 23). Lincoln: University of Nebraska Press, 1975. (a)

Giorgi, A. An application of the phenomenological method in psychology. In A. Giorgi, C.T. Fischer, & E. Murray (Eds.) *Duquesne studies in phenomenological psychology II*. Pittsburgh: Duquesne University Press, 1975. (b)

Harman, W. The humanities in an age of science. In F. Severin (Ed.), *Humanistic viewpoints in psychology: A book of readings*. New York: McGraw-Hill, 1965.

Harman, W. Notes on the theory of humanistic psychology. *AHP Newsletter*, (August) 1974, 1–2.

Hebb, D. O. What psychology is about. *American Psychologist*, 1974, *29*, 71–79.

Heider, J. Catharsis in human potential encounter. *Journal of Humanistic Psychology*, 1974, *14*, 27–47.

Hendrickson, G. High school morale and humanistic psychology. *Journal of Humanistic Psychology*, 1973, *13*, 69–75.

Husserl, E. *The crisis of European sciences and transcendental phenomenology*. Evanston, Ill.: Northwestern University Press, 1970.

Jourard, S. *The transparent self* (Rev. ed.). New York: Van Nostrand-Reinhold, 1971.

Kantor, J. R. *Principles of psychology* (Vol. 1). New York: Knopf, 1924.

Kelly, G. A. *A theory of personality*. New York: Norton, 1963.

Kelly, G. A. Humanistic methodology in psychological research. *Journal of Humanistic Psychology*, 1969, *9*, 53–65.

Koch, S. Psychology and emerging conceptions of knowledge as unitary. In T. W. Wann (Ed.), *Behaviorism and phenomenology*. Chicago: University of Chicago Press, 1964.

Koch, S. Psychology cannot be a coherent science. *Psychology Today*, 1969, (Sept.) *3*, 64–69.

Köhler, W. [The mentality of apes.] (E. Winter, trans.). New York: Harcourt, Brace & World, 1925.

Kolton, M. The humanistic treatment philosophy of innovative drug programs. *Journal of Humanistic Psychology*, 1973, *13*, 47–56.

Maslow, A. A philosophy of psychology: The need for a mature science of human nature. In F. Severin (Ed.), *Humanistic viewpoints in psychology: A book of readings*. New York: McGraw-Hill, 1965.

Matson, F. W. *The broken image*. New York: Braziller, 1964.

Matson, F. W. Statement of purpose of AHP by AHP leaders. *AHP Newsletter*, (April) 1974, 14–16.

May, R. Relation of existential to humanistic psychology. *AHP Newsletter*, 1965, *2*, 1, 4.

Merleau-Ponty, M. *The structure of behavior*. Boston: Beacon Press, 1963.

Misiak, H., & Sexton, V. S. *Phenomenological, existential, and humanistic psychologies: A historical survey*. New York: Grune & Stratton, 1973.

Philips, E. Characteristics essential for the emergence of problem solving behavior. *Psychology*, 1969, *6*, 19–29.

Pollio, H. R. *The psychology of symbolic activity*. Reading, Mass.: Addison-Wesley, 1974.

Radnitzsky, G. *Contemporary schools of metascience*. Töteborg, Sweden: Scandinavian University Books, 1970.

Reed, H. Learning to remember dreams. *Journal of Humanistic Psychology*, 1973, *13*, 33–48.

Richards, R., & Richards, A. *Homonovous: The new man*. Boulder, Colo.: Shields Publishing Company, 1973.

Roback, A. A. *History of American psychology*. New York: Library Publishers, 1952.

Rogers, C. The human dimensions of science. In F. Severin (Ed.), *Humanistic viewpoints in psychology: A book of readings*. New York: McGraw-Hill, 1965. (a)

Rogers, C. Some questions and challenges facing a humanistic psychology. *Journal of Humanistic Psychology*, 1965, *5*, 1–5. (b)

Rosenthal, R. *Experimenter effects in behavior research*. New York: Appleton, Century, Crofts, 1966.

Royce, J. R. *The encapsulated man*. New York: Van Nostrand-Reinhold, 1964.

Royce, J. R. On conceptual confusion in humanistic psychology. *Contemporary Psychology*. 1972, *17*, 704–705.

Severin, F. (Ed.). *Humanistic viewpoints in psychology: A book of readings*. New York: McGraw-Hill, 1965.

Severin, F. Third force psychology: A humanistic orientation to the study of man. In C. T. Morgan & R. A. King, *Introduction to psychology* (4th ed.). New York: McGraw-Hill, 1971. (Supplement, pp. 1–13)

Sutich, A. Introduction. *Journal of Humanistic Psychology*, 1961, *2*, vii–ix.

Why join the Association for Humanistic Psychology? *Journal of Humanistic Psychology*, 1974, *14*, back cover.

3

Thaddeus E. Weckowicz

THE IMPACT OF PHENOMENOLOGICAL AND EXISTENTIAL PHILOSOPHIES ON PSYCHIATRY AND PSYCHOTHERAPY

I came like water and like wind I go
Into this Universe and Why, not knowing
Nor Whence, like water willy-nilly
flowing

The Rubaiyat of Omar Khayyam

The preoccupation with existentialist themes, as illustrated by *The Rubaiyat of Omar Khayyam* from eleventh century Persia, is as old as humanity itself. It becomes more intense whenever there is a cultural crisis, when old values are questioned, when an existing social Weltanschauung is no longer meaningful or valid.

The rise of existentialism in Europe in the twentieth century is associated with the social upheaval of the two world wars, crumbling social and political orders, the rise of mass society, and the alienation of man both from his culture and from himself (Schact, 1970).

Thaddeus E. Weckowicz • Department of Psychiatry and Theoretical Psychology Center, University of Alberta, Edmonton, Alberta T6G 2E9, Canada.

It is difficult to assess the role of the phenomenological and existential traditions in twentieth-century psychiatry because neither phenomenology nor existentialism represents a unified school of thought, either in philosophy or in psychiatry.

Among the philosophers and psychiatrists who call themselves phenomenologists or existentialists, there are many different and often opposing views. Common in the views of all of them are a rejection of the traditional metaphysics of the body–mind relationship and a rejection of scientism, particularly the reductionistic, mechanistic version typical of nineteenth-century materialism. Furthermore, there is a rejection of naive objectivism and, in its place, an acceptance of man as the measure of things—not as an abstraction but as a living, feeling, concrete everyday human being—you and me.

It may be important, at this juncture, to ask in what way philosophizing is relevant to the practice of psychiatry. Psychiatry, as a medical specialty, is concerned with the concrete complaints of patients: finding the causes of their illnesses, restoring their health, and restoring them to the society. However, in practice, the psychiatrist is confronted at all times with problems which imply certain philosophical presuppositions. For instance, various theories of mental illness presuppose certain assumptions regarding mind–body relations. A diagnosis of hallucination implies epistemological presuppositions about perception. And views on the goals and techniques of psychotherapy imply philosophical assumptions about human nature: determinism versus free will, conformity to the society versus autonomy of the individual, and the rights of the individual versus the rights of the society. The psychotherapist is confronted with various ethical problems of value choice, definitions of happiness and goodness, and the ultimate concerns of man. These considerations have put psychiatry in a special position, unlike the rest of medicine, and have produced a keen interest, particularly among continental psychiatrists, in philosophical and ethical problems.

In this connection, some formulations offered by Jurgen Habermas (1972) are pertinent. Habermas proposed a classification of disciplines into empirical-analytical, hermeneutic, and empirical-critical. The natural sciences are empirical-analytical in their structure and intent; they aim at the discovery of universally valid scientific laws, at the prediction and control of events in the external world. in contrast, the humanities are based on the hermeneutic method, with the aim of explicating the symbolic meanings of intersubjective communications and social norms.

Habermas's third category, the empirical-critical disciplines, embraces the social sciences, including psychoanalysis. These disciplines aim at the explanation of human and social behavior. In pursuing the behavioral and social sciences, man continually constitutes or recreates himself as something new.

The progress of the natural sciences (the empirical-analytical disciplines) is embedded in the general progress of technology and is concerned with the material world, as was pointed out by C. S. Peirce (1935) in his lectures on pragmatism. Medicine, as an applied natural science, falls into Habermas's first category, the empirical-analytical sciences, and as a result is an integral part of general technological progress. The implicit acceptance of Cartesian dualism— the split into body and mind— has simplified issues for medicine. As a consequence, the body can be regarded, in a certain sense, as belonging to a person as an object, a thing, or a tool does; repairing it or "fixing it up," therefore, becomes an engineering problem. A physician or a surgeon can be seen as a body mechanic or a body engineer. The transaction between a physician and a patient can be regarded as a legal contract according to which the physician undertakes to repair the body, which is the property of the patient—the person. Admittedly, some areas are gray, such as the case of an assault on the body, which is construed as an assault on a person rather than on the person's property. There are also some conflicts about the goals, values, and underlying moral issues with which medical ethics are concerned. Such issues as performance of abortions on demand rather than for strictly "medical reasons," euthanasia, or the more general problem of the preservation of human life at any cost as against an insistence on the "quality" of life are undoubtedly ethical and moral issues. However, they can be relatively easily separated from medical technology as such.

It is not easy to place psychiatry and clinical psychology in any of the three categories proposed by Habermas. The psychiatrist or the clinical psychologist treats a person's mind, which, unlike his body, is identified with the person himself. In this way, the psychiatrist exerts some control over the patient as a person. Often the patient is at the same time both the subject and the object of the contract between himself and the psychiatrist. The psychiatrist often acts as an agent of the society and treats the patient against the patient's will. At the same time, the psychiatrist also treats the body, influencing the brain of the patient by administering drugs or electrical convulsive therapy. The psychiatrist, therefore, influences mind and body at the same time, breaking down the Cartesian model of body–mind dualism. To the extent that psychiatry is concerned with the physiology of the brain, it falls into the category of the natural sciences, Habermas's empirical-analytical class, and is embedded in human technological progress. It deals, therefore, with the value-free natural facts. On the other hand, particularly in the context of psychotherapy, psychiatry can be characterized as a hermeneutic enterprise since it is concerned with explications and clarifications of meanings and with semantics generally, as has been recently pointed out by Lacan (1966). This facet of psychiatry, dealing with explications of the private meanings of the expressions produced by the client, aims at the reconstruction of that client's past-life experience on the basis of temporal continuity of these meanings.

As the third alternative, and in accordance with Habermas's suggestion, psychiatry and clinical psychology could be regarded as an empirical-critical science concerned with both the biology of the human organism and the human symbolic world. Thus conceived, psychiatry and clinical psychology, together with other empirical-critical sciences, will participate in the dialectical process by which man, a product of biological evolution and the emergent human society, constitutes himself in a continuous self-creating act. By discovering the laws of human biology and explicating the meanings of symbolic productions and the norms of conduct, man acquires the self-knowledge that leads to constant evolution and growth. This organismic personal and societal growth, reflected in human consciousness, leads in its turn to more rational and saner behavior—the goal of positive mental health. Thus, in the dialectical interaction between the subjective and the objective, the boundaries between facts and values and between determinism and free will become blurred. A greater knowledge and a greater mastery of human and social behavior spell a greater freedom for man. The presupposition of the objective scientific observer examining a system from the outside has no place in the framework of the empirical-critical science. Man, the object of investigation, is also its subject. He constantly changes as the inquiry progresses. This is the position of Habermas, stemming from the Hegelian–Marxist tradition. It is presented here as an illustration of the complexity of the philosophical presuppositions and issues of psychiatry, clinical psychology, and psychotherapy which need to be explicated. The following outstanding philosophical issues can be discerned in the ongoing debates in the field of psychiatry and mental health: the body–mind relationship; determinism versus indeterminism of human behavior and, a related issue, free will and moral responsibility; the issue of value-free behavioral and social science; and the issue of autonomy of the individual versus conformity to the society. These are perennial problems of philosophy and indicate the relevance of philosophy to psychiatry and psychotherapy.

Before discussing the influence of phenomenology and existentialism on psychiatry, it is necessary to present briefly the issues with which the phenomenological and existential schools of thought are concerned.

First, what is the relationship between phenomenology and existentialism? Phenomenology, particularly Edmund Husserl's phenomenology, should not be identified with existentialism—although both are derived from the tradition of German idealism—since the intents and purposes of the two philosophies are different. Two problems posed by Immanuel Kant—the problem of the limitation of pure human reason, and therefore of human knowledge (Kant, 1966), and the problem of an apparent contradiction between the freedom of will of the noumenal (metaphysical) self and the causal determinacy of the phenomenal self (Kant, 1959)—have given impetus to many attempts at their solutions. Some of these attempts were based on rationalism (e.g., Fichte and Hegel), and some appealed to the irrational voluntaristic aspects of human experience (e.g., Kierkegaard and Nietzsche). Johann Gottlieb Fichte (1969), in attempting to bridge the gap between the Kantian things-in-themselves (noumena) and the contents of experience (phenomena), stated that the ego, by an act of creation, posited the objective world. Thus, the ultimate basis of human knowledge and action was an act of the transcendental ego of the subject positing the object. The dynamic acts of the human mind were more important than its contents. The mental act is of basic importance in both phenomenology and existentialism; both, however, reject the metaphysical assumptions of German idealism. To make a gross generalization, which is only approximately true, phenomenology has been mainly concerned with the first problem of Kant and has tried to lay a foundation for human knowledge which is absolutely certain and which therefore transcends the limits of Kantian pure reason. Existentialism has applied itself to Kant's second problem, namely how to reconcile the freedom of choice and moral responsibility with the causal determinism of the experienced world without postulating the Kantian deus ex machina in the form of categorical imperative and moral laws.

Edmund Husserl was an influential German philosopher who, using Franz Brentano's act psychology (Brentano, 1874), developed a school of phenomenological philosophy and started the so-called phenomenological movement. Incidentally, Franz Brentano, an Austrian philosopher under whom Husserl studied, also taught philosophy to young Sigmund Freud. Husserl attempted an in-depth analysis of the essential structure of the pure act of knowledge *(noösis)* of external objects *(noöma)* on the part of the transcendental ego and the structure of other "intentionalities" on the part of the ego toward these objects. His purpose was to lay the foundations of absolutely certain knowledge and to make philosophy a rigorous science. The immediately experienced *(Anschauung)* act of knowing, revealing the nature of things, replaced the Kantian and neo-Kantian synthetic *a priori*, based on the categories, of pure reason (Husserl, 1962).

Existentialism is a philosophy of the predicament of man or, to put it differently, a philosophy which examines the question: "What does it mean to be human?" Husserl was concerned mainly with epistemology, while the existentialists are concerned with ontology—the meaning and nature of *being*. Existentialists, then, have adopted Husserl's phenomenological method of the analysis of pure consciousness and applied it to the analysis of being. Heidegger's version of the phenomenological method—hermeneutic phenomenology—not only dealt with "here-and-now" consciousness but examined the totality of man's life (Heidegger, 1927). Spiegelberg (1960) has discussed the history of the relationship between the phenomenological and existentialist movements. While there has been tension and antagonism between the Husserlian phenomenologists and the existentialists in Germany, they have been closely associated with one another in France. In Germany, Karl Jaspers's version of existentialism (Jaspers, 1955; Jaspers & Bultmann, 1959) has been particularly critical of Husserlian phenomenology. Jaspers rejected Husserl's idea of scientific philosophy as a contradiction in terms. Instead of the phenomenological method, Jaspers, who had previously used only a limited descriptive phenomenology in the context of psychopathology, proposed a method of elucidation of existence *(Existenzerhellung)*. This method appeals to the Kierkegaardian leap of faith in the attempt to realize existence. Independently of the above, a controversy also developed between Husserl (1962) and Heidegger (1927) over the validity of hermeneutics as a method of scientific phenomenology. Some psychiatrists, including Eugene Minkowski, Erwin Straus, Kurt Schneider, Victor von Gebsattel, Henri Ey, Heinrik Rümke, and Jan van der Berg have used phenomenological methodology (mainly descriptive phenomenology) in its original Husserlian form in an attempt to understand various psychopathological conditions by analyzing immediate states of consciousness (Husserl, 1900; Spiegelberg, 1972). These can be considered phenomenological psychiatrists as distinct from existential psychiatrists.

To what, then, does the concept of phenomenology refer? First, it refers to an approach to science which stresses pure observation and description without preconceived ideas or attempts at causal and theoretical explanations. It registers naturally occurring types and groupings of phenomena. Thus, it is propaedeutic to any explanatory science. It refers secondly to a description of conscious states in all their richness and fullness (e.g., William James's stream-of-consciousness psychology or the stream-of-consciousness literature exemplified by James Joyce's *Ulysses*). Sometimes the term phenomenology is used to describe the epistemological position which claims that sensory data, conceived as brain-mind events or as the neutral "stuff" of experience, are the ultimate experiential reality. This usage is wrong; the proper term for this position is phenomenalism, and it should not be confused with phenomenology proper, which maintains that a world of real objects, and not a motley of sensory data, is given in the immediate experience. The third meaning of the word refers to Husserl's phenomenology.

Husserl's phenomenology identifies consciousness almost completely with intentionalities. Consciousness, with a few exceptional nonintentional experiences *(Erlebnisse),* consists of mental acts by which certain relations are established between the subject and the object. These acts are called "intentionalities." Consequently, consciousness is not a container filled with sensations and ideas from which the homunculus-ego infers the existence of the external world of objects (resembling a radar operator inferring the presence of planes and ships from the blips on a radar screen). Consciousness is open to the world of real objects; it is in the very relations of the subject to the objects. Consciousness is a dynamic activity (acts) rather than "stuff" (substance); it is "doing" rather than "being" (Husserl, 1900).

"Back to the things themselves" was the motto of the phenomenologists. They made a clean break with Cartesian epistemology and the Cartesian metaphysics of the body-mind relationship. According to the latter, body (*res extensa,* the machine) and mind (*res cogitans,* the ghost) were two entirely different substances (Descartes, 1931). The logical conclusion of Cartesian metaphysics and epistemology was solipsism. The call to return to the things themselves was meant to put an end to a metaphysical conundrum and an unsolvable riddle. After all, the ultimate reality is the concrete, immediate experience. Scientific theories are only abstractions of certain limited aspects of reality.

Husserl was concerned mainly with the problems of epistemology—the ultimate foundations of knowledge. He intuitively analyzed the meanings resulting from the subject intentionally relating to objects. His phenomenological method included *epoché,* suspending or bracketing judgment as to the physical or mental nature of objects and of the external world (Spiegelberg, 1960).

In discussing Husserl's phenomenology it is important to remember that his philosophical position shifted considerably from one period of his philosophical career to another. There is the prephenomenological period, the period of descriptive phenomenology initiated by *Logische Untersuchungen* (Husserl, 1900), the period of transcendental phenomenology initiated by *Ideas: General Introduction to Pure Phenomenology* (Husserl, 1962), and the final period of the radicalization of transcendental phenomenology, the period in which intersubjectivity and life-world *(Lebenswelt)* were stressed, as presented in *Cartesian Meditations* (Husserl, 1960) and *Die Krisis der europäinischen Wissenschaften und die transzendentale Phänomenologie* (Husserl, 1954). In the transcendental-phenomenology period, Husserl came very close to embracing the position of German idealism with its stress on the acts of the transcendental ego "constituting" the world. In the final period, the period of *Lebenswelt,* Husserl shifted his position toward that of philosophical realism. Other early phenomenologists, such as Alexander Pfänder, tended to reject Husserl's earlier idealist position and to subscribe to a more realist point of view (Spiegelberg, 1960). My remarks with regard to Husserl will apply mainly to the period of transcendental phenomenology.

In the early phase of descriptive phenomenology, Husserl used his method of phenomenological reduction to grasp the meaning of concrete objects and situations. Later, he went further and developed a second phenomenological method of eidetic reduction aimed at grasping the general essences of things and ideas, the so-called *Wesensschau* (which can be translated as "intuition of ideal essences"). This method, he thought, would lead to an absolute, noncontingent knowledge.

Many phenomenologists did not follow Husserl in his quest for

Wesensschauen but stuck to the descriptive phenomenology of concrete intentionalities (Spiegelberg, 1960). This is true of the phenomenological methods of Eugene Minkowski, Kurt Schneider, Erwin Straus, Jan van der Berg, and Maurice Merleau-Ponty (Spiegelberg, 1972). These phenomenologists are concerned not only with the problem of knowledge, but with the application of phenomenological method to the experiences of concrete individuals in their concrete worlds—to their feelings, to their perceptions, to their bodies, to their movements, and to their acts. Merleau-Ponty (1962, 1963) made an exhaustive phenomenological analysis of perception and of the structure of human behavior, taking as his point of departure man-in-the-concrete-world. The two are inseparable from one another. One can only separate man from his world by secondarily abstracting one from the other. Minkowski (1970) and Straus (1963) both described phenomenological time and space. Phenomenological time and space are different from the conceptual time and space of physics. They are time and space which, in the subjective duration and subjective perspective, are lived. Minkowski described phenomenologically the time and space of schizophrenics and depressives. Mayer-Gross (1914) and Rümke (1924) wrote papers on the phenomenology of normal and abnormal states of happiness. Schneider (1921) studied the phenomenology of love and sympathy, and von Gebsattel (1954) wrote on the phenomenology of obsessional compulsive states, depersonalization, and sexual perversions. Schneider and von Gebsattel were influenced by Max Scheler, another prominent member of the phenomenological movement and a very influential German social philosopher of the first quarter of the twentieth century. Scheler (1954) was less concerned than Husserl with the foundations of knowledge but more concerned with the problems of sympathy, ethics, and the hierarchy of values, conceived objectively.

Husserl, himself, as has been mentioned already, shifted his emphasis in the last phase of his work (the *Lebenswelt* phase) from the phenomenology of intentionalities of the transcendental ego to the phenomenology of man-in-his-concrete-world (Spiegelberg, 1960). Husserl's famous follower, Martin Heidegger, developed phenomenological methodology a step further (Spiegelberg, 1960). His hermeneutic phenomenology was meant to give insight to a wider panorama of the totality of human life. He also applied it to the existential themes—the meaning of life, the meaning of death, existential anxiety, and generally the problems of being.

These themes also occupied Søren Kierkegaard (1941, 1944), who, almost 100 years earlier, passionately attacked rationalism and objectivity in both philosophy and theology. He insisted on subjective or personal meaning of truth and saw man as condemned to loneliness, guilt, "sickness unto death," trembling in fear, and confronted with making choices for good and evil. Kierkegaard's contemporaries did not pay any attention to his writings, which were published at his own expense. They were discovered and became famous half a century after the death of this strange philosopher who was alienated from his age and society.

Another precursor of existentialism, Friedrich Nietzsche (1955), rejected the value system based on natural order and reason; he insisted, instead, that the superman (the "ideal" man) would create new values beyond good and evil. His aphoristic philosophy was directed against enlightenment, rationality, and philistine reasonableness. It penetrated into the dark abyss where the roots of reason and human existence were to be found. These existentialist themes were later taken up by Karl Jaspers (1955) and Martin Buber (1958) independently of Heidegger.

These themes were subsequently included in Heidegger's systematic philosophy and examined in the light of his method of hermeneutic phenomenology. In his most important book, *Being and Time* (*Sein und Zeit*, 1927), Heidegger is concerned with ontology—the problem of being in general. Human beings are a special kind of beings. They are beings who are conscious of their own being. Therefore, the analysis by hermeneutic phenomenology of the human consciousness of being will provide an insight into the general categories of being—the *existentia*. Heidegger asked the question: "What is the predicament of human beings, who are conscious of their being?" The predicament is in their finitude and temporality. Thrown into the world without the ability to exercise any choice in this matter, they are faced with the absolute certainty of their death, total dissolution, and nothingness. Heidegger calls the being which is conscious of its own being, which is always being-in-the-world, *Dasein*, literally translated as "there is." The method of intuitively grasping the meaning of *Dasein* in relation to the general problems of being is called *Daseinsanalytik*. It is an ontological analysis of *Dasein* or *Existenz*—not to be confused with Binswanger's *Daseinsanalyse* which is an attempt to establish philosophical anthropology. Each *Dasein* is characterized by an individuality, *Jemeinigkeit*, but his world is also the *Mitwelt*, which he shares with the others with whom he communicates. The *Dasein* is confronted by the facticity of his world, which to some extent limits his freedom, but he also has the possibility of making free choices and of facing his existence and his death. The most important choice is that of an authentic life as against an inauthentic life. The *Dasein* shows concern *(Sorge)* about his destiny; at the same time, he tends to escape into the facticity of the world. He tries to escape from anxiety *(Angst)* which is not a fear of any particular object or situation but is a fear of nothingness, the consequence of the temporality of human existence. However, death gives meaning to the human life and the human life gives meaning to death. The authentic existence has to squarely face this predicament. You have, after all, to live your own life and to die your own death, as was so poignantly portrayed by Leo Tolstoy in "The Death of Ivan Ilyich" (Tolstoy, 1960).

In later writings, Heidegger (1949) tended to disassociate himself from the existentialist movement and to regard himself as an ontologist. He became interested in the language of poetry, particularly that of Hölderlin, as a medium from which an insight into the meaning of being could be obtained. In using language as a source of wisdom, Heidegger shows a similarity to the so-called "ordinary-language" English philosophers, followers of the later Ludwig Wittgenstein—the Wittgenstein of *Philosophical Investigations* (1953). However, while Wittgenstein stressed the "publicness" of language games and was concerned with common language, Heidegger was concerned with the esoteric language of poetry, full of strange metaphors and neologisms—almost a private language—which he hoped would give him an insight into "being". Where the common-language analysis dissolved the problems of ontology and put them, together with other metaphysical problems, into the category of "pseudoproblems" (diseases of the language caused by its inappropriate use), Heidegger's analysis of the esoteric language of poetry was supposed to solve these problems.

Heidegger's philosophy made a great impact on a group of Swiss psychiatrists—Ludwig Binswanger (1963), Medard Boss (1963), and Roland Kuhn (1963)—and also on a group of young German psychiatrists—Heinz Hafner, Karl Peter Kisker, and Hubert Tellenbach (Spiegelberg, 1972). The latter group, under the leadership of Walter von Baeyer, formed the new Heidelberg school of psychiatry. While the older Heidelberg school limited itself to phenomenology, the new school has an existentialist orientation. The three Swiss psychiatrists were trained in Freudian psychoanalysis and have been practicing it as a method of psychotherapy. They added *Daseinsanalyse* as an anthropological framework to help them better understand their patients, to give them a new dimension, as it were, for a fuller and richer picture of man. While biological and psychodynamic factors accounted for some aspects of the life history of the patient, the *Daseinsanalyse* accounted for other aspects. Thus, an attempt was made to create a phenomenological anthropology, a framework within which human beings could be fully understood. Binswanger was one of Freud's early Swiss followers, and despite Binswanger's subsequent involvement with phenomenological existential movements, he and Freud remained on friendly terms, as reported in Binswanger's book, *Sigmund Freud: Reminiscences of a Friendship* (1957a). Binswanger's other important books—*Grundformen und Erkenntnis menschlichen Daseins* (1942), *Schizophrenie* (1957b), and *Melancholie und Manie* (1960)—have not yet been translated into English.

In his phenomenological anthropology *(Daseinsanalyse)*, Binswanger does not stress "being" as such but concrete being-in-the-world, the concrete individual-in-his-world. Thus, Binswanger's concerns are ontic rather than ontological, with concrete individuals rather than with general categories of "being." The accent of *Daseinsanalyse* is on the existentialist *Mitwelt*, the relatedness to other human beings, rather than on the *Umwelt* and the *Eigenwelt*.[1] The concept of "concern" is developed into that of "love." Love has spiritual connotations and transcends Freud's biological libido. It is an encounter between two unique individuals, a unique "I and thou" relationship, a "we-ness." Love, in its spirituality, transcends man's temporality.

English readers are familiar with the translation of the *Daseinsanalyse* of the schizophrenic patients, Ilse and Ellen West, translated into English in the Rollo May, Ernest Angel, and Henri Ellenberger book *Existence* (1958). Schizophrenic *Dasein* is characterized by the breaking apart of the consistency of natural experience, the splitting of experience into rigid alternatives, and the attempt to cover up the attrition caused by these tensions. Many English and American readers are taken aback by the flowery, metaphorical language of Binswanger and other *Dasein* and phenomenological analysts. This metaphorical language serves the same purpose as the language of poetry, namely, to create certain images

[1] In existentialist terminology, *Umwelt* is the world of man as a biological organism without self-awareness; *Mitwelt* is the world of social relationships and encounters with others; and *Eigenwelt* is the world of self-reflection and self-identity, the world in which man transcends his biological and social determinants.

which would convey metaphorically subtle meanings not transmittable by common or scientific language. One important innovation of *Daseinsanalyse* is the claim that the schizophrenic's psychic world can be understood in the same way as the psychic world of the psychoneurotic. According to the old Heidelberg school of psychiatry, as represented by Karl Jaspers's *General Psychopathology* (1963), only the personality development of a psychoneurotic can be understood either by the method of phenomenology or by Wilhelm Dilthey's method of *Verstehen-Psychologic* (psychology of understanding). The schizophrenic process was supposed to be incomprehensible. *Daseinsanalyse* claims to be able to understand the schizophrenic world intuitively.

Since the death of Binswanger, the most important representative of *Daseinsanalyse* has been Medard Boss who, however, calls his method phenomenological *Daseinsanalytik,* thus indicating a closer adherence to Heidegger. He has followed Heidegger beyond the *Being and Time* phase into the more purely ontological phase. Boss is also a psychoanalyst, who regards his phenomenological *Daseinsanalytik* as a frame of understanding rather than as a psychotherapeutic method. His book *Psychoanalyse und Daseinsanalytik* has been translated into English by Ludwig Lefabre under the title of *Psychoanalysis and Daseinsanalysis* (1963). Boss's *Daseinsanalytik* studies *Dasein* for its own sake in its full concreteness as an entity in relation to "being" and not just as Binswanger's being-in-the-world. Perhaps Boss's most important contribution is his phenomenological analysis of dreams.

Another important follower of Binswanger is Roland Kuhn (1954). He gave a phenomenological interpretation of the Rorschach test. His case study of Rudolf, the murderer of a prostitute, also appears in *Existence* (May *et al.*, 1958).

At this point, a few words must be said about Viktor Frankl (1968), who developed his method of existential analysis, or *ontoanalysis,* together with his method of *logotherapy* independently of the *Daseinsanalyse* of Binswanger. He is a prolific writer, and most English-speaking psychologists and psychiatrists are well acquainted with his views on the "will to meaning," the meaning of suffering, and noögenic neurosis. Noögenic neurosis is an existential neurosis suffered by people who find their lives devoid of meaning. The meaninglessness of some barren lives produces existential anxiety, resulting in neurotic symptoms. Logotherapy is the treatment for noögenic psychoneurosis. In contrast to *Daseinsanalyse, existential analysis* and *logotherapy* are psychotherapeutic methods aimed at helping as well as understanding the patient. Frankl perceives the doctor's role not only as one only of treating the body but also as that of ministering to the spiritual needs of the soul of the patient. Thus, the doctor reverts to the role of the medicine man in primitive society, where medical practice and the priesthood are not separated one from the other. Frankl is an existential philosopher who not only has preached his philosophy from an armchair but, like Socrates, has lived it. His experiences in a concentration camp produced his passionate commitment to the existentialist Weltanschauung.

So far, the main subject of discussion of this paper has concerned the existentialism of German-speaking countries. It is time to now turn to the French existentialist movement and its main exponent, Jean-Paul Sartre. Sartre, an existentialist, and Merleau-Ponty (1962, 1963), a phenomenologist, have had a great influence on psychology and psychiatry. Sartre's existentialism, as presented in his book *Being and Nothingness* (1956) as well as in several of his plays, short stories, and essays, is perhaps the most radical version of existential philosophy. It stresses subjectivity of experience, the absurdity of the human predicament, and the nothingness of consciousness. Conciousness, the *pour soi,* in contrast to inanimate objects, the *en soi,* can only attain being by relating to other objects. Sartre's most famous pronouncement is that "existence precedes essence." The meaning of this statement is that consciousness creates its own nature out of nothingness. By free acts and free choices, man transcends himself. To put it differently, man creates himself, or to put it still differently man is what he does; hence his aspiration to godliness.

Many Christian existentialists, such as Paul Tillich (1962) and Gabriel Marcel (1965), reject this position and assume a polarity between essence and existence. Paul Tillich, in *Systematic Theology* (1963), characterizes man's existence as a state of estrangement from his essential or ideal nature, which is one of unity with God. Even Heidegger, in *Sein und Zeit* (1927), is ambiguous on this issue, although he explicitly denies the notion of an essence of man, at the same time he talks of a state of "fallenness" *(Verfallen)* in which *Dasein* exists "inauthentically" and is divorced from its own nonrelational potentiality for being. According to Sartre, *pour soi* (human consciousness), in contrast to *en soi* (causally determined objects), is free and projects itself into the future by anticipating events. *Pour soi* can relive the past and project itself from the present to the future. Since freedom of action and choice have roots in nothingness, they produce "anguish" or existential anxiety, which tends to be suppressed by "bad faith," an approximate equivalent of Heidegger's inauthentic existence." The predicament of man is that he has to make free choices and establish his human dignity in a godless, absurd world, a world devoid of any purpose or grand design.

Sartre has developed a method for understanding concrete human beings and their psychological experiences. This method is called by him "phenomenological existential analysis" and is modeled on Freudian analysis. However, there are important differences. Sartre rejects Freud's psychological determinism; he rejects the notion of unconsciousness and substitutes for it the prereflective consciousness. He also rejects the division of psyche into id, ego, and superego, regarding it as a total gestalt. His most famous existential analyses are of Jean Genet, a thief who was also a literary figure (Sartre, 1952), of Baudelaire, and more recently of Flaubert. In later years, Sartre disassociated himself from existentialism and came closer to the position of humanistic Marxism based on the writings of the young Marx. Sartre's more recent views are presented in *Critique of Dialectial Reason* (Sartre, 1960).

Under the influence of phenomenology, particularly that of Merleau-Ponty and to a lesser extent that of Sartre, a group of French psychoanalysts, including Angelo Louis Hesnard (1957), Daniel Lagache (1956), Jacques Lacan (1966), and Antoine Vergot (1958), developed a phenomenological reinterpretation of Freudian psychoanalysis. In this reinterpretation, the concept of transference is deemphasized; instead, the concept of intersubjectivity, or existential encounter, is stressed. Freudian metapsychology is replaced by the framework of Merleau-Ponty's phenomenology—the phenomenology of the full-bodied, conscious man-in-the-concrete-world. Intersubjectivity, the encounter, or to use Sartre's term, the *pour autrui*, has played a crucial role in French phenomenology and existentialism. This theme was further developed by Alfred Schuetz (1932), the phenomenologically oriented social philosopher.

In the group of French psychoanalysts influenced by phenomenology and existentialism, Jacques Lacan is undoubtedly the most important. A Freudian psychoanalyst, he was originally influenced by the phenomenology of Sartre and Merleau-Ponty. In particular, Merleau-Ponty's concept of the consciousness–behavior structure as applied to human nonlinguistic and linguistic behavior was important for the development of Lacan's views. More recently, Lacan has to a great extent abandoned the immediately-given-in-experience structuralism of phenomenologists for the concept of hidden structure of the human mind, as postulated by Levi-Strauss (1963) and structural linguists (Mauriello, 1975). Lacan has developed a theory of symbolism based on de Saussure's (1974) linguistics and Levi-Strauss's structuralism. He has rejected Freud's reductionistic theory of the human mind and has replaced it by one of the dynamisms of symbols, the "signifier" and the "signified," embedded in the synchronic and diachronic structural matrix of language, customs, and social mores. Thus, biological dynamisms such as drives and instincts are replaced by the rules of behavior stemming from the linguistic and cultural structures. The "signified" of the unconsciousness is expressed by the "signifier" of the consciousness. The linguistic processes of metaphor and metonymy are particularly important in shaping the symbolic world of the individual. At times, Lacan tries to reconcile Merleau-Ponty's structure of behavior with de Saussure's linguistic structure and Levi-Strauss's structuralism.

In England, a group of psychiatrists at the Tavistock Clinic in London, under the leadership of R. D. Laing and D. G. Cooper, applied Sartre's and Merleau-Ponty's phenomenological analysis, Martin Buber's philosophy, and Alfred Schuetz's analysis of intersubjectivity to the understanding of schizophrenic patients and their interpersonal relationships. According to Laing (1960), the schizophrenic patient suffers from ontological insecurity; he dreads being annihilated as a separate self by being engulfed by the other. He fears that his identity has been destroyed by "implosion," "engulfing," or "petrification." His firm identity has never been established because in his interpersonal relationships he has never attained a true reciprocity but only a "pseudomutuality." He cannot relate to others and at the same time maintain his own identity. According to Laing, an understanding of the existential predicament of schizophrenic patients is important for their psychotherapy.

After this brief historical review of the phenomenological and existentialist contributions to psychiatry and clinical psychology, it is time to pause in order to take stock. One can ask the following question: What is the distinctive contribution of phenomenology to psychiatry in contrast to that of existentialism? The contributions made by these two philosophies are quite different. While pheomenological psychiatry can be regarded as being related to scientific psychiatry, existentialist psychiatry is concerned with a different dimension, a different aspect of reality from that with which science is concerned. Phenomenology, particularly descriptive phenomenology, carefully describes and classifies the mental phenomena to be investigated scientifically. It can be regarded as a preliminary step before scientific analysis of normal and abnormal phenomena can be undertaken.

The existentialist approach, on the other hand, is either antagonistic or indifferent to the scientific approach. Existentialism deals with a different dimension of the human condition from that with which science is concerned. It is concerned not with epistemic and technological enterprises but with the elucidation of existence and the ultimate concerns of man. It is concerned not with a description and explanation but with an active "living through." Existentialist psychiatry deals with the spiritual dimension of man, his living values and projects and the ultimate meaning of his life. Frankl (1968) maintains that there is a spiritual dimension to every neurosis and psychosis, with noögenic neurosis being a manifestation of existential frustration and therefore of a spiritual rather than a psychological or a biological nature. His method of logotherapy is supposed to deal with the existential frustration, existential vacuum, and frustration of the will to meaning. Its purpose is to make people conscious of their responsibility, their obligations, and the ultimate meaning of life and death. One could ask whether logotherapy, in spite of the two specific therapeutic maneuvers it uses—"paradoxical intention" and "dereflection"—can actually be regarded as a technique of psychotherapy. It is more in the nature of a philosophy of life, a point of view with which a person can be presented. Any specific techniques such as "paradoxical intention" and "dereflection" belong to psychotherapy and not to logotherapy; they only detract from the seriousness and honesty of the latter.

Perhaps existentialist therapy as a whole is a contradiction in terms, and therefore there could not be any existentialist therapy. A therapy presupposes a relationship between one person playing the role of an expert and the other the role of the client. The first person is supposed to do something to and manipulate the second person in order to obtain some change in the latter's behavior. Psychotherapy therefore is a form of human engineering. It turns a subject into an object and leads to an inauthentic existence. In contrast, a relationship leading to an authentic existence would be an encounter between two unique individuals who are equal, not one who is a patient and the other a psychotherapist. In such a situation the influence would be mutual. It should not be constrained by certain roles or certain techniques because each authentic relationship must be unique.

According to Rollo May (May *et al.*, 1958) there cannot be any special school of existential psychotherapy, existentialism is an attitude, an approach to fellow human beings. It is concerned with philosophical presuppositions and basic orientations rather than specific techniques. It is a humanistic attitude which is a corrective to soulless professionalism, it is an attitude with which specific psychotherapies are carried out. However, while existentialist attitude is compatible with insight elucidating psychotherapies, such as for instance psychoanalysis, it is not compatible with the behavior modification technique in which the client is manipulated as an object. May (May *et al.*, 1958; Patterson, 1973) discusses six characteristics or emphases associated with the existentialist attitude in a psychotherapeutic situation:

1. A flexibility of technique to take cognizance of the individuality of the client
2. An encounter between two unique individuals rather than a transference of the analysand onto the analyst
3. Reality and sincerity in the therapist–patient relationship—the client as "an existential partner"
4. Avoidance of behavior by the therapist that would impede or destroy the experience of the full presence of the other person
5. The aim of therapy being for the client to experience his existence fully
6. Confrontation of the client with free choices and commitments

As has already been pointed out, some types of psychotherapy are more compatible with the existentialist attitude than others. Van Kaam (1962) believes that, of all psychotherapies, client-centered therapy of Carl Rogers is the most compatible with the existentialist attitude and orientation. However, any psychotherapeutic technique remains a technique and can only be made more human by an awareness of the existential dimension in the relationship of the two parties in the psychotherapeutic enterprise.

It is time to turn to the American scene and to discuss a group of psychologists known under the general name of "humanistic psychologists." They started independently of the European philosophical tradition but have been converging toward existential psychology and psychiatry. Reference is made here to the "self," the "self-actualization," or the "third-force" psychologies of Abram Maslow (1962), Gordon Allport (1955), Erik Fromm (1955), Carl Rogers (1951), and a few others. I have not included Rollo May or Amedeo Giorgi (1970) in this group.

The first is mainly a translator and interpreter of European existentialism and the second is a phenomenological psychologist in the European tradition. Thus, both are outside the mainstream of American humanistic psychology.

Rogers is, of course, the most important among the humanistic psychologists, because he has developed a method of psychotherapy, and also because he has advocated a phenomenological approach—although based on a different brand of phenomenology than that of Husserl. The phenomenology of Rogers was modeled after that of Snygg and Combs (1949), who maintained that an individual's behavior is determined by his phenomenal field. This phenomenal field represents the self and the experienced world. Thus, Rogers's phenomenology should be classified as a brand of phenomenalism rather than as belonging to phenomenology proper. However, in recent years, as a result of cooperation with the philosopher-psychologist Eugene Gendlin (1962), Rogers has come much closer to European philosophical phenomenology and existentialist philosophy. Consequently, he puts a greater stress than in his earlier writings on the actual act of experiencing rather than on the contents of experience. Also, intersubjectivity, nascent in the therapeutic process, has become of paramount importance.

American humanistic psychologists stress "self" rather than "self-in-the-world." The process of self-actualization, stressed by these psychologists, can be interpreted in three ways. The first interpretation is the Aristotelian interpretation wherein human beings are endowed at birth with entelechy, or potency, to develop the essence of humanness. The development toward this goal is teleologically determined; the essence is already potentially present in entelechy and precedes or determines existence. Individual differences are accidents and are played down. The second interpretation stresses individual differences in the developmental or genetic endowment potentials. If optimal environmental conditions are provided, individuals will develop, divergently, their unique characteristics. Essence still precedes existence, but it is no longer the common human essence but a unique, individual essence. The third approach maintains that the individual is not determined by entelechy but that he transcends himself by his creative acts. The individual creates himself. Existence precedes essence.

Existentialism, at least the Sartrian version of it, espouses the third approach to self-actualization. It is not always clear where American humanistic psychologists stand on this issue. Some quotations from

Maslow will illustrate this point. In a little book entitled *Toward a Psychology of Being,* (1962) Maslow devotes a chapter to "What psychology can learn from existentialists." After indicating that American humanistic psychologists have been independently developing the same ideas as the European existentialists, or to put it in Maslow's words borrowed from Molière, "have been talking prose without knowing it" (Maslow, 1962, p. 10), he expresses skepticism about terms like "essence," "existence," and "ontology," as used by the existential philosophers and considers only the concept of personal identity as useful, because it "can be worked with empirically" (Maslow, 1962, p. 9). As far as the interpretation of the process of self-actualization is concerned, he states:

> The Europeans are stressing the self-making of the self in a way that the Americans don't. Both the Freudians and *the self actualization and growth theorists* [italics mine] in this country talk more about *discovering* the self (as if it were there waiting to be found) and of *uncovering* therapy (shovel away the top layers and you'll see what has been always lying there, hidden). To say, however, that the self is a project and is *altogether* created by the continual choices of the person himself is an *extreme overstatement* [italics mine] in view of what we know of, e.g., the constitutional and genetic determinants of personality. This clash of opinions is a problem that can be settled experimentally. (Maslow, 1962, p. 12)

Further, in connection with the time dimension and the orientation toward the future in existential philosophy, Maslow states:

> I think it fair to say that no theory of psychology will ever be complete which does not centrally incorporate the concept that man has his future within him, dynamically *active at this present moment* [italics mine]. In this sense the future can be treated as *a-historical in Kurt Lewin sense* [italics mine]. (Maslow, 1962, pp. 14–15)

It seems that the goals, situated in the future, are conceptualized as the Aristotelian "potencies" or "entelechies" determining the growth of the organism in a certain direction, thus implying that "the essence precedes existence." Allport (1955), in his book *Becoming,* also devotes a few pages to the problem of personal freedom and implies that although personal freedom is experienced subjectively, nevertheless, from an objective point of view, when all the factors are known, behavior is predictable and therefore determined.

Another important point of disagreement between the humanistic psychologists and the existentialists is the problem of human happiness. There is a kind of "Pollyannaish" optimism about the goodness of human nature and the world in the writings of American humanistic psychologists which is not shared by existentialists. A quotation from Maslow will illustrate the point:

> I don't think we need take too seriously the European existentialists' exclusive harping on dread, on anguish, on despair and the like, for which their only remedy seems to be to keep a stiff upper lip. This high I.Q. [*sic*] whimpering on a cosmic scale occurs whenever an external source of values fails to work. They should have learned from the psychotherapists that the loss of illusions and the discovery of identity, though painful at first, can be ultimately exhilarating and strengthening. (Maslow, 1962, p. 15)

A further illustration of this emphasis on happiness and well-being can be taken from Maslow's theory of motivation. Maslow (1954) divides human motives into those of deficit, as for example hunger and thirst, and those of growth, the most important of which is self-actualization. He maintains that the motives for deficit have to be satisfied before the individual can start self-actualizing himself. This is contrary to the beliefs of existentialists such as Frankl (1968), who found the meaning of life while he was in a state of extreme physical deprivation in a concentration camp. This also applies to the artist who creates great works of art while starving in a garret (Maddi, 1968). This point has also been stressed by Dabrowski (1964) in his theory of positive disintegration. Dabrowski maintains that new and higher personal values are created through suffering and disintegration of a previous, lower-level personality adjustment. This idea is in agreement with the general ethos of existentialism.

The humanistic psychologists believe that by investigating man and society scientifically, it will be possible to discover humanistic ethics based on the nature, and therefore the essence, of man. Further, they believe that when society is based on humanistic ethics, the "millenium" will arrive. This theme is particularly prominent in the writings of Erik Fromm (1955). Existentialists do not share this optimistic faith in a utopia. Furthermore, in many of the writings of humanistic psychologists, there is implied a quest for happiness, often identified with positive mental health. Existentialism, on the other hand, is not a philosophy of happiness; it is a philosophy with courage and dignity as its key values.

At this point one might ask what is the contribution of phenomenology and existentialism to humanistic psychology and more generally to humanism. The answer depends, of course, on the definition of humanistic psychology and humanism. The characterization "humanistic" is attributed to so many different systems of ideas that apart from pointing to man as the main concern it denotes very little. Obviously, Thomas Hobbes, John Locke, Jean-Jacques Rousseau, Immanuel Kant, Jeremy Bentham, John Stuart Mill, the young Karl Marx, the existentialists and the American humanistic psychologists, to mention only a few, all have been concerned with man, regarding man as the measure of all things. However, the different humanistic thinkers have often differed a great deal in their conceptions of man. By and large, two traditions, going back to the beginning of the nineteenth century, can be discerned.[2] One has its roots in the philosophy of the Enlightenment and of rationalism, in the scientific revolution, and in faith in social reforms, progress, and the goodness of man. This was typically represented by the English utilitarians. This humanism is optimistic. It believes that through scientific discoveries, through social reforms and progress, man will become liberated from hunger, poverty, sickness, ignorance, and superstition. Man will become the master of the world and the master of himself. He will replace God of traditional religion as the pinnacle of being. The code of ethics based on the commandments of God will be replaced by the humanistic ethics based on the ideal nature of man. Autonomous morality will replace heteronomous morality. This type of humanism seeks the liberation of man through a struggle against orthodoxy, the established religion, and through striving for social progress. Its two main pillars are rationality and the scientific method. Alfred Adler, Erik Fromm, and even B. F. Skinner can be mentioned as examples of humanistic psychologists in this tradition.

The other humanistic tradition is rooted in the romantic cult of the unique individual and his inwardness. It stresses the importance of feelings and of the spiritual, intuitive, mystical, and aesthetic experiences. It is based on the philosophy of irrationalism and voluntarism. It stresses the autonomy of the individual, his self-actualization, his artistic creativity, and his absolute freedom. It perceives man as pitted against society, which is intent on crushing him and turning him into

[2] Humanism originally denoted the intellectual current associated with the Renaissance period of the fifteenth and sixteenth centuries and characterized by a revival of interest in the classical Greek and Roman cultures. It also meant abandoning the scholastic preoccupation with God and theology for an interest in man and his worldly affairs. By the beginning of the nineteenth century, the concept of humanism had ceased to be predominantly associated with classical scholarship.

a mindless robot.[3] This second humanistic tradition is basically antiscientific. With some qualifications, it can be said that existentialism belongs to this latter humanistic tradition.

At times, it seems that the so-called American humanistic psychologists, such as Maslow, attempt to use incompatible ideas belonging to the two traditions of humanism when they talk about creating a science of humanistic psychology and applying the scientific method to the problem of free will, ultimate values, creativity, and mystical experience. Juxtaposing incompatible ideas can lead to insolvable contradictions and endanger the whole enterprise. Perhaps both European existentialism and phenomenology, with their background of philosophical sophistication, will be helpful to American humanistic psychologists in reexamining their philosophical presuppositions and clarifying their concepts. In the applied field of psychotherapy, the influence of existentialism has already been very profitable, as for instance in the case of the Rogersian client-centered counseling (Patterson, 1973).

I would like to conclude this chapter with a few remarks on the way in which I see the roles of existentialist and phenomenological psychiatry in the total psychiatric and clinical-psychological enterprise. Rollo May and his coauthors (1958) referred, in their well-known book, to "existence" as a new dimension in psychiatry. I think that this position is correct. Phenomenology and existence are dimensions which can be accommodated with other dimensions or points of view and which do not exclude them. They provide additional depth and insight into the phenomenon of mental illness. They do not exclude biological and psychodynamic approaches. A book entitled *Existential Foundations of Psychology* (1966) by Adrian van Kaam, a Dutch existentialist psychologist who came to America and is presently at Duquesne University, and who has also had training as a Rogersian therapist, is very useful in this connection. Van Kaam takes an existentialist point of view that encompasses the totality of man-in-his-world. Within this general, encompassing view, there can be differentiated perspectives, narrower or broader, dealing with particular aspects of man—the biological, social, psychodynamic, and so on. These perspectives abstract certain aspects

[3] The "romantic" humanists have tended to glorify the "encounter" between unique individuals, the unique relationships of "romantic love" and friendship between two individuals or in a small group. They have tended to distrust secondary social groups and social institutions. The encounter group is a present-day manifestation of this tendency.

of the concrete man and are of limited scope and usefulness. However, they serve a purpose.

Not everybody will like this point of view of philosophical "pluralism" or "perspectivism"; some might even consider it the old "eclecticism" revisited. They may prefer "philosophical monism" instead. They are perfectly entitled to feel so; after all, it is their free choice.

References

Allport, G. W. *Becoming.* New Haven: Yale University Press, 1955.

Binswanger, L. *Grundformen und Erkenntnis menschlichen Daseins.* Zurich: Niehaus, 1942.

Binswanger, L. [*Sigmund Freud: Reminiscences of a friendship.*[(N. Guterman, trans.). New York: Grune Stratton, 1957.(a)

Binswanger, L. *Schizophrenie.* Pfullingen: Neske, 1957.(b)

Binswanger, L. *Melancholie und Manie.* Pfullingen: Neske, 1960.

Binswanger, L. Heidegger's analytic and its meaning in psychiatry. In J. Needleman (Ed. trans.). *Being-in-the-world.* New York: Basic Books, 1963.

Boss, M. [*Psychoanalysis and daseinsanalysis*] (L. B. Lefabre trans.). New York: Basic Books, 1963.

Brantano, F. *Psychologie vom empirischen Standpunkt.* Leipzig: Dunkker & Humblot, 1874.

Buber, M. [*I and Thou*] (R. S. Smith, trans.). New York: Scribners, 1958.

Dabrowski, K. [*Positive disintegration.*] (J. Aronson, trans.). Boston: Little, Brown, 1964.

Descartes, R. The meditations. In *The philosophical works of Descartes* (E. S. Haldane & G. R. T. Ross, trans.). London: Cambridge University Press, 1931.

Fichte, J. G. [*The science of knowledge.*] (A. E. Kroeger, trans.). New York: Appleton, Century, Crofts, 1969.

Frankl, V. L. *Psychotherapy and existentialism: Selected papers on logotherapy.* New York: Clarion Books, 1968.

Fromm, E. *The sane society.* New York: Holt, Rinehart, & Winston, 1955.

Gendlin, E. T. *Experiencing and creation of meaning.* Glencoe, Ill.: Free Press, 1962.

Giorgi, A. *Psychology as a human science.* New York: Harper & Row, 1970.

Habermas, J. [*Knowledge and human interests.*] (J. J. Shapiro, trans.). London: Heinemann, 1972.

Heidegger, M. *Sein und Zeit.* Halle: Niemeyer, 1927.

Heidegger, M. Holderlin and the essence of poetry. In W. Brock (Ed.), *Existence and being.* Chicago: Regnery, 1949.

Hesnard, A. L. *Psychoanalyse du lien interhumane.* Paris: P.U.F., 1957.

Husserl, E. *Logische untersuchungen.* Halle: Niemeyer, 1900.

Husserl, E. *Die Krisis der europäischen Wissenschaften und die transzendentale Phänomenologie.* The Hague: Nijhoff, 1954.

Husserl, E. [*Cartesian meditations.*] (D. Cairns, trans.). The Hague: Nijhoff, 1960.

Husserl, E. [*Ideas: General introduction to pure phenomenology.*] (A. Lauer, trans.). New York: Collier, 1962.

Jaspers, K. [*Reason and existenz.*] (W. Earle, trans.). New York: Noonday Press, 1955.

Jaspers, K. [*General psychopathology.*] (J. Hoening & M. W. Hamilton, trans.). Manchester: Manchester University Press, 1963.

Jaspers, K., & Bultmann, R. *Myth and christianity*. New York: Noonday Press, 1969.
Kant, I. [*Foundations of the metaphysics of morals*.] (H. J. Paton, trans.). New York: Liberal Arts Press, 1959.
Kant, I. [*Critique of pure reason*.] (N. Kemp Smith, trans.). New York: Anchor Books, 1966.
Kierkegaard, S. [*Concluding unscientific postscript of the "philosophical fragments*."] (D. F. Swenson, trans.). Princeton, N. J.: Princeton University Press, 1941.
Kierkegaard, S. [*The concept of dread*.] (W. Lowrie, trans.). Princeton, N.J.: Princeton University Press, 1944.
Kuhn, R. *Die Maskendeutungen im Rorschachversuch*. Basel: Karger, 1954.
Kuhn, R. Daseinsanalyse und Psychiatrie. In H. W. Gruhle & R. Jung (Eds.). *Psychiatrie der Gegenwart*. Berlin: Springer, 1963.
Lacan, J. *Ecrits*. Paris: Seuil, 1966.
Lagache, D. Psychoanalyse et psychologie. *L' évolution psychiatrique*, 1956, *21*, 269–295.
Laing, R. D. *The divided self*, London: Tavistock Publications, 1960.
Levi-Strauss, C. [*Structural anthropology*.] (C. Jacobson & B. F. Schoepf, trans.). New York: Basic Books, 1963.
Maddi, S. R. *Personality theories: A comparative analysis*. Homewood, Ill.: Dorsey, 1968.
Marcel, G. *Being and having*. London: Collins, 1965.
Maslow, A. H. *Motivation and personality*. New York: Harper & Row, 1954.
Maslow, A. H. *Toward a psychology of being*. New York: Van Nostrand, 1962.
Mauriello, V. *Unmasking Lacan*. Paper presented at the Second Annual National Scientific Meeting of the Canadian Psychoanalytic Society, Toronto, June 6, 1975.
May, R., Angel, E., & Ellenberger, H. F. *Existence*. New York: Basic Books, 1958.
Mayer-Gross, W. A. Zur Phänomenologie abnormer Glucksgefuhle. *Zeitschrift für pathopsychologie*, 1914, *2*, 588–601.
Merleau-Ponty, M. [*Phenomenology of perception*.] (C. Smith, trans.). New York: Humanities Press, 1962.
Merleau-Ponty, M. [*The structure of behaviour*.] (A. L. Fisher, trans.). Boston: Beacon Press, 1963.
Patterson, G. H. *Theories of counselling and psychotherapy*. New York: Harper & Row, 1973.
Sartre, J. P. *Critique de la raison dialectique*. Paris: Gallimard, 1960.
Saussure, F. de. [*Course in general linguistics*.] (W. Baskin, trans., C. Bally & A. Sechehaye, Eds.). Glasgow: Fontana/Collins, 1974.
Schact, R. *Alienation*. New York: Doubleday, 1970.
Scheler, M. [*The nature of sympathy*.] (P. Heath, trans.). New Haven: Yale University Press, 1954.
Schneider, K. Pathopsychologiche Beitrage zur phanomenologischen Psychologie von Liebe und Mitfuhlen. *Zeitschrift für der gesamte Neurologie und Psychiatrie*, 1921, *65*, 109–140.
Schuetz, A. *Der sinnhafte Aufbau der sozialen Welt*. Vienna: Springer, 1932.
Snygg, D., & Combs, A. W. *Individual behavior*. New York: Harper, 1949.
Spiegelberg, H. *The phenomenological movement—a historical introduction*. The Hague: Nijhoff, 1960.
Spiegelberg, H. *Phenomenology in psychology and psychiatry*. Evanston, Ill.: Northwestern University Press, 1972.
Straus, E. [*The primary world of senses: A vindication*.] (J. Needleman, trans.). Glencoe, Ill.: Free Press, 1963.
Tillich, P. Existentialism and psychotherapy. In H. M. Ruitenbeek (Ed.), *Psychoanalysis and existential philosophy*. New York: Dutton, 1962.
Tillich, P. *Systematic theology*. Chicago: University of Chicago Press, 1963.

Tolstoy, L. [*The death of Ivan Ilyich and other stories.*] (A. Maude, trans.). New American Library, 1960.
van Kaam, A. Counseling from the viewpoint of existential psychology. *Harvard Educational Review*, 1962, *32*, 403–415.
van Kaam, A. *Existential foundations of psychology*. Pittsburgh: Duquesne University Press, 1966.
von Gebsattel, V. *Prologomena zu einer medizinischen Antropologie*. Berlin: Springer, 1954.
Vergot, A. L'intérêt philosophique de la psychologie freudienne. *Archives de Philosophie*, 1958, *21*, 26–59.
Wittgenstein, L. [*Philosophical investigations.*] (E. M. Anscombe, trans.). Oxford: Blackwell, 1953.

II

EXPERIENCING AND EPISTEMOLOGY

4

Joseph Lyons

DISCONTINUITIES

OR THEORY AS PRAYER

Erwin W. Straus died in June 1975, at the age of 83. I had the privilege of working with him for ten years, learning from him and sharing his vision of a humanistic science of man that would be both honest—that is, phenomenologically sound—and useful—that is, existentially valid. This paper is a salute to his memory.

In the beginning there is a person's awareness. Both logically and psychologically, any datum or collection of data must start at this point. How curious that it should have taken the discipline of psychology a full century, at least, to swing back to accepting such a statement. But now that we have the statement, and now that it provides respectability for the area of cognition and the significance of meaning and values, we see that no threat is posed to a painfully built temple of behavioral science. The loudly heralded behavioral revolution, as we now see, was a methodological counterrevolution and nothing more.

The topic of experience, or ongoing awareness, now reenters psychology as a legitimate area of empirical inquiry, which it ought to have been in any case. More important, the process of awareness now takes on a special role: we begin to understand that awareness functions within the person as the screen through which all inquiry must pass—including, of course, inquiries of psychology itself. A first consequence is that psychology itself is redefined. It is not simply a science of people's

Joseph Lyons • Department of Psychology, University of California at Davis, Davis, California 95616.

behavior but more exactly, a science of the behavior of persons when they are observed as persons; still more precisely, it is a science of the behavior of persons when they are observed by other persons.

And here, at the very beginning, we come to what seems an insuperable difficulty. It is a difficulty that is specific to states of awareness and that arises out of our accepting them as sources of data. If our data were, as contemporary empiricists would have it, entirely "objective" and nonexperiential, analytic approaches would then be appropriate, as would their effluvia—continuities, dimensions, quantities, discrete and equivalent units. But this is hardly the case when the data, about myself or about other persons, are apprehended in the form of experience. Then, everything takes on such characteristics as qualities, values, colorings, and uniqueness—in short, *dis*continuities. In his recent reflections on the body and its formative processes, Stanley Keleman puts it this way:

> Everything in the human being points to discontinuity. We are pulsating all the time. . . . Laughing and crying, orgasm and ejaculation are pulsatory, rhythmical. The muscles extend and flex. I open and close. I love and I don't love. My feelings come and go. I *am* my discontinuity—my connectedness and disconnectedness. (Keeman, 1975, p. 41)

The fact of discontinuity extends, equally, to the relations between awareness and its target. If my awareness were, as empiricists would have it, simply one more term in a natural series, then it would be inconceivable, in principle, for there to be a gap between the ego pole and the object pole of my field of experience. I want to begin by discussing three such instances of discontinuity—the case of Nirvana, the case of the madman, and the case of playing God.

Two Extreme Cases

Occasionally, and disconcertingly, we are told that someone has passed through a period of complete ego loss. Temporarily freaked out on whatever path he is pursuing, the person comes back to our earth and claims for that period some absolute and separated status of experience. It is the ultimate experience, he insists, reminding us in passing that in the original Sanskrit the word Nirvana means "blowing out a light."

We question him eagerly, but he says only that he has been "out of it." We pursue the matter, for we are understandably anxious to find out about heaven without paying the cost of the trip. Unfortunately, all that our pilgrim can do is to shake his head and say, over and over, something like "Wow!" What we usually assume, then, is that his recent experience has consisted of a nearly total ego loss. Normally, as we know, ego functions are needed in order to talk to oneself or report to another person about what happens. On principle, then, it is not possible to talk sensibly about one's experience of ego loss. That would involve the use of these functions to deal with their absence—to use speech to say the unsayable or to compose in music the sound of silence.

It may be that the matter has to be dropped at this point. It appears that no links are possible between our states of ongoing, everyday experience—the states in which we talk about Nirvana—and the state that our friend has just passed through. Even language, that great aboutness device, that ultimate set of machinery for allowing us to stand in one place and refer to another place, fails us. Our friend seems to have no words at this moment for what must have happened before. The experience is discontinuous and unreachable.

In the second case, which is a little more familiar to us as psychologists, we try to find out from the madman what his condition is like. Now, it may or may not be true that the schizophrenic has taken up a position at the very extreme of some dimension of human relatedness, but let us agree that he has seriously tried to cut all his ties with others, to cease being a living presence to them, to drop out of human company. Whether he succeeds at this is always questionable, but for our purposes at this point, the schizophrenic seems to be standing where we can spot him yet on the other side of an impassable gap. And so we are led to ask him, eagerly, "Hey, what is it like?" Or, if the schizophrenic should ever return to our company—that is, achieve a remission, or be cured, or recover, whatever term one wishes—we are led to ask, even more eagerly, "Tell us, what *was* it like?"

Once, in my own days of innocence and eagerness as a clinical researcher, I took part in an interview of sorts with a mute catatonic patient. We had learned the intriguing fact that such patients, if heavily overdosed with sedatives such as sodium pentothal (the so-called "truth serum"), will often, and paradoxically, be aroused to activity. This seemed to us an absolutely perfect experimental arrangement. We would take this man who had cut himself off from our human company and coax him or soften him or bludgeon him (however you choose to understand the action of the drug) into crossing the gap, or at least calling over to us to tell us what it was really like.

We gave this man the drug and watched him soften, relax, even smile at us, and the interview commenced. I will not take your time with its details; we spent the better part of an afternoon taking turns in questioning him, and the full record is in print (Lyons, 1960). But the fact is that at no time did we ever engage in conversation with this man. At no time did there take place a dialogue of even minimal import to his history or ours; he was very careful to skirt that contingency. He told us a number of impersonal facts, each one a datum that was already available for all our scrutinies in the hospital files. On one or two occasions he slipped to the level of trivia or gossip or chitchat. But in all, he said nothing that we, or he, could respond to in a personal sense, or have a feeling about, or add to that store of the momentous which makes up the history of even the meanest human life.

What he did do, when finally he was pushed beyond the limits of even his own timeless patience, was to offer a brief answer to our repeated question. We kept asking him, "But Rocky, why haven't you talked all these months?" To this, he finally answered, "Well, there wasn't much to say." It sounds like a slightly weary wisecrack, but I am sure that he did not mean it as a joke. I believe that it is, like the exclamation "Wow!", the only message that one can send between discontinuous states.

Talking to God

Suppose that someone you know has the chance to play God for a month. He prepares for it as best he can, looks forward to the beginning of his celestial term, and then one day, as of 9 a.m., he is God. You too have been waiting for the occasion, so you hurriedly call over to him, "Hey, God, tell me—what is it like?" Would your friend be silent? And would you, perhaps, renew your request with greater urgency? "Please tell me. I've always wanted to know. What is it really like to be God?"

You might continue, in innocence and eagerness, finally in passion and impatience and even anger, but I think there would be no way at all that your friend God could tell you about his tenure. If he were to try, he would, I think, conclude with great sadness, "Well, you really wouldn't understand." Nor could he finish his term as God and then, joining you over a quiet drink, give you a retrospective account of what that month had been like. He might just sit there and stare into space and say, over and over, "Wow!" Hearing this message once more, it might finally occur to you that perhaps we here on earth should learn to attend better to instances of the inarticulate.

Notice that you did in fact speak to God but that you were probably wasting your time trying to start a dialogue. Does this mean that you had no right to expect any response at all? We can get a first answer to this question by considering an instance that is very familiar to us—our attempts at communication with human beings who are engaged in playing God. If I write to the White House, I am not either offended or surprised when I get a form letter in return that says, neatly and impersonally: "Thank you for your letter of recent date. Please be assured that your views will be taken under consideration." Indeed, I would be quite shocked to receive from the White House a computerized form letter that was more personal in tone, for example: "Dear Joe, What a surprise to hear from you! How have you been? Why, only this morning Nancy was saying over breakfast, 'You know, we haven't heard from Joe Lyons in a long time.' "

No, when I try to communicate with God, the very most that I can expect is a *sign,* not in the form of a responsive and personal answer but an indication that I have been heard. As Walter Ong (1970) has said, "If you believe you can *make* God appear or manifest himself, you're substituting magic for faith."

This begins to suggest what it is that I do not do in my communications with God. I may plead for intercession so that my ticket number will be picked in the draw of the Irish Sweepstakes, but I do not precede this prayer with an inquiry about my chances. I do not say "Hey, God, what is the ticket number that will come up when they make the draw?" Like everyone else, I recognize that God is not in possession of any information. Nor do I ever ask, under different circumstances, "Listen, God, tell me frankly—I mean, don't be afraid of hurting my feelings. What do you really think of me?" For we also assume that God has no opinions.

Clearly, this is a most curious situation. Communication of a sort appears to take place, but it seems to be between two participants who have no contact. Their relationship is built around a gap between them. In the ritual that then occurs, communication from below takes place in a set form, with a specified manner of address and with restricted expectations. The communication from on high, on the other hand, has to take place in its own way and at its own pace, as though there could be no clear admission that God's thunderous word is in response to the mere voice of a human. The ritual reply from on high can happen immediately, or much later, or seemingly not at all. It can take the form of a flash of lightning, a fire in a bush, a disembodied voice, even the destruction of a city; it can occur in a waking vision or a sleeping dream. Its shape can be a messenger, often in disguise. Its significance can be contained in an obscure sign which itself requires further interpretation. Between God and man, then, there is no responsive, two-way communication. Rather, two interlinked modes of communicating subsist, the one hidden from yet in touch with the other. This is how the discontinuous is breached.

Bridges

Although it may not be known to God, to the catatonic, or to the mystic, there are quite similar ways of calling across a gap that separates us from what seems discontinuous with our normal state. Apparently, we are not completely cut off from these places. Though they seem unreachable, they are in some ways close at hand. For one thing, to despair over whether one can bridge a gap is in some sense to come to grips with it. If the presence of discontinuity poses a problem for us when we face it, it becomes a significant part of our personal history. And most important, in both the case of the Nirvana experience and the experience of the catatonic, it is the gap itself which bounds and therefore in some sense defines the nonnormal experience. Precisely because we agree that we cannot define such an experience, it is in some way both discontinuous and reachable. The existence of more or less formalized ways for bridging these gaps suggests that this answer has occurred to others as well. I would like now to consider briefly two such contrived means for addressing a discontinuity.

The Koan

This pseudoincident, widely used in Zen teaching, has been defined as "a public document setting up a standard of judgment." By means of an exercise involving intensive contemplation of the koan, a disciple is led through personal crisis toward enlightenment. It is even possible that by a heroic effort the disciple can burst through the situation, as it were, into a state of complete understanding.

The form of the koan consists of no more than a question put by the disciple to the master and the answer—or often the failure to answer—by the master to the disciple. In a still briefer form, it can consist of a question-answer stated by the master, with, of course, no answer from the openmouthed disciple. For example, the disciple might ask if there is "Buddha nature" in a dog, and the master might answer with the single word *mu,* which in this connection has no sensible meaning at all; in English he might have said, "Ah!"

How are we to understand this? Surely not by assuming that the interchange is part of a coherent discourse between equals. In fact, it is not meant as part of a discourse at all. For the situation of the master—which is what determines the structure of the koan—is unusual and far from enviable. He is required to teach just that which, by his own insistent claim, cannot be taught in any ordinary sense. Every question put to him by a disciple, then, threatens his position. He cannot offer a coherent reply, for then he would be stepping out of his special position as a Zen master; yet he cannot refrain from replying, for he has set himself up as a master who would train his disciples. Between himself and his disciples there is a gap, in the form of a discontinuity which is both unbridgeable and passable.

The master resolves this dilemma by staying firmly within the situation and also by using his own unenviable position in a special way. He turns the interchange into a representation of the very heart of his own teaching. Since it is teaching that which cannot be taught yet must be learned, the koan which is made out of their learning-teaching says just that: "Here is our joint situation; here is the discontinuity in it. Do you now see where I am in it, and therefore where you are?" If the disciple grasps this, then he has leaped across a gap.

The Parable

Much closer to our Western way of thinking is another mode of crossing an unbridgeable gap, the parable of the New Testament. There is a revealing passage (Matt. 13:11, 13) in which Christ is asked by his disciples why he speaks to ordinary folk in parables. "He answered and said unto them, Because it is given unto you to know the mysteries of the kingdom of heaven, but to them it is not given. . . . Therefore speak I to them in parables: because they seeing see not; and hearing they hear not, neither do they understand."

The structure of the parable is not at all like that of the koan. It seems to have the form of a little moral tale, yet with its stark and dramatic opening and the absence of an orderly ending, we can guess that it is not a story which is meant to stand by itself. Rather, it is meant to be only an example such that what it says is much less important than what it implies—and it does the latter not explicitly but by pointing elsewhere. Like the koan, it is a device for representing, which it does by translating a truth that is not understood into an example that is. For ordinary folk, it thus makes the ineffable understandable.

The koan and the parable are alike in the respect that they are both methods for helping someone to make contact across what seems an unbridgeable gap—the learning-without-teaching situation of the Zen disciple or the presence of the divine for the human followers of Christ. The target is discontinuous with the everyday experience of these followers, yet the gap can be breached. In the Zen teaching, the koan allows the saying of the unsayable; in the teachings of Christ, the parable permits an understanding of the ineffable. Both require that the follower approach the gap naked and innocent, without knowledge, foreswearing the opportunity to talk about the discontinuity. And because the human experience of major discontinuities has always been in religious matters, both the koan and the parable are devices for religious teaching.

Praying

The "natural" device in religion for breaching the discontinuous, then, should be prayer. We generally associate the form of this act with its modern version, although in fact this developed as recently as the twelfth century. At that time, under the influence of Franciscan monks, the position of the individual penitent was institutionalized as the proper way to talk to God. Derived in part from the posture of a liege in the presence of the feudal master, it required the individual to kneel with hands together and head bowed and to talk in a low voice or even silently.

Praying is unilateral. It takes the form of a request, not a question or a command. It is never a part of a dialogue, and it is never the opening line of an action sequence. Here again, the posture peculiar to prayer tells us something important about its nature. For the physical stance of prayer in all religions, in every era, differs frrom action stances in that we tend toward bilateral symmetry in prayer. We prostrate ourselves, hands close to our sides or stretched out evenly ahead of us; or we stand with feet together, head bowed, and arms hanging by our sides; or we assume a position almost like attention, with palms pressed together at the midline and eyes closed; or we rest on our knees with head bent and hands together—all of these are positions in which the left and right sides of the body are in approximately the same stance.

This matter of symmetry and asymmetry in bodily posture is most curious and quite unnoticed. Among practically all animals, particularly those which cannot move freely in water but must make their way on land, the normal stance for movement and action is bilaterally asymmetrical. The feature becomes evident very soon after birth. In the human neonate, the initial position can involve lying on the back, arms and legs akimbo, and head flopped adventitiously to one side or the other. But as it begins to engage in meaningful action, the infant's postures become increasingly asymmetrical; one side or the other is emphasized at each instant of movement, and the two sides do not assume the same position even at rest.

The inference to be drawn here is that action of any sort, whether taking a position or engaging in purposeful movement, whether resting or doing something, has as a necessary concomitant a bilateral asymmetry of posture and stance. If we consider our own posture at any moment or look around at others, we can note the universality of asymmetry—sometimes to an extreme degree, as in adolescents who are beginning to test out new boundaries of purpose and freedom. As repeated studies have shown, even when we stand still or sit we are typically shifted toward one foot or one buttock. If we were to try to walk with perfect bilateral symmetry, our gait would resemble that of a robot or, more familiarly, the movie version of Frankenstein's monster. And if we stop moving and assume a bilaterally symmetrical pose, it resembles standing at attention—or being at prayer. As many social groups have intuitively recognized, in order to represent the stance of "No action in the world" or "Taking no sides," one places the body symmetrically; and so we have the full lotus position of oriental meditative disciplines or the position in which a corpse is often placed, with hands folded evenly across the chest.

Prayer, then, means to be in a special stance that we assume in talking to God. It is a position that says we are not about to engage in action, since we all know that, by its nature, action calls for an appropriate response or reaction. Our purpose in praying is not to do anything on our own, nor to initiate an interchange in which we take turns with God in some back-and-forth sequence of word or deed, nor even to gather some useful data. Yet we do not stand there dumbly; we are convinced that we assume this position for a purpose, often, indeed, for the most solemn purpose of our existence. It is a very special position, clearly unworldly. No wonder that from its earliest appearance in human society, it required a temple put aside for its enactment. When we pray, we stand on mysterious ground.

Discontinuity and Excarnation

Prayer must thus be viewed as the prototypical mode of address to that which is discontinuous with our experience. Now I want to consider the notion of discontinuity in a broader sense, in its most general relation with awareness or inner experience.

It has been argued, by Julian Jaynes (1973) among others, that what we now refer to as a person's inner experience is a relatively recent phenomenon, as human history goes. No more than a few thousand years ago, in Western culture, inner experience—that is, my own ongoing knowing of the meaning and sources of what goes on with me—was located in the gods, particularly in the goddesses called muses. The poet or bard, singing to us, could well be blind, since he had no need of sight; all he had to do was sing with the voice of the muses, speaking in their tongues.

Our modern conviction that our inner experience is really located in our heads may be no more valid than that of the Greeks. For inner experience, so-called, is clearly not a substance or a thing that requires a place. It might be better understood, perhaps, as that aspect of my life-in-action which arises from some inspirational source, and I suspect that as a source or wellspring, Olympus will do as well as my brain. Our contemporary insistence, at least in Western culture, that the source of one's individual experience is to be found in material form inside the skull may be more historically determined than we like to think. It may well be a consequence of that momentous shift within European culture over the past few centuries in which God was dethroned and then relocated inside the individual person as a self.

But one wellspring is as good as another, until it runs dry; it need only help us to see things straight. If our premise is that inner experience is not material, even though it may be realer than real, then we are entitled to conclude that it does not require a location, but a source. Experience, like heaven, is no more than a state of mind.

Now for some consequences of this premise. I understand our awareness as *excarnated*. This is Erwin Straus's term (1959). He coined it to refer to a basic characteristic of thinking—that it constituted a way of lifting oneself out of the sense-bound, body-bound moment. Thinking is an out-of-the-body trip. To this I would add, so is all our inner experience; in imagination, in thought, in fantasy, in memory, in all the operations we call cognitive, we break free of our incarnated state and soar, as far as we are able, into realms that never were and perhaps never could be.

A number of miracles follow on this fundamental characteristic of our experiencing selves. On the one hand, inner experience is a mode of freedom from the physicality of senses and body; yet equally, all our experience arises from, interlinks with, and returns to its sources in our bodily selves. We refer to this miraculous juncture when we say that each of us possesses, and is possessed by, both a living body and a lived body. Thus, though in all our inner experience we seem to soar beyond our senses and our bodies, the one target of experience that we know best and return to first and most often is the body as it is lived.

In its most fundamental aspect, then, all our experience is discontinuous because, being excarnated, it is addressed to the physical, to the world of things-as-is. Our experience in-the-world has the form of a one-sided yet dual interchange in which the two sides intertwine across a gap, affecting each other but never meeting. *In experience, we pray to the world.* This is more immediately and evidently true in regard to my experience of my own body as target. I know my body intimately, in a way that is almost prior to organized knowing, yet I cannot ever come to know it, because at the very instant that I assume a position in which some objective knowledge of my body is possible, it disappears as though offended or transgressed, as though I had committed the mistake of touching the sacred. There is a similar result if I try to give up what I know *of* my body and attempt to grasp it immediately, directly, even materially, because after all I am part of it; that is, if I try to come to terms with my body by *being* my body, as in states of free reverie, dream, blind emotion, or even habit, then I find that I cannot know it at all. My body disappears again, swirling back down the throat of my own action.

It seems that the only way I can maintain a continuing, knowing contact between my ongoing awareness and the state of my body is by having the first respectfully address the second in a kind of somatic prayer. And it may even be that, historically, prayer was the first instance of organized excarnation from which all others were learned.

Creating the Other

There is a further consequence of the status of experience as excarnate: it is the characteristic of objects which are discontinuously apprehended as not existing until brought into being by my experiencing. When I address them, I breathe on them. In an important sense, I create them.

Consider the "objects" of my thinking or imagining. These are not objects in the sense of being resident somewhere, taking up space, waiting to be touched by my action as a stone might wait on the ground to be moved by my foot. Rather, they are creations of my thinking, my imagining, my fantasy. Here the process and its object are one; thinking *is* thoughts, no more and no less. The other side of the coin, as a consequence, is that my experience is not a fixed, thinglike or machine-like process which runs its course, spewing out objects as products but not being affected by them. My experience needs its own objects as environment and will, in turn, be affected by them and set up relations with them.

In the realm of the spiritual, this fact of my creating is called *faith*. God is my very own creation. If I do not believe or if I fail in my side of this mysterious bargain, then God will never appear. We might see this, if we so choose, in Michelangelo's Sistine Chapel painting, *The Creation of Adam*. The mortal man is shown reclining, it is true, but already half roused. He has placed his left arm on his knee and has brought his hand into position to receive, or perhaps to find, create, or accept, God's outstretched touch at the moment of creation. It is hard to say who is the creator here.

The most common version of this phenomenon of creation, yet the one that we seem to understand the least, is that special target of experiencing, the other person. It seems to me difficult enough to understand how I am able to address my own body; yet it is incomparably more difficult to understand how I can address another person. I mean by this not to address another person as a physical object nor even to address another person as a living, purposeful creature but to address another person as an individual who is like me, who is moved in ways that I am, who is (as I am always certain) addressing me in return in the same way. How do I manage to create myself in a different but similar guise? What is it that very young children know and demonstrate in talking to themselves?

The other person is close to me yet separated by a gap, myself but not, of course, myself, reachable in some ways yet always in other ways a mystery, public to me yet private to himself just as I am to myself. In addressing this other person, I find myself continuously creating and re-creating an other. Facing a discontinuity that I would breach, I find only the bare beginnings of surety, only the first hints of a fixed, solid truth on which I can depend. Everything that I can know, following this beginning, will then result from two directions I may pursue: either I impale the other person on my prejudices and thus constrain him, making him more thing than being or I create him as an impression, compounded of my thinking and imagining, mixed equally of my hope and fear and prayer. If I emphasize the first direction, I will run no risks but make no gains. I will myself be as fixed with that person as I have made him. I will enforce between us a ritual in which we are bound together by habit or primitive passion.

But if I pursue the second direction, allowing the other person to be what I imagine, to become my creation, and if I then make my own response, whatever that may be, then the other will become my myth, quite literally the creature of my needs and failings, my wishes and my mysterious ways of knowing. Most of all, there will be no truth involved in what we know of one another. No matter how I twist and turn, I will never be able to settle to my final satisfaction whether that person is in fact as I imagine him to be or whether my impression of him is a product of my own thinking and feeling. I will never be able to apportion the correct fractions of truth between the reality of that person and my projection.

We cannot easily live with the uncertainity involved in this latter direction, not in that most charged and significant of arenas, our interpersonal relations. So we settle most often for some aspect of the simpler and more primitive direction in creating the other. We lean on our stable prejudices rather than risk falling in a dance of our own creation.

The Rememberer

The problem of memory provides an excellent example of the issues involved in accepting experience as excarnated. Before the time of the Greeks, in pre-Christian Coptic or Judaic thought, for instance, the faculty of remembering was considered a miracle on a par with dreaming. This may be difficult for us to grasp, so embedded are we in a certain limited way of thinking about this question. But for pre-Christian thinkers, the act of remembering was a mode of addressing God or the attendant spirits, just as surely as one did so in a dream or a vision. The rememberer was not simply, and somehow, in touch with his own mental contents; he was not engaged in using one part of his psychic apparatus to contact another part, much as a dog might use its left hind leg to scratch the front of its right ear. That general notion, with all that it requires by way of assumption, came about much later.

Even as late as the first century A.D., in the final flowering of Hellenic thought in Rome, Plutarch viewed remembering as a faculty of the soul. In his work on oracles, he remarks, "Of things past, none is or subsists, but all things are born and die together, [and the soul] laying hold upon them, I know not how, invests things not present with visible form and existence" (Plutarch, Moralia). They are all around us, these "remembra," as we may call them; it is we who make them come forth or create them as in a vision whenever we exercise that special faculty of memory which is the converse, and equivalent, of foreknowing.

Following their understanding of Aristotle, Christian thinkers turned the creative act of remembering into a complex, two-sided conception. There is, on the one hand, a mechanical faculty, allied to the senses which operate in the present, by which one turns one's attention inward, using one part of the psyche to operate on another part. Then there is, on the other hand, a collection of stored impressions or contents which were left over from one's past life and action. The latter notion, that progressive imprints are made in the brain, made the concept of *memory trace* fundamental to any theory. This concept is with us yet, in all its weaknesses and contradictions—although on at least two occasions, in the writings of Karl Lashley (1960) and Erwin Straus (1966), it has been all but destroyed. In Western thought, it is not the act of remembering but the process of memory which constitutes the problem, the process being made up of a collection of traces plus a built-in hook for dragging them back to the present awareness.

In its most recent and virulent form, as a theory of memory banks and their informational contents, we are offered the ultimate version of the mechanical memory. Bedazzled by the technology of computers and tape recorders, contemporary American information theorists depict an elaborate mental museum. Bits of information, all chopped up into the same size, are packaged into "chunks," screened, categorized, stored briefly in short-term banks, and then taken out, presumably one chunk at a time, to be filed away in long-term storage. Who accomplishes all these jobs is never mentioned; the employees of the inner museum are forever anonymous. We may wonder: Do *they* remember their instructions? And if they do, are there, then, still smaller, still more deeply hidden homunculi in *their* heads which in turn. . . ? But in that line of thought lies only scientific chaos, and so it must be suppressed.

There is, however, an alternative theoretical possibility, its recent history extending back to the early thought of Freud. It appears most clearly in current Soviet experimental research (Smirnov, 1973) in which a distinction is made between voluntary memory, or memorizing, and involuntary memory, or remembering. The former is what is usually studied in the psychological laboratory, where subjects are made to learn something, usually in rote fashion, are told they will be tested on it later, and then, after varying interval conditions, are assessed in regard to how much they have retained. It is an arrangement precisely calculated to support the conception of the memory process as an elaborate kind of tape recorder. The Soviet experimenters, who recognize that in real life most remembering begins with a kind of involuntary "learning," have used a different paradigm. Their subjects are observed in the course of certain activities, are subjected to various intervening conditions, and are then tested to see what they have remembered. In the American laboratory, the independent variable is usually the interpolated condition; in the Soviet laboratory, the independent variable is more likely to be the relation between the original "learning" situation and the subsequent remembering situation. Thus, they have shown that school children who participate in play activities and then are tested for recall in the laboratory remember significantly more than those who are told to do the same thing in the laboratory and then are tested for recall of it on the playground.

Memory, in this alternative view, is not merely a sort of learning in the absence of reinforcement. Rather, it is my individual way of addressing my own past—a past which is itself creation that cannot be separated from my remembering. Therefore, my remembering will depend in part on the significance and the place of the original activity in my ongoing history; that fact, in turn, keeps changing as my history develops, in part depending on the relation between that former situation and the situation in which I now engage in remembering and in part depending on how I now choose to address, and so create, this aspect of my history. Aristotle put it succinctly in 330 B.C.: "For whenever one exercises the faculty of remembering, he must say within himself, 'I formerly heard this' or 'I formerly had this thought' " (Aristotle, *Parva Naturalia.* [*On memory and reminiscence.*] Sec. 449b, nos. 23–24). Only a creature which has a personal past and can be reflective about it, relate that reflectiveness to its ongoing present, and then link both aspects to its own self can be said to remember. Otherwise one simply changes with time and learning, as a dog does, or one simply repeats, which is what the tape recorder does, or one simply retains an impression, as the sand does of the footprint.

As he so often did, Freud understood a portion of this problem. He saw clearly that a theory of remembering must also encompass a theory of forgetting. Unfortunately, although he began to understand the many modes of forgetting, he could not free himself from a mechanical, associationist view of remembering. Contemporary explanations in American psychology fail equally; they offer the computer as a model, ignoring the fact that it is a machine which is unable to forget. Both aspects, the remembering and the forgetting, are needed in a theory of memory, because they are two versions of the same kind of act—that mode of addressing myself across the gap of my own past, "investing things not present with visible form and existence," exactly as I might do in other forms of prayer toward the discontinuous. This act is not a product of memory but a dividend of remembrance.

Theory, Violence, and Learning

There are many different avenues open to us as human beings as we go about our individual engagements in the world, as we construct our own meaningful lives, and as we make and remake our careers as historical beings. In this paper I have discussed one of these avenues in its many facets—that we find ourselves facing a gap, addressing its mystery, and maintaining the gap while speaking to that which is discontinuous with our sense-bound ego state. In this act, of which prayer is the prototype, we do not demand but allow; we present ourselves as though open to a gift. Whatever reply we then hear is not a reaction, not a response, and surely not an echo. It comes to us from the other, but it is an other that we ourselves create by being gifted enough to reach toward and then understand the reply.

Two forms of such address seem to have arisen at very early dates in human culture. They are expressed in every language in a pair of related terms: *to ask for*, or to seek help, and *to ask about*, or to seek knowledge. In our own culture, where the split between the two has been quite marked for more than two centuries, we no longer even see them as related. Indeed, we might consider it almost offensive to suggest that at their roots, in the prototypic human act of creating one's world, prayer in religion and theory in science might be one and the same.

Theory making is our contemporary way of asking questions of nature; it is therefore, as we hope, our way of penetrating into the unkown. But I would suggest here that as a human act it is also remarkably similar to praying. For theory is, like prayer, a one-sided endeavor; I do not ever engage in a dialogue with nature. If I were to act as a good scientist should, all I could do is use the appropriate mode of respectful address—that is, the correct application of theory—in order that nature might then be revealed to me. And, as in the case of prayer, whatever answer then comes back to me is largely of my own making.

It may be asked skeptically: Is this comparison of theory and prayer really no more than a suggestive analogy? Do I have any solid basis for claiming that theory is indeed a form of prayer?

The answer to this question can be found by looking more closely at the forms of our knowing about the world. I suggest that if our knowing is to be meaningful at all, and relevant to the way things are, such knowing cannot ever be gained by receiving truth in the manner of making a withdrawal from an account whose contents are known. World-relevant knowing is not to be gained by a process of accepting presented facts without a seeking activity on our part. Nor can we hope to arrive at some form of the truth by simply stumbling across a discovery that is already organized and present for us. Rather, our knowing has to come about in the course of meeting specific requirements, which can be outlined as a series of steps,

First of all, our knowing must be organized in a sensible relation to what *might* be there to be found. The model for this stage, in terms of an older and perhaps better established activity, consists of our procedure as we approach an oracle of our choosing: we find out about the appropriate temple; we enter it in a state of preparation; and we anoint ourselves so as to be ready for the occasion. It is the first function of theory to accomplish these steps for us in regard to our knowing.

Following this, we must address ourselves to the world in a mode, and by means of an approach, which is coherent as well as relevant to our seeking. This, the second function of theory, follows the requirement in prayer that we find and deliver the proper prayer, with the proper stance, for the occasion at hand.

Finally, we must commit ourselves to a participative exchange in which our taking is also an engagement and a giving of ourselves. In everyday affairs, the model for this activity is that utterly noncommercial transaction that we find in the interchange of love. Allen Wheelis (1971, p. 81) tells us, in perhaps too masculine a metaphor: "The world to us is a woman in our arms; we may know her but will change her, and in being known she changes us. . . . We should not boast of conquest—modesty better becomes our achievements in knowing—mindful that she whom we held yesterday may surprise us today with qualities born of the embrace." This process we call learning.

Prayer implies no action. Theory, however, because it enables us to build a history of increasingly world-encompassing knowledge of the world, can easily plunge us into the danger of putting it all to the test in action. In theory, of course, theory is nonworldly, and scientists, taking refuge in this aspect of theory, are prone to boast of the worldly purity of their efforts. "Don't blame me for the consequence of the bomb," they will say. "We didn't drop it. We only made it." But in fact, theory, as handmaiden to modern science, has increasingly dirtied itself in the messy affairs of the world.

As we know, science and religion, at odds throughout the Middle

Ages, finally declared a truce following their Galilean wars. A division of territories was proclaimed in which science received the world and religion gained jurisdiction over souls. It turned out to be a one-sided bargain, for all that religion received was that contemporary version of the soul, modern man's anxious self. Since then, science has aimed at pure doing, at accomplishing, above all at control. As Erling Eng (1972) has noted in a discussion of Husserl's late view of contemporary science, it became "a European form of action, even of violence within the horizon of the everyday world" (p. 276). The consequence, as we can see all around us, is a total technology, which now threatens to overwhelm us with its products and destroy us with its tools.

Yet, theory, as the systematic and world-encompassing form of prayer, might well serve simply as our way of addressing the mysteries of nature rather than the mysteries of God or man or oneself. Toward the end of his life, Wilhelm Reich (1973) began to have a sense of this as his vision came to include all of the universe. He saw the universe as a "functional" whole, as a "vigorous, free, and still lawful and harmonic world. . . a tangible, full pulsating world, perceivable and measurable at the same time" (p. 66). This is not the impersonal or ideal world of contemporary science, but the *human world,* as Erwin Straus called it. It is not an array of mere things that we call to our purposes, that we manipulate and use and finally destroy in a continuing sacrifice to our power and achievement. Rather, it is a *Lebenswelt* which is continuingly created out of our meaningful action and interaction, which is built out of the gifts that breach our discontinuities.

Reich (1973, p. 66) was able to say, "The single way out of the chaos is, then, the shaping of life-forms according to the laws of the living," but having achieved this vision, it was his strange and tragic fate to find his vision trapped in the context of the mechanistic physics of the nineteenth century. Like J. B. Rhine, he sounds like a bad dream had by Helmholtz. Reich was defeated, in large part, by himself; he was left staring across a gap which had become a threat rather than a promise as he himself became, in the end, the ultimate paranoid scientist, trapped in his own high-energy world of demons.

Theory, misused as power, can thus turn into violence or mechanism. But my thesis in these pages has been that we can avoid this danger in science and that we can in the process build a humanistic psychology if we are willing to base it on forms of prayer as the prototype of meaningful human encounter. Prayer, in this sense, is the fundamental act of the infinitely varied human world in all its forms: as personal meeting, as communication, as sympathy and love, as understanding, as the knowing of one's own history and especially as the sense of one's own body, and finally as theory when it is in the service of understanding rather than power. It is when we act in these ways that we come to know the answers to our prayers.

References

Eng, E. Body, consciousness, and violence. In A. Tymieniecka (Ed.), *Analecta husserliana* (Vol. 2). Dordrecht, Holland: D. Reidel, 1972.

Jaynes, J. The origin of consciousness. In D. Krech (ed.), *The MacLeod symposium.* Ithaca, N.Y.: Department of Psychology, Cornell University Press, 1973.

Keleman, S. *Your body speaks its mind.* New York: Simon & Schuster, 1975.

Lashley, K. S. In search of the engram. In D. Beach (Ed.), *The neuropsychology of Lashley: Selected papers.* New York: McGraw-Hill, 1960.

Lyons, J. An interview with a mute catatonic. *Journal of Abnormal and Social Psychology,* 1960, *60,* 271–277.

Ong, W. J. *The presence of the word.* New York: Touchstone/Clarion, 1970.

Reich, W. *Ether, God, and Devil.* New York: Noonday, 1973.

Smirnov, A. A. *Problems of the psychology of memory,* New York: Plenum Press, 1973.

Straus, E. W. Human action—response or project. *Confinia Psychiatrica,* 1959. 2, 148–171.

Straus, E. W. On merory traces. In E. W. Straus, *Phenomenological psychology.* New York: Basic Books, 1966.

Wheelis, A. *The end of the modern age.* New York: Basic Books, 1971.

5

John Charles Cooper

WHY MAN IS PRIOR TO SCIENCE IN ANY SCIENCE OF MAN

THE EPISTEMOLOGICAL ORDER OF VALUE AND FACT

Introduction

Harold G. Coward and Joseph R. Royce, in their original[1] contribution to this volume (pp. 109–134) entitled "Toward an Epistemological Basis for Humanistic Psychology," discuss the difference between traditional empirical twentieth-century psychology and the newly developing humanistic psychology in terms of the distinction Martin Buber makes between "I–It" and "I–Thou." They observe correctly that for some two centuries the empirical questions of natural science have provided the dominant framework for Western thought in general and the specific development of psychology as well. This rigid empirical viewpoint has

[1] Due to space limitation, Coward and Royce removed all references to Buber. However, since Cooper is actually quoting Buber, there is no inconsistency in what follows (see Buber, 1958).

John Charles Cooper • Dean of Academic Affairs, Winebrenner Theological Seminary, 701 East Melrose Avenue, Findlay, Ohio 45840.

given us a one-dimensional concept of man, and because of this we have largely lost any vision of man as a total being, dividing him, intellectually, into various systems, stimuli, and responses.

Much contemporary thought has been in revolt against this one-dimensional vision for the past several decades. Thinkers from many disciplines, including literature, drama, art, religion, philosophy, and psychology itself, have protested against the reduction of man to a mechanistic object. Coward and Royce, speaking for this more holistic, existentialist outlook observed:

> In studying human nature we need to, as Buber put it, take out from a man all we can about the color of his hair or his eyes, his nerves, his thought, etc., and to do this we need the presuppositions, questions and methods of scientific psychology. But, having taken out all the pieces as it were, we will not have an understanding of man as human until we also open ourselves to approaches which exceed the limits of current scientific conceptualizations and methodologies, for such learning will result in the transformation and extension of our own limits of awareness. The inclusion of the "I–Thou" perspective within the study of psychology is not only essential if the enterprise is to be true to its name, but it will also result in an opening of new vistas similar to what happened in Greek philosophy when Socrates shifted the level of discourse from the earlier question of Thales, "What is the world made of?" to questions of purpose and value. Socrates's questions were disconcerting, says Suzanne Langer (1948, p. 19), because they were not aimed at merely describing the motion and matter of a thing, but rather to see its purpose. The aim of the humanistic or third force in contemporary psychology is to effect a similar shift--a shift which values and builds on the needed first steps of scientific psychology (of knowing man by abstracting his component parts), but changes the presuppositions and questions so that they are directed towards the knowing of man in his full humanity--in a holistic and empathetic "I–Thou" way. (Coward and Royce, personal communication)

It is my contention not only that this humanistic outlook is justified by our intuitive sense that man is being shortchanged by positivistic and empirical presuppositions but that the very order of knowledge, the way we do come to know anything that we do know, demands the recognition that man is prior to science, that a human being in his or her totality exists before any observations are made and any hypotheses formulated. The data, the Pointer reading, the hard facts of the natural-science outlook are not really so hard after all; the facts themselves are the results of human values. We do not need to apologize for a holistic science of man. The nature of knowing itself, the basis of science, demands a humanistic psychology.

Fact

In the general, positivistic world of science, experimental psychology and behaviorism in particular, facts are facts and values are somewhat uncertain. That is a fact which can be demonstrated, observed, and measured, both now and in the future by other, independent observers.

Moritz Schlick, in his essay, "Meaning and Verification" (1936, p. 339) observes:

> Verifiability means possibility of verification. . . . [I] call "empirically possible" anything that does not contradict the laws of nature. . . .
>
> . . . The results of our consideration is this: Verifiability . . . is the sufficient and necessary condition of meaning.

Schlick therefore identifies meaning with verifiability, which for him as a logical positivist is a matter of logical order, of the proper phrasing of sentences that directly refer to what is observed. We are in the presence of the "look-and-see world" of the pragmatist and the behaviorist.

Somehow this is not fully satisfying. One wonders how we are to deal with values, love, hate, aspiration, hope, and other human experiences if we are limited to these epistemological processes. A human philosophy, a science of man, and a humanistic psychology are impossible with a logical-positivistic foundation. And yet man, with all his needs and interests, exists and must be studied. Humankind *is*, and above all is a value-observing, meaning-creating enterprise. If there is to be a human science, a humanistic psychology, with any philosophical basis of support, we must therefore reinvestigate the foundations of knowledge. Perhaps "facts" are not as simple, or as basic as the positivists and behaviorists would have us believe.

Coward and Royce, in their chapter in this volume, have attempted to focus on the epistemological issue involved in laying a firmer philosophical foundation for humanistic psychology. It is not clear that these commentators have done more than raise the epistemological issue. Coward and Royce do move close to the epistemological area, however, in dealing with the controlled observation that is the scientific answer to the problems of observer bias in common-sense observation. They state that empirical repeatability is the scientific requirement that guards against this observer bias (Coward & Royce, this volume, p. 111, citing Royce, 1970).

As I will discuss in the following section, I do not believe that controlled observation, institutionalized in the laboratory experiment for most of the sciences, including much of psychology, is a real guarantee that what Coward and Royce call observer bias—and what I call the presence of human values—is removed by the laboratory method. It is a little like building a house out of mud, then becoming aware that mud is less than beautiful. At first we might mix the mud with some coloring material so that we have a lovely pink or blue mud house. But it is still mud. Later we learn to create our own building material, mixing clean earth and water under controlled conditions. We press this sanitized material into bricks, bake and cure them, and build our houses according to elaborate plans. Now we have attractive, regularized houses built of mud bricks. Later we may add stucco to the walls of our house, hiding the mud bricks, but deep inside, the walls and foundations of our house are still composed of mud. As the years pass, we may paint over the stucco, give it new names, and forget about the interior of the walls and foundations. But under all the elaborate covers, and beneath all the sophisticated techniques, even centuries afterward when we build steel skeletons which are then covered with bricks, our dwelling—which I take to be a model of human science—is still integrally related to the mud wall shelters of our primitive past.

This is an illustration or parable, to be sure, and such stories lose their force when they are expressed in prose. But for the sake of clarity, I want to point out that the basic mud that runs through this story is my symbol for human intentionality, for the basic values that a human mind puts on some event or item in the public world, thus selecting it out for observation, classification, analysis, and use. I am saying that every fact that comes to us as a fact, all data that we collect as data, all processes that we investigate come to us, first as individuals and then to the community of discourse we call the realm of science, because those events or elements had value for a human being. All our grand systems of human activity, every science, are built from observations that have been selected by the human mind. Science does not have feet of mud; it is completely built of mud, the precious mud of human values. We can cover over these values and call them facts, but under the paint and the stucco, the mud is there.

Just here is the connection between epistemology and methodology—in all the sciences and particularly in psychology. The view of epistemology developed here implies that there can be no completely objective methods in studying anything, least of all man. Therefore, the import of what is said here is to stress the need for a total approach to the total human being, who is first of all one who sees distinctions in the public world and selects elements and events of that world for development on the basis of a prior valuation process. Values precede facts. Man is a purposeful creature. Mankind proceeds not randomly but on the basis of interests, desires, wants, needs, whims, purposes, and goals. Such values in man demand our attention because they are of supreme value and interest to us. It is entirely possible that these inner values are cognitively prior to the phenomena we recognize in the world. Many great philosophers were aware of this, or at least were vaguely aware of this situation. Because of this awareness, Plato spoke of innate ideas and attributed them to the presence in man of an immortal soul. Kant recognized that the raw stuff of experience was organized by the human mind, adding the noumenal to the phenomenal elements of knowledge. Aristotle spoke of all human epistemological transactions as purposeful. In recent years, the existentialist Paul Tillich agreed. The conclusion of my investigation is that Aristotle was right.

Purposes and Values

In Book 1, Chapter 1 of *Metaphysics,* Aristotle offers a universal statement that may be the only "all, without exception" sentence that remains true after empirical examination: "All men by nature have a desire to know." Later in the same book, observes that: "In man, experience is a result of his memory, for many memories of doing the same thing end in creating a sense of a single experience. Experience seems almost the same as science and art."

The Sophist, Polus, observes the same thing about the empirical basis of science, or knowledge, in Plato's *Gorgias.* For Polus, experience (that is, empiricism) is all. He says: "Experience produces art but inexperience only luck."

There is no recognition of the noumenal element of memory in Sophism. The Sophists in general were not concerned with what Kant later called the noumenal, the synthetic function of pure reason, nor were they troubled by the axiological questions of human knowledge, by the values and the source of values which to some degree, though in differing respects, all men hold. But Aristotle was concerned with value, above all with the overarching value of the end or purpose of every activity from the movement of a limb to the movement of the universe. Aristotle (*Metaphysics,* Book I) called that supreme value simply "the good."

> For one who desires knowledge for its own sake will desire above all what is most genuinely knowledge and that is the knowledge of what is best to know. And the things best to know are first principles and causes. For through them and from them all other things may be known but not they through the things covered by them. [There is an asymmetrical relationship between universal and particular insights into the nature of experience, Aristotle holds.] Supreme then among the sciences and superior to all subordinate science is that which knows the end for which everything takes place, which is the good for each thing and, as a whole, the highest good for all nature.

Since Aristotle rejected the hard-line interpretation of Plato—that there is a supermundane world (or heaven) parallel to this world that is the goal of the immortal soul after death—he was perplexed as to the origin and relative order of value and fact.

Aristotle's problem was the same as our problem, since we, too, are confronted by the reality of values as determiners of the meaning of empirical data and of human experience, and we, too, choose to deal with values without recourse to a heaven as their source. Our difference from Aristotle—and from the thoughtful Immanuel Kant—is that many twentieth-century philosophers and psychologists are unaware of the issue. We cannot say with Aristotle, "the study of truth is partly hard and partly easy" (*Metaphysics,* Book II, Chapter I). For most of us, there is a desire to know the facts about whatever is at issue, a thrust to gather data, to find something "hard" that can be measured, although we are often unable to say just what it is we are measuring or just how our instrument is a suitable tool to measure that particular kind of thing. We do whatever we can with everything we have and think little about the value of what we do and nothing at all of Aristotle's teleological question, "Why?" The recent controversy over I.Q. tests is an obvious example. Strong believers in the value of these tests for predicting academic and vocational adaptability and success are now confronted with moot charges that such instruments measure only the conditioning of those tested by white, middle-class values. Supposedly value-free instruments prove to have a distinct priority of values over the factual data contained in them.

All such embarrassing instances of the priority of values over facts simply add weight to the claim that the positivistic approach to man is mistaken and inadequate. A truly human science or humanistic psychology would begin from a base that includes the recognition that values—the values of the observing, searching, selecting human being who pursues science, philosophy, or psychology—are prior to and, indeed, create the "facts" discovered. But for those who insist on a mechanistic model for man and deny the importance of the inner, subjective world, these negative and positive instances are crushing. It would seem that a way of "doing science" (practicing psychology) that does not recognize the primacy of human values, and allow for it in its method, is not really "scientific" (or objective) at all. Only humanistic psychology, in this view, even comes close to the much desired "objectivity" which can only result from understanding all the subjective factors involved in a situation and compensating for them.

Negative Instances

There are a number of familiar situations in social psychology that provide negative instances, "backward proof," of the priority of values over facts in the epistemological process. Like it or not, what we feel about the world and how we see the world (in terms of world-view or outlook, often represented by the German term Weltanschauung) determines what we see and what we find in the world. This may not be universally true, but its popularity as an epistemological method calls into question any strict insistence on a classical, value-free empiricism.

The first example is drawn from human prejudice. Whites who belittle blacks may be participants in a society where many blacks are responsible citizens, moral, industrious, and intelligent. However, prejudiced persons see only black irresponsibility, immorality, and laziness. They see what they expect to see, what their "values" tell them about the world. In similar fashion, radical blacks see all whites as exploitative, and radical anticommunists see communist plots everywhere, from the waterworks to the legislative hall.

The second example is drawn from human emotions, particularly those of hate and love. A person who actively dislikes another only infrequently recognizes good qualities and noble actions on the part of that other. A man or a woman who is "in love" rarely notices the warts on the beloved until the passion passes. We see a reflected image of our inward values when we look on the face of the enemy or the form of the beloved. The field of literature is our record of folly.

The third example is drawn from human needs. Plato recognized the "passions" or "appetites" as an element in the makeup of the human soul. We are all aware of the changes in personality and the thinking process brought on by strong sexual excitation or by an unrelenting feeling of hunger or thirst. When one is fully nourished and in a state of self-possession, one takes notice of the world around, of the beauty of the sky, the nature of the countryside, the faces of other people. But when one is sexually aroused, one's intentionality is narrowed down to the proverbial "main thing." When a group of us offered a course in pornography and sexuality at Bowling Green University, Ohio in 1972, we began by giving the participants a little test involving their responses to 100 photographs taken from American magazines. Each student was tested separately and asked to check whether the photograph spoke to him or her of sex "not at all, a little, a moderate amount, or a lot." One young man checked that a photograph of a can of tomato soup spoke to him of sex "a lot." When asked why, he replied that he was horny and in that condition everything spoke of sex! I suspect that he was not an atypical case. Facts are skewed completely out of context when the organism insists on its needs. These organic movements become overarching values, or value facts, that take priority over everything else. Anyone who has taken a written examination while hungry recognizes the truth of this statement.

Positive Instances

That values often are prior to, and determinative of, the data that comes to the mind from the phenomenal world can be shown by the positive instance of attention to the point of view of the observer in any epistemological transaction. That the knowledge process is more than noting "pointer readings" is borne out by the work of Werner Heissenberg. Our seeing something, our simple physical presence, changes the world we are observing. Nuclear physicists recognize this relationship, although cultural anthropologists sometime seem oblivious to it. The point of Heissenberg's insight is that there is no value-free or purely objective scientific knowledge. Stating data in mathematical propositions by no means removes the existential infection, the introduction of values, purposes, viewpoints by the simple physical presence of the observer. All data is purposefully gathered data, already given some value by its collector. Even the most meaningless raw observations have the basic meaning of having been observed, of having some minimal value because they have come under the gaze of human intentionality. The digesting of data and its integration into other data is but an upgrading value.

The Priority of Meaning (Value) over Data in the Epistemological Transaction

For Paul Tillich, the major theologian and philosopher of religion of the mid–twentieth century and one of the more popular promoters of existentialism, meaning is the chief category of anthropology and the key issue in epistemology. Tillich's idea of meaning is not simply axiological but that it is the fulfillment of human existence in the creativity of what he calls "spirit." In Tillich's view, which borders on the mystical (and which he called "belief-ful realism"), the principles of the macrocosm are given in the microcosm. Sometimes Tillich referred to his epistemology as "self-transcending realism." His major work on this subject is the still untranslated monograph, *Das System der Wissenschaften nach Gegenstanden und Methoden. Ein Entwurf* (1923).

Tillich opposed both idealism and realism in his epistemological work. He suggested a critico-dialectical method which presupposes the autonomy of the spiritual (i.e., the culture-creating dimension of human personality) from every immediately existing thing. Tillich believed that this method transcended both idealism and realism. In his essay "Religions philosophie" (1925), Tillich observed:

> [The critico-dialectical method] need not assume that the mind gives its laws to nature. Nevertheless it cannot hold an epistemological realism to be true. It cannot assume that nature gives laws to the mind. It must assume that the principles of meaning to which consciousness submits itself in intellectual activity are at the same time the principles of the meaning of existence expressed in the meaning-oriented consciousness. If it hopes nevertheless to avoid the difficulties of an exclusive idealism as well as a doctrine of pre-established harmony, then it is best to speak of the meaning-fulfillment of existence through the activities of the spirit. On the basis of this premise, which is ultimately nothing other than a self-intuition of the spirit as spirit and not as existence, the critico-dialectical method develops the universal forms of meaning, which are at the same time functions of the mind and principles of meaningful reality. (my translation)

Tillich holds that what is needed to understand the real nature of the act of knowing is a method of phenomenological intuition joined to a dynamically developed critical method, which he calls the metalogical method. This metalogical method aims to apprehend the import inhering in the forms (i.e., noumenal, synthetic mental processes), presupposing a creative human power to set up norms. It aims to grasp both form and import (meaning). This method unashamedly seeks to reach back to the ultimate principle that gives meaning to existence. Such a method is akin to mysticism, which seeks to intuit the absolute in its relationship to the relative—the one in the many. The basis of any mysticism, of course, is the belief that the principles of the macrocosm are given in the microcosm; as William Blake has it: "To see a world in a grain of sand"

But this outlook also underlies the empirical method. The particular studied carefully tells us about the whole. The peculiarities of one shark, particularly when we study a sample number of individual sharks, tell us about the whole family of sharks. If every shark we studied was blue, it would be neither mystical nor empirical to hold that some sharks are white. The basic epistemological factor here is an inchoate belief in the interconnection of all things and in their basal uniformity, an interconnection and uniformity which is open to understanding by the human mind. Where mysticism and empiricism part company is not on the apprehension of forms (species, types, normal curves, etc.) but on the apprehension of import, the eliciting of meaning from human experience. Empiricism denies meaning except in terms of utilitarianism; mysticism affirms meaning in terms of human participation in a spiritual whole; and Tillich affirms meaning in the fulfillment of the human longing for the meaning of existence through the awareness of spirit or the power of self-transcendence seen in the act of knowing. What is transcendent about the act of knowing is the awareness of the basal unity of subject and object beyond the "over-against" stance of man in the world, his discontinuous relationship to the other and to things. Tillich declares:

> It has not been recognized that there is a break-through to a new method here, to a new fundamental attitude of mind, namely, the metalogical-dynamic method. The implication for the implementation of metalogic is that while the dynamic of the elements of meaning can indeed be expressed in symbols derived from the affective side of the conciousness, the goal of this symbolism is the intuition of the forms of meaning filled with living import, not of any independent metaphysical entities. For the elements of meaning belong together; there is no import apart from a form, and no form without import. (my translation)

Thus, Tillich's philosophical efforts are motivated by a desire to present a conception of the meaning of life—the foundation of all values—as it is disclosed by a direct interaction with concrete actuality. The temptation of intellectuals is to divide reality into hard data and subjective values in secular empiricism or to disrupt meaning by the introduction of metaphysical entities or transcendantal abstractions in supernaturalism (traditional theology) and idealism. These methods create a new view of actuality out of themselves and then set it up over and against the actuality given in experience.

But Tillich felt that the true function of the intellect is to comprehend the truth of actuality. This attempt should not end in formalism but rather should lead to the awareness of the power and vitality of the real as it fulfills itself in meaningful creativity.

The Epistemological Paradox

Jean Paul Sartre, in *Being and Nothingness* (1956), defines both facticity and value. He tells us that facticity is the necessary connection of the "for-itself" with the "in-itself," hence with the world and its own past. Value is said to arise as the for-itself constitutes objects as desirable. More specifically, value is the beyond of all surpassings as the for-itself seeks to be united with its self. It is what the for-itself lacks in order to be itself. Connecting both facticity and value is transcendence, which is the process whereby the for-itself goes beyond the given in a further projection of itself.

In observing this, Sartre takes us back to the insights of Aristotle in *The Metaphysics*. Man desires to know, particularly to know the first principles and causes of things—including himself. Man is not an unmoved, noninvolved observer. He desires to know the good, the overarching purpose of his being in the world. Value is that which surpasses all facts, a transcendent process by which man projects himself forward in the world, through time, in pursuit of his own evolving maturation—the fulfillment of himself in the end for which he was made.

Amazingly, in both Aristotle, who denied the existence of an immortal soul, and in Sartre, who declared himself an atheist, consideration of the relationship of value and fact led to reflections on God. Aristotle says:

> On such a first principle depends the heavens and the natural world. And its life is like ours when for a brief moment it is at its best. . . . Life also belongs to God, for thought as actuality is life, and God is that actuality. (*Metaphysics*, Book VII, Chapter 7)

And Sartre concludes:

> The act is not its own goal for itself; neither does its explicit end represent its goal and its profound meaning; but the function of the act is to make manifest and to present to itself the absolute freedom which is the very being of the person. This particular type of project, which has freedom for its foundation and its goal, deserves a special study. It is radically different from all others in that it aims at a radically different type of being. It would be necessary to explain in full detail its relations with the project of being-God, which appeared to us as the deep-seated structure of human reality. But such a study cannot be made here; it belongs rather to an Ethics and it supposes that there has been a preliminary definition of nature and the role of purifying reflection . . . it supposes in addition taking a position which can be moral only in the face of values which haunt the For-itself. (Sartre, 1956, p. 581)

Fact or value? Value or fact? Man desires to know meanings, not bits of information. Man lives by meanings and is a meaningful, meaning-creating creature. Few people have sacrificed themselves for facts; even Galileo retracted what he knew were facts when pressed by the Inquisition. But many persons have died for their values. It is not facts but values that come into conflict. There is a clue here somewhere.

References

Buber, M. *I and thou*. New York: Scribners, 1958.

Sartre, J. P. *Being and nothingness* (H. E. Barnes, trans.). New York: Philosophical Library, 1956.

Schlick, M. Meaning and verification. *Philosophical Review*, 1936, *45*, 339–369.

Tillich, P. *Das System der Wissenschaften nach Gegenstanden und Methoden. Ein Entwurf*. Gottingen: Vanderhoeck und Ruprecht, 1923.

Tillich, P. Religions philosophie. In M. Dessoir (Ed.), *Philosophie in ehren Einzelgebieten*. Berlin: Ullstein, 1925.

6

Harold G. Coward and Joseph R. Royce

TOWARD AN EPISTEMOLOGICAL BASIS FOR HUMANISTIC PSYCHOLOGY

It may be that each period in the history of human thought manifests a dominant philosophic presupposition or Weltanschauung. The general populace, and even some of the educated who should know better, are culturally conditioned to uncritical acceptance of whatever way of thinking happens to be dominant at the time. As Susanne Langer (1948, p. 15) aptly puts it: "such implicit 'ways' are not avowed by the average man, but simply followed. . . . They constitute his outlook; they are deeper than facts he may note or propositions he may moot." Langer goes on to show that the adoption of a particular way of thinking effectively limits the kinds of questions one can ask. Thus, each age produces its own questions, which in turn generate the particular academic enterprise of that era.

For roughly the past two centuries the empirical concepts and questions of natural science have provided the dominant frame of mind for Western thought. By treating the subject of study as a detached object to be observed, described, and quantified, considerable manipulative

---

Harold G. Coward • Department of Religious Studies, University of Calgary, Calgary, Alberta T2N 1N4, Canada. *Joseph R. Royce* • Theoretical Psychology Center, University of Alberta, Edmonton, Alberta T6G 2E9, Canada. The preparation of this paper was partially supported by a Canada Council Grant (#55-56118) on psychological epistemology to Joseph R. Royce.

power over our natural environment has been achieved. However, while contemporary Western science (and its technology) has many humane accomplishments to its credit, the limitations inherent in its presuppositions are today increasingly entering the awareness of both the scholar and the ordinary person. The consequence of these changes in outlook is a shift from an unquestioning acceptance of the empirical presupposition (as our dominant mode of knowing) toward what Royce (1964) has called unencapsulation and what the sociologist Sorokin (1941) calls an integral culture—a perspective in which other modes of knowing and being, along with the empirical, are regarded as legitimate. Since what we have just described is the cultural context in which humanistic psychology was nurtured, it is not surprising that it should demand that psychology be redirected toward an understanding of man in his full humanity. It is toward the clearer formulation of humanistic psychology's new presuppositions and questions that this book and this chapter address themselves.

Toward Clarification of the Terms Scientific and Humanistic in Contemporary Psychology

Perhaps the first step required is a conceptual clarification of the terms "scientific" and "humanistic" such that those within the third force are clear about themselves and those working within empirical scientific psychology are clear as to the different focus being taken. Such conceptual clarification is crucial for both sides if mutual trust, respect, dialogue, and complementary effort is to be established.

On Scientific Psychology

Historical and philosophical analysis indicates that a science typically develops via four successive stages: (a) prescientific philosophical speculation, (b) exploratory observation (empirical), (c) the development of more mature methods of experimentation, both qualitative and quantitative, and (d) theoretical unification, such as mathematical rationalization (Royce, 1957, 1978a). Physics, for example, has passed through all four stages, and biology appears to be somewhere just beyond the third phase, having achieved relatively little overall theoretical unification. Psychology has barely tapped the fourth phase and can be characterized in the late twentieth century as being somewhere between phases two (empirical) and three (experimental). Thus, although a mature science involves a mutual meshing of both the rational (theory) and the empirical (facts), it is clear that since contemporary psychology is primarily empirical in its orientation an analysis of the nature of scientific observation will provide the key to what we mean by the word "science" in psychology.

Such an analysis is presented in compressed form in Table 1. In this table, we see that scientific observations encompass a very wide range, including field studies and case studies at one extreme and laboratory experiments at the other. Although scientific methodology emerged out of common-sense observations, it is obvious that such observations are completely uncontrolled and are, therefore, strongly influenced by the biases and idiosyncrasies of the observer. Thus, "controlled observation," involving the isolation and assessment of the effect of relevant variables, is the scientist's answer to the problem of observer bias. The implication is that the experimental designs, sophisticated qualitative and quantitative analyses, and instrumentation techniques of science result in replicable observations and that "empirical repeatability" is the key epistemic requirement of empirical science (Royce, 1970).

What are we to conclude from the panorama of scientific methodology as presented in Table 1? One conclusion is that, although the laboratory experiment is the sine qua non for controlled observation, there are degrees of repeatability using all types of observation, including investigations conducted under the relatively uncontrolled conditions of the field and the clinic. This is true in a wide range of sciences, including astronomy and geology, a wide range of medical and biological specialties, and psychology and other behavioral sciences. Thus, the major point is that the term "science," as used both within psychology and outside it, connotes a much broader meaning than the restrictive stereotype which is conveyed by such terms as "experimental," "quantitative," and "precise." While valid extensions of scientific methodology to include the biological and behavioral domains have been impressive, contemporary "scientism" has also led to overextensions and the development of pseudosciences. The point is that the liberalized view of science has resulted in serious conceptual confusions, particularly in the writings of humanistic psychologists (Royce, 1972). This confusion includes gross misunderstanding of the rigorous demands of scientific methodology.

It should be noted that there is similar misunderstanding of the

Table 1. A Synthesis of Scientific Methods of Observation

Type of observation	Brief description of type of observation	Examples of types of observation	Conditions of observation	Equipment and other tool aids in observing	Degree of "control" of observations	Relative scientific validity of knowledge gained (repeatability)	Comments
Observation in daily life	Common sense	See sky, trees, animals; reflect on one's thoughts	Relatively undirected, uninformed observing; observations relatively random	None	Completely uncontrolled	Completely speculative	Can lead to "hunches" which should be checked by more "controlled" observation
Observation in the field	Naturalistic	Bird watching; observing a riot; watching social behavior of monkeys in natural habitat	Man knows "what to look for" in his observing; selects what he will see	Minimal (e.g., binoculars)	Variables free to vary without control, but may be specifiable and their effect estimated	Good description of phenomena; knowledge of operating variables speculative, and "predictability" is therefore highly questionable	The observer must not be detected by what is being observed
Observation in the clinic	Case study	Medical, psychological clinics	Clinician can "recognize" what the accidents and forces of nature randomly present to him	Many diagnostic aids; precision relatively weak	Variables free to vary without control, but may be specifiable and their effect estimated	Good description of phenomena; knowledge of operating variables speculative, and "predictability" is therefore highly questionable	Stress is on the single case, and the major interest is applied

Semilaboratory observations	"Standardized" conditions of observation	Psychological test; observation dome	Man specifies the conditions but does not "control" the variables; variables free to vary under the specified conditions	Many aids which make observing clearer	Variables free to vary, but are specifiable, and their effect can be estimated with reasonable accuracy	Probability of repeatability is reasonably high but with considerable variation in degree of error in prediction	Statistical analysis leads to determination of the contribution of each variable
Predicted observation in nature (field or clinic)	Naturalistic experiment	Astronomical observation of position at a given time	Nature provides "controlled" experiment for the "informed" man	High-powered instruments of great precision	Variables so well known that predictions of what will occur are confirmable	Precision only slightly less accurate, in general, than in the laboratory experiment	Scientist limited by time, since he can make observations only when nature provides the conditions for observation
Laboratory observations	Experiments	Speed of sound or light	Man artificially "controls" relevant variables in the laboratory	Maximal use of equipment; present tendency is toward complete automation to the point where laboratory man may only read a few dials and meters	Most completely available "control" devised by man or nature to date	Highest validity possible, because "controlled" experimental findings are repeatable within very small degree of error	No experiment is ever completely "controlled", but this fact does not detract from the value of experimentation

Note. From *The Encapsulated Man* by J. R. Royce. Copyright 1964 by Van Nostrand. Reprinted by permission.

rigors of scholarly and creative work in the arts and the humanities. Although this is not news to anybody who has made a serious commitment to these disciplines, it is unfortunately true that many scientists, including psychologists of both scientific and humanistic persuasions, are convinced that only science is rigorous. Koch (1976, p. 146) speaks to this point as follows:

> [S]ome psychologists will no doubt . . . be appalled by the implication that psychology in certain of its reaches (and, indeed, as regards some of its "core" areas . . .) must turn out to involve modes of inquiry rather more like those of the humanities than the sciences. Perhaps they will feel that humanistic knowledge is "soft" knowledge, based on soft intellectual disciplines, while scientific knowledge and research discipline is hard. But musicology is hard (in several senses), as are classics, comparative philology, biblical archeology, and responsible forms of literary criticism. And philosophy—even logic and the philosophy of science—is typically assigned to the humanities.

On Humanistic Psychology

As indicated in the introduction, the third-force movement in psychology can be viewed as part of a broader cultural demand for a more meaningful existence. The core theme of the more academically oriented leaders of the movement is that psychology's conception of man has been too limited and reductionistic, that particularly in his overconcern for method and control the psychologist's view of man has been dehumanized or de-meaned. The key protest is that a conception of man which is devoid of meaning is less than human. Thus, our analysis of the humanistic literature reveals two broad patterns of concern under the rubric of humanistic psychology: (1) a concern for an adequate theory of man and (2) a focus on how to alleviate "the human condition."

The latter group is practically oriented—they want to work actively to alleviate the human condition in individuals, groups, or even societies. In their roles as therapists, counsellors, and so on, they comprise one of the originating factors of the third-force movement. The tradition cites Jung, Adler, and Fromm as positive influences, while Rogers, Frankl, and May are notable contemporary names. The thrust of their approach involves the relationships between therapists and patients and has variously been called growth therapy, logotherapy, and other names. The therapist's task has also been phrased in terms of helping the patient *become* the best version of her or himself. Similar concerns at the societal level are exemplified in the writings of Maslow (1965) and

Winthrop (1962). Maslow makes a case for "eupsychia"—a psychologically healthy culture which will come about as a result of individual psychotherapy combined with mass techniques for educating society about the "humanness" of being. Winthrop, picking up the spirit of Maslow's speculations, reports on the existence of "experimental communities" which exemplify alternatives of "humanized," cooperative living. Such communities provide examples of group-oriented efforts toward reducing the effect of the "pathological normalcy" of our time (e.g., the dehumanizing effects of robotization, bureaucratization, urbanization) and, in effect, provide a form of group psychotherapy.

The second subgroup among humanistic psychologists is guided by a desire to elaborate on the definition of man. Since they are, in principle, devoted to basic research, they are primarily concerned with developing a viable theory of man, more precisely "meaningful man," and ask the question: Are scientific methods adequate, or must one resort to nonscientific means? Most humanistic psychologists opt for science, although, in general, they have produced relatively little empirical data. Furthermore, close scrutiny of what they actually mean by scientific method is not clear. However, it would be reasonable to conclude that what they have in mind is what we have called an extended or liberalized notion of science—an approach which is more like case study and naturalistic observation than controlled laboratory observation (see Table 1). The major point is that the "scientifically" oriented group does not see the term "humanistic" as set in opposition to the term "scientific." Rather, they want the term "humanistic" to denote a unique subject matter (e.g., meaning), heretofore neglected, which is to be scientifically explored.

We have identified six clusters of concern in contemporary humanistic psychology. These are summarized in Figure 1. We have already alluded to the two applied groups where the relevant action involves human betterment via either the individual or society (the right side of the figure). Let us now focus our attention on the tree structure at the left side of the figure. As previously indicated, most humanistic psychologists recommend a scientific attack on humanistic problems. A distinction can be made between those aspects of man which reveal themselves in relation to other men and those aspects which are characteristic of the individual. Within the former category, interpersonal relations are critical. Topics such as love, valuing, and altruism are viewed as modes of encounter. The literature also suggests that research

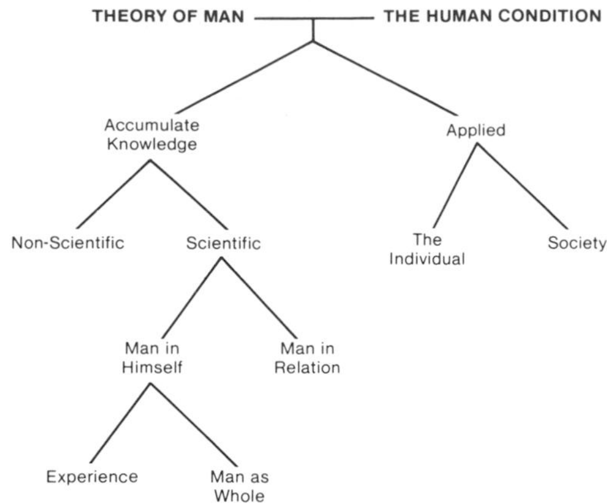

Figure 1. The major concerns of humanistic psychology.

should focus on "the truly major events in man's life" (Bugental, 1965). Within the latter category, individual characteristics, are such problems as identity (self-image, self-insight, self-growth) and experience. We make special note of the term experience and what it might denote because it constitutes a subject matter for which humanistic psychology might have a unique claim. Furthermore, there are also implications for the development of novel methodologies, a point which cannot be made easily with respect to the subject matter mentioned above. The term "phenomenology" is most often used to characterize the methodological aspects of "experiential research" (notable advocates of this approach include Giorgi, 1970; Graumann, 1974; MacLeod, 1970).

The remaining category refers to nonscientific knowledge acquisition. This category probably includes the largest segment of humanistic writings, ranging from the symbolic projections of the individual via dreams, projective tests, and biographies to parallel group projections as manifested in Jungian archetypes, mythology, and other literary and artistic forms. Although these authors frequently protest that their efforts are scientific in principle, it is our view that it is more accurate to characterize efforts in this category as either humanistic in the sense of like-the-humanities or as prescientific and/or nonscientific philosophic speculation. Major concerns include the reality and epistemic validity of everyday human experience, the nature of values, and what it means to be human. At its deepest level, nonscientific, humanistic writings move in the direction of existential philosophy. At their best (e.g., Bugental, Rollo May, Erich Fromm, and Henry Murray), such efforts constitute insightful webs of wisdom about the nature of man; at their worst, they are dogmatic beliefs which are authoritatively announced as the medicine we all need if we are to be spiritually saved.

It is our view that the heart of humanistic psychology lies in this cluster of concern and, further, that it is this branch of the humanistic tree which is the most conceptually confused.

The Complementarity and Continuity of Scientific and Humanistic Psychology

Although philosophic issues concerning the humanities and the sciences are old, they are just beginning to be joined in the context of modern psychology (Royce, 1965, 1970, 1976, 1977). The kind of analysis which is called for can be briefly alluded to by way of Figure 2. On the left side of this figure we see the humanities as concretely involved *in* life, as opposed to scientific abstractions which are derived *from* life. And, parallel to the ultimate theoretical goal of science, we see that the humanistic disciplines ultimately aim at making overarching statements (i.e., metaphoric-rational) regarding man-in-the-universe. However,

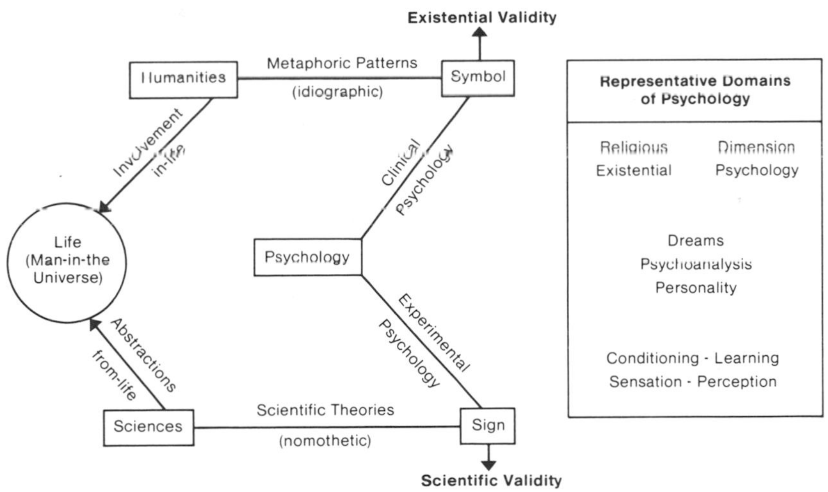

Figure 2. Psychology at the crossroads. (From *Psychology and the Symbol* by J. R. Royce. Copyright 1965 by Random House. Reprinted by permission.)

and this is the main point, the humanities speak through a symbolic rather than a sign language. Hence, the emerging statements take the form of metaphoric patterns or symbol systems rather than scientific theories, and the truth-giving quality of such statements follow the epistemological criteria of symbols rather than signs. As used in this context, the essence of the sign–symbol distinction is that the sign reveals a one-to-one correspondence (that is, *A* means *B*, and not *C*, *D*, or *E*) whereas the symbol provides a one-to-many relationship (that is, *A* may mean *B*, *C*, *D*, or *E*, or any combination thereof).

Another difference between the sciences and the humanities has to do with what is being processed. For example, the natural sciences deal with matter–energy processing, and the humanities are focused on value processing and meaning. If we add information processing to the matter–energy and meaning categories we have a three class taxonomy for describing process (e.g., see Miller, 1976). If we also introduce different levels of investigation, such as the inorganic, the behavioral, and the cultural, we can elaborate further on what is being processed. All this is summarized in Table 2.

According to this table (see behavioral-mental) psychology is, in principle, primarily concerned with information processing. While there is increasing awareness that it is information which is crucial at the behavioral level, psychology has tended to follow the inorganic and organismic, matter–energy paradigm of traditional science. And although scientific psychology has been aware of how important it is to

Table 2. The Relationship between Level of Investigation and What Is Being Processed

	Processing categories		
Level of investigation	Matter–energy	Information	Meaning
Inorganic	+ +		
Organismic	+ +	+	
Behavioral-mental	+	+ +	+
Behavioral-social		+ +	+ +
Social-cultural		+	+ +

process meaning, it has found this problem to be essentially intractable; humanistic psychology is focused on meaning, regardless of its intractability. However, most psychologists, including the humanists, have uncritically accepted epistemic attitudes which were originally developed for dealing with matter–energy processing. Unfortunately, humanistic psychologists have not been any more successful in dealing with the problem of meaning than their predecessors. According to Table 2, information processing constitutes a bridge between the processing of matter–energy and meaning, and psychology constitutes a bridge between the organismic and cultural levels of analysis. It is conceivable that investigations which involve an appropriate adaptation of information concepts could move toward the processing of meaning. The point is that the psychology zeitgeist is currently undergoing a paradigm shift away from behavioral matter–energy processing toward information–meaning processing (e.g., the emergence of cognitive psychology), and we can therefore anticipate that this issue will at least receive more attention. However, the concern for meaning continues to be "the" problem, whether psychologists call themselves scientific or humanistic (e.g., see Koch, 1976).

While our analysis has focused on the differences between the sciences and the humanities, it should also be pointed out that there are similarities. In fact, it would not be unreasonable to think of the sciences and the arts as two poles of a knowledge acquisition continuum (Royce & Powell, 1978). A rough characterization would place the natural sciences at one extreme, followed by the behavioral and social sciences. Physics and chemistry could serve as prototypes of the natural sciences, with the biological sciences following. Psychology and anthropology are prototypical behavioral sciences, and sociology is a good example of the social sciences. The next large grouping along the continuum would include such humanities as philosophy, theology, drama, and literature. And, finally, such artistic forms as painting, sculpture, and music would fall at the other extreme. We have purposely held back from the mention of history because of its middle position on the continuum. As we see it, history is the best disciplinary prototype for dealing with the scientific-humanistic issue in psychology, because history epitomizes the dilemma of the two cultures, with its desire to generate laws so that it can predict the future, on the one hand, and its fidelity to unique (i.e., nonreplicable in principle), idiographic events on the other hand. Thus, to the extent that a Toynbee-like analysis can generate replicable patterns concerning the affairs of men, history takes on the characteristics of a science. The humanistic version of history, on the other hand, claims that although accurate prediction of events is not possible we can sharpen our interpretations of the past, that "meanings" do emerge, and that the study of history improves our understanding of man.

Our main point here is that the major source of contemporary conceptual confusion concerning humanistic and scientific psychology is epistemic in nature. In particular, it is our view that scientific psychology (although it involves metaphorism) relies primarily on the epistemologies of rationalism and empiricism whereas humanistic psychology (although it also involves rationalism and empiricism) is primarily dependent on metaphorism (Royce, 1965, 1967, 1970, 1974; Royce, Coward, Egan, Kessel, & Mos, 1978).

Elsewhere, Royce (1978b) has expressed the contrast between scientific and humanistic knowledge via the logic of linear combinations of components. More specifically, on the assumption that a knowledge claim K can be operationalized, it can then be represented as a vector in three space, where E, R, and M refer to empiricism, rationalism, and metaphorism, and W_1, W_2, and W_3 refer to the weights to be assigned to each of the three epistemic components. The general case is therefore indicated as

$$K = W_1E + W_2R + W_3M \tag{1}$$

It should be noted that Equation 1 is idealized and simplified in that the combined weights add up to unity and there are no correlational, interactional, or error terms. Given these conditions, we can now succinctly contrast scientific (K_S) and humanistic knowledge (K_H) via Equations 2 and 3, as follows:

$$K_S = .4E + .4R + .2M \tag{2}$$

$$K_H = .1E + .1R + .8M \tag{3}$$

As developed earlier, the major contrast is the predominance of rationalism and empiricism in the case of scientific knowledge and the importance of metaphorism for the humanities. It should also be noted, however, that all three epistemologies are involved in both classes of knowledge. For empirical confirmation of the above, the reader is referred to Royce and Smith (1964), Smith, Royce, Ayers, and Jones (1967), Mos, Wardell, and Royce (1974), and especially Royce, Mos, & Kearsley

(1975), which summarizes the available empirical evidence on the psychoepistemological profile.

Epistemological Issues

Having distinguished between the terms "scientific" and "humanistic," let us now focus on the humanistic side and examine the new philosophic basis which is being assumed. Its dawning, based on Cassirer's (1953, 1955, 1957) philosophy of symbolic forms, was brought into focus more than 30 years ago by the philosopher Susanne Langer (1948, p. 29): "A new philosophical theme has been set forth to a coming age: an epistemological theme. . . . The power of symbolism is its cue, as the finality of sense-date was the cue of a former epoch." Langer goes on to point out how the sense data of science function as a sign language to directly indicate the specific object or part of an object being studied. A symbol differs from a sign in that it does not merely indicate or announce the sensory presence of an object but points the investigator toward an understanding of the meaning or purpose of the object (Langer, 1948, p. 61). This illustrates how the new philosophy involves a shift from a purely empirical focus on the sense object to the perhaps more difficult question of its meaning or purpose in human life.

This shift from sign knowledge to symbol knowledge is elucidated in another way by Wilfred Cantwell Smith (1974). He points out that human knowledge is of two kinds: (1) the study by man of the material world and (2) the study of man by man. While the principle of objectivity is a foundation of the former (science), the latter (the humanistic study of man by man) necessitates not a rejection of objectivity but a going beyond it. What is implied here is not a return to subjectivity as the logical alternative to objectivity but rather the inclusion of and moving beyond both prior positions to what Cantwell Smith calls "critical corporate self-consciousness." By this he means a knowledge characterized by awareness of "a particular human condition or action as a condition or action of itself as a community, yet of one part but not the whole of itself; and [an awareness] of it as it is experienced and understood both subjectively (personally, existentially) and objectively (externally, critically, analytically . . . scientifically)" (Smith, 1974, p. 3). Furthermore, one aspect of corporate self-consciousness is that both the observer and the subject transform each other through the relationship itself. Thus, there is a necessary, dynamic open-endedness to humanistic knowledge. This is due to the fact that the mind cannot view itself externally. From the objective or empirical viewpoint, this has long been seen as an insuperable flaw to be minimized by every technique possible. From the humanistic viewpoint, however, the "participation of the knowing mind in the humanity that it seeks to know is an asset, and not merely an inescapable fact. . . . [I]t helps us to know" (Langer, 1948, pp. 19, 45).

The subjective empathic nature of the knowing process is receiving increasing attention from a variety of investigators. One statement which is particularly germane is that of the philosopher Dorothy Walsh (1970, p. 265), who points out that "humanistic knowledge is knowledge as realization, that is, the realization of the qualitative character of some actual or possible lived experience." The title of Walsh's paper is "Knowing by Living Through," where "living through" is participative and existential, a kind of knowledge which is not the same as informational "knowledge about." Walsh (1970, pp. 267–268) makes a distinction between "experiencing in the sense of living through, and experiencing in the sense of simply being aware of. We can be aware of a color, but we would not normally speak of living through the experience of apprehending a color." Accordingly, lived experience is something more than just experience. The "something more" is, in our judgment, an existential characteristic which she describes with the term "realization." We think Walsh's concept of realization is related to the existential concept of authenticity, as both are concerned with the extent to which humanistic understanding probes the depths of existential reality. For example, mere recognition is too superficial; it suggests that the knower is at the abstract, informational level of awareness rather than the gutsy, lived-through level required for full realization.

Michael Polanyi (1958, 1967, 1969) extends this perspective still further; it is his view that all knowledge acquisition (including the findings of science) is a highly personalized skill. He makes two points of direct relevance to a humanistic epistemology. First, all knowing requires a deep indwelling or personal participation of the knower in the known. Such indwelling is directed toward knowledge of the integrated whole rather than knowledge of particular pieces. As Polanyi puts it, "*we experience a man's mind as the joint meaning of his actions* by dwelling in his actions from the outside" (Polanyi, 1969, p. 152). The second point Polanyi makes follows from the first and establishes the necessity of hierarchical levels of knowing directed by a controlling purpose. For example, "in themselves the parts of a machine are meaningless; the machine is comprehended by attending *from* its parts to their joint function, which operates the machine" (Polanyi, 1969, p. 152). The parts, viewed in themselves, are controlled by the empirical laws of nature; when seen as a whole, however, they are controlled by the operating principles of the whole. Applied to humanistic psychology, this analysis suggests a hierarchy of knowing with each higher level controlling the several ways that the parts of the lower levels can be integrated. An important point here is that Polanyi avoids any reductionism of the lower levels to the higher. Full recognition is given to the controlling principles or laws of the lower level, with the higher integration merely interacting with lower levels. Reductionism in the opposite direction, from the higher to the lower, is also guarded against by Polanyi's insistence that it is the higher levels which provide the functional principles for the integration of lower levels.

Perhaps an illustration will put this notion into perspective. In prose speech, five different levels can be observed: (1) voice production, or sounds, (2) the combination of sounds into uttered words, (3) the joining of words to form sentences, (4) the working of sentences into a consistent style, and (5) the content of the text itself. Each level, although possessing its own inherent laws, exhibits indeterminate boundary conditions open to control by the higher level. The uttered sounds can be combined in many possible patterns to form words, words are controlled by grammar to form sentences, sentences are selected by the dominant thought of the paragraph, and so on. "Consequently," concludes Polanyi, "the operations of a higher level cannot be accounted for by the laws governing its particulars forming the next lower level" (Polanyi, 1969, pp. 154–155). Words cannot be derived from phonetics, nor grammar from words, nor style from grammar, nor thought content from style. Polanyi (1969, p. 155) applies this to all living beings as follows:

> All living functions rely on the laws of inanimate nature in controlling the boundary conditions left open by these laws; the vegetative functions sustaining life at its lowest levels leave open, both in plants and animals, the possibilities of growth and also leave open in animals the possibilities of muscular action; the principles governing muscular action open their integration to innate patterns of behaviour; such patterns are open in their turn to be shaped by intelligence, and the working of intelligence can be made to serve the still higher principles of man's responsible choices.

In Polanyi's analysis of human experience, each level contains an inherent dualism or tension between the laws of its own component particulars and the integrating principles being imposed by the next higher level. This is extrapolated upward so that even the highest level of knowing has its indeterminate upper boundary. Thus, reality is unknowable in its totality—or, to put it in Polanyi's language, reality is indeterminate.

Metaphorism as an Epistemological Basis

The thinking of Polanyi, Walsh, Cantwell Smith, Cassirer, and Langer seems consistent with the suggestion that metaphorism can provide an epistemological basis for humanistic psychology. A careful discussion of the epistemological characteristics of metaphorism can be found in *The Encyclopedia of Philosophy* (Beardsley, 1967). A metaphor is characterized as differing from the literal or sign language of empiricism in that there is a novel or unusual tension between the terms involved (e.g., as in the phrase "logical space"). The metaphorical combination is seen as something more than just an arbitrary juxtaposition of words—it opens up or evokes a new sense of meaning (in purely nonsense combinations, such as "ungrammatical space," there is oddity but no opening up of new meaning). In this opening up of new meaning, "metaphor is a convenient, extraordinarily flexible, and capacious device for extending the resources of language, by creating novel senses of words for particular purposes and occasions" (Beardsley, 1967, p. 286). Literature effectively illustrates this sense and use of metaphor. As Robert West (1971, pp. 136–137) puts it,

> Whereas scientific language is perspicuous because ideally its terms have fixed and positive signification, literature's successes depend largely on the free use of terms that are fertile with simultaneous suggestions. Ambiguous these terms often are, but instead of baffling the mind they enable a growing comprehension.

Take, for example, T. S. Eliot's evocative and yet precise description of contemporary life as "measured out by coffee spoons" (in his poem *The Lovesong of J. Alfred Prufrock*). Such metaphors do not record facts or establish logical relations; rather, they use commonplace words in new and imaginative juxtapositions so as to manifest a meaning much deeper than the commonplace. The point is that the "artful" in literature is focused on the metaphoric use of language. And, though style is an aspect of art, it, along with other aesthetic properties, is in the service of exploring reality through the nuances of language. If you will, language is the tool or the medium by means of which the literary artist makes "discoveries." And, says the philosopher Richard Kuhns, the difference between the philosopher and the poet is that the philosopher wants to analyze language reductively whereas the poet "is forever a maker of worlds; to him language can never be exhausted" (Kuhns, 1971, p. 272).

As we see it, the artful use of language is inexhaustible for at least two reasons: (1) the limitless possibilities in the imaginative juxtaposing of words, which continually provide us with new metaphors, and (2) the extension of literary endeavor to include, in principle, all aspects of human experience, including the ineffable. The point is that, while reality undoubtedly includes the unspoken (e.g., see Lyons, this volume), human awareness of a given aspect of life is usually enhanced when it has been linguistically articulated, and the skillful use of metaphoric language is the literary artist's way of adding to human consciousness.

In addition to the fertile opening up of new meanings, a metaphor can also be described as "a condensed shorthand, by which a great many properties can be attributed to an object at once" (Beardsley, 1967, p. 286). Whereas empirical language is one to one in nature, a metaphor provides a synthesis of several units of observation into a single image or symbol. Polanyi's (1967) notion of levels of meaning and language, the way in which the primary meaning of a term has the possibility of many new combinations in its upper boundary area, is one explanation of how metaphors are created. In Polanyi's more technical philosophic language, the person *A* (the thinker; e.g., T. S. Eliot) sees a *B* (coffee spoon) as bearing on a C (life) or else uses a B for the purpose C ("coffee spoons for measuring out life"). For Polanyi, the function of such metaphors is only possible because of the notion that we know more than we tell. The way in which we fashion the metaphor indicates that knowledge of the whole was in some sense already potentially present within the knowing consciousness. What the metaphor does is to present enough of that tacit knowledge so that personal recognition occurs, as when the police artist puts together a juxtaposition of facial features which is close enough to, but always less than, the reality so as to evoke recognition from us. Essentially, the components of the metaphor in their juxtaposition function by pointing our minds toward the more complex integration already potentially present within our experience (Polanyi, 1967). It is an integration, however, which cannot be explicitly verbalized; rather, it is tangentially or indirectly evoked within one's consciousness. A metaphor has power through its ability to nondiscursively communicate such complex tacit knowing. Eanst Cassirer points out that a metaphor functions on the principle of *pars pro toto*—the part not only evokes the nondiscursive whole but becomes and is the whole. The component parts of the metaphor do not simply integrate in a "logical addition" fashion but function by creating or manifesting something new. In that new creation the parts no longer have their old status but are now transformed into a new whole (Cassirer, 1946, p. 6). Such a new metaphor is exactly what Langer (1948), following Cassirer, calls "a new key" which provides the assumed philosophical basis for an epoch. Warren Shibles (1971), a recent philosopher, follows a similar line of thought and argues that every basic definition or philosophical presupposition is best understood as a metaphor which can then be given discursive expansion into a philosophical system or position.

The above discussion suggests that there are two fundamentally different (but complementary) classes of language and knowing, literal and metaphorical. It is our thesis, furthermore, that the former is best suited to the expression of empirical truths whereas the latter alone is capable of expressing transempirical, humanistic truths. However, some critics of humanistic knowledge take the view that the only knowledge there might be in nondiscursive statements are those claims which can be stated discursively. It is, of course, true that one can make propositional statements about nondiscursive material. For example, it has been said that the playwright Harold Pinter has elevated the "pause" to a line of dialogue. That is a propositional claim concerning an important aspect of Pinter's plays. The meaning of that statement is clear, but it is by no means the whole truth. The half truth is that various propositional statements exist in the lines (and pauses) of a play and, further, that drama critics write about plays and playwrights in propositional form. But none of all that is the "metaphoric pattern" called a play. Such propositions are merely those aspects of the totality called a play which can be "reduced" to propositional form. The play itself is stated via a symbolic language and is essentially metaphoric rather than literalistic (i.e., propositional) in nature. More specifically, the full power and meaning of a pause in the context of a Pinter play is conveyed metaphorically, and the claim is that more is conveyed than can be "reduced" to literalistic or propositional statements. That which is conveyed has to do with a segment of existence, and further, whatever is conveyed occurs because of the experiential (i.e., nonverbal) involvement of the audience in what is being presented (i.e., represented; note the ritualistic-mythic implications of the dramatic form) on the stage. The total statement (i.e., the metaphoric pattern) is the play itself. The typical response the artist gives when asked to explain a work is to indicate that what he or she had to say is presented via the work itself. The artist, by conscious design, does *not* speak discursively or literally. Insisting that the author simply tell us (i.e., propositionally) what he or she had in mind is a category mistake (i.e., it demands that poets speak "scientifically," and/or that scientists speak poetically).

The above analysis gives strong support to Royce's distinction between scientific and humanistic psychology and to his suggestion that humanistic psychology be founded on a metaphoric epistemology. In regard to metaphoric knowing, the involvement or participation of the knower in life situations is stressed by Cantwell Smith, Langer, Walsh, and Polanyi. There is also general agreement as to the differences in the kind of discourse: literal, discursive, or sign language in the case of science, and metaphorical, nondiscursive, or symbolic language for the humanities. But there is one issue (one of the most difficult and significant problems for humanistic psychology) which has not yet been faced—the question of a criterion or a norm for valid knowledge. For scientific psychology, the criterion of observable repeatability has proven to be an effective (even if imperfect) discriminator of true from false empirical-knowledge claims. What parallel criterion of humanistic knowledge can be established? It is to this crucial question that the remainder of this paper addresses itself.

How Can We Justify Knowledge Claims in Humanistic Psychology?

While the metaphor has the great virtue of enabling us to speak about those essential human experiences which seem to transcend the limits of empirical and rational knowing, there are certain dangers to be faced. The unique ability of a metaphor to combine several levels or aspects of meaning into a single image or symbol not only opens the way to possible misunderstandings but also makes the establishment of a criterion for valid truth extremely difficult. For example, misunderstanding can occur when the reader or hearer reads into the metaphor something quite extraneous, in spite of the demand that careful attention be paid to the context in which the metaphor occurs. Since "the actual meaning of a metaphor in a given context consists of those marginal meanings pushed into prominence, or at least not cancelled out, a metaphor is highly sensitive to its context" (Beardsley, 1967, p. 286). Consequently, metaphors must not be used in logical argument if misunderstanding is to be avoided (Beardsley, 1967, offers the following helpful example: suppose all *A* are *B*, and suppose that *B* are metaphorically *C*; if it is therefore logically concluded all *A* are metaphorically C, there will be misunderstanding). However, even if the reader understands the metaphor in its intended contextual sense, the question of epistemological validity still remains. We see two properties which must be developed further if we are to have a better understanding of humanistic-knowledge claims: (1) existential validity and (2) the multiple meanings of the metaphor. Let us begin with existential validity.

Existential validity has to do with unmasking the realities of human existence. Requirements such as "universality" and "authenticity" and such concerns as "values" and "meaning" are central to a thorough elaboration of existential validity as an epistemic norm. Thus, various analysts of the problem of humanistic knowledge have focused their attention on the existential significance of such terms as authenticity, realization, and intension. "Authenticity," it has been argued, unmasks the superficial and demands that the empathic-participative aspect of humanistic knowing penetrate to the depths of being-in-the-world. "Realization" involves crossing over a (not well understood) threshold of "living through" understanding. And "intension" (not "intention") has to do with "intensifying awareness" via the power of the metaphor. Cassirer sees "intension as *the* defining quality of metaphoric in contrast to logical knowing." It is his view that in logical determinations the fundamental relation is an extending hierarchy of concepts: "each separate 'specimen' of a species is 'contained' in the species; the species itself is 'subsumed' under a higher genus; but this means, also, that they remain distinct, they do not coincide" (Cassirer, 1961, p. xv). In metaphoric knowing, however, it is not concentric expansion but the opposite movement of "intension" which takes place. The mental view is not widened but compressed or distilled into a single focal point of high intensity significance or meaning. At this level of knowing, the differences, which are defined and highlighted in logical thinking, have faded away and every part of the whole is experienced as the whole itself.

Whereas discursive knowing shifts our attention from the thing or event to its structure, the nondiscursive or metaphoric approach strives for intensive awareness of the thing itself. Robert West illustrates this contention by referring to literature. The author, with a gifted eye, shows us not only man as he is, but what he may become. "He acquaints us convincingly with some real experiential possibilities, possibilities real because they are just such as conceivably may have once been actual or may come to be so" (West, 1971, p. 134). We respond to a story such as Hemingway's *The Old Man and the Sea* because it evokes within us the realization that the capacity for such courage, heroism, and perseverance is present within each of our natures. Such an immediate, personal response is one aspect of validation, and it would also be included in what Ernst Cassirer refers to as "the concrete universals of humanistic knowledge."

> This concreteness, directness and wholeness are precisely what distinguish the logic of the humanities from the traditional logic of abstract universals. Initially, the universals in either logic are all those vaguely concrete concepts of our everyday thought. But, as the logic of the humanities advances, these universals acquire ever richer, subtler, and more concrete wholeness; whereas the logic of the natural sciences works continually toward *isolation of generalized aspects*. (Cassirer, 1961, p. xiv)

One way to move in the direction of "existential universality" is via Wilfred Cantwell Smith's concept of "corporate critical self-consciousness." By this he means a knowledge which goes beyond the limitations of misplaced objectivity on the one hand and mere subjectivity on the other hand. In the following quote, his point is that humanistic-knowledge claims must be validated both by the persons directly involved and by external critical observers:

> We are talking about the study of man by man. By corporate critical self-consciousness I mean that critical, rational, inductive self-consciousness by which, within a community of persons, constituted at the minimum by two persons, the one being studied, the one studying, but ideally by the whole human race, is aware of any given particular human condition or action as a condition or action of itself as a community, yet of one part but not of the whole of itself; and is aware of it as it is experienced and understood simultaneously both subjectively . . . and objectively. . . .
>
> In objective knowledge, that first observer's understanding has done justice to what is observed is testable by the experience of a second and third observer. In corporate critical self-consciousness, that justice has been done to the matter being studied is testable by the experience of the subject or subjects. Often the former—another observer—is in principle not available; since unlike what obtains in the world of matter, no human situation is truly repeatable. In any case, it is inadequate; partly because all observers are inherently less than the whole of mankind; and partly because it is intrinsic to human experience that experience appears differently, and in fact is different, from the inside and from without. (W. C. Smith, 1974, pp. 304)

Thus, humanistic knowledge must be personal rather than impersonal as in scientific or objective knowledge. Being personal means participating (as fully as one's sensitivities allow) in the perspective of the person and/or symbolic form under study—"to know not only what a man does . . . but what he refrains from doing; what he dreams of doing, what he fears to do; what he does with exultation, hesitation, guilt, or boredom. An action is not understood unless one discerns what courage went into it, what routine, what integrity or duplicity, what choice" (W. C. Smith, 1974, p. 8). Anyone who has learned another language (especially one from a different cultural context, such as Chinese or Sanskrit for a Westerner) knows that it is not just a matter of equating word meanings; one must know the unstated assumptions inherent in the language (and possibly the culture) if there is to be true understanding. Thus, existential validity requires that the knowledge in question be shared (corporate) and that the knower's description of it be confirmed by the critical assent of the person who is being known and/or those who are most intimately involved in the production of a given symbolic form (e.g., painters, writers, or other art experts). Humanistic knowing requires that we use every means possible (all available objective and subjective techniques) to, as it were, experience reality from within the shoes of the other person (empathy)—to participate as fully as possible in the other's consciousness—and then to verify by critically comparing the understanding so reached with the understanding of the other person. Humanistic truth is a truth which can be recognized, assimilated, and critically validated by both persons (or groups) in the knowing relation—the knower and the known. Cantwell Smith (1974, p. 13) offers an example which will likely be current in the experience of each of us.

> The verification test of any statement about women in society would be whether both men and women, insofar as they are rational; and a body of investigators, insofar as they are methodologically sophisticated, critical, scientific; could all three endorse it. The goal is the corporate critical self-consciousness of a community of persons . . . who can say, and feel and mean: some of us are men, and some of us are women, and the situation among us who are women is such-and-such.

This is the critical corporate dimension of our human self-consciousness, and it is judged to be a major aspect of existential validity in humanistic knowledge. It discriminates in the sense of consensual validation, since in cases of false knowing (e.g., as in cases of delusion, projection, paranoia, etc.) there would be no critical corporate agreement achieved.

As to the multiple meanings of metaphorism, let us see if a recent proposal by Royce (1976, 1977) can accommodate this problem. The essence of Royce's proposal, put forward under the rubric of "constructive dialectics," is that viable alternatives should be retained until exhaustive critical analysis can point the way to a resolution. Thus, the multiple meanings of a rich metaphor would first be identified and then critically analyzed. As a result of such detailed analysis, some of the "interpretations" would be found wanting and would be temporarily or permanently cast aside. The remaining, more viable "interpretations" would receive further critical analysis—in particular, a dialectic analysis. The term "dialectic" implies a direct confrontation of alternatives with the intent of revealing strengths and weaknesses. If a given alternative shows sufficient weaknesses, it may be dropped because of insufficient viability. Subsequent effort must either provide an overriding synthesis which makes special cases of the alternatives and/or show the complementary roles of the viable alternatives. Dialectic analysis is, of course, endless, for the resulting synthesis now becomes a thesis against which an antithesis will eventually be developed. Thus, there are no final resolutions, only plausible theses which best accommodate the available evidence for a given duration of time.

As a final word on "constructive dialectics," it turns out that in the more extended analysis of the entire domain of psychology this approach is relevant to scientific psychology as well. In particular, there are two important foci of dialectic analysis in science—the interaction between data and theoretical conceptualizations and the rivalry between alternative theories. Thus, new data may necessitate the modification of old concepts and/or the introduction of new ones, and changes in conceptual structure usually lead to new observations. Similarly, the dialectic analysis of theories will force a direct confrontation as to the adequacy of the alternatives. In the present context, the point is that the alternatives undergoing analysis in science are viable *theories*, whereas the alternatives undergoing analysis in humanistic psychology are viable text *meanings* (Royce, 1976, 1977). This means that extended conceptual analysis is common to both approaches, but in the first case, the focus is on scientifically meaningful constructs, and in the case of humanistic psychology, the demand is for existentially meaningful concepts and text interpretations. Thus, the formal procedures of dialectic analysis are the same, but the epistemic norms relevant to scientifically valid concepts are different from those which are appropriate for humanistic-existential understanding.

In conclusion, we are saying that the key to humanistic knowledge is that it teaches "us to see more subtly and profoundly" (Cassirer, 1961, p. xiv). All artistic and other humanistic forms share this concern for a deeper, more sensitive, "tuning in" to one or another of life's wavelengths. If the artist is a painter, he or she wants to make us more aware of color, space, and visual form. If the art form is music, the demand is for greater sensitivity to the nuances of sound combinations. And as we move away from abstract artistic forms to the more concrete and life-laden humanities, such as literature and drama, the existential aspect of humanistic knowledge comes into sharper focus. The point is that the novel or play serves as a metaphor—an analogy (formally comparable to a model in science) about a significant segment of life. The implication is that a "great" novel or play is "great" because its portrayal, although fictional, is authentic and penetrating. Thus, the great novel or play invites us to "live through" vicariously and, through the power of the metaphor, to come away with a deeper understanding of man and the human condition.

Acknowledgment

We wish in particular to acknowledge the assistance of Michael Katzko, Center Graduate Research Assistant. His summary of the relevant literature via Figure 1 provided the basis for the text in the section *On Humanistic Psychology*.

References

Beardsley, M. C. Metaphor. In *The Encyclopedia of Philosophy* (Vol. 5). New York: Macmillan, 1967.

Bugental, J. F. T. *The search for authenticity*. New York: Holt, Rinehart & Winston, 1965.

Cassirer, E. *Language and myth*. New York: Dover, 1946.

Cassirer, E. *The philosophy of symbolic forms* (Vol. 1). New Haven: Yale University Press, 1953.

Cassirer, E. *The philosophy of symbolic forms* (Vol. 2). New Haven: Yale University Press, 1955.

Cassirer, E. *The philosophy of symbolic forms* (Vol. 3). New Haven: Yale University Press, 1957.

Cassirer, E. *The logic of the humanities*. New Haven: Yale University Press, 1961.

Giorgi, A. *Psychology as a human science*. New York: Harper & Row, 1970.

Graumann, C. F. Psychology and the world of things. *Journal of Phenomenological Psychology*, 1974, *4*, 389–404.

Koch, S. Language communities, search cells, and the psychological studies. In W. J. Arnold (Ed.), *Nebraska Symposium on Motivation* (Vol. 23). Lincoln: University of Nebraska Press, 1976.

Kuhns, R. *Literature and philosophy*. London: Routledge & Kegan Paul, 1971.

Langer, S. K. *Philosophy in a new key*. New York: Mentor, 1948.

Lyons, J. Discontinuities: Or, theory as prayer. In J. R. Royce & L. P. Mos (Eds.), *Humanistic psychology: Concepts and criticisms*. New York: Plenum Press, 1981.

MacLeod, R. B. Psychological phenomenology: A propaedeutic to a scientific psychology. In J. R. Royce (Ed.), *Toward unification in psychology*. Toronto: University of Toronto Press, 1970.

Maslow, A. H. *Eupsychian management: A journal*. Homewood, Ill.: Dorsey, 1965.

Miller, J. G. *Living systems*. New York: McGraw-Hill, 1976.

Mos, L. P., Wardell, D., & Royce, J. R. A factor analysis of some measures of cognitive style. *Multivariate Behavioral Research*, 1974, *9*, 47–58.

Polanyi, M. *Personal knowledge*. Chicago: University of Chicago Press, 1958.

Polanyi, M. *The tacit dimension*. London: Routledge & Kegan Paul, 1967.

Polanyi, M. *Knowing and being*. Chicago: University of Chicago Press, 1969.

Royce, J. R. Toward the advancement of theoretical psychology. *Psychological Reports*, 1957, *3*, 401–410.

Royce, J. R. *The encapsulated man*. Princeton, N. J.: Van Nostrand, 1964.

Royce, J. R. (Ed.). *Psychology and the symbol*. New York: Random House, 1965.

Royce, J. R. Metaphoric knowledge and humanistic psychology. In J. F. T. Bugental (Ed.), *Challenges of humanistic psychology*. New York: McGraw-Hill, 1967.

Royce, J. R. The present situation in theoretical psychology. In J. R. Royce (Ed.), *Toward unification in psychology*. Toronto: University of Toronto Press, 1970.

Royce, J. R. On conceptual confusion in humanistic psychology. *Contemporary Psychology*, 1972, *17*, 704–705.

Royce, J. R. Cognition and knowledge: Psychological epistemology. In E. C. Carterette & M. P. Friedman (Eds.), *Handbook of perception* (Vol. 1): *Historical and philosophical roots of perception*. New York: Academic Press, 1974.

Royce, J. R. Psychology is multi: Methodological, variate, epistemic, world-view, systemic, paradigmatic, theoretic, and disciplinary. In W. J. Arnold (Ed.), *Nebraska Symposium on Motivation* (Vol. 23). Lincoln: University of Nebraska Press, 1976.

Royce, J. R. Toward an indigenous philosophy for psychology. *The Ontario Psychologist*, 1977, *9*, 16–32.

Royce, J. R. How we can best advance the construction of theory in psychology. *Canadian Psychological Review*, 1978, *19*, 259–276. (a)

Royce, J. R. Three ways of knowing and the scientific world view. *Methodology and Science*, 1978, *11*, 146–164. (b)

Royce, J. R., & Powell, A. Toward a theory of man: A multi-disciplinary, multi-systems, multi-dimensional approach. In *The Sixth International Conference on the Unity of the Sciences*. New York: International Cultural Foundation Press, 1978.

Royce, J. R., & Smith, W. A. S. A note on the development of the psycho-epistemological profile. *Psychological Reports*, 1964, *14*, 297–298.

Royce, J. R., Mos, L. P., & Kearsley, G. P. *Test Manual for the psycho-epistemological profile*. Edmonton: University of Alberta Printing Office, 1975.

Royce, J. R., Coward, H., Egan, E., Kessel, F., & Mos, L. Psychological epistemology: A critical review of the empirical literature and the theoretical issues. *Genetic Psychology Monographs*, 1978, *97*, 265–353.

Shibles, W. *Metaphor: An annotated bibliography and history*. Whitewater, Wis.: Language Press, 1971.

Smith, W. A. S., Royce, J. R., Ayers, D., & Jones, B. The development of an inventory to measure ways of knowing. *Psychological Reports*, 1967, *21*, 529–535.

Smith, W. C. *Objectivity and the humane sciences*. Paper presented at the Frontiers and Limits of Knowledge Symposium at the annual meeting of The Royal Society of Canada, Toronto, June 1974.

Sorokin, P. A. *The crisis of our age*. New York: Dutton, 1941.

Walsh, D. Knowing by living through. *Philosophy and Phenomenological Research*, (December) 1970, 265–272.

West, R. H. Literature and knowledge. *The Georgia Review*, 1971, *25*, 125–144.

Winthrop, H. Humanistic psychology and intentional community. *Journal of Humanistic Psychology*, 1962, *2*, 42–55

III

PARADIGM AND METHOD

7

Harold G. McCurdy

THE DUALITY OF EXPERIENCE AND THE PERPLEXITIES OF METHOD

The inadequacy of a mechanistic psychology such as dominates the academic scene today has long been recognized. Not by polemics, however, can relief be expected; nor will a loosely conceived humanistic psychology provide the remedy. New ideas are required which will neither abandon reason in favor of undisciplined emotion nor drive a wedge between science and life. The general direction of the effort we should be making is clear: the mathematical mode of thought, a signal feature of modern science, must be liberated from its enslavement to mechanistic principles and technological ends, and the general matrix of experience in which it is embedded must be recovered, valued, explored. I will argue that the human mind is at least dual in its tendencies, and that grave perplexities of method issue from this fact, and even more from the neglect of it.

Let us begin with the mathematical tendency. When we hold in our hands two cylinders of lead shot or two buckets of blueberries or two of anything else and heft them, we pass the judgment that they are equal or unequal in weight. The judgment has an immediate, intimate, personal quality; we feel it as we pronounce it; the objects are in our

Harold G. McCurdy • Department of Psychology, University of North Carolina at Chapel Hill, Chapel Hill, North Carolina 27514.

hands pressing on them, smooth or rough, hot or cold, broad or narrow. The judgment hardly seems abstract, and yet it is, in fact, a singling out of an aspect of the total experience. Even before terms like "heavier" and "lighter" entered language, our forbears ages ago must have been aware of the distinction as they lifted or failed to lift the stones they used as tools, weapons, and monuments. We are capable, and possibly they were as well, of going beyond "heavier" or "lighter" to "much heavier" or "much lighter," or even to "twice as heavy," "ten times heavier," and so on. In corporate endeavors we say, "It would take two men to lift this stone" and so on to larger numbers. There we have units of measurement, concrete living units, with a practical relationship to a real, resistant world. Perhaps our remote ancestors could say, "Here is a ten-man stone" and make good sense to their comrades.

But we long ago passed beyond this style of assessing weights to one employing instruments and depending on visual discrimination of symmetry or scale divisions. For our two hands, we substitute two unfeeling metal plates or pans, for our shoulders and arms, a pivoted bar from which they hang, and for the feeling of weight, a visual levelness or tilt of the bar or the position of a pointer against an inscribed scale. Sight substitutes for muscular effort, and judgment is made on objects no longer so intimately ours. We move toward greater abstractness. If we have doubts about the weighing device, we can test it by returning to the earlier mode of procedure; we can, that is, if the objects are large enough or small enough or of a kind that we are not afraid to handle. But the mechanical instrument improves on the more intimate procedure in various ways: it can deal with things too heavy or too light or too dangerous for us to compare by handling; it can reveal to the eye minute differences far beyond the capacity of the primitive muscular balance; and it can provide us with regularly spaced intervals of difference as units of measurement (such as ounces or micrograms) which alter our language toward greater precision and carry us into delicate mathematical operations. Number becomes a sovereign fact in the material world. We assign weight numbers to everything, even atoms, the earth, and the stars, which no man's hand has ever weighed or ever can.

A weighing instrument is easily comprehended as a projection of the living human body in one of its functions into another material form. Numbers, on the contrary, though represented by material marks, are clearly not material objects. Nevertheless, they are as truly ours as our weighing instruments, discovered or invented by us long before written history; and they are as truly ours as the primitive global experience of which they are a part even yet, when we allow them to be. In that last clause I admit the tendency of our mathematical thinking to break free of sense-rooted experience and take on independent existence.

Let us consider another example where the movement, rather than going from kinesthesia to a visual pointer reading and thence into pure mathematics, begins within the visual mode. A nautilus shell on the beach attracts our attention. We admire and examine it, taken with its color and form. The experience is immersed in a general consciousness of the sea and shore and sky, the flying birds, and the people in the surf—that is, the total visual panorama, along with the wind sweeping over us, the smell and taste of the sea, the feel of the shell in our hands, and the comments of bystanders. If we carry the shell away with us, we change that context, and the result may be that the shell is diminished and impoverished in our eyes, as Emerson describes it in "Each and All":

> I wiped away the weeds and foam,
> I fetched my sea-born treasures home;
> But the poor, unsightly, noisome things
> Had left their beauty on the shore
> With the sun and the sand and the wild uproar.

But at this point, or even before while the sea is still roaring near by, the mathematician abstracts the beauty of the shell and sees it as a spiral long familiar to geometers. The spiral placed on Cartesian coordinates yields an algebraic equation, an object for the mind rather than for the eye. To the eye, the equation bears no resemblance whatsoever to the spiral; and yet, if one knows the rules, the equation can be translated back into the visual spiral form which it represents. The translation backwards stops there, however, as far as mathematics is concerned. No clearcut rules carry us from the linear spiral to the nautilus shell, or from the shell on the collector's shelf back to the seaside from which it came, or from there into the sea itself and to the original shell-constructing living animal that inhabited it. The algebraic equation is a restricted statement of a limited aspect of our experience, not of the totality.

I have been illustrating the continuity between common global experience and the mathematical rarefaction of it; but it will not do to overemphasize continuity at the present stage of our intellectual history. We are the heirs of Galileo, who made a sharp distinction between the primary qualities of weight, hardness, and motion and the secondary qualities of color, sound, taste, and smell and relegated the latter to the limbo of the nonmathematizable side effects of the mathematizable primary qualities. It is a curious historical fact that the mathematical devices used by Galileo for dealing with weight and motion had been developed, at least rudimentarily, by thinkers who appear to have wished to unite rather than separate the various categories of experience that tend to be polarized into opposites. As we can read in A. C. Crombie's *Medieval and Early Modern Science* (1967), the Aristotelian separation of quantity and quality into categories so antagonistic that mathematics could not reach from one to the other, much less back again, was challenged as early as the twelfth century by Peter Lombard, (ca. 1100–1160) "who opened the question by asserting that the theological virtue of charity could increase and decrease in a man and be more or less intense at different times" (Crombie, 1967, p. 85).

In the fourteenth century, a number of scholars worked at the problem. Basically, the approach was correlational: graphical methods were used to show a variation in one dimension as against another. The variables were qualities as well as quantities. Nicole Oresme (d. 1382) was one of the most notable of these mathematizers. "It has been claimed," states Crombie, "that he anticipated Descartes in the invention of analytical geometry. Leaving aside the obscure question whether Descartes had any direct or indirect knowledge of Oresme's work, it is clear from the latter itself that Oresme had other ends in view than those of the 17th century mathematician" (Crombie, 1967, p. 92). Indeed, a glance at the contents of Oresme's *Tractatus de Configurationibus Qualitatum et Motuum* in Marshall Clagett's (1968) translation reveals that it is primarily the intensity and configuration of qualities of the soul, or qualities of things to which the soul attends, that concern him. The acceleration of falling bodies is a relatively minor topic. Unfortunately, his discussion remains at an abstract speculative level, and he develops no empirical handles on the phenomena by which they might have been brought into line with his graphical scheme. Nor did any successor carry on persuasively in the direction he had marked out. Extensions of his method, according to Crombie, became "elaborately subtle and in practice sterile" and were ridiculed by humanists such as Pico della Mirandola (1463–1494), Erasmus (1467–1536), and Luis Vives (1492–1540). Galileo, in the seventeenth century, narrowed Oresme's enterprise to a concern for the mechanics and kinematics of tangible bodies, ruling out practically everything that Oresme was trying to deal with (beauty and friendship, for instance). Under the double impact of humanistic ridicule and the instant success of the mechanistic science of Galileo and Newton, the humanistic mathematics of Oresme faded away in the general occultation of everything medieval; and the humanists of the twentieth century, if we are to believe C. P. Snow, do not even know enough to ridicule their mathematical scientific colleagues across an Oxford table or realize why it is that humanists are on the way to being replaced by computers.

I suppose the nearest relative of Oresme in recent times is D'Arcy Thompson. Thompson was unusual in his combination of Greek and Latin scholarship (humanism in the Renaissance sense) with mathematical biology. P. B. Medawar expresses the opinion that he was "an aristocrat of learning whose intellectual endowments are not likely ever again to be combined within one man." Medawar makes a pointed contrast between Thompson and others who have made "two or more separate and somewhat incongruous reputations, like a composer-chemist or politician-novelist." The singularity of Thompson is that he "comprehended many things with an undivided mind" (cited in Thompson, 1958, pp. 219–220). Medawar finds this marvelous unity not altogether commendable; he charges Thompson with "a certain perversity of reasoning"—in preferring, for example, curvilinear to straight-line representations of growth rates by using arithmetic rather than logarithmic grids—and damns his science by praising his literary style, which, he says, is full of old-fashioned eloquence, graces, and decorative matter out of keeping with real science. If I am not mistaken, it is not so much Thompson's style of writing which annoys Medawar as it is his willingness to express the mind's nonmathematical tendency along with the mathematical in the same discourse. This other tendency of the mind can be called the poetic, and I will illustrate it first of all from Thompson himself.

In 1917, the year of the first publication of Thompson's *Growth and Form,* he was invited to give the Huxley lecture at the University of Birmingham. How ironical that in the name of Huxley, who advocated a mechanical model of man, at the very center of industrial England, and during the first great mechanized war, Thompson chose to speak on the beauty of the nautilus shell and concluded his address with these words, which his daughter says "made a deep impression on the audience as D'Arcy delivered them leaning forward on his hands with his eyes alight":

> What is it that the physicist and the mathematician and the biologist alike, resting from their labours, see looking out of Mother Nature's eyes? They see dimly what Plato and Pythagoras and Aristotle and Coleridge and Wordsworth saw clearly and many another whose eyes are anointed with divine clay. You may call it what you please! You may call it Entelechy; you may call it the Harmony of the World; you may call it the élan vital; you may call it the Breath of life; or you may call it as it is called in the storybook of Creation and in the hearts of men, you may call it the spirit of God. (Thompson, 1958, pp. 156–157)

This is not the way the Nobel Laureate Crick talks today, nor Medawar. It was out of an undivided mind that Thompson was able to speak thus. In his hands he held the nautilus shell, and his mind ran from there to the mathematics of the equiangular spiral, identified by him as a discovery made by Descartes in 1638, and also, simultaneously, to the significance of the nautilus as an emblem of unseen being. This is the nature of the undivided mind: it is both mathematical and poetical. In our divided culture, it may be easier to announce that the nautilus shell is mathematically translatable into an equiangular spiral and an algebraic equation of the form $r = \theta \log a$ than to argue that it is an emblem of God or, as Oliver Wendell Holmes makes of it in his once-famous poem, an emblem of the soul; but nevertheless, the human mind moves in the second direction as naturally as in the first, and the two directions are not interchangeable. Yet they do interact.

We can become aware of the interaction even while trying to attend exclusively to geometry. Geometry deals with forms. A form may not be a quality of quite the same order as color, melody, virtue, or charity, but still it is not entirely a matter of quantity. The fact of a cube, a sphere, a cone, or a pyramid is not exhausted by giving linear and surface dimensions and the volume. There are two considerations at least that have puzzled those with mathematical intentions. One, recognized by the Pythagoreans themselves and hushed up as a scandal or sacred mystery, is the fact that it is impossible to have any unit of quantity that would fit equally well both the sides and the hypotenuse of a right triangle. Indeed, the melodies of the lyre were more amenable to Pythagorean analysis than the triangle and the circle, those basic geometrical forms. A second problem, recognized no doubt from time immemorial, has been pointed to by David Hume (1751/1957, p. 110):

"Euclid has fully explained all the qualities of the circle, but has not, in any proposition, said a word of its beauty."

Hume's reflections on this problem are a tribute to the fact that the mind is not entirely mathematical, but they unfortunately have the effect of shutting up the mind in itself, in subjective separation from the object which in the mathematical mode of procedure it handles as an undenied part of the reality. Hume declares:

> The beauty is not a quality of the circle. It lies not in any part of the line whose parts are equally distant from a common center. It is only the effect which that figure produces upon the mind, whose peculiar fabric or structure renders it susceptible of such sentiments. In vain would you look for it in the circle or seek it, either by your senses or by mathematical reasonings, in all the properties of that figure. (Hume, 1751/1957, p. 111)

Hume goes on to the complexities of architecture and, asking where the beauty is, answers that it "results from the whole when that complicated figure is presented to an intelligent mind susceptible of those finer sensations. Till such a spectator appears, there is nothing but a figure of such particular dimensions and proportions—from his sentiments alone arise its elegance and beauty" (Hume, 1751/1957, p. 111).

The same line of argument is extended to moral qualities, "and we must at last acknowledge that the crime or immorality is no particular fact or relation which can be the object of the understanding, but arises entirely from the sentiment of disapprobation which, by the structure of human nature, we unavoidably feel on the apprehension of barbarity or treachery" (Hume, 1751/1957, p. 111). We encounter in Hume the modern dividedness of mind which is one of the consequences of identifying the real (the "scientific") with that which can be sensed and mathematized. Thus, the building in Hume's illustration is allowed to exist with all its mathematical features before the sensitive spectator arrives but has no beauty until then; or rather, it never has beauty as a property of its own as it has weight, mass, and mathematical proportions but only the power (Locke's term) to stimulate in certain susceptible minds the illusion of having it. Against Hume's extreme subjectivism there have been, of course, some attempts to give beauty, if not morals, objective status by mathematizing it, as for example in the work of Hogarth, Fechner, and Birkhoff. The adequacy of these attempts has often been questioned, and no one, as far as I know, has ventured to mathematize beyond beauty to the more emblematic features of the perceived world.

The duality of the mind under discussion here is a prominent theme of Wordsworth's great poem, *The Prelude*. The symbolic center of his treatment of the theme is a Quixotic dream figure fleeing across a desert on camelback from an impending tidal wave, his mind intent on preserving two precious objects—a shell, representing poetry, and a stone, representing mathematics (Wordsworth, 1959, Book V, lines 55–139). Wordsworth himself was primarily concerned with creating and preserving poetry. But several times in this long poem he pays poetic respects to mathematics. He does so in the famous lines on the statue of Newton which conclude with

> The marble index of a mind forever
> Voyaging through strange seas of Thought, alone.
> (Wordsworth, 1959, Book III, lines 62–63)

He does so more elaborately in lines 115–167 of Book VI. Especially worth our attention is what he says there about the power of "geometric science" to allay sorrowful feelings as it lifts the mind above "melancholy space and doleful time" and to calm the spiritual perturbations of the poetic mind, "beset With images, and haunted by herself." It is well known how important to Wordsworth were his images, especially those "spots of time" which awaken the soul to an awed recognition of "moving about in worlds unrealized." Gigantic supernatural forms, boundless mists, howling winds, and roaring seas, intimations of meanings entirely beyond the range of the senses, characterize such moments. The dreamer in the dream of the camelrider is bidden to hold to his ear the shell of poetry, "so beautiful in shape, In colour so resplendent":

> I did so,
> And heard that instant in an unknown tongue,
> Which yet I understood, articulate sounds,
> A loud prophetic blast of harmony;
> An Ode, in passion uttered, which foretold
> Destruction to the children of the earth
> By deluge, now at hand.
> (Wordsworth, 1959, Book V, lines 92–98)

At the end of Book V he further describes the poetic experience:

> Visionary power
> Attends the motions of the viewless winds,
> Embodied in the mystery of words:
> There, darkness makes abode, and all the host
> Of shadowy things work endless changes,—there,
> As in a mansion like their proper home,
> Even forms and substances are circumfused

> By that transparent veil with light divine,
> And, through the turnings intricate of verse,
> Present themselves as objects recognized,
> In flashes, and with a glory not their own.
> (Wordsworth, 1959, Book V, lines 595–605)

Milton and Shakespeare, Spenser and Dante are doubtless exemplars for Wordsworth of the mind working poetically, but looming high above their grandeurs and complexities in this passage must be the *Apocalypse* of St. John, where the prophetic visions begin with "a great voice behind me like a trumpet speaking," or in another simile, "like the voice of many waters." In Wordsworth's own culminating vision in *The Prelude* of a night of full moon and stars above a billowy ocean of mist over a hundred hills, the climax of the experience is in "the roar of waters, torrents, streams Innumberable, roaring with one voice!" (Wordsworth, 1959, Book XIV, lines 59–60). It is the privilege and the burden of the poet's mind to hear this mighty voice or its lesser kindred and to render what it says in his native language—to be spoken and heard not simply scanned on a page by the eye. Of opposite character is "geometric science," a calm soundless realm of pure abstractions, "an independent world Created out of pure intelligence" (Wordsworth, 1959, Book VI, lines 166–167).

The duality of experience arising from the two opposite directions of the mind has now been sufficiently indicated, though by no means fully explored. The mathematical direction is toward a focused clarity achieved by stripping away most of common experience, particularly the passions; the poetic direction is toward infinite meaningfulness loaded with sensory and passionate content—the images which according to Wordsworth constitute the poet's burden. This duality of experience has somehow to be acknowledged and incorporated into any psychology which aspires to humanistic completeness.

Method, experimental and mathematical, has been the mark of scientific work for centuries; and method would indeed seem to be indispensable if the ideal of cooperation between many workers in a scientific community for the building of knowledge is to be realized. Following that line in psychology would simply mean that mathematics would be extended far beyond the typical psychophysical problems where it first gained a beachhead into problems of meaning, of sentiments, of the evolution of individual poetic systems, and all the rest that has hitherto been considered out of bounds, though undoubtedly present in human life. In our present historical context, the thought arouses dreadful images of men turned into machines, and with good reason, since our scientific posture today is not that of a Nicole Oresme but more that of a Dr. Frankenstein. Yet here I am saying that the mathematical tendency is no less human than the poetic and no less rooted in our common experience, and that its specialization as an adjunct to mechanics is not absolutely necessary, however historically fated it may seem to be. The fact that mathematics has been so extensively applied to industrial and military ends should not imply that a mathematical examination of the harmonies of the lyre is a betrayal of music into the hands of the enemies of music. Mathematics can clarify without necessarily producing an atom bomb. What we call the dehumanization of man is really more a function of the poetic than of the mathematical tendency. The image of man-as-machine or of the universe as a vast mechanical death engine is itself poetic, though indeed horrible; horror is a part of human experience brought to full expression in the poetic operations of the mind but not in the mathematical.

Still, having said all this in favor of extending mathematical or quasi-mathematical method farther into the psychological realm, I am uneasy and perplexed. To go from comparing weights held in the hands to the use of balances and numbers is a transition not too jarring; nor is going from a nautilus shell to the Cartesian equiangular spiral and its numerous mathematical properties. But to go from the voice of many waters speaking visions and prophecies in the same mathematical direction seems almost fantastically absurd. Can we expect any genuine continuity here, or is there not rather an unbridgeable, fixed chasm or a taboo, at least, which would be lethal if defied?

I am both attracted and repelled by the argument of T. E. Hulme in his *Speculations* (1924) that the principle of continuity has been pushed too far—attracted where the argument warns us against flattening out reality to a dead level of materialism and repelled where it seems to propose that our mere humanity is an utter nothing from the perspective of the divine. But the warning is useful. Even if we stick to the realm of "geometric science," as Wordsworth calls it, we must admit discontinuities on a purely logical basis; and that there have been, and still can be, prodigious discontinuities in human and cosmological history is surely believable. The poet David Jones, in his preface to *The Anathémata*, refers to what he and his friends in the 1920s called "the break." This break had to do with "something which was affecting the entire world of sacrament and sign" (Jones, 1965, p. 16). It is clearly related to the contrast Hulme makes between the religious attitude of the Middle Ages and the modern post-Renaissance secular attitude.

So much for history. As for "geometric science," consider a Euclidean isosceles triangle, its three angles totaling, by definition, 180°. Let its base be as wide as you please, a foot, a mile, a parsec. Let its two sides lengthen out, the angle at the apex decreasing at any speed you please as the angles at the base increase. An observer of the apex would see the lines of the two sides drawing closer together and approximating a single line; but at the moment the angles at the base each became 90°, and not a moment before, this apparently single line would spring apart into two lines, exactly as far apart as the base is wide, without any intermediate condition between one and two, or between no separation and separation of a foot, a mile, a parsec. We have a discontinuity! An observer at the base might speak of a continuous, gradual change or, since the difference between an angle of 90° and one of 89° 59′ 59.99″ might be imperceptible, of an unchanging status quo. But the observer at the apex would speak of an abrupt, cataclysmic change, destroying, let us suppose, the most important love union of his life as his partner instantly receded or totally vanished into the distance. If such a thing can happen in the geometric realm where logic teaches us that it is inevitable, given the conditions, how can we assume that nothing comparable applies to the obscurer realm of the dynamic mind? My assumption that the mathematical tendency and the poetic tendency are but two expressions of a basic mental unity may be fallacious. The duality might be there from the beginning; the two tendencies might be quite opposed, even before their difference becomes clear in Euclid's *Elements*, on the one hand, and St. John's *Apocalypse*, on the other. It is a matter of some interest that Descartes, the chief advocate of mathematical method in the history of Western science, was presented in a dream at the outset of his career with a choice between the mathematical and the poetical. He chose the mathematical way, but he also made a vow (which he kept) to go on a pilgrimage to the shrine of Our Lady of Loretto.

Not without a sense of daring did I myself undertake years ago to be methodical, and even mathematical, in the analysis of poetic writings. My objective was to learn something about the structure and functioning of personality, and my guides were Freud and Jung. They had convinced me that dreams and poetic works were drawn from the same depths, and they identified these depths as belonging to personality and had, from their own researches on dreams and poetic fiction, constructed personality theories. I followed them, but shrank from being as poetic as they were in handling, in the name of science, such materials. It seemed to me necessary to show more respect for the problem of method and, in particular, to save the phenomena—that is, to take seriously the content and structure of the manifest dream or manifest art work, however emblematic it might be of the dreamer's or poet's intention according to the imagination of the interpreter, whether Freud, Jung, or some other. In short, I took the mathematical rather than the poetic direction of mind in dealing with poetic materials. I thought that one might discover something by following such a course; and I assumed that whatever was discovered would have some bearing on the nature of human personality, in view of the assurances I had derived from the theories of Freud and Jung.

I will now present a few outcomes of this line of work to illustrate the possibilities. Taking as my unit of analysis the dramatis personae of the fictional writings I studied, I discovered that if I assigned them weights (character weights, I called them) the relation between these weights within the poetic system—a given author's collection of novels or dramas—was such that one could describe the relationship by an exponential curve. The weight of a character was determined by counting the number of lines of speech attributed to him or her in a drama or by counting the number of pages on which he or she appeared in a novel. To facilitate comparison from work to work, I arbitrarily set 100 as the weight of the character having the highest number of lines or pages and figured the other weights as a proportion of that. For example, in the 32 plays by Shakespeare which I studied, the character weights of the twelve most voluble characters within a play, on the average, were 100, 63, 52, 40, 35, 30, 25, 21, 18, 15, 12, 10. Very similar results were obtained by line count for the plays of Marlowe and Sophocles and by page count for the novels of Charlotte Brontë. Curves for these four authors, constructed on a grid with character weight on the ordinate and rank order on the abscissa, are enough alike to suggest that we are dealing with a general ordering tendency of the authorial mind. To be sure, the curves are based on averages. The range in the 32 Shakespeare plays is from 100, 25, 25, 16, 13, 11, 11, 9, 7, 6, 6, 6 for *Henry V* to 100, 96, 88, 73, 72, 62, 56, 53, 51, 46, 25, 22 for *Midsummer Night's Dream*. In no case, however, does the curve depart radically from the exponential form of the average curve; for example, *Midsummer Night's Dream* is far from the possible extreme of equality among all the characters, and no curve is a straight line or convex. Moreover, the hint of emotional dynamics (the influence of mood on structure) provided by the above comparison of plays at either end of the character weight range is borne out by further examination, for the leading characters of the tragical and historical plays are more distinctly separated from the others within their plays than are the leading characters of comedies.

This kind of analysis of poetic works and my purpose in doing it (namely, to probe into personality structure) will not appeal to everyone, as various critical remarks have made me aware not to mention the stronger evidence of total indifference. But, ignoring this negative fallout, I would call attention to the similarity between my procedure in regard to literary materials and the procedures of those trying to assess the weight of ordinary ponderable objects. As discussed above, the primitive natural way to compare object weights is to balance the objects in the two hands; from there we move to mechanical balances and precise units of measurement which we treat mathematically. Presumably, this change of means for evaluating weights does not alter the fundamental reality with which we were concerned when we merely hefted the objects; on the contrary, the reality seems to come more sharply into focus. Similarly, when I count lines of speech and use this relatively mechanical means for arriving at weight values (and hence, in a way, dramatic values) for the characters of a Shakespearean play, I am simply substituting a more objective procedure for the initial feeling I had that one character does dominate the stage more than another and that there is some sort of graduated relationship within the whole set of characters. Any conscious reader of Shakespeare would be aware of the ordering which the counting procedure makes more obvious and precise and thus more susceptible of mathematical treatment. When the figures are set before us, we may occasionally be surprised at the order revealed, but not in the main. As much as we value Cordelia in *King Lear* we are scarcely likely to disagree with the line count which puts Lear at the top of the quantitative heap rather than Cordelia. Perhaps it is more troubling to find Othello in second place to Iago with a weight of 80 to Iago's 100. Yet is it, finally, absolutely unjust? There can be all sorts of reasonable disputes about the discrepancies between intuitive judgments and the results reached by line count; and, of course, there are problems of the accuracy of the line count. Nevertheless, if the mathematical tendency of the mind which has given us refined measurements of the weight of physical objects was not perverse in so doing, neither is it perverse in subjecting poetic objects to a similar treatment. Yet just that question does arise, I believe, in the minds of literary scholars and humanists in general, or would, if they attended to such matters at all. Is it not perverse, or at best irrelevant, to go at the poetic plays of Shakespeare in such a manner?

I will return to this question. First, however, I wish to exhibit a few other results of this mathematical style of approach to poetic works and also to dreams, which might seem to be even less promising. I do not claim any ultimacy for these results. I do think that they are suggestive of what might prove to be of great significance if more able and more determined investigators proceeded along the same line.

With numerical weights attached to Shakespearean characters, it is possible to answer such questions as whether gradual or abrupt changes occurred over the period of authorship and whether correlations can be found between the various quantities and between them and external events. For example, Shakespeare gave noticeable attention to the father–son relationship in 15 of the 32 plays examined. Before *Henry IV* (written when Shakespeare was about 33) the matter is rather incidentally handled in six plays, in four or five of which some kind of reproach is implicitly or explicitly directed against the sons for failing to live up to paternal hopes and wishes. The father–son relationship reaches a sudden peak in *Henry IV*. Then, from the first part of *Henry IV* through *Macbeth* (when Shakespeare was about 39), not excluding the school lesson incident in *Merry Wives of Windsor* (interlude though it is), serious reproaches and difficult demands are laid on the sons by the fathers, and the sons are in general under strong compulsion to justify their existence. In the last three of the 15 plays (Shakespeare between 45 and 48), there is again a change; in these plays, it is the fathers who are under reproach, and the concern is with the recovery of sons who have been lost.

Such is my impression as a reader of the plays, but this impression is supported and strengthened by using the character weights, crude as they may be as indices of what is going on in the plays. Taking each play as constituting a unit, determining the total weight of the 12 leading characters, dividing this weight into the weight of the father (or fathers, in *Hamlet*, *Macbeth*, and *Winter's Tale*), and then comparing the six plays from *Comedy of Errors* to *King John* (Shakespeare between 28 and 32) with the nine plays from *1 Henry IV* to *The Tempest* (Shakespeare between 33 and 48), I found the average proportional weight of fathers in the latter group to be greater at a statistically significant level, the *F* based on a square root transformation being 6.51 where 4.67 is at the 5% level of confidence. There is a similar sharp turning-point at *Lear* (Shakespeare 41) in father–daughter relations, statistically speaking. Taking the 14 plays dealing with this relationship and proceeding as in the other case, with a division made at *Lear* where the father–daughter relationship achieves a heightened emphasis in comparison with the preceding nine plays, I obtained an *F* of 12.71, exceeding the 1% level of confidence, for which the required value in this case is 9.65.

Precisely why these changes should occur in Shakespeare's plays (and, according to the general theory that guided me, within the personality of Shakespeare himself) I am not prepared to say. Maybe we are catching a glimpse of psychic dynamics that would be paralleled in many other developing personalities. Maybe particular events in Shakespeare's history precipitated the changes; it does appear significant to me, for example, that *Henry IV* was written very near the time of the last illness of Shakespeare's father. The matter of concern to us in the present context is that the numerical indices do not contradict, and indeed seem to clarify, the intuitive impression, just as the use of a measuring instrument like the balance gives precision in many instances to what we already knew more vaguely (McCurdy, 1953).

I have occasionally taken a brief look at the question of whether poetic works have any correlation with the dreams of their authors. The two instances I have formally, though very incompletely, examined are the German dramatist Christian Friedrich Hebbel (1813–1863) and the Bohemian novelist Franz Kafka (1883–1924). Both writers sporadically recorded their dreams. From Hebbel's diary I took 65 useable dreams and applied a simple analysis. In regard to the dream actors, I found that 82 were human, 17 animal; of the human actors 70 were male, 12 female; of these 47 male and 7 female actors were familiar to the dreamer, 23 male and 5 female actors were unrecognized by him; of actors who could be called "famous" (e.g., God, Napoleon) there were 29, all male. Such simple categorizations can be used in various ways. One question that interested me was the ratio of male to female characters. From various kinds of inquiries, I have concluded that on the average the male imagination is more densely populated by male than by female figures. The tendency is marked in Hebbel's dreams. The ratio of male characters to the total of human characters is .85, whereas for 127 University of North Carolina male undergraduates the same ratio is .62. Pursuing the matter further, I noted that the ratio for Hebbel's 42 dreams of 1836–1840 was .81 and for his 14 dreams of 1846–1850 was .94. I asked myself then if the upward trend was also to be found in his dramas and made a spot check with two dramas separated by an interval of 14 years, *Judith*, composed in 1839–1840, and *Gyges*, composed in 1853–1854, that is, at about the periods of the dream samples just mentioned. A rough-and-ready estimate of the page space devoted to the female characters (and hence for the male characters, by subtraction) yielded a male/total ratio for *Judith* of .59 and for *Gyges* of .74. The trend is the same, though the absolute values are lower. The two dramas also seemed to confirm the trend noted in the dreams of an increase of fearful emotion over time, this being a topic I looked into because the category "fearful" stood out in Hebbel's dreams as compared with the dreams of my group of undergraduates and because it doubled in numerical value between the periods 1836–1840 and 1846–1850.

My own research into dreams in these and other instances tends to agree with Calvin Hall's proposition that dreaming and waking life are fundamentally akin. From data of his, I can also add one more bit of evidence that there is a correlation between an author's dream and his literary works, in some respects. Utilizing *Dreams, Life and Literature: A Study of Franz Kafka* (1970) by Hall and Lind, and making some calculations of my own, I find that the ratio of aggressive actions to the total of aggressive and friendly actions combined is .39 in Kafka's *Amerika* of 1912, .50 in *The Trial* of 1914, and .53 in *The Castle* of 1921—a steady increase. Hall and Lind's appendix giving the text of Kafka's dreams permits the construction of a corresponding series for the dreams (see Table 1). The trend toward increased aggressiveness is present in the dreams as in the novels.

Table 1

	1910–1911	1912–1913	1914–1917	1920–1923
Number of dreams	10	8	11	8
Aggressive acts	1	5	6	8
Friendly acts	4	4	8	5
A/A + F	.20	.55	.43	.61

After these few examples of mathematical excursions into literature and dreams, I return to the question of whether it is perverse or irrelevant to make such studies. The question would not arise if it were not for that other direction of the mind, the poetic. It would not arise because there would be no poetic works to examine; and, more important for our present deliberations, it would not arise because the mathematical tendency would be unopposed. No one can be strictly and simply a mathematician. The great Newton, who expressed contempt for poetry, had his poetic moments. That is to say, he set himself and his mathematical works in the humbling vastness of the universe, imaged as an ocean of truth roaring at his feet while he, like a little boy, gathered a few pebbles of knowledge cast up on the sand; and he set the universe in turn within a spiritual empire of which God was the head and countless intelligent beings both visible and invisible were the ministers, kept in order by acts of will rather than by mechanical arrangements and the inverse-square law of gravitation; and in doing so he far outran the limits of mathematics.

The poetic, which takes off from any facts whatsoever toward an evaluation of them as beautiful or ugly powers or as the signs of beautiful or ugly powers, which in short seeks out the meaning of facts, cannot rest in mathematics or be comprehended by it. And so, when a reader is fully engaged in reading a Shakespearean play in the poetic mode, as any appreciative reader at some time or other is bound to be, the intrusion of the mathematical tendency may be unwelcome. In a profound sense, to read Shakespeare mathematically is not to read him at all. The problem is not just that the mathematical focus excludes too much of the variety and immediacy of experience, as when the nautilus shell in its native habitat is reduced to the Cartesian equiangular spiral (the equivalent of excluding the sound of Shakespeare's musically chiming words and the stir of the dramatic action), but that the whole poetic drive toward the creation of aesthetic and metaphysical meaning, the vivification of life by the establishment of events within an organic system or a historical plot leading to heaven or hell or ultimate mystery, is denied. When one is in pursuit of meaning, it is not enough to be given experimental facts and mathematical analysis; it is like asking hungrily for bread and being given a stone.

It is here that we must look for the cause of the discontent that is expressed not only in impatience with the scientific game and a call for a humanistic psychology but also in eruptions of violence such as have marked the youth movement. There is a restless search for meaning because the poetic tendency of the mind has been suppressed. One solution, appealing to a minority, has been to swing over recklessly to an exotic poeticism with a strong Oriental aura, renouncing science and common sense and calling on the devils and pagan gods for salvation with the aid of drugs and magic rituals. Another, more popular solution has been to sink down as far as possible into the primitive immediacy of the senses, seeking the comfort of animal or infantile indefiniteness in regard to both tendencies of the mind. Neither solution can be satisfactory, each being too one-sided or undeveloped to be fully human.

Psychology goes on in the midst of and as a part of the total human scene. More and more people turn to it for help. New disillusionments occur and must continue to occur as long as psychology remains stuck in the old ruts. But what does that mean? It does *not* mean that psychology should give up mathematical method. On the contrary, mathematical method should be extended to the limit, in the confidence that when it is applied to music, the plastic arts, and literature and to creative products and processes in general it will yield new insights, as much as it does when applied to the swing of the pendulum and the motions of the planets.

At the same time, in some manner, the other direction of the mind must be granted admission not only to our private fantasies but also to our textbooks and research publications. The psychoanalysts have indeed given rather free rein to this tendency and have developed a rich mythology, but without due attention to investigative method or mathematical reasoning. Furthermore, the mythology is notably lacking in two features which I think are desperately needed: (1) a cosmological frame, extending from the interdependent life forms and materials of the earth to the vast extraterrestrial realities of the sun and the moon, the planets and the stars, and other aspects of our galaxy and the other galaxies beyond; and (2) a conception of human society, both as it has been and is now, and as it might be in its ideal state. Diseased as human beings undoubtedly are, they do exist in an orderly universe of great complexity and very energetic *thereness,* and they do aspire to a right relationship with this universe and with one another. To grasp the nature and significance of the individual human being placed thus within a universe of unknown extent and destiny, and within a teeming human society of billions of members carrying along the results of hundreds of thousands of years of history, requires a generous dramatic imagination, along with respect for everyday realities like the stone that Dr. Johnson kicked in his desperate argument against a misty solipsism and also respect for the mathematical powers of the mind that teach us about abstract patterns and their behavior in cosmic and human affairs. Granted something like this, present in intention even if not worked out in detail, we could all specialize as much as we please—as factor analysts, computer programmers, designers of laboratory experiments on visual acuity or the kneejerk, Pythagorean anatomists of poetry and so on—without running the danger of withering the life we are trying to investigate.

I do not wish to leave hanging the proposal that we should expand psychology into the cosmological and the social, developing a dramatic model of the human being instead of a mechanical one as we do so. Over ten years ago, in *Personality and Science* (1965, especially in Chapter 2), I did what I could along this line in brief compass. So far as I know, that effort has not affected anyone else's theoretical ponderings, and so, though I must work in briefer compass here, I return to the theme as if it were an absolute novelty. Once again I urge attention to literary art. (Wundt, who is celebrated in the histories as the founder of experimental psychology, urged something similar and wrote an enormous *Völkerpsychologie* to back it up, holding that only a small portion of the business of psychology could be brought into the laboratory; but perhaps that has been forgotten.)

If we take works of literature seriously, we must realize that they are always saying something about our place in the universe and in society. It is true that they say different things, each being the expression of a unique point of view, but there are common features, too. One of the commonest is the presence of some conscious "I" in the midst of various complexities, trying to solve problems, escape dangers or tedium, deal with particular things and persons, achieve through them gratifications often delayed or denied, and so forth. Also very common is an implied or explicit conception of the meaning (or meaninglessness) of the cosmic or social context within which these activities occur.

If we turn from narrative or dramatic literature to life as we ourselves live it or witness it being lived, the general impression is the same: human life is a drama. All the world is a stage, and we are the players. What takes place has little to do with S-R bonds, ids and superegos, test scores, and the rotation of factors, but much to do with hopes and fears, loves and hates, bodily and spiritual couplings and uncouplings, projects and careers, deceits and discoveries, moral dilemmas, pride and humiliation, apathy and violence, curses and prayers, and so on. These are all terms of relationship, of dramatic relationship. And what are they related to? They are related to people who are conscious "I's" variously connected in loose or tight organizations and to various other animate and inanimate beings, the ends and means of various sorts of strivings, wishes, and regrets. Furthermore, all these activities of conscious beings occur within some kind of setting—in a room, in a desert or forest, on earth, in a machine bound for the moon or Mars, on the moon or Mars, or elsewhere, but always in some area, a tiny precise corner or vague cloudland, of a vast domain of which it may be understood that God or chance is the ruling power above all.

The quality of this setting—whether it hinders or favors, fosters or is indifferent to heartfelt desires—is momentous. Often its quality is correlated with the psychic condition of the actor, perhaps changing by interaction from resistant to compliant, from mild to harsh, from forbidding to indulgent, and so on, in resonance with the actor's own acceptance or rejection. Here we touch on religion. There comes to mind an experiment performed by Francis Galton, who pinned up a drawing of Punch and paid daily homage to it, as if it were an idol. The experiment was soon abandoned because Galton began to feel that Punch was growing powerful and malevolent. I know of a group of college students who for the fun of it installed themselves in a reputedly haunted house and invoked the evil spirits. The evil spirits came—at least, an uncanny cold wind blew across them—and one of the party went into shock, and all were afraid. I mention these examples to indicate that our dealings with the environment are not always nonvitalistic. Bachelard's book, *The Poetics of Space* (1964), is probably not known to many professional psychologists, but the title alone should be suggestive to all of us as we contemplate the astronauts and cosmonauts in their space capsules repeating "A-OK!" and asking for the baseball scores or reporting to the Russian public that they did not see God up there. One can be a hundred thousand miles from earth in the region of the solar winds and cosmic rays and never leave the party line of Americanism or dialectical materialism; or one can sit by a smoky peat fire in County Cork and hold converse with the hosts of heaven, with or without the intermediation of Dante.

Beyond the incorporation into psychological theory of such actualities as I have adumbrated, there is one more step, possibly far more difficult, that should be made by those aspiring to a humanistic psychology. They should publicly reveal as clearly as they can their own point of view, their own faith or unfaith. Are they Marxists? Let it be said and explained. Are they Christians? Let it be spelled out. Are they dwellers in limbo, unable to tell right from left, up from down? Confessing it may enable the auditor or reader to understand better whatever else is communicated. As we tell others about themselves in general, let us be open about ourselves in particular. Of course, in one way or another the truth is bound to come out. The question is whether we can be cooperative about it, whether we can articulate consciously the vision which our own poetic tendency creates or accepts as true. Our period of history is characterized by visions of doom. Wordsworth's dream figure, frantically riding to preserve his precious shell and stone from destruction, was only a precursor. In our generation, the atom bomb has awakened the deepest fears of mankind. Typical is the 1950 television pronouncement of Einstein on the coming of the hydrogen bomb. He is reported by C. P. Snow to have said:

> If these efforts should prove successful, radioactive poisoning of the atmosphere, and hence, annihilation of all life on earth will have been brought within the range of what is technically possible. *A weird aspect of this development lies in its apparently inexorable character. Each step appears as the inevitable consequence of the one that went before.* And at the end, looming ever clearer, lies general annihilation. (Snow, 1967, p. 90)

Snow comments on the italicized sentences: "They are utterly true. The more one has mixed in these horrors, the truer they seem" (Snow, 1967, p. 90). The poetic tendency of the human mind, the synthesizing creative tendency, is treated in these words of two of our most revered scientific prophets as an impersonal force moving relentlessly toward the destruction of the life that bears it; for the hydrogen bomb, with all its appanage of refined instrumentation, is as surely a human creation as any self-destructing machinery put together by Jean Tinguely. To say that the creation of the hydrogen bomb and its annihilating use are inevitable and inexorable is to propose a psychological theory which brings in Thanatos as an absolutely demonic mechanized factor within the great world machine which the imagination of science has been building up for the last several hundred years. Was this, indeed, Einstein's vision of the ultimate truth? Is it C. P. Snow's? Is it ours? If not, what is our vision?

In the tenth century it was widely expected throughout Europe that the world would come to an end by fire in the year 1000. When, in spite of the terrible portents which had fed the expectation, the year 1000 came and went without bringing total destruction, the soaring spires of the Gothic cathedrals began to rise in a reaction of relief and gratitude. Are the prospects for the year 2000 as good? Whatever else we may say in our textbooks about human nature, we should occasionally insert a footnote on its capacity for gratitude as demonstrated in this one great outpouring of energy which resulted in those marvelous artifacts of stone and glass where whole communities of people once gathered together to celebrate a spiritual order rainbowing above their darkness.

References

Bachelard, G. *The poetics of space*. Boston: Beacon Press, 1964.

Clagett, M. *Nicole Oresme and the medieval geometry of qualities and motions*. Madison: University of Wisconsin Press, 1968.

Crombie, A. C. *Medieval and early modern science*. Cambridge, Mass.: Harvard University Press, 1967.

Hall, C. S., & Lind, R. E. *Dreams, life and literature: A study of Franz Kafka*. Chapel Hill: University of North Carolina Press, 1970.

Hulme, T. E., *Speculations*. New York: Harcourt Brace, 1924.

Hume, D. *An inquiry concerning the principles of morals* (C. W. Hendel, Ed.). Indianapolis: Bobbs-Merrill, 1957. (Originally published 1751.)

Jones, D. *The anathémata*. New York: Viking, 1965.

McCurdy, H. G. *The personality of Shakespeare: A venture in psychological method*. New Haven: Yale University Press, 1953. (Reprinted by Kennikat Press, 1973).

McCurdy, H. G. *Personality and science: A search for self-awareness*. New York: Van Nostrand, 1965.

Snow, C. P. *Variety of men*. London: Macmillan, 1967.

Thompson, R. *D'Arcy Wentworth Thompson, the scholar-naturalist, 1860–1948*. London: Oxford University Press, 1958.

Wordsworth, W. *The prelude* (E. de Selincourt, Ed.; 2nd ed. rev. by H. Darbishire). Oxford: Clarendon Press, 1959.

8

Donald Kuiken

DESCRIPTIVE METHODS FOR INQUIRY IN HUMAN PSYCHOLOGY

The label "humanistic psychologist" is as flattering and dangerous as the biblical Joseph's robe. Some members of the psychological family suspect their younger brother of gaudy display while they diligently and scientifically pasture the flock. A few encourage a protective tolerance of the fanciful and ambitious dreamer. Still others are anxious to oust the interloper–but will be satisfied to sell him to Ishmaelites headed for the nearest growth center.

The fact is that Joseph has not demonstrated remarkable skill in interpreting his alternative vision of psychology's future. The vision still lacks complete articulation. Presently, humanistic psychologists constitute a diverse community which shares an amorphous but recognizable disciplinary matrix (Kuhn, 1970) with commitments to certain metaphysical statements, symbolic generalizations, and scientific values, but without identifiable research paradigms for systematically assessing the adequacy of these propositions. To elaborate, humanistic psychologists are united in their commitment to some metapsychological statements which have both a heuristic and an ontological status—for example, "Human actions can be understood in terms of their meaning for the person." Also, most humanistic psychologists agree to some basic generalizations, at least in their most abstract form—for example, "The

Donald Kuiken • Department of Psychology, University of Alberta, Edmonton, Alberta T6G 2E9, Canada.

experience of choice facilitates fulfillment of human potential." And there is virtual unanimity on some statements pertaining to scientific value, such as "When facing the choice between an efficacious methodology for trivial phenomena and a barely adequate methodology for significant phenomena, the latter is the preferred option." But in contrast to the persistence of these themes, there is no corresponding shared commitment to exemplary or model research paradigms (Kuhn, 1970) by which humanistic psychologists can systematically examine and evaluate their generalizations.

It is possible to regard this unfinished disciplinary matrix as a vision without substance. Critics can with some justification point to humanistic psychologists' lack of exemplary research paradigms as an inability to systematically clarify, qualify, or revise their propositions—an inability which makes the discipline resemble "nothing but" a reversion to philosophical speculation of "just another" contemporary social movement. From another perspective, the challenge is to articulate a research approach which is commensurate with the other components of the disciplinary matrix. This possibility has not been addressed either directly or concretely enough for reasons that are worth considering in more detail.

Responses to A-Meaningful Psychology

The history of psychology, even prior to its formal institutionalization as a science nearly a century ago, is embellished with controversy about whether a scientific model based largely on the modern theoretical and empirical achievements in natural science is adequate for meaningful inquiry into the most significant human experiences and actions. In perhaps the most acidic and informed critique available, Koch (1959, 1964, 1974) has argued that the imported (and mistaken) conception of science which has dominated psychology since its inception has had extremely restrictive consequences for problem selection and, when actually applied to problems of genuine significance, has had a trivializing effect on accepted "solutions."

The aim of Koch's argument, then, and a common denominator in critiques by humanistic psychologists, is the misleading conception of science and the correspondingly misleading prescriptions for exemplary research paradigms. Since this conception is increasingly extended into the value-laden and time-honored domains of aesthetics, moral development, and so forth, the most prevalent of Koch's twin chimerae of restriction and trivialization is almost certainly the latter. This trivialization takes the form of models of human conduct which obscure and dull rather than clarify and enrich our discriminatory resources. The deadening impact of these models on our sensibilities almost certainly, in turn, affects our attitudes and moral behavior toward other persons.

The preceding attempt to condense the most frequent complaints about established psychology is unrepresentative in one respect. It suggests that the imported conception of science in psychology has produced trivialized images of man and that these trivialized images are responsible for atrophied moral judgment. In this description, a root cause of contemporary a-meaning (Koch, 1974) in psychological thought and of the concomitant decline in the quality of human interaction is the conception of appropriate scientific methodology—the area in which humanistic psychologists have been critical but unable to provide a practicable alternative. Indeed, they seem more inclined to treat the symptoms of their malaise by providing alternative images of man, moral prescriptions corresponding to these images, and rather vague conjectures about alternatives to current scientific praxis.

Thus, one means by which psychologists have identified themselves as humanistic is their opposition to the moral implications of established psychological models and by their alternative and more humane imperatives. As the dictionary definition implies, what is "humane" in their imperatives depends on which qualities they believe distinguish man from other animate beings and, further, which of these specifically human qualities they value most highly. For example, the notion of psychological health, or "full humanness" (Maslow, 1971), which guides the therapeutic and educational endeavors of humanistic psychologists is framed in discussions of aesthetic sensitivity, authenticity, the capacity for nonutilitarian I–Thou relationships, complementarity in self-reliance and self-surrender, and so on (cf. Jourard, 1974; Mahrer, 1978; Maslow, 1954; Rogers, 1961). These are potentials to be actualized in a humanistic (I prefer humane) ethic, and their actualization is a justifiable goal regardless of their amenability to scientific scrutiny.

The connection with methodological questions only emerges with the fact that to assess the course of change and its alignment with these moral imperatives requires a methodology appropriate for these phenomena. Humanistic psychologists, however, have usually reverted to traditional forms of assessment, implicitly admitting their lack of an alternative conception of science or explicitly indicating that their task is to assimilate their inquiry to the established conception of science. As a result, for example, the psychometric instrument usually used as a criterion measure of self-actualization (Shostrom, 1966) does not and, for methodological reasons, probably could not include direct measures of aesthetic sensitivity or genuineness although such concepts are part of the multidimensional complex called psychological health. And in studies of client-centered therapy (Truax & Mitchell, 1971), the practically ubiquitous judges' ratings of accurate empathy (a component of I–Thou relationships) founder on the question of whether other more global stylistic characteristics are actually being rated (Chinsky & Rappaport, 1970). In sum, the attempts to operationally define these goals for change have resulted in operations which very likely miss the subtleties of the phenomena and, therefore, unwittingly subvert the goal of making them the legitimate object of psychological inquiry.

Other humanistic psychologists have found moral problems not only in the image of man spawned by traditional psychology but also in the traditional conception of science *per se*, particularly as an experimental enterprise. For example, Matson (1966; 1973) is highly critical of the exploitation and manipulation that characterize much contemporary psychological research. Alternatively, in arguments based on both scientific value and social value, he proposes that inquiry should involve the knower and known in the dialogical *verstehen* described by Martin Buber. Similarly, but in a more forthrightly ideological statement, Habermas (1971) argues that logical empiricism in the social sciences is typically guided by utilitarian interests in control (not simply for the sake of testing explanatory hypotheses) and that the human sciences should instead be maximally relevant for emancipation, that is, social criticism and self-understanding. The scientific strategy appropriate for this kind of human science should include a hermeneutic approach to understanding the meanings people give to their actions and communications. The preceding are two examples in which moral imperatives are linked closely to a critique of established methodology and to alternative visions of human scientific inquiry. The alternatives provided, however attractive and recurrent in the literature, have been too vague to guide the development of a concrete and systematic praxis for psychological inquiry.

A second means by which psychologists have identified themselves as humanistic is their opposition to traditional psychology's chosen subject matter and their interest in another range of phenomena—especially those which are usually regarded as the domain of the humanities. The social sciences have typically been concerned with man solving his bio-social problems and the image of man derived from this study is usually one of an adapting, learning, information-processing individual. In contrast, the students of the humanities and some humanistic psychologists have been concerned with man when he is attempting pointed commentary on how he is living and the meaning his life has to him. For example, H. Murray (1968) and others in the psychoanalytic orientation have pointed to the similarities between the meaning and aspirations reflected in myths and those reflected in people's more mundane dreams and fantasies. Also, Bugenthal (1965) and other existential psychologists and psychotherapists have found that the literary and philosophical conceptualizations of the existential givens in the human condition highlight and clarify the central dilemmas being faced or avoided in more ordinary lives.

Methods of inquiry supportive of these trends resemble the text-interpretive strategies of the humanities, with emphasis on the meanings and significance of dream reports, projective test responses, clinical-interview and biographical information, and, not surprisingly, myth and literature *per se*. Despite the marginal reliability and construct validity of even the more systematic of these efforts (e.g., the TAT), these interpretive skills continue to be exercised and to receive attention because they are perhaps our only access to the self-reflective thought samples whose poignancy compares to that found in the humanities. De Charms (1968) has suggested that analysis of such self-reflective thought samples could be the methodological basis for a more human psychology, but to date this remains little more than a possibility. This, I believe, is because when these interpretive strategies are used by humanistic psychologists, they eagerly go far beyond the subtle skill of explicating intended meanings to the more questionable art of inferring significance. It is irrelevant here whether this inferred significance is found in destructive libidinal urges or in self-actualizing tendencies; in either case the interpretation usually goes beyond intended meanings to explanations of intended meanings based on personality, pathology, history, and so on. This uncritical mixture of speculative causal explanation and explicative description of intended meanings is a part of the psychoanalytic legacy in existential and humanistic psychology. It hardly represents a radical reconsideration of methodology.

A third basis for claiming the title of humanistic psychologist is support for the basic tenet that experience must and can be given more serious attention in an empirical scientific psychology. Phenomenological philosophy, it is usually argued, can provide a basis for a revised but empirical inquiry into human experience. The result has been a potpourri of both constructive and misleading claims (Kockelmans, 1971). One of the latter is the virtually axiomatic claim that what is present in the phenomenal field determines subsequent behavior (cf. Snygg & Combs, 1949). When this claim is reduced to hypothesis rather than axiom, it acquires a status which, except for its highly general form, is no longer differentiable from the cognitive theories of behavior that predominate in virtually all areas of contemporary psychology except those harboring the most rabid Skinnerians. This form of theorizing even includes cognitive formulations of S-O-R paradigms in social and personality psychology (Bandura, 1977; Mischel, 1973; Phares, 1973). Except in their axiomatic form, then, theoretical formulations which include description of the person's experiences do not set humanistic psychologists apart from the mainstream. This does not mean that humanistic psychologists have no alternative cognitive theoretical formulation to offer, but it does mean that to make their alternatives clear—even to themselves—they must look much more closely at recent literature in which choice, intentions, and so on are part of the theoretical framework. If this were done, it would probably reveal that the kinds of experience humanistic psychologists include in their theories are markedly subtler (e.g., "not being understood" rather than "aversive consequences") and call for more serious attention to a phenomenology which is not theoretical but methodological in import.

The phenomenologically based efforts which are more directly addressed to methodological questions are those which emphasize careful and rigorous descriptive analyses of experience. Primarily, what is proposed is a description of people's experience by explication of the intended meanings of their verbal communication (cf. Giorgi, 1970; McCleod, 1970; Valle & King, 1978). As Giorgi (1971) suggests, the development of this methodology is a risk because it is based on a phenomenological philosophy which itself is not fully developed. Nonetheless, there are provocative, if not profound, examples of this type of method available in the work of Van Kaam (1966), Giorgi (1971), and Coliazzi (1973). It is unlikely that the developmental state of phenomenological philosophy has caused these applications to be generally ignored by humanistic psychologists; they have had many occasions to invoke its ontology for their purposes. Yet, despite their desire to deny the privileged epistemological position of logical empiricism, they have generally ignored the implications of philosophical phenomenology for an alternative systematic and empirical enterprise.

If the preceding cursory review is accurate, humanistic psychologists have not critically and creatively advanced methods appropriate for their expanded concern with experience. Koch's pointed remarks vis-à-vis the recent past in psychology should consequently be taken to heart by humanistic psychologists as well.

> Even those committed to the acknowledgment of experiential events and to the use of experiential variables in their systematic work tended, because of the climate prevailing in that interval, to avoid direct discussion of the many methodico-creative problems that must be joined for effective development of a psychology that takes experience seriously. The paucity of direct considerations of such issues, say in the writings of the classical Gestalt psychologists or of Lewin (at least the writings of these men while in America), is in a way astounding. There are, after all, open and important questions having to do with the relations between experience and "report," optimal techniques for experiential observation, prospects for methods of observer training which might increase the sharpness and reliability of experience-language (this in turn depending on more general issues in the psychology of language), the formulation of adequate independent and dependent (experiential) variable categories, optimal modes for integrating behavioral and experiential data, and many others. These are no simple problems; they are not "methodological" in the idle, role-playing sense: the fate of psychology must be very much bound up with progress toward their resolution. (Koch, 1964, p. 35)

The Need for Development of Experiential Description

An attempt to expand the range of methods by which psychologists can systematically study experience requires initiative from both those actively involved in research and those engaged with the philosophical issues. To date, philosophers have been more willing than psychologists to take such initiative, and the concrete implications for methodology which can be derived from the work of persons like Dilthey and Husserl are still largely undeveloped by psychologists. Even humanistic psychologists have only dimly perceived the need, let alone the concrete possibility, of a viable and systematic strategy for dealing more effectively with experience.

Few psychologists would argue that there are no mental events (such as pain, attitudes, etc.), and few would rule them out as at least part of the proper subject matter of psychology. However, whereas the structuralists assumed that mental events were largely available to awareness and, hence, to introspection, most contemporary psychologists are justifiably suspicious of the range of man's transparency and no longer give him the status of authority on his own mental events (cf. Nisbett & Wilson, 1977). Instead, mental events are usually given the status of hypothetical constructs which are inferred from relatively concrete behaviors (e.g., types of errors in problem solving) or from some type of rating scale (e.g., rated mood or liking). There is no need to eliminate this strategy from the psychologist's repertoire, but there is a need to provide a perspective which will help decide when it is appropriate and when other strategies are necessary.

An observed behavioral response (e.g., performance on a concept-learning trial) may be appropriate, although not always efficient (Lieberman, 1979), when the inferred psychological event (e.g., hypothesis testing) is of interest regardless of whether it is available to the subject's reflective awareness. However, if the subject's reflective awareness is the phenomenon of interest regardless of its veridicality, the behavioral indicator alone is insufficient. The addition of rating scales (e.g., "To what extent did you believe hypothesis X?") is appropriate if the researcher wants the subject to introspect on an aspect of his experience regardless of whether that introspection would have occurred without introduction of the rating scale. However, if the phenomenon of interest is whether a certain aspect of mental life is present in experience without instigation by the investigator's leading questions, some other form of access to the subject's awareness is necessary. Content analysis of a subject's free or open-ended introspection, if reliable, can be helpful in such circumstances (e.g., "How did you try to learn the items on this trial?"; cf. Karpf & Levine, 1971).

Similarly, if conscious intentions, plans, reasons, and so forth are to be seriously considered as potential explanations for behavior (Harre, 1977; Harre & Secord, 1973), then the strategy of inferring them from overt behavior is inappropriate. To know whether a subject did have a plan or reason for behavior rather than unconciously acting *as if* there was a plan or reason is a discrimination that not only can but must be made by examining the content of the subject's reports of plans and reasons. The strategy of asking the subject is especially appropriate when more than one type of reason or plan may account for a given pattern of concrete behavior. And again, when the object of interest is whether these aspects of mental life are in awareness without the obtrusiveness of an inquiring researcher, the content analysis of a subject's unfettered introspections may be methodologically desirable.

The preceding arguments for careful use of introspective reports are quite conventional except for the suggested use of content analysis of freely reported introspection. This recommendation, too, may seem conventional because content analysis already has an established history (Holsti, 1969) and because subjects' introspective reports of their hypotheses and strategies have already shown some utility in predicting subsequent behavior (Ericsson & Simon, 1978, 1979; Lieberman, 1979). In short, the limited use of introspection is already a feature of contemporary psychology, perhaps reflecting the "new mentalism" (Paivio, 1975).

However, the recommendation to use content analysis of freely reported introspection in psychological research is more complex in practice than increasing the use of procedures that are currently available to us. In fact, Lieberman's (1979) recent argument for limited use of introspection misleadingly implies that the principal problem is the unambiguous definition of already known categories of verbal meanings. For example, if the researcher were interested in analyzing introspective reports for a preconceived construct, such as enjoyment of rhythm in the experience of poetry, he or she might survey a sample of introspective reports to develop appropriate content categories whose reliably judged presence defines enjoyment of rhythm. This strategy is potentially very useful but, in many cases, premature. Especially in the areas most significant to humanistic psychologists (e.g., aesthetic experience) it seems more appropriate to acknowledge our relative ignorance of the characteristic features of subjects' verbalizable experience. A reflection of our ignorance is the crudity of strategies commonly used to discern significant features of experience. Usually, psychologists rely on extrapolation of theory designed for a highly dissimilar situation (e.g., applying Hull's drive theory to clinical anxiety) or on their own speculative and/or empathic efforts (e.g., what seems inconsistent to the researcher should arouse dissonance in the subject). Although it is not necessary to forego these attempts to guess the nature of significant components of others' experience, the more empirical effort of systematically describing them seems warranted. The latter, however, will require more extensive exploration of descriptive strategies for discerning and determining characteristic features of introspective reports.

Systematic description prior to explanatory experimentation is not unfamiliar to psychologists. For example, an ethologist's first step in research is to collect an ethogram (i.e., a purely descriptive collection of a species' behaviors without concern for the causal basis of the behaviors). This emphasis on preliminary descriptive effort has influenced psychologists in a variety of areas in which a few now advocate naturalistic observation prior to explanatory experimentation (Willems & Raush, 1969). When considering the possibility of systematic use of introspective reports, however, little is available beyond McCleod's (1970) suggestion that such description is propaedeutic to a significant explanatory psychology. The exception, perhaps, is the psychological phenomenology explored by Van Kaam (1966), Giorgi (1971), and Coliazzi (1973). The following proposal is akin to but certainly not identical to these latter explorations.

A Prescription for Describing Experience

What follows is a strategy for collecting and analyzing freely reported introspection in a wide variety of situations. It is not universally applicable and is only one of many similar strategies which may prove useful. The goal of this strategy is to discern the types of experience reported in a particular situation and to delineate the defining features of each type. The resulting content categories might provide new discriminations which are of interest in their own right or they might be used in further descriptive and/or experimental research, as indicated in a later section. First, however, the technique itself will be described, accompanied by a hypothetical example.

The first step, abstractly put, is as follows: *A plurality of persons in a particular situation is encouraged to reflect on their own experience and to describe this in a verbal form which is understandable to others.*

A plurality . . . . The first differentiating characteristic of this strategy is that the data are derived from a plurality of persons rather than only one person, as is frequently the case in the descriptions found in clinical work in the existential–phenomenological tradition (e.g., Binswanger in Needleman, 1967). Further, although it may be desirable that the investigator also engage in this process to better understand the context of the subjects' communications, what is proposed here is an examination of the subjectivity of subjects, not investigators.

. . . of persons . . . . The class of biological organisms included in this kind of study must obviously possess the capacity for what Harre and Secord (1973) suggest are the two minimal defining characteristics of persons—that is, the capacities to direct their attention to their own subjectivity and then to communicate in linguistic form the contents of that awareness. Variations in these capacities due to age, pathology, and so on will, as in any research, affect the nature of the results, but the absence of these characteristics precludes this kind of analysis.

. . . in a particular situation . . . . A researcher can specify the particular situation for which introspection is to occur by asking the subject to reconstruct a situation which has particular psychological significance, such as a situation in which the subject felt understood (Van Kaam, 1966). This technique has the advantage of eliciting introspection about experience in naturalistic settings with clear psychological significance but the disadvantage of taxing the subject's memory for what may be elusive subjective events, thereby resulting in incompleteness of introspective reports (Ericcson & Simon, 1978). On the other hand, the researcher might construct a situation which has psychological significance to the subjects and rely on more immediate recall, such as the experience of a verbal learning experiment (Coliazzi, 1973; Giorgi, 1971) or repeated reading of selected poems (Collier & Kuiken, 1977). Or, if the act of communication does not interfere, the experimenter could construct a situation and ask the subject to describe his subjectivity in its here-and-now immediacy (see the example below).

. . . are encouraged to reflect on their own experience . . . . Depending on the particular situation, several means are available to encourage reflection. In the situation requiring reconstruction of an event, the interview format can be used. Or, when the situation is constructed by the researcher, specific but open-ended questions can be asked. Also, a variety of instructions can be used to obtain reports which are concurrent with change in subjects' experience of a constructed situation. Ericsson and Simon (1978, 1979) review evidence suggesting that several features of requests for introspective reports detract from their veridicality. First, requests for general rather than particular types of information seem preferable. Particular probes can interfere with recall and induce post hoc inferential activity in retrospective reports. Further, particular probes can interfere with the subjects' attention to the situation and induce inferential activity in concurrent reports. Second, requesting that subjects explain their mental events also interferes with accurate

reporting, perhaps again by inducing inferential activity. Third, as the classical introspectionist experiments revealed, training subjects for scrutiny of certain contents of experience can interfere by inducing thoughts and inferences that would not otherwise be present. However, we do not presently know whether or under what circumstances rehearsal or training for the subject is appropriate. It is a skill to suspend evaluation and explanation of our conscious mental events and simply describe them. Training subjects in such a skill could minimize such interference with the subject's descriptive effort.

. . . and to describe this in a verbal form which is understandable to others. Of course, the subjects and researcher must be members of the same language community. An assumption of this procedure is that the meanings of the subjects' verbalizations are sharable—a consequence for which both the subjects and researcher are responsible through exercise of their language skills. It must also be recalled that, individual differences aside, there are limits to the power of language to attain this sharing of verbal meanings. No verbal assault on the subtleties of experience is guaranteed of success.

To exemplify this stage of the process, five persons were asked to focus on the changes in their experience of a colored photograph of Rembrandt's *Aristotle Contemplating the Bust of Homer*. They were asked to describe these changes as they occurred in their immediate experience of the painting so that they could be tape-recorded. A brief warm-up exercise in this procedure preceded the one-and-one-half-minute introspection period with the painting itself. Afterwards, subjects were asked to report any changes in their experience that occurred during that time but which they had omitted disclosing. For ease of exposition, the following example includes only one person's reported experience of the central focus of the painting, that is, the figure of Aristotle and the bust of Homer.

> The first thing that I notice is the piece of statuary and the apparent band around the person's head and then I shifted to the man standing with his hand on the person. . . . I just started looking at the face of the man looking at the statue and it strikes me as a very pensive, and perhaps even sad look. The eyes are rather heavy and despairing. The statue, on the other hand, seems to be [sic] rather bright or happy look on the face and it seems to me an interesting contrast, that this inanimate object is kind of happy and the person is not. I just started noticing the clothes on the man which strike me as interesting also. The man seems a bit out of proportion as I look at him; his hands seem to be too big for his face and for his body. [The request to report omissions occurred here.] Well, as I was looking at the picture and

> describing the emotion on the statue's face and on the gentleman's face, I began to wonder if I was being a little bit introspective about it or projective about what I was seeing, particularly thinking about how I've been feeling this week . . . sort of pensive and sort of sad a lot of the time. I wondered if that was really on the face or if I was just drawing that onto the face. Then I rejected that and decided it was really on the face.

With this kind of raw "data" from a number of persons, the second stage in the descriptive process occurs as follows: *The researcher surveys a series of particular instances of such descriptions and attempts to explicate constituent features of the subject's communicated meanings.*

The investigator must now bracket his theoretical presuppositions, as well as the evaluations and explanations, in order to interpret the meanings of the subject's verbal communications. The task is to determine the meanings of the subject's communications as they have been presented by the subject. Presented meanings are those to which, by convention (e.g., usage rules, customs, formal necessities, etc.), we have learned to expect an affirmative answer when we ask the paraphrasing question, "Did you mean to say such and such?" Thus, it is the subject's presented meanings that are the criteria for valid interpretation. This does not mean that presented meanings are only those of which he was explicitly conscious at the time of speaking, but it does mean that he is able to become explicitly conscious of them on immediate reflection. For example, if a person says, "My car ran out of gas," he may assent to the paraphrase, "Do you mean to say that your car's gas tank is empty and its engine stopped running?" On the other hand, "Do you mean to say you had to leave your car to walk to a filling station?" asks about a probable truth but is excluded because it is not what the subject meant in his original statement but, rather, is an implication or probable consequence of that statement. Also excluded are unconscious meanings to which the subject would not assent by virtue of ignorance or self-deception (e.g., "Does that mean that you really wanted to cause a traffic jam?").

In these respects, the present position differs from the traditional *verstehen* and hermeneutic disciplines (cf. Radnitzky, 1970) in which both implications and unconscious meanings have their place. The usually speculative nature of implications and unconscious meanings is likely to lead to unreliable judgments, and inferences about unconscious meanings frequently deteriorate into unconscious causes or explanations of the presented meanings. Consequently, they have no place in a descriptive effort of this kind.

On the basis of his understanding of these presented meanings, the investigator now lists the constituents of the subjects' communications, that is, those natural meaning units which differentiate the subjects from each other according to their varying perspectives on a concern shared by all or almost all of the subjects. For example, each of the subjects in the example described his experience as if sharing a common concern with the identification of the psychological state or activity of Aristotle, although they speculated according to their individual perspectives what might be the object of his reflection (e.g., classical mythology), the content of his emotional state (e.g., sad and despairing), and so on. The task, then, is to describe these various perspectives clearly and simply but in a manner that is understandable without consulting those portions of the subject's communication not being summarized in a given constituent. To the extent possible, the summary should include the subject's own words. Also, when essentially the same perspective is shared by more than one subject, only one statement is listed, but it should be phrased in such a manner that it typifies each individual perspective; that is, it should be one to which each subject would give assent as an accurate paraphrase of his own perspective. Finally, in some cases more than one perspective may be presented by a single subject. These are listed separately if, and only if, each resultant constituent differentiates the subject's perspective from other subjects' perspectives.

Constituents can range in complexity from single simple sentences to complex configurations of sentences. Also, they may include content from widely separated segments of the communication, although typically they do not. What is "natural" about these units is not that they are distinguishable episodes in the sequence of the communication but rather that they represent meanings that cohere around a common concern.

When these criteria were applied to the five descriptions in our sample, the following constituents were obtained.

1. Psychological incongruities, polarities, or contrasts:
   a. The inanimate object, the bust, seems bright and happy in ironic contrast to the animate being, Aristotle, who seems pensive and perhaps even sad.
   b. Aristotle has one hand on his waist, symbolizing his pride, and the other hand on the bust, symbolizing the reverse, his reverence.

   c. Aristotle is physically oriented toward the bust of Homer but he is gazing past it.
2. Inferences about the psychological state or activity of Aristotle:
   a. The face of Aristotle, especially the eyes, seem rather heavy and despairing.
   b. Aristotle seems somewhat contemplative and reflective.
   c. Resting his hand on the bust suggests Aristotle's empathy and understanding.
   d. Aristotle might be reflecting on Homer as his mentor in classical mythology.
3. Outstanding perceptual features of the figures:
   a. Aristotle's hands seem disproportionately large for his face and body.
   b. The use of light, coming from the left, illuminates the hand resting on the bust of Homer.
   c. There is a certain resemblance between the bearded features of Aristotle and Homer.
   d. Aristotle's clothing is striking in its appearance.
4. Self-reflection occurring during the experience of the figures:
   a. I wondered whether the emotions I saw in the bust and in Aristotle were projections of my own emotions, but decided they were part of the painting.
   b. I was tempted to speculate on what Aristotle was thinking but tried to return to perceptual experience of the painting.
   c. Perhaps because I was defensive, I did not have strong emotional reactions to the painting.

Perhaps other common concerns and perspectives could be discerned by other investigators. The effort to be exhaustive in describing the constituent features of subjects' meanings will succeed or fail depending on the sensitivities of the investigator. The double difficulty is attaining description which is sensitive to nuance without at this stage interpreting implications and unconscious meanings of subjects' communications.

The basic unit for subsequent analysis, then, is the constituent—that is, the presented meaning of a common concern from the perspective of a particular individual. It is comparable to the basic constituents obtained in the phenomenological reduction of other investigators (cf. Coliazzi, 1978) except that here no attempt is made to form a comprehensive list of natural units. Instead, constituents chosen for further examination are restricted to those which reflect common concerns in subjects' experience.

The next step is as follows: *The investigator, to the extent possible, discerns and delineates types of introspective reports in terms of their constituents.*

A type, as defined here, is the synthesis of a number of constituents to form a relatively independent cluster of more or less concurrent constituents. The minimal conditions for discerning and delineating types are these: there must be relative independence of constituents which identify different types; the constituents identifying a particular type must be more or less correlated; and, if mutually exclusive type definitions are desired, individuals must be differentiable by unique type definitions. The presence or absence of these conditions can be assessed by using one or more of the variety of numerical clustering algorithms available (Sneath & Sokal, 1973), including Q-type factor analysis. For example, the constituents in the example can be regarded as traits which are absent from some descriptions and present for others. The entire array of such discrete dichotomous traits can be used to assess the similarity of any pair of individuals in the sample, using a correlation coefficient (or perhaps some other similarity index). By correlating all pairs of individuals in this way, the investigator produces a matrix of similarity coefficients which can then be subjected to Q-type factor analysis or some other clustering method. The more or less independent clusters derived from this analysis can then be subjected to some form of discriminant analysis in order to isolate the constituents that identify a particular type of introspective report.

There is, of course, no guarantee that the numerical algorithms will provide compellingly clear differentiations of clusters, and since I am only currently executing an initial project using this methodology, chances of success cannot be estimated at this time. It is possible, however, to compare this strategy with a similar one which has occasionally been used in psychological research. The array of constituents defined here is analogous to the concourse of communications on a topic in Q-technique (Stephenson, 1953, 1972), although in the case of the latter these can be gleaned from essays and books on a topic and not simply from introspective reports. Whereas the present type differentiation is derived from the original sample of introspective reports, in Q-technique the concourse is Q-sorted by a new sample of subjects and then factor-analyzed for types. An important difference between the present methodology and Q-technique is that, in the latter, other persons' communications on a topic are presented for Q-sorting and can cause retrospective alterations of the reported experience. When, as in the present strategy, a person's unfettered introspective reports are used, other persons' introspective reports are not available to exert such influence.

The use of numerical clustering algorithms for type identification is the primary feature differentiating the present strategy from that outlined by phenomenologists such as Van Kaam (1966) and Coliazzi (1978). Their procedures for identifying constituents are virtually identical to those used in the present strategy. However, they attempt to integrate the entire array of constituents—obtained from a plurality of subjects—into a single, exhaustive description that captures the essential features of all subjects' reports. Using a similar strategy, Collier and Kuiken (1977) obtained clearly incompatible constituents from different subjects, indicating that efforts at integration obscure fundamentally different types of experience. The search for resolution to this problem led to the present proposal. Despite the use of numerical aids, usually anathema to phenomenologists (Giorgi, 1970), this strategy might best be described as an attempt to obtain a precise and systematic means of identifying what Husserl called morphological essences, that is, the more or less invariant structures of class concepts (Husserl, 1967). Confirmation of this point lies outside the scope of this present chapter.

The final step is as follows: *The clusters of constituents defining types are described in their typicality and structure to define content categories.*

The constituents which differentiate one type from another are only candidates for status as defining features of these types. It is possible to simply use factor scores to define types, but this might blur the discrimination of patterns of constituents which define a coherent and psychologically meaningful construct. Imagine, for example, that Q-type factor analysis of our hypothetical sample produced a type-identifying factor which was discriminable from other types because of the more or less consistent presence of the following constituents:

1. The inanimate object, the bust, seems bright and happy in contrast to the animate being, Aristotle, who seems pensive and perhaps even sad.
2. The face of Aristotle, especially the eyes, seems rather heavy and despairing.
3. Aristotle's hands seem disproportionately large for his face and body.

4. I wondered whether the emotions I saw in the bust and in Aristotle were projections of my own emotions but decided they were part of the painting.

It is possible to use these constituents and those clearly associated with other types to develop the defining characteristics of the type. For example, by finding that "Aristotle might be reflecting on Homer as his mentor in classical mythology" is a constituent which is not located in the hypothetical factor referred to above, we might conclude that the latter is defined by inferences about Aristotle's emotions rather than inferences about his thoughts and musings. Or, if we were also to find that "Aristotle has one hand on his waist, symbolizing his pride, and the other hand on the bust, symbolizing the reverse, his reverence," is a constituent which identifies another factor, we might conclude that the type is defined by virtue of some self-conscious "projection" rather than a more intellectual interpretation of "symbols." By contrasting the constituents of different types in this way, it is possible to more specifically describe what aspects of the constituents are the essential or defining features of the type.

A second source of information is the relationships among the constituents themselves. It is plausible, at least, that items 1 and 2 in the example above are simply related as part to whole. It is also plausible that the attention to emotional contrasts and disproportionate perceptual features are both manifestations of subjects' apprehensions of incongruity. This kind of synthesis involves a process of alternating between (1) using the constituents to apprehend the meanings of the whole, that is, the constituents identifying the type, and 2) using this understanding of the relationship between the parts to determine the contextual appropriateness of all the part–whole relationships. The result should be an account of the structure of the type which accounts for most, if not all, of the constituents.

Using these two sources of information about the meaning of this particular type, a tentative definition of the type is prepared. Consider the following definition and example:

Type I. Incongruity apprehension and self–other differentiation

Defining Features. The subject reports ironic juxtaposition of emotional expressions and incongruities in perceptual features of the painting. He considers the possibility that projection may be responsible for his experience of the emotional expressions and makes final evaluation of the meanings in the painting after considering this.

Example (reconstructed from the example protocol on pp. 170–171): I just started looking at the face of the man looking at the statue and it strikes me as a very pensive, and perhaps even sad look. The eyes are heavy and despairing. The statue, on the other hand seems to have a rather bright or happy look on its face. It seems to me an interesting contrast that the inanimate object is kind of happy and the person is not. I wonder if I am being a little projective about what I am seeing particularly thinking about how I have been feeling this week . . . sort of pensive and sad a lot of the time. I wonder if that was really on the face or if I am drawing that onto the face. I reject that and decide that it was really on the face.

Preliminary type definitions of this kind can be elaborated or amended by attempting type categorization on another set of subjects' experiential reports. Such examination might indicate, for example, other types of incongruity which can clarify the abstract definition and provide other specific examples. This same sample and the articulated definition can then be presented to another judge for the purpose of training in the necessary discriminations, following which interjudge reliability can be assessed using conventional procedures (Holsti, 1969).

The procedure outlined (and idealized) in this section is intended as a guide toward definitional richness and precision for experiential reports. But the work of precise and subtle definition is underdetermined by rule. Perhaps there is, for example, no absolute rationale for stipulating *a priori* what terms should provide the basis for definition—even though that kind of stipulation has characterized some of the dogma (seldom actually practiced) about "observables" in psychology. The critical issue, regardless of whether the definitional base is "object language" or, as here, constituents of presented meanings, is reliability of reference. It is typically assumed that "observables" provide the most reliable reference, and consequently, there are repeated efforts to translate subjective meanings (e.g., emotional states) into peripheral or physiological processes (e.g., GSR) or more simply to make the peripheral or physiological processes (e.g., arousal) the fundamental phenomena with the concomitant loss of the subject matter of original interest. The present *a priori* stipulation of constituents of presented meanings as a basis for definition is intended to counter these prevailing tendencies.

Also, there is no absolute rationale for stipulating the use of clustering algorithms to discern and delineate types of introspective reports. The critical issue here is that somehow the minimal criteria for type definition be met. That is, there must be relative independence of constituents which identify different types; the constituents of a particular type must be more or less correlated and, if mutually exclusive type definitions are desired, individuals must be differentiable by unique type definitions. To these ends, the clustering algorithms are useful tools because the preceding criteria, being relative, make extreme demands on the investigator for judging the degree to which they can be met. However, if the experiential reports are such that the discerning investigator can meet these criteria without this tool, he should do so. The goal is to differentiate rich and yet precise content categories, not to make use of a particular technique.

Conclusion

If humanistic psychologists are to take experience more seriously than is the case in established psychology, descriptive efforts of the kind prescribed here should be an important part of their program of inquiry. The history of psychology, and science more generally, indicates that the profundity of a given explanatory system is largely a function of the careful and systematic description which precedes it. Psychoanalysis, for example, still has an impact on psychology not because of the fruitfulness of its energistic explanatory notions—now generally in disrepute—but because of the rich and detailed descriptions of symptoms and defense mechanisms which continue to elicit response from those psychologists who take man's capacity for self-deception seriously. Similarly in developmental psychology, Piaget's impact is attributable to the power of rich description of developmental stages to suggest interesting explanatory hypotheses.

The general disrepute of descriptive efforts in psychology, although increasingly questioned (Willems & Raush, 1969), is an archaic remnant of a conception of science which glorifies a limited range of scientific activity. In the "accomplished" sciences, there is mathematization, experimentation, and explanation; so, psychologists count, experiment, and theorize. What, however, of the descriptive efforts that characterize some of the important developments in the natural sciences we are so eager to emulate? A historical example from the biological sciences will highlight possibilities too infrequently considered by psychologists—including humanistic ones. In the eighteenth century, Linnaeus developed a description of the defining features of species, orders, families, and so forth by careful examination of many candidates for these classes. Although he not only developed categories but, very significantly, arranged them hierarchically, he was aware that his was not a satisfactory system. It took the genius of Darwin in the nineteenth century to interpret Linnaeus's hierarchy as a family tree and to begin to examine the "intergrades" of species. Darwin himself did not undertake experimentation *per se* although he developed a theory of natural selection which explained the succession of species–intergrades–species, which he painstakingly observed and described. The attempt to experimentally examine the causes of this sequence via artificially induced mutations awaited twentieth-century advances in genetics.

The first point here is that Linnaeus did precede Darwin and Darwin did depend on his, and others', taxonomic efforts. These efforts, therefore, were not idle enterprises. The second point is that taxonomy need not be "mere description." Although Linnaeus developed a hierarchy and Darwin specified developmental sequence, the former did not and the latter did inspire an explanatory theory with profound implications. The third point is that experimentation assessing the causal explanations of species change was a late development whose profundity depended largely on the context of preceding descriptive work.

Parallel implications can be drawn for descriptive efforts of the kind advocated in this paper. First, "mere" description of types is not an idle enterprise. An attempt to systematically define types of experience in psychologically significant situations can fail for many reasons, but efforts which are successful can reveal new discriminations which are of interest in their own right. Second, efforts which go beyond content categorization to hierarchization or developmental sequence are more likely to suggest theories which merit further development and which point to specific areas requiring more detailed description. Third, experimental explanatory examination of the changes in frequency of occurrence of different types or of sequences of development of types can follow in a rich and meaningful way from these descriptive efforts. This experimental effort is likely to be as profound as the descriptive efforts which precede it.

So, the successful descriptive effort might eventually enable Joseph to announce himself to his experimental brethren again. Only then can the constructs with which he works be more firmly anchored in actual experience, and the kinds of discriminations he makes will then be more subtle than before. This is a rather modest attainment perhaps, but its general unavailability in contemporary psychology makes it a silver cup worth placing in Benjamin's bag of grain.

References

Bandura, A. Self-efficacy: Toward a unifying theory of behavioral change. *Psychological Review*, 1977, *8*, 191–215.

Bugenthal, J. F. T. *The search for authenticity*. New York: Holt, Rinehart, & Winston, 1965.

Chinsky, J., & Rappaport, J. Brief critique of the meaning and reliability of "accurate empathy" ratings. *Psychological Bulletin*, 1970, *75*, 379–382.

Coliazzi, P. F. *Reflection and research in psychology: A phenomenological study of learning*. Dubuque, Iowa: Kendall-Hunt, 1973.

Coliazzi, P. F. Psychological research as the phenomenologist sees it. In R. S. Valle & M. King (Eds.), *Existential-phenomenological alternatives for psychology*. New York: Oxford University Press, 1978.

Collier, G., & Kuiken, D. A phenomenological study of the experience of poetry. *Journal of Phenomenological Psychology*, 1977, *7*, 209–225.

De Charms, R. *Personal causation: The internal affective determinants of behavior*. New York: Academic Press, 1968.

Ericsson, K. A., & Simon, H. A. *Retrospective verbal reports as data*. C.I.P. Working Paper No. 388, 1978. (Available from Department of Psychology, Carnegie-Mellon University.)

Ericsson, K. A., & Simon, H. A. *Thinking-aloud protocols as data*. C.I.P. Working Paper No. 397, 1979. (Available from Department of Psychology, Carnegie-Mellon University.)

Giorgi, A. *Psychology as a human science: A phenomenologically based approach*. New York: Harper & Row, 1970.

Giorgi, A. A phenomenological approach to the problem of meaning and serial learning. In A. Giorgi, W. A. Fischer, & R. von Eckartsberg (Eds.), *Duquesne studies in phenomenological psychology* (Vol. 1). Pittsburgh: Duquesne University Press, 1971.

Habermas, J. *Knowledge and human interests*. Boston: Beacon Press, 1971.

Harre, H. The ethogenic approach. In L. Berkowitz (Ed.), *Advances in experimental social psychology* (Vol. 10). New York: Academic Press, 1977.

Harre, H., & Secord, P. F. *The explanation of social behavior*. Totowa, N. J.: Littlefield, Adams, 1973.

Holsti, O. R. *Content analysis for the social sciences and humanities*. Reading, Mass.: Addison-Wesley, 1969.

Husserl, E. *Ideas: General introduction to phenomenology* (W. R. Boyce Gibson, trans.). London: Allen & Unwin, 1967.

Jourard, S. *Healthy personality: An approach from the viewpoint of humanistic psychology*. New York: Macmillan, 1974.

Karpf, D., & Levine, M. Blank trial probes and introtacts in human discrimination learning. *Journal of Experimental Psychology*, 1971, *90*, 51–55.

Koch, S. Epilogue. In S. Koch (Ed.), *Psychology: A study of a science* (Vol. 3). New York: McGraw-Hill, 1959.

Koch, S. Psychology and emerging conceptions of knowledge as unitary. In T. W. Wann (Ed.), *Behaviorism and phenomenology*. Chicago: University of Chicago Press, 1964.

Koch, S. Philosophy of science of human behavior. In S. C. Brown (Ed.), *Philosophy of psychology*. New York: Macmillan, 1974.

Kockelmans, J. J. Phenomenological psychology in the U.S.: A critical analysis of the actual situation. *Journal of Phenomenological Psychology*, 1971, *1*, 139–172.

Kuhn, T. S. *The structure of scientific revolutions*. Chicago: University of Chicago Press, 1970.

Lieberman, D. A. Behaviorism and the mind: A (limited) call for a return to introspection. *American Psychologist*, 1979, *34*, 319–333.

Mahrer, A. R. *Experiencing: A humanistic theory of psychology and psychiatry.* New York: Brunner/Mazel, 1978.

Maslow, A. H. *Motivation and personality.* New York: Harper Brothers, 1954.

Maslow, A. H. *The farther reaches of human nature.* New York: Viking, 1971.

Matson, F. W. *The broken image.* Garden City, N.Y.: Anchor Books, 1966.

Matson, F. W. AHP committee on human policies: Statement of purposes. *Journal of Humanistic Psychology,* 1973, *13,* 15–18.

McCleod, R. B. Psychological phenomenology: A propaedeutic to scientific psychology. In J. R. Royce (Ed.), *Toward unification in psychology.* Toronto: University of Toronto Press, 1970.

Mischel, W. Toward a cognitive social learning reconceptualization of personality. *Psychological Review,* 1973, *80,* 252–283.

Murray, H. The possible nature of a "mythology" to come. In H. Murray (Ed.), *Myth and myth making.* Boston: Beacon Press, 1968.

Needleman, J. *Being-in-the-world: Selected papers of Ludwig Binswanger.* New York: Harper & Row (Torchbooks), 1967.

Nisbett, R. E., & Wilson, T. O. Telling more than we can know: Verbal report on mental processes. *Psychological Review,* 1977, *84,* 231–259.

Paivio, A. Neomentalism. *Canadian Journal of Psychology,* 1975, *29,* 263–291.

Phares, E. J. *Locus of control: A personality determinant of behavior.* Morristown, N.J.: General Learning Press, 1973.

Radnitzky, G. *Contemporary schools of metascience.* Göteborg, Sweden: Akademiforlaget, 1970.

Rogers, C. *On becoming a person.* Boston: Houghton Mifflin, 1961.

Shostrom, E. L. *Manual for the personal orientation inventory.* San Diego: Educational and Industrial Testing Service, 1966.

Sneath, P. H. A., & Sokal, R. R. *Numerical taxonomy.* San Francisco: Freeman, 1973.

Snygg, D., & Combs, A. W. *Individual behavior.* New York: Harper, 1949.

Stephenson, W. *The study of behavior: Q-technique and its methodology.* Chicago: University of Chicago Press, 1953.

Stephenson, W. Applications of communication theory: II. Interpretations of Keats' "Ode on a Grecian Urn." *Psychological Record,* 1972, *22,* 177–192.

Truax, C. B., & Mitchell, K. M. Research on certain therapist interpersonal skills in relation to process and outcome. In A. E. Bergin & S. L. Garfield (Eds.), *Handbook of psychotherapy and behavior change.* New York: Wiley, 1971.

Valle, R. S., & King, M. (Eds.). *Existential-phenomenological alternatives in psychology.* New York: Oxford University Press, 1978.

Van Kaam, A. *Existential foundations of psychology.* Pittsburgh: Duquesne University Press, 1966.

Willems, E. P., & Raush, H. L. (Eds.). *Naturalistic viewpoints in psychological research.* New York: Holt, Rinehart, & Winston, 1969.

IV

INTERDISCIPLINARY PERSPECTIVES

9

Harry Garfinkle

THE ANTHROPOLOGICAL FOUNDATIONS OF A HUMANE PSYCHOLOGY

Introduction

The term "behavior" strikes me as singularly inappropriate to serve as the defining parameter of a humane psychology. To begin with, the prefix "be-" denotes a reactive rather than an enactive function in the English language. If psychologists were to use the term "endeavor" along with "behavior," then they would at least be utilizing a technical term with a prefix that carries a sense of active implication (i.e., the prefix "en-"). In epistemological terms, we would then be dealing with a psychology of action as well as reaction, for with "behavioral psychology" we are locked into (no pun intended) John Locke's "tabula rasa," or passive way of experiencing sense data. And though Skinner's brand of operant conditioning at least introduces the element of biofeedback into the classical-conditioning approaches of Pavlov and Watson, we are still essentially dealing with a ratological view of psychology—one which fails to recognize that although human beings are a species of animal they have in the course of their evolution become differentiated in certain specific ways from the rest of the animal kingdom and might, therefore, just merit a psychology with a difference.

Harry Garfinkle • Department of Educational Foundations and Theoretical Psychology Center, University of Alberta, Edmonton, Alberta T6G 2E1, Canada.

Put somewhat differently, we can recognize with Razran (1971) that "there is unmistakable evidence that in man, and presumably in higher animals, the mechanisms of conditioning interact significantly with conscious categories," (p. 14) and further that "awareness, affects, images and meanings are, it is believed, the minimum conscious categories needed for a behavior plus consciousness approach to the mind" (p. 15). In incorporating "endeavor" and its adaptation-level-of-organization term "consciousness" (Appley, 1971) as well as the active experience-processing-and-integrating term "cognition" into the requisite foundations of our psychological paradigm, we are in effect moving from a sensory psychology (Paradigm I) to a cognitive psychology (Paradigm II). And we are effecting a primary paradigm shift and reorientation in the prospectus of psychology, from B. F. Skinner's (1974, p. 208) "A scientific analysis of behavior must, I believe, assume that a person's behavior is controlled by his genetic and environmental histories rather than by the person himself as an initiating creative agent" to precisely the position that he is denying. Or, to cast it affirmatively, it is a matter of accepting Ross Stegner's contention, that "it is important to remember that psychological processes are modified by the nature of the organism, that behavior is often active, not merely reactive" (Appley, 1971, p. 208). A psychology in which "endeavor" would be the key term would then have "experience" as its transactional term and "conscious endeavor," "coconscious behavior," "subconscious homeostasis," and "unconscious neurergia" as its phenomenal, analytical, configurational, and biofeedback components.

This would be a step forward in overcoming the reductionism that characterizes behaviorist psychology, but it is not enough. The terms "behavior" and "endeavor" are both inadequate for a humane psychology for they still carry the implication that psychology is a science dealing with "individuals" rather than with "social persons." They must, therefore, be embedded in turn in a psychology of "conduct" (Dewey, 1930) in which the organismic level is recognized as being characterized by performance norms that are qualitatively different from and not equatable to the mechanistic reactions and cybernetic enactions to which human beings under constrained conditions can be reduced (Koestler & Smythies, 1969). The human being in this socially expressive psychological formulation (Paradigm III) has consequently to be seen in life cycle developmental terms—and in terms of a psychoneurological organization of the body in which the "brain" functions not just as an "associative" organ, as it does in behavioral psychology, or as an "integrative" organ, as it does in endeavoral psychology, but as an "executive" organ.

In this sense, Paradigm I psychology is essentially empiriological in its epistemological provenance, Paradigm II psychology is essentially phenomenological, and Paradigm III psychology is essentially semasiological. Internal stimuli in this context then function as symptoms and external stimuli function as signs. These, in turn, are invested with meaning and as signals, symbols, scales, syndromes, and semiotics serve to facilitate the organism's interpretation of, and acclination to, its environment. The human being in this psychological perspective thus learns not only what is impressed on *its* senses and what *it* finds to be aversively and felicifically utilitarian but also how to seek out the means which will enable *him or her* to realize *his or her* full potential. In short, while a mechanism or a cybernism has only a programmed "it" identity, a higher organism has a generic and sexual identity as a "he" or a "she" who can learn how to learn better.

A psychology of conduct thus allows the human being to have a dialectical personality, which is more than just a sense of objective individuality and an awareness of subjective identity. And, again, a step forward has been taken in encompassing the humanness of being human in this modeling of a requisite humane psychology. But this too is not enough. Even when the subject of our psychology has been individualized, privatized, and personalized, we have not yet realized the species-being properties which pertain to the quality of being a human being—that is, the qualities inherent in being anthropologically classified as *Homo sapiens sapiens*. A psychology of comportment (Paradigm IV) must consequently be developed to encompass the behavioral, endeavoral, and relational aspects of human existence. And comportment in this sense also becomes the pandectic term for the psychological processes analytically identified as operating within the biocenosis in which all earthly species are ensconced. The following social parameters must consequently be recognized as the field conditions for all individual actions: (1) synecological web-of-life interspecific relations; (2) demecological intraspecific relations; (3) socioecological interdemic relations; (4) autecological intrademic relations (Schwerdtfeger, 1963, 1968, 1977). Figure 1 presents this biocenotic network in schematic form.

In the context of a Paradigm IV psychology, sociobiology and evolutionary speciology become the key processes within which the em-

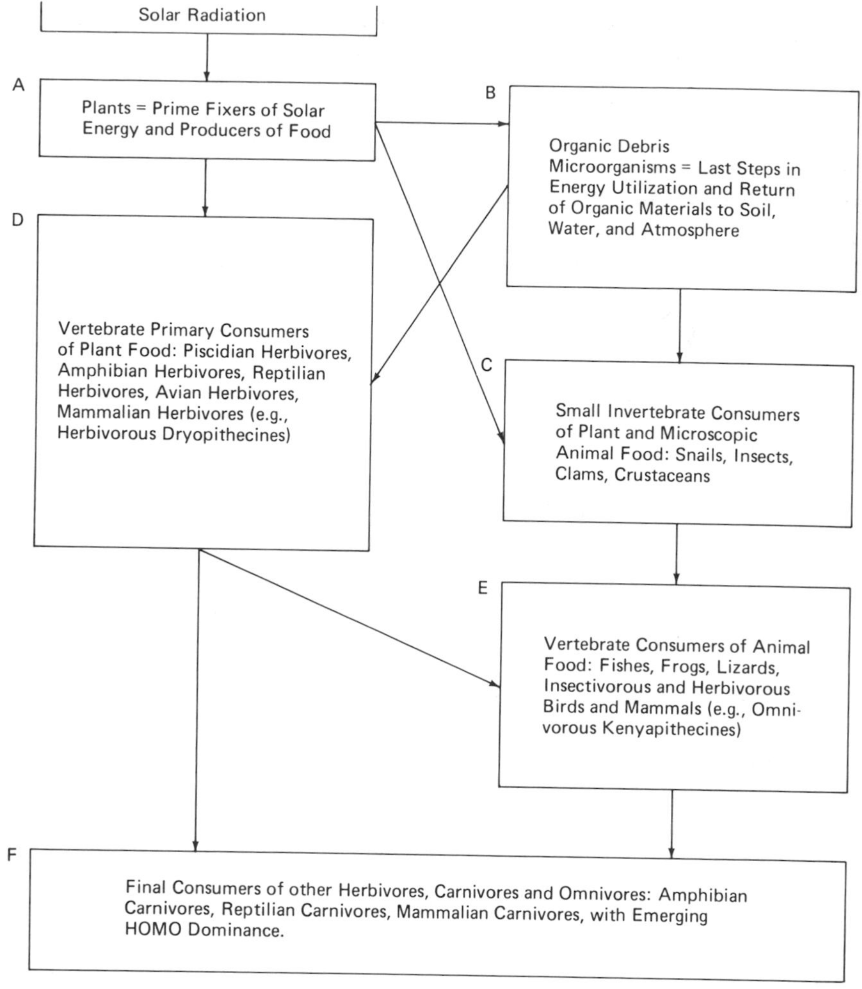

Figure 1. A schematic model of the earth as a biocenosis. (Adapted from Figure 26, *Life of the Past*, by G. G. Simpson, 1953.)

piriological, phenomenological and semasiological ways of coping with the environment are carried on; and comportment is delineated in terms of a species-specific form of ethological consciousness. Ethograms (Wescott, 1970) then represent the biogrammatic way of "being and becoming human" (Count, 1973). Books like *Lemur Behavior* (Jolly, 1967), *The Mountain Gorilla—Ecology and Behavior* (Schaller, 1965), and *My Friends, the Wild Chimpanzees* (van Lawick-Goodall, 1967) are indicative of what primate psychology in the modality of ethological consciousness has to encompass. And books like *Studying Behavior in Natural Settings* (Brandt, 1972), *Naturalistic Viewpoints in Psychological Research* (Willems & Raush, 1969), and *Ecological Psychology: Concepts and Methods for Studying the Environment of Human Behavior* (Barker, 1968) are similarly indicative of what a humane psychology in the modality of ethological consciousness needs to consider.

But when all is said and done, the ethological consciousness only includes the parameters necessary to get at the psychological features that are to be found in the comportment of the primates at the preanthropine state of evolution. We would still have to identify the psychological characteristics that came into being in the intervening evolutionary grades between the preanthropines and ourselves. This is a matter of some 20 million years of evolution, and the changing nature of hominid nature during this period resulted in our attaining a psychological makeup at variance in a number of significant ways with that which characterizes all other primate genera. Eliciting the psychological characterization of the humanization grades which lie between the putative ancestral forms common to both the hominids and the pongids who now inhabit the earth consequently makes up what will be referred to as "the anthropological foundations of a humane psychology."

What this amounts to is the realization that up to Paradigm IV psychology we have been coming to terms with what all social mammals can be said to share, but now, with Paradigm V psychology, we are finally moving into what distinguishes the human way of living from that of all other creatures. We are consequently concerned with "the evolution of man's capacity for culture" (Spuhler, Gerard, Washburn, Hockett, Harlow, & Sahlins, 1959), with the transformation of the "biocenosis" into an "oikoumene," the changeover from acclinative evolution to accommodative humanization, and the incorporation of ecological processes into economic prospectives. Karl Marx and Friedrich Engels, V. G. Childe, and Darcy Ribeiro (Ribeiro, 1970) have, in this connection, been among the pioneers in bringing about this shift in perspective from a psychology represented in root metaphors derived from a model of science based on the physical sciences (Paradigm I, morphology), the chemical sciences (Paradigm II, physiology), the geological sciences (Paradigm III, embryology), and the sociobiological sciences (Paradigm IV, speciology) to one based on the human cultural sciences (Paradigm V, anthropology). This means that a minimally adequate scientific psychology of the human species must be more than empiriologically grounded in intersubjectively objectifiable experience, more than phenomenologically grounded in hermeneutically unpacked explicitation, more than semasiologically grounded in meaningfully structured socialization, and more than ethologically grounded in acclinatively viable evolution. It must, in an all-encompassing sense, be historiologically grounded in accommodatively successful enculturation.

Finally, in our attempt to be true to the complexity of human existence in some sense of the idea of authenticity, it is necessary to realize that the hominization transformation into humanization is not just another specialized part of the general evolutionary process that characterizes all biological populations. Nor is the apeiron,[1] in which historical events take place, only cumulatively affected by the course of the accommodative modifications introduced by the human species. Human affairs are, instead, valuationally, morally, communally, and praxially regulated. The patterns of culture by which human beings live do not, à la David Hume's Paradigm I assumption, pose a bifurcation between facts and values. Rather, they are made up of choices regarding the extent to which the accoutumation process will allow for deviations from the established mores or traditionally transmitted customs of the social formation under consideration. Human history is consequently a record of achievement in the enhancement of the degrees of freedom by which human beings in a social formation can continue to live. Culture, in this sense, works against deterministic necessity and absolute constrenatory authority, with the result that human history is a saltatory process with quantum qualitative jumps in the moralization of the human condition. A Paradigm VI psychology would consequently embed the historiological apeiron of "humanization" in an axiological prospective of "jeshuralization" (from the Hebrew *jeshur* or yosher, meaning universal justice or righteousness) and result in the "human" psychology standards of Paradigm V being measured by the "humane" psychology criteria of Paradigm VI.

It is the thesis of this chapter, then, that an adequately scientific

[1] The term "apeiron" comes from Anaximander (Diels, 1934–1937). I am using it to convey the idea that change in the historical domain is dialectical and that, in a saltational sequence, each new synthesis represents a unity of contrarieties at a higher level of organization than existed before. "Culture" consequently entails the axiological transvaluation of the earlier historical conditions, the reconstitution of the already established social institutions, and the transfiguration of the prior forms of human nature and personality.

psychology of the human species must be a Paradigm VI psychology. It must, furthermore, go beyond the anthropoidally human to the humanely and ethically human psychic nature of the sapient societies/populations/persons who now occupy the earth. For reasons which will be indicated in the text of this study, I intend to use a periodization of

Table 1. Stages in the Formation of the Modern Human Consciousness

I. Anthropoid comportment—the preculturation stages	
1. Preanthropine grade	Represented by Dryopithecine fossils, more than 18,000,000 years old—the ethological consciousness
II. Hominid comportment—the protoculturation stages	
2. Alloanthropine grade	Represented by Kenyapithecine fossils, less than 18,000,000 years old—the kinesiological consciousness
3. Paraanthropine grade	Represented by Ngororapithecine fossils, less than 12,500,000 years old—the eidological consciousness
4. Protoanthropine grade	Represented by Australopithecine fossils, less than 7,000,000 years old—the eicological consciousness
III. Hominine culture—the socioculturation stages	
5. Eoanthropine grade[a]	Represented by *Homo habilis* (habiline) fossils, less than 4,500,000 years old—the lavorological consciousness
6. Archaeanthropine grades[b]	Represented by *Homo erectus* (pithecanthropine) fossils, less than 1,750,000 years old—the dybological consciousness
IV. Human culture—the ethnoculturation stages	
7. The paleoanthropine grade	Represented by *Homo sapiens "aboriginalis"* fossils, less than 300,000 years old—the phasiological consciousness
8. The mesoanthropine grade	Represented by *Homo sapiens "regionalis"* fossils, less than 150,000 years old—the mimetological consciousness
9. The neoanthropine grade	Represented by extinct *Homo sapiens sapiens* fossils, less than 50,000 years old—the cenemological consciousness
10. The holoanthropine grade	Represented by ancestral *Homo sapiens sapiens* forms, less than 15,000 years old—the praxeological consciousness

[a] Four phases, some of which may well merit "grade"-level status: (1) pre-Oldowan habilines—Africa; (2) Oldowan habilines—Africa; (3) post-Oldowan habilines—Africa; (4) Eurafrasian migrating habilines—Java.

[b] Seven phases, some of which may well merit "grade"-level status: (1) developed Oldowan pithecanthropines—Africa; (2) post-Oldowan pithecanthropines—Africa; (3) European Clactonian pithecanthropines—Britain; (4) South East Asian Trinil pithecanthropines—Java; (5) Central Asian Choukoutien pithecanthropines—China; (6) Eurafrasian Acheulean pithecanthropines—Germany; (7) Eurafrasian developed Acheulan pithecanthropines—Spain.

ten hominization/humanization/jeshuralization grades to cover the changing nature of human nature from its preanthropine to its holoanthropine characterizations. Table 1 represents, in outline form, the essence of the hypothesis that governs this presentation.

Stage 1: The Preanthropine Grade of Hominoid Consciousness

The baseline for the preanthropine grade of hominoid consciousness consists of the comportment characteristic of the primate demes of the Dryopithecines who inhabited the Southern European and Eastern and Central forests of Africa more than 18 million years ago. Their place in the biocenosis was that of small mammalian herbivores (box D in Figure 1), and this condition carried with it the specific set of synecological, demecological, socioecological and autecological interrelations which it is the job of the paleoecologist to fill out (Howell & Bourliere, 1966). The Dryopithecines are selected as the possible ancestors of both the hominids (fossil and living human beings) and the pongids (chimpanzees and gorillas), even though there are also some pongoid and hominoid affinities in the Pliopithecines of the same period. However, the exact combination of progenitors, while desirable, is not basic to the argument being developed in this chapter; my concern is with the succession of grades rather than the clades of descent (A. Jolly, 1972, p. 62–63). This period, 18 million years ago, represents the time when the process of continental drift which brought Africa, Arabia, Eurasia, and India together in one continuous land mass was terminated (Bishop & Miller, 1972). The ensuing movement of flora and fauna, brought about by these geomorphological changes, eventuated in new climax successions, with the result that the Dryopithecines, who had meanwhile undergone a three-continent-wide adaptive radiation, variegated natural selection, and the extinction, reliction, adaptive succession, and acclination of some of their migrating populations, subsequently gave rise to a number of new alloprimate evolutionary lines.

Since today's chimpanzees and gorillas continue to inhabit an ecological niche very similar to that of the Dryopithecines, they will be treated here as the successful representatives of the 18-million-year process of adaptive succession, and an ethogram based on today's pongids can, with corrections for what is known about their Miocene ancestors, serve as the point of departure for the deviations to be identified within the subsequent evolutionary grades of the hominoid succession. It is also fortunate that many of the Kenya Dryopithecine fossils such as "Proconsul" (though probably closer in type to the yet-to-evolve pongids than to the yet-to-evolve hominids) were found in fairly full skeletal form, *in situ,* in strata that stretch back some 20 million years. They are thus available for a realistic reconstruction of the biocenotological conditions of the time. There are also over 700 specimens of the period to draw on (Simons, 1972) so that a fairly complete morphological reconstruction is possible.

Paleoecologists, paleontologists, and sundry biological experts, therefore, have their work cut out for them in order to come up with a model of the processes of natural selection, social selection, and sexual selection that were operative within the biocenotological settings that contained the Dryopithecines, They must delve into such questions as the nature of interspecific and intraspecific competition and cooperation, congregation and separation, coordination and isolation, subgroup interpenetration and rejection, commensalism and contestation. The answers must, in turn, be linked via socioecological structural reconstructions to the autecological conditions in effect within each of the contact troops being studied; these then lead to more questions relating to domination and subordination, agonation and succoration, and the sex, age, health, and strength resolution patterns within the troop.

The diurnal and nocturnal cycles of representative troop members would then have to be investigated in order to determine how the days of the year were spent and what the patterns and schedules (padules) pertaining to eating, drinking, defence against predators, resting, sleeping, playing, grooming, and so on were like. The familial and sexual relations between the sexes and ages would, furthermore, have to be probed in order to assess the nature of the courting, conjugating, and mating patterns of the troop and the ensuing relations of parentalism, fraternalism, filialism, age-grading, and sex-typing (Kummer, 1971). Similarly, the whole field of intergroup, intragroup, and intermember communication would have to be reconstructed, and the links between proxemics and hierarchics clearly delineated. Finally, the range of variation in feeling tone, from celebration and collective festiveness to stressful choric vocalization, would have to be identified and incorporated into our model of preanthropine conduct. On these grounds, an ethogram could then be constructed (Wescott, 1968, 1970).

It may seem like a presumptive claim to allege that from the *in situ* anatomy of a number of skeletons it is possible to model the physiological and sociobiological psychology of primates who lived 20 million years ago, but this is precisely what paleoecology is all about (Dolhinow, 1972). There is, however, support of a different nature from the theory of "encephalization" (Noback & Moskowitz, 1962). It has been established experimentally that the more refined general senses require the integrative activity of the cerebral cortex and that, for example, the loss of weight discrimination induced by the ablation of the postcentral cortex is greatest in man, less in the chimpanzee, and least in the monkey, so that "a sequence in degree of encephalization with respect to this modality is indicated in these three species" (p. 210). The sequence is similar for many other psychological modalities (Noback & Moskowitz, 1962).

We could then reason that since some 20 million years ago neither the pongids nor the hominids had yet attained their present day specializations, a grade level of neural systemic organization close to that of the orangutans, who branched off into their own ecological niche some 22–24 million years ago, might serve as our possible baseline. Composite alternatives could be constructed from other hylobatid, pongid, and hominid forms to serve as comparable bases for simulation purposes. But these few hints are perhaps enough to indicate that a paleoecology, a paleosociobiology, and a paleopsychology can all be constructed to serve as the basis of getting at the evolutionary departures that we are about to identify.

Ethology, as a study of the comportment of animals in their natural setting where interbreeding populations are under the selection pressures of the environment, serves as well in this grade as a psychological parameter. "Environment" is, however, only a background term covering the determinate impact of influences stemming from the larger cosmos and the biosphere; in the foreground we have, in addition, to focus on the impact of the range, the habitat, and the "milieu" in which social interaction takes place and in which the ethological consciousness takes shape. Every newborn primate is therefore inducted into a preexistent ethos, and every new generation modifies to some extent its received ethos padules (patterns and schedules). In the baseline society that we are starting with, we can therefore recognize that there was a structure to the troop's social organization, that there was a set of traditional transmissions in the troop's social organization, that there was individuality, play and grooming, dreaming and festiveness in the troop's social differentiation, and that there was the ability to engage in implement-using comportment in the troop's social instrumentation. Life within that socialized set of bonds therefore constituted the ethos of the preanthropine grade of psychic consciousness; and expressed as the modal padule, we have the putative Dryopithecine ethogram whose subsequent reconstitution this chapter will try to chart.

Stage 2: The Alloanthropine Grade of Hominid Consciousness

Fossils with humanlike mandibles and teeth-wear patterns show up in the paleontological record between 14 million *(Kenyapithecus wickeri)* and 10 million *(Ramapithecus punjabicus)* years ago, and they are probably acclinated forms from the process of continental drift and climatic dessication that came to a head some 18 million years ago. The Indian fossils would, by present evidence, appear to represent an evolutionary line that became extinct, but the African fossils are part of a continuing sequence of adaptive radiations. It is likely that the formation of the Great Rift Valley some 15 million years ago again forced some of the survivors into new ecological niches, and their subsequent acclination to edge-of-forest biocenotological conditions represented a further departure from the forest conditions in which the preanthropines had their habitat. Since the teeth of our fossil specimens show that their possessors had moved from a herbivorous to a more omnivorous diet (from box D to box E in Figure 1), we can recognize that they were also party to modified forms of synecological, demecological, socioecological, and autecological social acclination, social organization, social celebration, social communication, social instrumentation, and social differentiation. Whether lacustrine, woodland clearance, broken forest, or peneplain forest adapted, these East African alloforms of the Ramapithecines were moving into new biogeographical conditions, and within their midst we would probably find the ancestral populations that represent the next grade of hominid consciousness.

Given a cline that was part arboreal and part savannal, the challenges of their changed territorial habitat resulted in adjustments by the Ramapithecines to the new scale of their ecozone. In systems terms, we would have to recognize that their social organization would consequently entail a modified set of variations in the troop's comportment, consisting of band-on-ground and band-in-tree whole–part relationships, of tree member–member and ground member–member relationships, and of various band–coalition–member, whole–composite-part–individual-element relationships. Attainment of the regulatory order required to maintain this more complex form of social organization is the basis for the hypothesis being advanced here to the effect that these hominids are to be credited with a structure of social complexity in which the social comportment of the previous grade began to be incorporated into new levels of social organization. It will take two more hominization grades to effect the transition from social comportment to social custom, but it is already evident that the commensalism of the Ramapithecines, the type specimens for the alloanthropine grade of hominid consciousness, entails a different group sustenation padule than that which characterized the Dryopithecines, the type specimens for the preanthropine grade of hominoid consciousness. Aramorphic-selection outcomes in the direction of a change in the ingestive, digestive, and eliminatory organs of the body are therefore consequential to the selection pressures operating in these new ecozones.

If we now treat the sociobiological structures established by the alloanthropine bands as their molar form of social organization, we can at the same time identify the level of social experience, in its endeavoral, behavioral, and latency (conduct-based) aspects, as constituting the psychobiological organizational level of each Ramapithecine band. Encephalization would also proceed in the direction of enhanced selected forms of motility, visual acuity, dexterity, and social communication through affective vocalization and an expanded repertoire of body-motional gestures (mands). By shifting to an incipient ground-dwelling existence, the alloanthropines made visual display an important means of socialization and compounded their means of multimodal communication. The result was the emergence of the new form of consciousness which I would designate as "the kinesiological consciousness" (Birdwhistell, 1970).

Living on the ground also changed the primate reproductive pattern and probably resulted in an augmented birthrate and an increased population. This would have put pressure on the continuation of the traditional arboreally based and herbivorously specialized diet of the alloprimates' ancestors and probably led to their assuming a more variegated omnivorous type of alimentation pattern. Troop organization being duolocal, we can also postulate a development in communicative skills. Wescott suggests (1970) that five of the 17 diagnostic criteria of language that he lists are common to all social mammals, and these suggest the sources for subsequent emergence of the other features of a protolanguage and then later a fully articulated language:

1. Referentiality, or the specific designation by a signal of an object (as opposed to the mere expression of emotion)
2. Productivity, or the capacity of the communication system to generate new signals (usually by recombining old ones)
3. Displacement, or reference to things which, being absent in place or time, are not immediately perceptible
4. Multimodality, or the use of signals both to make statements and to give commands
5. Multicanalization, or the use of two or more alternate sensory channels for the transmission of synonymous messages

The representation in consciousness of these more complex forms of association and communication is consequently my warrant for postulating that instead of an ethogram type of biogram it is now necessary to speak of a "kinesogram" and a "*bittewelt*" as carrying the weight of the psyche's enhanced interrelatedness with its *auswelt* (synecologically integrated), *umwelt* (demecologically integrated), *mitwelt* (socioecologically integrated), and *merkwelt* (autecologically integrated).

Stage 3: The Paraanthropine Grade of Hominid Consciousness

Some 12.5 million years ago, Asia was once again joined to North America, and a new wave of floral and faunal migration got under way. This altered the succession climaxes and again resulted in a changed biocenotological balance. Dessication increased in East Africa, and we have evidence in the Ngorora Formation of the transition of at least one species of hominid from a forest clearance habitat to an open savanna ecozone. This is the kind of environment that the gelada and hamadryas baboons are adapted to, but among the hominoids, only the chimpanzees, at a later date, skirted this kind of habitat. We are, however, on very thin ice in generalizing about this grade since as of the beginning of 1974, we are dealing with a single molar. On odontological evidence, its characteristics seem to fall between those of *Ramapithecus* and *Australopithecus*, the ensuing grade prototype, so that "*Ngororapithecus*," living about 9 million years ago, will for the present have to stand for the movement of the hominids to an open-country environment.

Thus, if in the previous grade the emphasis was on the dietary changes which resulted in aramorphic developments in the direction of an omnivorous form of dentition and metabolism, in the paraanthropine grade the stress is on the changes in the locomotor mechanism which made it possible for an erstwhile arboreally adapted species to become terrestrially acclinated. With several million years of natural, social, and sexual selection, the outcome was the emergence of an increasingly upright bipedal hominid. There are, to be sure, open-country fossil hominids from about four to one million years old, but they would appear to have reverted to an herbivorous diet since their teeth are specialized for seed-eating, and they are no longer on the main evolutionary hominization line. C. J. Jolly (1970) has reconstructed their ethology as graminivores. We are, however, in need of a placeholder to represent the hominization of the first hominid ground dwellers, and this function *"Ngororapithecus"* will have to fulfill until he or she has more fossil company.

Open-country living is also significant in sociobiological terms, for it entails a further increase in scale. As against forest-dwelling groups of 10–50 monkeys, some of the baboon troops living under savanna conditions number over a hundred. Because tree cover is possibly some distance away, a defense and warning system functions among the baboons, and there is a greater degree of whole-troop movement and organization. The process of assuretation thus puts a premium on protection and directional mutuality since a dash for the trees at the first sign of danger is no longer possible. The organization of feeding and sleeping arrangements for a hundred band members necessarily leads to complexification in the nature of the social relations required, and we can posit that the first hominids to have faced survival on these terms must have also attained some form of regulatory and differentiated social structure. This suggests that deployment and logistics problems had then to be resolved, and this set of circumstances serves as my basis for concluding that another step in the direction of a more complex form of social organization, the movement to the incorporation of comportment into the context of culture, was taken during this hominization grade.

To understand the concomitant psychological changes, we would then have to consider how the greatly enlarged paraanthropine bands, with ethological (affect-tone) and kinesiological (gesture-mand) forms of communication, would have developed in their new ecological setting. I therefore accept the hypothesis that open-ground movement would have put a premium on carrying—the very young, perhaps some food, perhaps some implements—over long distances and that the social organization making this possible represented a second hominization step (Bartholemew & Birdsell, 1953).

The imaging of the whole–coalition–part social relationships prevailing in the band would also have involved the acquisition of a series of subconscious and coconscious gestalts in which social status, social distance, and social territorial-utilization constellations would have all had to be implicitly recognized and acted upon. Response set would then have been triggered by an enhanced metacommunication level of signaling; and warning reminders would increasingly have taken the place of actual agonistic contests. All of this can be represented by the statement that such imagings entailed the development of eidola in the mind, and I would therefore posit the emergence at that time of an "eidological consciousness." Description of the modal padules (patterns–schedules) and mands (body gestures) making up the composite comportment/conduct of each troop member would then be described in terms of an "eidolagram" and by the *"gangwelt"* that represented the life routines, choices, and innovations of paraanthropine life in the East African savanna some nine million years ago.

Stage 4: The Protoanthropine Grade of Hominid Consciousness

Australopithecine fossils of what is here being designated as the protoanthropine grade of hominization show up from about five million years ago. The preceding four million years are, for the moment, paleontologically fallow. *Australopithecus robustus* and *Australopithecus boisei,* in their predominantly herbivorous sustentation patterns are probably no longer in the mainstream of hominid evolution, but *Australopithecus africanus,* in the period between seven (?) and four million years ago, may have been a part of the continuation of the aramorphic developments in the direction of a more humanlike masticatory pattern and the more humanlike locomotary pattern already underway in the previous grades. In any case, *Australopithecus africanus* mandibles, teeth, pelvises, and limb bones are more like our own than those found in any prior fossils; and by their increasing frequency in the paleontological record, it is possible that by this time the hominids had become a more dominant genus in the biocenosis. It is also likely that they had effected the full transition from forager to predator (box E in Figure 1), even though the greater part of their diet may still have been of vegetable origin. They had, by the location of their fossil remains, become acclinated to open-grassland (veldtland) living where, facing the danger of felid, canid, and hyaenid carnivores, they had themselves been selected for speed in locomotion. Le Gros Clark's analysis (1978) is that they had become upright in their running stance, though not yet in their walking pose.

The use of the hands becomes the new basis for survival in this grade; power grip and precision grip ability are central to the paleontological questions requiring resolution (Napier, 1960). Dart (1957) proposed that regular use of tools came into prominence at this time and spoke of the "osteodontokeratic" culture (bone, tooth, and horn) of the Australopithecines. The confirmatory evidence is certainly weak, but the implemental use of animal remains is likely. The presence of selected palm-sized pebble stones from river beds some five to eight miles away in conjunction with the fossil remains of the protoanthropines has also given rise to the supposition that this was the eolithic age (the dawn of the stone age) in which the artifacts were, though probably still nature fashioned, hominidally selected and effectively used. Pebble "tools" with one or two sharp edges have been designated as instances of Kafuan technology (van Riet Lowe, 1957), and as such, they represent the formal start of the archaeological record.

Sociobiologically, there is also indirect evidence of a change in social organization. Analysis of the children's teeth that have been found indicates that the period of infancy was being prolonged, and this suggests that some form of proveniation and protection had been developed to make this extended non–self-feeding period possible. And although it is not always possible in the fossil record to determine who is predator and who is prey, some of the lair sites contain both Australopithecine and other, possibly scavenged, animal bones. Thus, if small game predation and carrion scavenging were being carried on, the social model for the hominids of this grade would no longer have been the baboon troop; instead, the lion pride or the wolf pack would have to be invoked. And if food was being brought to individual lairs, we would have to posit a band form of predation organization along with, possibly, a familial form of consuming organization, built around an extension of the female's succoring padule.

The attainment of a social structure based on band assuretation, band proveniation, and mating-pair and offspring bonding along with the encephalization of sexual conduct thus brings to a head the complexification of social relations intended by the term "comportment." From this grade on, socialization at the societal level and familiarization at the familial level will create the dialectic for the choices (later values, mores, and ethics) facing the newly weaned hominid child. Socialization will thus come to determine the band's more general form of social relationships—that is, those involved in the social-selection padules inherent in acclination—while familiarization will increasingly come to represent the primary group's mediation of the lifeways of the larger social unit in its regulation of the next generation's internalization of the troop's comportment padules and mands.

Along with these changes in ecological acclination and societal organization, there were also concomitant changes in the Australopithecine psychobiological makeup. Expressed in the form of a Guttman scale, we can say that when the ethological consciousness was (as a result of encephalization catching up with the outcomes of selection) compounded within the kinesiological consciousness, hominid *mouthedness* and some new emotional and sensorimotor patterns of social and environmental coping were effectively enhanced. When this synthesis was, in turn, compounded within the eidological consciousness, hominid *footedness* and some time-binding and mnemonic abilities were enhanced. And finally, as a result of the manipulatory skills emergent and selected for at this grade, the encephalized correlates in the brain for *handedness* and an integration of affective identification, visual acuity, locomotor speed, and finger dexterity began to take hold. The result was an increasing ability to produce prefigured models of tools (icons), sought-for useful settlement sites *(eikes)*, and more important, the increased ability to pass these on as learned traditions to the next generation.

I propose, therefore, to designate the psychic synthesis of the ethological consciousness, the kinesiological consciousness, the eidological consciousness, and the newly emergent ability to foreshadow the form of reality to be constructed in concrete practical form as the "eicological consciousness" and its ambience as the *"tatwelt."* Hominids able to effect this kind of synthesis can thus be seen to have left the rest of the animal kingdom behind, and their representative lives would, by the termination of this grade, be portrayed in an "eicogram."

Stage 5: The Eoanthropine Grade of Hominine Consciousness

Homo habilis, the type specimen for the eoanthropine grade of primate hominization, is for some anthropologists still a nebulous representative (Brace & Korn, 1971). The habiline prototypes are either subsumed under the previous level or sunk into the next grade. In historically denotative terms, the makers of the tools of the Oldowan technical tradition are, however, the ostensible placeholders of this stage of hominine evolution and are, by my criteria, the earliest primates to merit the hominine status of the genus *Homo.* Flourishing between 4.5 and 1.5 million years ago in the period of Pliocene–Pleistocene transition (and surviving for a while longer in the face of pithecanthropine competition), the habilines probably attained the status of primary predators in the biocenosis of that period (from box E to box F in Figure 1). In all likelihood, they also began that set of migrations which carried the hominines to Europe, Asia, and other parts of Africa.

They became regular tool users and systematic hunters and gatherers, and for that reason I would suggest that the term "ecology" is no longer suitable to describe their survival patterns and that the term "economy" should, from this grade on, be used to detail the context in which they lived. In this usage, I am referring to a hypothesis first presented by Friedrich Engels in an essay entitled "The Part Played by Labour in the Transition from Ape to Man" (Engels, 1878/1954) as well as to the ideas of historical materialism roughed out by Marx (1858/1973). Marx, in his amplification of Feuerbach's notion of the nature of "species man," accepted the contention that human beings, as social animals, had to guarantee (1) their *means of subsistence* and (2) their *relations of reproduction;* but then, leaving the biological reductionism of his contemporaries behind, Marx averred that as sociohistorical beings the human species had also certain distinctly human characteristics in the form of (3) the *forces of production* that they utilized and (4) the ability to organize their *social relations* of production in accord with the potential of the age in which they lived. The integration of these four elements is in Marx's terms, what is meant by a general economic mode or, in its specifics, a social formation. These terms will, therefore, from this point on serve as the basis for the periodization of the rest of the hominization grades to be adduced.

Specifically, organized hunting and gathering provided *Homo habilis* with the means of subsistence required; and cooperative social organization regulated the relations of reproduction, which is another way of saying that the ethological forms of comportment were now embedded in what I shall refer to as the lavorological forms of collaboration/culture. The Oldowan tool-making tradition would then have become the basis for the means of production by which the habilines' food supply was enhanced and their social organization was protected, while the division of labor along age and sex lines, for hunting and gathering and helping and preparing purposes, would have represented the formalization of their social relations. On this basis, *Homo habilis* can be recognized as having incorporated his ecological acclination (readapting to a new cline) requirements into his economical "accommodation" (fitting into a general mode) requirements. Thus, instead of speaking of habiline food-getting activities as predation and foraging, we shall henceforth recognize the quantum jump in their sustentation patterns and refer to them instead as hunting and gathering.

In psychobiological terms, too, we can register a quantum jump in purposeful activity. If we examine the Oldowan artifacts, we can classify them as possible scrapers, perforators, cutters, strikers, choppers, and missiles. The question therefore arises: What kind of intelligence is represented by the ability to fashion such an assemblage of useful tools? Subsuming the changes in conscious control already encephalized during the previous three anthropine grades, we would have to recognize that affect, memory, movement, and performance had all been reintegrated into the higher unity of skill. Then skill, in the sense of regularized competence in communication, cohabitation, proveniation, assuretation, manipulation, and artifaction, could be expressed in terms of padules (patterns and schedules) and mands (body-coordinated movements) which constituted habiline social performance as labor. And labor, when internalized as the new level of consciousness attained at the eoanthropine grade, would be manifest as the "lavorological consciousness" and its ambience as the *"werkwelt."*

To express all of these qualitative changes, we are thus in need of terms that will convey the idea that the ecodeme was being incorporated into an economy, that comportment was in the process of being encompassed in collaboration, and that acclination was in process of being absorbed by accommodation. Hence, this is the grade which marks the transition from the protocultural to the cultural stage of hominid consciousness. The subsequent stages in the nature of human nature will therefore be dealt with under the heading of "humanization" rather than by the more genetically denotative term "hominization." This means that humanization via culture will subsequently have an increasingly greater impact in determining the course of hominization via heredity. Finally, with labor as the basis of the eoanthropine social formation, the lavorological consciousness, expressed in a lavorogram, and represented by its ambient *"werkwelt,"* will entail a valorization of the padules and mands by which life was regulated and secured. Accommodation will then become the educational form of cultural transmission from one generation of habilines to the next, and the internalization of this whole transformed way of living will characterize the emerging psychic makeup of the habilines of our eoanthropine grade of humanization.

Stage 6: The Archaeanthropine Grade of Hominine Consciousness

The archaeanthropine grade of hominine evolution is represented in Africa by fossil finds in the eastern, southern and northern parts of the continent, in Europe by fossil finds in Germany and Hungary, and in Asia by fossil finds in Israel, Java, and China. Artifacts of the developed Oldowan and early- and middle-Acheulean traditions—the two main technical styles characteristic of the achievement registered by the archaeanthropines—are even more widespread. It is interesting to note that artifacts of the more advanced tool-making tradition, the Acheulean, appear first in Africa; and the bones of their makers may be about 1.5 million years old. In all probability, accommodation to the hunting of medium to large herbivores on the African plains was accompanied by selection for a larger, more agile, more dexterous, speedier hominine with a larger cranial capacity and, concomitantly, an improved technical repertoire.

At the same time, the hominines of this grade underwent a bifurcated set of selection pressures in Africa and Eurasia. While Africa was beset with alternate pluvial cooling and interpluvial warming, even dessicating, periods, the northern hemisphere underwent the processes of glaciation and melting referred to, in their European provenance, as the Donau, Gunz, Mindel, Riss, and Wurm glacials and interglacials. Then, when aridity resulted in severe selection pressures in the southern hemisphere, warm temperate conditions prevailed in the north; and when glacial conditions put the northern populations into a stressful relationship with their environment, wetter conditions prevailed in Africa. This resulted in population movements north and south, consequent cohabitation on the part of previously isolated populations, and changes in the course of archaeanthropine evolution. We would thus have to recognize the existence of a small form of Pithecanthropine in East Africa (cranial capacity to 750 cc), a somewhat larger form which reached around to northern and western Africa and into west central Europe and southeast Asia (cranial capacity to 900–1000 cc), and a still larger form in China and central Europe (cranial capacity to 1250–1350 cc).

About 500,000 years ago, between the Gunz and Mindel glaciations, fire was harnessed in Eurasia, and it may have become the all-important factor in the survival of *Homo erectus* in the cold conditions of these temperate and betimes even frigid latitudes. We thus find that Peking man *(Sinanthropus pekinensis)*, living for at least 70,000 years in the shelter of a number of caves at Choukoutien, had hearths at the mouths of three of them. Evidence of fire has also been found at a number of sites in France and Hungary. For *Homo erectus "prometheus,"* fire thus became the means of making the northern latitudes tolerably habitable, providing warmth, light, protection against wild predators, resistance to bone damp, a home base for hunting and gathering expeditions, and the opportunity to come together for convivial forms of social celebration. In time, it also became a means for roasting and cooking food and an aid to tool making. Since there is as yet no evidence of fire-making ability at that time, fire-tending would consequently have led to a less nomadic existence and possibly to the noumenal feeling of being "at home" somewhere, while the rest of the range would have been differently marked as hunting and gathering territory. Thus, a mental shift from experiencing the world in terms of padules (mental patterns–schedules) to reflecting the world in terms of chorules (choreal or place-bound schedules) was one significant psychological outcome of these developments. The development of an *"innerwelt"* to modify the rigidity of the habiline *"werkwelt"* was possibly another.

It is difficult to determine the social organization of the different *Homo erectus* demes, extended as they were over three continents, but recognizing that they were generally able to hunt the herbivores of the plains and the forests allows us to make some analogical comparisons between their lifeways and those of hunting and gathering peoples today. Three recent books, *Man the Hunter* (Lee & DeVore, 1968), *The*

Hunting People (Coon, 1971), and *Hunters and Gatherers Today* (Bicchieri, 1972), are seminal for this purpose. Stone age archaeological reconstructions provide a further anchor for the ethnological suppositions being drawn.

An archaeological reconstruction of conditions some 400,000 years ago at the caves of Choukoutien reveals that in the three caves that were graced with hearths there may have been about twenty people living at any one time—skeletal remains of over 40 individuals have been found. In the same context, some 70% of the animal bones found were of the local variety of deer, so this would appear to have been the main staple food, although there were remains of about 45 other species of animals as well (Black, de Chardin, Young, & Pei, 1933). Some of the human remains were those of children and older people (over 40) who were too young, too old, or too handicapped to hunt or gather much food so that some form of eleemosynary bonding must have prevailed as the basis for their support. Whether this was accompanied by stable genealogical relationships as well is still an open question, but it suggests that humanity was living "by more than bread alone." In theoretical terms we are thus looking at the probable transition from a social formation based on accommodation to one based on consouciation (extended care for all in-group members). The relations around each hearth involved three-generational contacts, and the relations between the hearths may have also begun to be regularized in kinship terms. Moreover, all the skulls found have been carefully broken open and the brain marrow presumably removed. Perhaps the distinction between related dead kin and edible kine was still in the process of being clarified.

Collective labor and the means of communication thereto did, however, tie the group together, and we can speculate about the linking up of each band and their nearest human collaterals. We can also try to construct models of individual and small-group deportment within each cave in response to the exigencies of their society's economic and social mode of life. Life was harsh, and 50% of the deme probably died before the age of 14, so that it would have been necessary to bear four children per family simply to maintain the ongoing population level. The continued evolution of *Homo erectus* has, therefore, to be reconstructed by a judicial weighting of the ecological, demographical, and socioeconomic variables involved.

The cranial capacities of the skulls found at Choukoutien vary from 915 to 1225 cc, while some of those at Vertesszollos, in Hungary, are above the mean for modern European man (1325 cc). This represents a virtual doubling of the cranial capacity of the archaeanthropines in the course of a little more than a million years and indicates the likelihood of a considerably more developed neurophysiology and psychology than that which characterized the previous grade of hominines.

The Russian physical anthropologist V. V. Bunak (1959), for one, has tried to gauge the quality of the mental activity and speech development that might have gone along with *Homo erectus*'s enlarged brain, and he has come up with the following hypothesis: In the area of mental activity, there was a considerable development of the visual, proprioceptive, and tactile forms of perception, as these would have had to be kept in mind, so to speak, in order to carry through the extended succession of operations required to produce choppers and skin cutters. In the area of speech development, working from endocasts and from inferences regarding the level of communication attendant on their socioeconomic mode of production, he places the archaeanthropines in the early-speech stage, suggesting that they had gone beyond shouts and calls to polysemantic but still unsyntactically used blade articulations, vowels, and vibrants. With fire, they would also have had a greater load of envisioning and imagining experiences; and it is evident that some of their tools were finished, in aesthetic terms, beyond the call of functional utility. Ralph L. Holloway, Jr. (1969) has also proposed a neurophysiological social-behavioral model for reconstructing fossil man's grade of psychosocial development.

To characterize the change in consciousness resulting from all this, I have been struck by the fact that more than skill, more than utility, was now involved—that, in fact, labor animated by noumenal, affinal, and aesthetic considerations now seemed to pervade the archaeanthropines' lifeways. I have therefore taken over Richard Landers's (1966) term "dybology," in order to suggest the development of an "innerwelt," or weltanschauung, in which even the inanimate world was cognitively treated as if it was infused with animate spirit, and I would therefore credit the archaeanthropines with the evolution of the "dybological consciousness." Then, instead of speaking of labor in the functional-survival sense, we can speak of industry as labor cognitively infused with imagination, extended time-binding memory, aesthetic appreciation, social identification, and individualization in competence and regularity of performance; and we can treat industry, in this sense, as the emergent characterization of this grade's psychological attainment. The processes of socioeconomic accommodation would then gradually lose their strictly deterministic weighting, and the less necessitarian form of consouciation, in which dybological considerations modified collaboration into custom, would instead come to prevail in hominine psychosocial lifeways. The complex representation of this new social reality would then take the form of a "dybogram," and its ambience, an *"innerwelt."*

Stage 7: The Paleoanthropine Grade of Human Consciousness

In the paleoanthropine grade of human evolution, we move from *Homo erectus* to *Homo sapiens*. The glacial advances and retreats and the succession of desert and grassland cover of the Pleistocene epoch greatly accelerated the rate of natural, social, sexual, and cultural selection. The forced movement of populations east and west, north and south, and around mountains, deserts, and water barriers resulted in a general mixing of geographical races, organized societies, technical traditions, and psychic orientations. Migrations thus occurred which, in the Mindel–Riss interglacial period, resulted in peoples from Asia, Africa, and Europe coming together for the first time.

In my own estimation, however, control of fire was the most important factor making for the appearance of the new evolutionary grade. In the sense that man is what he eats, the use of fire in roasting meat and cooking rough vegetable matter reduced the time required to chew and digest what was being eaten while increasing the energy output of ingested food. By 300,000 years ago, the overall recession and reduction of the human masticatory apparatus was well under way, and with every improvement in the preparation of food, the power required of the hominine jaws to process it was also reduced. This also resulted in the reduction of the musculature required to hold the human head in place atop the spinal column and in a shift in the position of the foramen magnum vis-à-vis the skull and the spinal column. The fossils found at Montmaurin, in France, at Steinheim, in Germany, and at Swanscombe, in England, are, though incomplete, probably the remains of the earliest members of *Homo sapiens*.

With ecological changes and advances in technology, also came changes in social organization. In the ethnographic record, historical accounts of big-game and herd-game hunts involve anywhere from 25 to 300 people. To use the technique of the swamp-directed fire drive or the valley corral involves the cooperative efforts of a lot of people; and since the food supply from a successful kill (e.g., bones of 20 elephants have been found at one kill site) would have allowed a large population to engage in concentrated feasting before the meat went bad and other scavengers and predators closed in, a new scale of social organization had to come into being with this grade. If later practice is any guide, the occasion of the big-game hunt would bring together peoples (clans?) who would in other parts of the year carry on their sustentation activities in smaller social units (bands, households). At the time of coming together, they may have also initiated the exchange of gifts, mates, and traditions. These larger social amalgamations may initially have been of a temporary nature; but at some point in time, these arrangements were formalized into regularized and regulated endogamous and exogamous mating patterns, with the consequent intensification of the affination and affiliation obligations that came into being. They then moved from genealities to ethnicities requiring some form of political organization to handle their big-game hunts. Once instituted and supported by tradition, these social relationships could then be passed on to the next generation as traditional grouping arrangements, incest taboos, nubile-adolescent controls, and so forth. The origins of many of mankind's later political and kinship patterns thus had their beginnings in the socioeconomic conditions faced by the paleoanthropines between 300,000 and 150,000 years ago.

In the demological sense, the mixing of the *Homo* populations from three continents resulted in an alteration in gene pool qualities and frequencies, and the resultant populations were those we now characterize as the progenitors of the subsequent sapient grades. And with genetic reassortation, changes in the structuralization of the brain occurred, including alterations in the neurochemistry attendant on the cognitive and communicative functions. From the hypothesis that what was done with brain-handedness to shape tool conventions was also done in the realm of brain-cognitiveness to shape mentation traditions and in the realm of brain-communicativeness to shape utterance codes, we can adduce the transition from ostensive to abstract forms of cognition and from phonic to morphemic forms of communication. And although the evidence is still circumstantial, the resultant process of encephalization cumulatively taking form over these 150,000 years probably resulted in the development of the coordinative functions of the premotor region of the cerebral cortex (Bunak, 1959, p. 318). At the same time, in regard to speech, the lower jaws became lighter, the vocal organs became thinner, the tongue became more flexible, and the syllabic differentiation of initial and terminal phonemes became a part of the human speech repertoire. In fact, speech and intelligence in their neurophysiological foundations are probably the main aramorphic characterizations of the sapient grades.

In psychological terms, these outcomes can be expressed by stating that the development of human consciousness during this evolutionary grade depended very much on the integration of the ecological, sociological, lavorological and dybological forms of psychic orientation within the context of the projective forms of verbalization represented by the encephalization processes referred to above. Phasis, in the sense of the coordinated production of polysyllabic sounds, would then have become the means for expressing the polysemantic notions that the aboriginal *Homo sapiens* populations were increasingly capable of producing. Thought and language would then both convey a composite, connotative message compounded of the expression of an action, the acting subject, the object of the action, the aim of the action, the means of the action, the wish for the action, and the emotional, motor, and imaginational concomitants of the action. The ability to respond to the cultural compulsive, compounded of customs, traditions, and codes prevalent in the economic mode in which the paleoanthropines lived, by means of thoughtful assessment and vocal designation, and embracing the many-sided complex referred to previously, is what I propose to designate as the "phasiological consciousness," with its ambience, the "*rituswelt.*"

The quantum jump entailed in the transition from the archaeanthropine to the paleoanthropine grade thus represented an advance in both the intellectual and the communicational potential available within the human community. The morphemic expression of intellectual images and social chorules meant that there had been a great advance in the ability to handle intentional and directional forms of information and that traditions, customs, and codes would henceforth be carried as transgenerationally transmitted conventions. And just as in the previous grade accommodation had been given the fillip of flexibility represented by its continued manifestation within the context of consouciation, now consouciation was to be given a further degree of openness by being incorporated within the framework of asseveration, the basis of theory.

Homo sapiens "aboriginalis" could thus be seen as living in an economic mode of big-game and herd-game hunting and gathering, to which mode each generation was accommodated but with the latitudinal awareness that there were noumenally envisaged alternatives governing the social arrangements to which each community in society was consoucially assimilated. And now, within this humanization grade, a higher degree of embeddedness, in the form of public knowledge, was acquired as communicated convention was attained. Asseveration, in the sense intended here, therefore, betokens a kind of Whorfian relatedness between economy, community, and koinonia, with phasiologically conveyed convention serving as the social-psychological cement. Production, imagination, and language expressed in new social relations of a political nature could then be modified in the context of an ethnocultural form of society, ethnicity in this case being the label for the classificatory (conventionally instituted) kinship arrangements which brought these three parameters into a new sociohistorical synthesis. The psychological counterpart of these new social arrangements would then be their synoptic internalization, communicative expression and ritual transmission in the form of a "phasiogram," and their ambience, in the *"rituswelt."*

Stage 8: The Mesoanthropine Grade of Human Consciousness

As the paleoanthropine grade of human evolution covers the humanization changes attending the onset, peak, and retreat of the Riss glacial (the Kanjeran pluvial in Africa) in the period between 300,000 and 150,000 years ago, so the mesoanthropine grade of human evolution covers the humanization changes attending the onset, peak, and retreat of the first phase of the Wurm glacial (the Gamblian pluvial in Africa) in the period between 150,000 and 50,000 years ago. Ecological changes of tectonic and climatic origin further compounded the natural selection pressures facing the human populations of Europe, Asia, and Africa; and migrations followed by genetic drift resulted in the formation of new geographical races. In paleontological terms, we are consequently dealing with Neanderthaloid forms in Eurasia, Shanidar and Palestinian forms in southwestern Asia, Rhodesioid forms in sub-Saharan Africa, Mapa forms in southern China, and Solo forms in Indonesia. Toward the end of this period, there also appear the Kanjeran forms of northeastern Africa, the Border Cave forms of southern Africa, the Skhul-

Tabun forms of the Middle East, and the Sarawak forms of southeast Asia; and we are well on our way to the fully sapient forms of the next grade.

Big-game hunting and herd hunting continued as before, but as the glaciers advanced from the north and descended from the higher altitudes of the Pyrenees, the Alps, the Carpathians, the Caucasus, and the Himalayas, pockets of Neanderthal populations were trapped and forced to spend tens of millenia in isolated accommodation. During this time, too, the Sahara became a desert barrier, and the populations to the south of it were likewise forced into a relatively long period of isolation. India, China, and southeast Asia were also isolated during extended parts of this mid-Pleistocene period. We therefore have, for the first time in history, the existence of populations in the major ecozones and climes of the eastern hemisphere; and the human oikoumene henceforth includes differentiated forms of acclination, consolidation, accommodation, consouciation and asseveration.

Such a distribution meant that ecozones previously left behind in times of glacial and dessicational stress had now perforce to be accommodated to. This put a premium on hardihood and led to selection in favor of gerontomorphic forms. It also resulted in improvements in approvisionation, arraimentation, habitation, pyrotention, and social organization in the cultural sphere. The availability of proboscidean ivory tusks and various forms of deer antler also resulted in new technological achievements. Most important, however, was the development of a wood/bone hammer stone for striking a wedge placed on the edge of a prepared core in order to remove very thin, yet strong, flakes. This is the Mousterian technique pioneered by some unknown Neanderthaloid population, and it gave the Neanderthaloids the means to make very effective spear heads and the ability to pierce the toughest animal hides with greater striking power, and from a greater distance, than ever before.

Particularly in the area north of the Eurasian mountain glacial line, the amalgamation of cooperating groups for big-game hunting became a year round activity, and this led to permanent clan and lineagelike ethnic political arrangements. It is even possible that the deployment of outlying populations was consciously organized so that there would be hospitality centers in whatever part of the range the hunters and gatherers might find themselves, and thus, extended-kinship structures of an attenuated nature like the tribe may have come into existence.

Developments such as these put a premium on cooperation and organization and probably resulted in new forms of ethnic socialization and assimilation. Courting and mating celebrations keyed, in all probability, to the spring foaling time of the great herds also created a noumenal bond between the mesoanthropines and the flora and fauna which were basic to their survival. Transgenerational and transrange mutuality thus became firmly established.

As for the means of production, tools and weapons of bone supplemented those of wood and stone; and along with the Mousterian technique, the first backed blades and burins and the first composite tools in the form of attachable projectile points were invented. The making of clothes with fastenings of bone or wood further attests to the advances being made, as does the improvement in the construction of shelter. Facilities for transport and storage also appear in the archaeological record of this period. Fire seems to have been under better control, and possibly towards the end of this stage pyrofaction took the place of pyrotention.

All this would be part of the lavorological or workaday consciousness of each growing child, but it would receive an amplified fillip from the assimilation processes of socialization, familiarization, and transgenerational genealization and ethnocization within which the accommodation, consouciation, and asseveration processes had become ensconced. Familiarity with the environment, the group's economic domain, and the social milieu would then lead to the acquisition of discriminatory knowledge relevant to what foods were safely edible, what remedies were suitable for what ailments, and what raw materials could be fashioned into what utilities. All peoples have some culinary and medicinal ethnoscience of their own, and even without the ability to name the various specimens being used, the selection principles for the proper discrimination of what was useful and what was harmful were already being learned and passed on. There is evidence, too, of trepanning, limb surgery, dental extraction, and other forms of medical practice. In some syncretic way, these activities then became enmeshed with the endogamous and exogamous rules of marriage, conjugation, and classificatory kinship that were operative, and the whole package of tradition was asseverationally passed on to the next generation by rites of passage and other forms of accoutumation and codification.

In dybological terms, both inanimate and animate, human and nonhuman, but personified, objects and forces were in some instances endowed with animate properties, protean strengths, malevolent injuring propensities, and talismanic protecting powers, or credited with possession by a dybbuk (an indwelling spirit taking possession of an individual or natural object). By the same token, aesthetic, ethical, and spiritual nuances also began to register as fixations and pellucid expressions. The elements of the cosmos and the relations inherent in social communication all became intertwined with various forms of ceremonial ritual, and these abutted the more operationally functional aspects of the cultural compulsive.

The burial of the dead began to be practiced; in some cases, this was accompanied by strewing the bodies with flowers, coloring them with red ocher, ringing them with horns, leaving chunks of meat in the grave, flexing all the bodies in a particular body pose, and the introduction of other sepulchral conventions. Some of the burials consisted of headless bodies, and others suggest some form of ritual cannibalism; there is even evidence of what might be taken as a bear cult analogous possibly to that practiced by some of the Siberian peoples in propitiation for dispossessing the bear from his hibernal cave. It is also likely that fire as a kind of shaping magic took hold of the Neanderthal's imagination. The noumenal and the ceremonial, the social and the phenomenal, and the technical and the cosmic were all conjoined, and a new form of dybological expression was receiving both inner and outer expression in the emergent form of consciousness of this humanization grade. Particular forms of "identification" were thus beginning to take noumenal shape even among communities with similar modes of production.

In the field of asseveration as well there are significant advances in this grade. Bunak (1959, p. 319) refers to it as "the second early-speech stage" and suggests that it included the mastering of dental, labial-dental, and other articulations made with the forepart of the oral cavity. These were attached to a much wider ethnoscience repertoire relating to different states of nature, degrees of warmth and cold, arctic day and night conditions, male and female usages, the expanded tool kit made of stone, wood, bone, antler, and other animal and plant by-products, the methods of preparing skins for clothing, the funerary complex, the weaponry complex (spearhead, bolas, clubs, handaxes) the making of fire, the preparation of food, the rearing of children, the maintenance of the kinship structure, and whatever else had become sufficiently fixed to be passed on as convention from one generation to the next. This included the valorization of the padules attendant on the work routines, the moralization of the familiar chorules tied to the group's traditional forms of cooperation and genealogical identification, and the virtualization of intermember relationships by the rites of passage which created a form of emotion-laden work, kinship, and hygiene as the means whereby significant information, values, mores, and imculturated meanings were communicated both collaterally and lineally and impressed as desirable ethnic virtues. Then "praxis," as the unity of practice, theory, and politics, began to supercede industry.

The articulation of experience, derived from external natural *signs* and biocenotically conditioned *signals*, was integrated with the information conveyed by internally originating *symptoms* and intentionally conveyed *symbols*. More numerous and differentiated words and sentences, *syntagms*, with a greater polysemantic linkage of the past, present, and future, were also developed and transmitted; and more of the group's cultural repertoire, in the form of *semiotics*, became subject to conscious signification and transgenerational transmission and identificatory initiation. I have, therefore, designated the psychic development of this stage as being characterized by the "mimetological consciousness," its integrated description as being represented by a "mimetogram," and its ambience, by the *"prachtwelt."*

Stage 9: The Neoanthropine Grade of Human Consciousness

Fossil forms from some 40–50 thousand years ago, classified by paleontologists as those of *Homo sapiens sapiens*, have been found in the Middle East and in other parts of Europe, Asia, and Africa as well. Their origins are unclear, but some fossil remains found in Israel (Tabun, Skhul) would appear to represent admixtures of neanderthaloid and sapient physical features. Some in Rhodesia (Broken Hill) have, in a parallel way, a number of modern and Rhodesioid features; and there are reported finds in China showing similar combinations. Some of the earliest New World and Australian finds, dating back 35,000 years, may also be the products of such unions. Taking, for the present, the tricontinental hub in the Middle East as the probable center of widest demographic combination, it is possible to trace migrations from that source along the North African and East African coastal areas, along the European Mediterranean and Transmontane areas, and eastward into southern and central Asia. Gradually, by displacement, reliction, absorption, and intermarriage, modern man, in all his racial variants, came to occupy the earth. By the end of the Pleistocene, the oikoumene included all of the continents.

As sustentation specialization according to the possibilities of each ecozone had already taken place in the previous grade, the period between 50,000 and 15,000 B.P. witnessed the intensification of the processes of approvisionation. There was a change also in the socioeconomic mode from hunting and gathering to food collecting. This meant that practically everything that was edible was being eaten, such that, where feasible, fishing, fowling, shellfish collecting, and sea mammal hunting came to supplement the food derived from herd hunting and gathering. With the onset of the second Wurm interstadial, southern France was to be engulfed once more by arctic conditions, but with its tundra herds as the core of its provisions, it was a veritable Garden of Eden in terms of food.

The changes in the ecological balance were also accompanied by changes in social organization, and sociologically speaking, totemistic forms of organization (confederacies) came into existence in those parts of the earth where cooperation and mutual aid between a number of specialized food-collecting communities (tribes) were institutionalized. Each totem, in general, was symbolically linked to some food source, and the totality of the totems represented the totality of the approvisionation arrangements in effect in a given territory as well as the integrated political organization necessary to perpetuate the confederacy living in it. The corroboree, as instituted among the Australian aboriginal tribes, is probably indicative of the kind of celebration that originated during this period. It entails the exchange of gifts, mates, pledges of solidarity, and information about the food collecting possibilities of the territory, and it becomes the occasion for examining the past year's movements and projecting the next year's activities. The techniques of settlement archaeology are now contributing a great deal to our understanding of the social relations of this period.

The neoanthropine grade of human consciousness, then, resulted in the appearance of the ninth form of embeddedness to become so transculturally fixed as to constitute a cultural universal. Here, we are consequently dealing with the changes in psychic makeup that resulted from asseverative encephalization, competence and performance becoming integral parts of *Homo sapiens sapiens's* further evolution. With this stage, it is clear that mankind achieved a fully articulated form of speech, and differentiation by the sonority of sounds and by the way they were pronounced came to characterize the speech of all sapient populations; intonation, with variation in pitch, force, intensity and duration, became the basis of conveying meaning through culturally formulated semiotics. Mentally, this was paralleled by the ability to set the subject and its action apart in the mind and to establish what we now refer to as the subject–predicate relationship. The *syntagm*, or composite reality-relating sentence, then capped the semasiological repertoire. It is, however, not yet clear at what point the "paradigm" in which words—parts of speech—carrying the delineative loading of nomenalized concepts in all of their declensional and conjugational inflections were also worked into the language. The presence of composite tools does suggest, however, that the human species was developing a new kind of cognitive capacity and was learning how to convert signals into symbols with which to cope with changing social reality. We can therefore speak of the "cenemological consciousness" and its ambience, the *"sprichwelt."*

With artistic media, it also became possible for human beings to represent reality peremptorily; with magical media, it was possible to command reality imperatively; and with instrumental media, it was possible for human beings to test reality interrogatively. These supplemented the older forms of declarative information-conveying communication and exclamatory condition-reflecting communication; and the language took on a new compound of emotional, phatic, aesthetic, voluntaristic, noumenal, and phenomenally coded expression. Vernaculars were in the making; and they could henceforth be used for the virtualization of the wish-fulfilling psyching that the ethnicity under consideration was trying to bring under control. Adaptive and acclinative comportment, assuretative consolidation, accommodative collaboration, and assimilative consouciation were all compounded within the consciousness of asseverative social convention, and this new psychosocial synthesis was reflected in each individual's "cenemogram" of his or her culture's unity and expressed in each koinonia's linguistically articulated *"sprichwelt."*

The human *"sprichwelt"* is, therefore, the transcendant resolution by fully sapient men and women of the prior psychic synthesis of the *auswelt–umwelt–mitwelt–merkwelt–bittewelt–gangwelt–tatwelt–werkwelt–in nerwelt–rituswelt–prachtwelt* already encephalized. It represents the counterpart in language and consciousness of the tool to make tools; and in its syntagmatic and paradigmatic developments (distributional combinations [syntactics], significational combinations [semantics] and referential combinations [pragmatics]), it became the universal propaedeutic common to all linguistically bonded communities. In addition to the five features previously listed, human psychic competence henceforth acquired the neuropsychological substrate for the following forms of articulation (Wescott, 1970, p. 78).

1. Stratification, or simultaneous occurrence of signals on two different levels—a higher level, containing words and phrases which have referential meaning, and a lower level, containing sounds or letters which lack such meaning but help distinguish the words and phrases that have it
2. Dichotomy, or divisibility of most utterances into a subject, which presents a topic, and a predicate, which comments on that topic
3. Pantopicality, or capacity to transmit messages on any subject imaginable
4. Lengthlessness, or capacity to extend discourse indefinitely
5. Prevarication, or capacity deliberately to transmit false information
6. Soliloquism, or the tendency to talk to oneself (usually inaudibly or invisibly) and thereby to solve problems without having to consult others
7. Deuterism, or the ability to transmit signals which refer only to other signals and hence to "talk about talking"
8. Digitality, or the all-or-none discreteness of low-level signals, such as sounds or letters
9. Cenemism, or utilization of signals which, while not referential themselves, help comprise longer signals which are referential
10. Grammaticality, or obligatory ordering of signals (such that a change in order may lead to a disruption of the message)
11. Interrogation, or use of a specific type of signal for the solicitation of information
12. Negation, or use of a specific type of signal for the denial of a concurrent assertion

Furthermore, with this grade of cenemological humanization, we also attain the baseline common to all surviving holoanthropine peoples;

Table 2. The Encephalization of the Human Consciousness

Axiological developments	Epistemological developments	Ontological developments
1. Preanthropine (Dryopithecine) acclination	Herbivoration, proxemiation, imagos	The ethological life-style
2. Alloanthropine (Ramapithecine) assuretation	Omnivoration, kinesiation, mands	The kinesiological life-style
3. Paraanthropine (Ngororapithecine) coordination	Open-ground feeding, exploration, transportation, eidola	The eidological life-style
4. Protoanthropine (Australopithecine) cooperation	Scavenging, predation, manipulation, implementation, icons, eikes	The eicological life-style
5. Eoanthropine (*Homo habilis*, habiline) accommodation	Small- to medium-game hunting and gathering, instrumentation, elaboration, artifaction, artifacts	The lavorological life-style
6. Archaeanthropine (*Homo erectus*, pithecanthropine) consouciation	Medium- to big-game hunting and gathering, stylization, imagination, artisanation, designs	The dybological life-style
7. Paleoanthropine (*Homo sapiens "aboriginalis"*) asseveration	Big-game and herd hunting and gathering, objectivation, notions, visions	The phasiological life-style
8. Mesoanthropine (*Homo sapiens "regionalis"*, neand-rhod-solo-etc.) hygenation	Specialized ecozone hunting and gathering, traditional transmission, rituals	The mimetological life-style
9. Neoanthropine (*Homo sapiens sapiens*, extinct) glossiation	Specialized food collecting, articulation, arts	The cenemological life-style

Table 2 represents the encephalization of the human consciousness common to all subsequently evolving human demes.

Stage 10: The Holoanthropine Grade of Human Consciousness

The retreat of the third Wurm glacial and the termination of the Gamblian pluvial mark the end of the Pleistocene epoch and the beginning of the Holocene (recent) geological epoch. During the period from about 20,000 to 13,000 years ago, the Eurasian climate was arctic, with tundra and snow-covered plains lying between the glaciers. During these centuries, Atlantic cyclones swept across northern Africa and southwestern Asia with the result that the Saharan, Arabian and Iranian areas that are desert today were well-watered grassy plains (Turner, 1941). Only a contracted area to the south of these plains was desert, and to the south of this area, in the wake of the increased amount of rainfall, tropical forests and jungles covered a large extent of central and south Africa. North and South America were also populated during this period. Some 13,000–15,000 years ago, then, we are at the point in history where we are dealing with the ancestors of all the peoples on the earth today; and in order to bring out this global cultural commonality, all of the inhabitants of the oikoumene will be designated as living by the holoanthropine grade of human consciousness.

The geological unity of this epoch is, however, too gross for our purposes; it has been periodized by historians in a number of different ways. In this context and in line with the historical principles being used here, it will be treated in terms of a sequence of nine emergent socioeconomic modes of civilization. Nine concomitant enconscientation paragons will also be adduced, each of which has entailed and will entail some new value being incorporated in the shaping of human consciousness. Table 3 summarizes these developments.

The delineation of the past 15,000 years by some common denominator is obviously a difficult task, but I would like to try out the transcultural praxialization–jeshuralization process for historical size and suggest that the nine phases of the transfiguration process listed in Table 3 are, by the ninth phase, converging on an emerging "jeshurogram" in which enconscientation will be giving way to conscientization as the dominant characterization of the human psyche, in ways analogous to the prior incorporation of encephalization in the apeiron of

Table 3. Phases in the Transfiguration of the Holoanthropine Grade of Human Consciousness

1. Upper Paleolithic sociocultural modes of civilization	Represented by post-Wurm/Gamblian *Homo sapiens sapiens* koinonia, less than 15,000 years old (e.g., the Azilian cultural succession), the praxeological consciousness
2. Mesolithic sociocultural modes of civilization	Represented by relocating migrant koinonia, less than 13,000 years old (e.g., the Natufian cultural succession), the eponymological consciousness
3. Neolithic sociocultural modes of civilization	Represented by domesticating and cultivating koinonia, less than 11,000 years old (e.g., the Jarmo cultural succession), the sacerdological consciousness
4. Chalcolithic sociocultural modes of civilization	Represented by metallurgically based, conquering social formations, less than 7,500 years old (e.g., the Halafian cultural succession), the polemological consciousness
5. Bronze Age sociocultural modes of civilization	Represented by river valley hydraulic integrating social formations, less than 5,700 years old (e.g., the Sumerian cultural succession), the suzerological consciousness
6. Iron Age sociocultural modes of civilization	Represented by iron tool, land-clearing social formations, less than 3,800 years old (e.g., the Hellenic cultural succession), the juridological consciousness
7. Industrial Age A sociocultural modes of civilization (capitalist subphases I–VII)	Represented by steel-technology-powered, science-guided social formations, from about 1450 C.E. on (e.g., the Italian cultural succession), the ideological consciousness
8. Industrial Age B sociocultural modes of civilization (socialist subphases III–VII)	Represented by hydroelectric powered, "praxis"-guided social formations, from 1917 C.E. on (e.g., the Soviet cultural succession), the anthropological consciousness
9. Industrial Age C sociocultural modes of civilization (jeshuralist subphases V–VII)	Represented by the clean-flow-powered, "chessed" guided social formations, from 2075(?) on, locale unknown, the jeshurological consciousness

enconscientation. However, when conscientation begins to depend more and more on conscientization, the shaping of human consciousness is increasingly the result of the internalization of reflective practice (technology), critical theory (axiology), and universally normative politics (praxeology) as the basis of the newly constituted cultural compulsive.

All of the preceding is thus premised on the hypothesis that one of the long-term secular trends of human history is the institutionalization of *jeshurological criteriologies* (chassidegms) which provide the humanization norms for the institutionalization of *praxeological criteriologies* (apothegms). These in turn provide the legitimization norm for the institutionalization of particular *methodological criteriologies* (paradigms), which in turn provide the warrantability norms for the *apeirological criteriologies* (apeiregms) in which human beings work out their historical problematic. There are also teleonomic, synergetic, and cybernetic feedback loops linking these four criteriologies. And it goes without saying that there are a great many hidden modifications at issue from the elements, structures, processes, and modulations at work within the cosmosphere–geosphere–biosphere grounding conditions for the emergence of the cenotosphere–ecosphere–anthroposphere background for the human creation of the econosphere–affinosphere–semasiosphere–noemosphere–cenemosphere–praxeosphere complex now operating on the human psyche at the various consciousness levels of influence. Finally, the projection that is being hypothesized in this chapter is one to the effect that the changing nature of consciousness resulting from the enconscientation–conscientization transfiguration can be charted in the course of the seven subphases of cultural modification that make up the capitalist–socialist–jeshuralist industrial ages.

In ways not yet understood, it is also characteristic of the human neocortical and nervous system organization to catch up in psychological expression with the outcomes in culture stemming from the transgenerationally socially institutionalized padules and chorules made flexibly accessible to humanity by the encephalization–enconscientation–conscientization augmentations that constitute the record of human history. Following Rosenzweig's work on learning (Rosenzweig & Bennett, 1976) to the effect that intelligent problem solving in chicks can be registered in recordings made of what goes on in their forebrains whereas in chicks engaged in routine species-specific activities there is no distinctive record in the encephalogram, we can also make a case for the cumulative effect of human creative activity. The innovators in the human imculturation transformation can thus, in a certain sense, alter the synaptic-dendritic patterns at work in the innovators' brains; and if these protagonists survive better in the natural–social–sexual–cultural selection problematic, then cumulatively the course of human evolution is, in a *de facto* sense, being teleologically and then teleonomically altered. Anthropologists can already point to groups and individuals who can direct the contents of their own dreaming, raise their incidence of psionic susceptibility, control their body temperatures, and endure degrees of pain and pressure which were once considered fatal. The evidence from the study of aphasia also carries the implication that inverse speech ontogeny, such as (1) names before technical terms, (2) technical terms before common terms, (3) connectives before contentives, (4) fricatives before frictionless continuants, (5) linguals before nasals, (6) continuants before stops, (7) stops before vowels, (8) vowels before prosodics, and (9) phonemes before syllables (Wescott, 1967), can offer possible clues as to the actual order of semasiological and glossal encephalization.

The cenemological consciousness, which is the baseline for all subsequent holoanthropine-grade psychic developments, is, therefore, itself compounded of unevenly integrated glossal elements derived from the phasiological, semasiological, mimetological, and newly emergent cenomological phases of enconscientation. We thus have to recognize that the glossal design features, which Chomsky (1968) and Lenneberg (1967) have dealt with under the heading of "the biological foundations of language," only became such after the process of encephalization had occurred. Then, of course, they were subject to dialectical modification in historical time and thus became genetically incorporated in later hereditary facilitation. This means that between 300,000 and 15,000 years ago (the period of sapient evolution prior to the present grade) these linguistic features were, first of all, the outcomes of sociocultural improvements in communication that, along with ongoing parallel ameliorations in consouciological or aiutological (succor, support, and defense) relations, technological (standardized forms of elaboration) relations, and noumenological (imaginative projections of variations on empirical reality) relations, became incorporated into the cultural compulsion under which successive millenia of the genus *Homo* have continued to live. Effective social conduct and comportment, having thus been embedded in the culturally modifiable social milieus dealt with in this chapter as being successively characterized by the processes of collaboration, accoutumation, conveniation, and cenemiation, had thus to be socially instituted before they could become prevailing cultural compulsive of the given social formations.

Societies with the forms of institutions which gave them a survival advantage therefore endured, and in them the padules and chorules of the ongoing lifeways became the bases of the sensorimotor psychic habits which subsequent encephalization eventually registered through psychobiological expression. And since the motor regulatory neurons in the brain spark generalized movements of the bodily maintained segments before the adjustive control functions of the brain have established neural connections with them, there is a polygenerational hereditary delay between their padulated socialization and familiarization, their imculturation and enculturation, and their encephalization within a particular human lineage. Only after a cycle of this whole process has been effected, by which time a new humanization grade is in the course of coming into existence, is it possible to speak of performance as reflecting the biological potential consequently built in as emergent species-specific competence.

It is necessary, moreover, to remember that these linguistic and other putative cultural universals were the outcomes of a continuing saltationally padulated and chorulated accommodation–consouciation–asseveration–articulation process before they also came to be maintained as the outcomes of a continuing evolutionary process. Each of the social modes listed in Table 3 therefore represents new sociocultural modifications which, in some later historical phase, took on the characteristics of appearing as encephalized or psychoneurologically supported features of *Homo sapiens sapiens's* psychic makeup. The differential cultural incidence of various forms of aphasia, agraphia, agnosia, apraxia, and sexual and ethnic lateralization would thus appear to be one form of prima facie evidence in support of the hypothesis being presented here.

With the sociohistorical roots of competence established, we can return once again to the pandemic historical process jeshuralization, which is being brought into use as the neologism for the synoptic integrations that occurred within the holoantropine grade of enconscientation. In its subsumptions, it includes the humanizationally changing modal, increasingly reflexive, deontologically realizable, regulative, cognitive, and performative functions of life in society. But it does so at the level of conscious chassidology, apotheology, praxeology, and apeirology, so that by means of this form of consciousness the growing potential of the human species can be deliberately and purposefully realized. Jeshuralization thus represents the process of holoanthropine humanization whereby the social transvaluation of human consensus into human communion occurs. This results in the further transculturation of human consciousness and the transformation of human nature from its characteristic modal form in the terminal Upper Paleolithic sociocultural formations to the new transfigured form which may be characteristic of our descendants in the sociocultural modes of the Third Industrial Age. Table 4 consequently summarizes the changes in the nature of the human

Table 4. The Transculturation of the Human Consciousness

Axiological/jeshurological modifications	Epistemological/praxeological modifications	Ontological/apeirological modifications
1. Upper Paleolithic corroborization	Food collecting–food lardering ethnoscience	The totemological life-style
2. Mesolithic eponymization	Incipient domestication/ cultivation mythologies	The nomadological life-style
3. Neolithic sacralization	Domestication and cultivation theogonies	The choreological life-style
4. Chalcolithic hierarchization	Subjugation and surplus appropriation theurgies	The polemological life-style
5. Bronze Age legitimization	Hydraulic irrigation theomachies and theosophies	The suzerological life-style
6. Iron Age axialization	Hard-soil plow culture metaphysical philosophies and theologies	The diasporological life-style
7. Industrial Age A capitalization	Capitalist paradigmatic technologies and sciences	The patriological life-style
8. Industrial Age B collectivization	Socialist apothegmatic technologies and sciences	The comitological life-style
9. Industrial Age C ecumenization	Jeshuralist chassidegmatic technologies and sciences	The ecumenological life-style

man psyche that have come into being, and are in the process of coming into being, in the course of the last 50,000 years; it represents the preliminary unpacking of the anthropological foundations of a humane psychology.

References

Appley, M. D. (Ed.). *Adaptation—Level theory*. New York: Academic Press, 1971.

Barker, R. C. *Ecological psychology: Concepts and methods for studying the environment of human behavior*. Stanford: Stanford University Press, 1968.

Bartholemew, G. A., Jr., & Birdsell, J. B. Ecology and the protohominids. *American Anthropologist*, 1953, *55*, 481–498.

Bicchieri, M. G. (Ed.). *Hunters and gatherers today*. New York: Holt, Rinehart, & Winston, 1972.

Birdwhistell, R. L. Kinesics and context—Essays in body motion and communication. Philadelphia: University of Pennsylvania Press, 1970.

Bishop, W. W., & Miller, J. P. (Eds.). *Calibration of hominid evolution*. Edinburgh: Scottish Academic Press, 1972.

Black, D. R., de Chardin, T., Young, C. C., & Pei, W. C. *Fossil man in China: The Choukoutien cave deposits, with a synopsis of our present knowledge*. Mem. Geological Survey of China, Paleontologia sinica, Series A., No. 11, 1933.

Brace, C. L., & Korn, N. *Atlas of fossil man* (2nd ed.). New York: Holt, Rinehart, & Winston, 1971.

Brandt, R. M. *Studying behavior in natural settings*. New York: Holt, Rinehart, & Winston, 1972.

Bunak, V. V. Present state of "The problem of the origin of speech and the early stages of its evolution." *The Journal of World History*, 1959, *5*(2), 310–324.

Chomsky, N. *Language and mind*. New York: Harcourt, Brace, & World, 1968.

Clark, W. E. Le Gros. *The fossil evidence for human evolution* (3rd ed., revised and enlarged by B. G. Campbell). Chicago: University of Chicago Press, 1978.

Coon, C. S. *The hunting people*. Boston: Little, Brown, 1971.

Count, E. W. *Being and becoming human*. New York: Van Nostrand, 1973.

Dart, R. A. *The osteodontokeratic culture of Australopithecus Prometheus*. Pretoria, Transvaal Museum Memoir No. 10., 1957.

Dewey, J. *Human nature and conduct*. New York: Modern Library, 1930.

Diels, H. [*Ancilla to the pre Socratic philosophers*] (K. Freeman, trans.). Oxford, Eng.: Basil Blackwell, 1952. (Originally published, 1934–1937.)

Dolhinow, P. (Ed.). *Primate patterns*. New York: Holt, Rinehart, & Winston, 1972.

Engels, F. *Dialectics of nature*. Moscow: Moscow Foreign Languages Publishing House, 1954. (Originally published, 1878.)

Holloway, R. L., Jr. Culture: A human domain. *Current Anthropology*, 1969, *10*, 395–412.

Howell, F. C., & Bourliere, F. (Eds.). *African ecology and human evolution*. Chicago: Aldine, 1966.

Jolly, A. *Lemur behavior: A Madagascar field study*. Chicago: University of Chicago Press, 1967.

Jolly, A. *The evolution of primate behavior*. New York: Macmillan, 1972.

Jolly, C. J. The seed eaters: A new model of hominid differentiation. *Man*. (London, New Series), 1970, *5*, 5–26.

Koestler, A., & Smythies, J. R. *Beyond reductionism: New perspectives in the life sciences*. New York: Macmillan, 1969.

Kummer, H. *Primate societies*. Chicago: Aldine, 1971.

Landers, R. R. *Man's place in the dybosphere*. Englewood Cliffs, N.J.: Prentice-Hall, 1966.

Lee, R. B., & DeVore, I. (Eds.). *Man the hunter*. Chicago: Aldine, 1968.

Lenneberg, E. H. *Biological foundations of language*. New York: Wiley, 1967.

Marx, K. [*Foundations of the critique of political economy (rough draft)*] (M. Nicolaus, trans.). Harmondsworth: Penguin Books, 1973. (Originally published, 1858.)

Napier, J. R. Studies of the hands of living primates. *Proceedings of the Zoological Society of London*, 1960, *134*, 647–657.

Noback, C. R., & Moskowitz, N. Structural and functional correlates of encephalization in the primate brain. *Annals of the New York Academy of Sciences*, 1962, *102*, 210–218.

Razran, G. *Mind in evolution: An east-west synthesis of learned behavior and cognition*. Boston: Houghton Mifflin, 1971.

Ribeiro, D. The culture-historical configurations of the American peoples. *Current Anthropology*, 1970, *11*, 403–434.

Rosenzweig, M. R., & Bennett, E. L. *Neural mechanisms of learning and memory*. Cambridge, Mass.: M.I.T. Press, 1976.

Schaller, G. B. *The mountain gorilla—Ecology and behavior*. Chicago: University of Chicago Press, 1965.

Schwerdtfeger, F. *Okologie der tiere: Autokologie, demokologie, synokologie* (3 vols.). Hamburg: P. Parey, 1963, 1968, 1977.

Simons, E. L. *Primate evolution*. New York: Macmillan, 1972.

Simpson, G. G. *Life of the past*. New Haven: Yale University Press, 1953.

Skinner, B. F. *About behaviorism*. New York: Random House, 1974.

Spuhler, J. N., Gerard, R. W., Washburn, S. L., Hockett, C. F., Harlow, H. F., & Sahlins, M. D. (Eds.). *The evolution of man's capacity for culture*. Detroit: Wayne State University Press, 1959.

Stagner, R. Introduction to Section V (Social psychology and personality). In M. H. Appley (Ed.), *Adaptation-level theory: A symposium*. New York: Academic Press, 1971.

Turner, R. E. *The great cultural traditions: The foundations of civilization* (2 vols.). New York: McGraw-Hill, 1941.

van Lawick-Goodall, J. *My friends, the wild chimpanzees*. Washington, D. C.: National Geographic Society, 1967.

van Riet Lowe, C. The Kafuan culture. In J. D. Clark (Ed.), *Third pan-African congress on prehistory*. London: Chatto & Windus, 1957.

Wescott, R. W. *The divine animal: An exploration of human potentiality*. New York: Funk & Wagnalls, 1969.

Wescott, R. W. Man without 'speech.' Speculations on hominid protoculture. *Anthropological Journal of Canada*, 1970, *8*(2), 27–32.

Willems, E. P., & Raush, H. L. (Eds.). *Naturalistic viewpoints in psychological research*. New York: Holt, Rinehart, & Winston, 1969.

Additional Readings

Ackerman, R. *The philosophy of science*. New York: Pegasus.

Adam, G. (Ed.). *Biology of memory*. New York: Plenum Press, 1971.

Alsbert, P. *In quest of man*. New York: Pergamon Press, 1970.

Altman, J. *Organic foundations of animal behavior.* New York: Holt, Rinehart, & Winston, 1966.

Altmann, S. A. *Social communication among primates.* Chicago: The University of Chicago Press, 1965.

Altmann, S. A., & Altmann, J. *Baboon ecology: African field research.* Basel: S. Karger, 1970.

Amosov, N. M. *Modeling of thinking and the mind.* (L. Finegold, trans.). New York: Spartan Books, 1967.

Arbib, M. A. *The metaphorical brain.* New York: Academic Press, 1971.

Arieti, S. *The will to be human.* New York: Quadrangle Books, 1972.

Armstrong, D. M. *A materialistic theory of mind.* London: Routledge, 1968.

Aronson, L. R., *et al.* (Eds.). *Development and evolution of behavior—Essays in memory of T. C. Schneirla.* San Francisco: W. H. Freeman, 1970.

Ashby, W. R. *Design for a brain.* New York: John Wiley, 1960.

Attinger, E. O. (Ed.). *Global systems dynamics.* Basel: S. Karger, 1970.

Ayala, F. J., & Dobzhansky, T. C. *Studies in the philosophy of biology.* London: Macmillan, 1974.

Bartley, S. H. *The human organism as a person.* Philadelphia: Chilton Book Co., 1967.

Bateson, G. *Steps to an ecology of mind.* New York: Ballantine Books, 1972.

Bateson, G. *Mind and nature.* New York: E. P. Dutton, 1979.

Becker, E. *The revolution of psychiatry.* New York: The Free Press, 1964.

Bellairs, R., & Gray, E. G. (Eds.). *Essays on the nervous system.* Oxford: Clarendon Press, 1974.

Bernstein, B. *Class codes and control.* St. Albans: Paladin, 1973.

Birdsell, J. B. *Human evolution: An introduction to the new physical anthropology* (2nd ed.). Chicago: Rand McNally College Publications, 1975.

Blinkov, S. M., & Glezer, I. I. *The human brain in figures and tables.* New York: Plenum Press, 1968.

Brace, C. L., & Metress, J. (Eds.). *Man in evolutionary perspective.* New York: John Wiley, 1973.

Braidwood, R. J. *Prehistoric men* (8th ed.). Glenview, Ill.: Scott Foresman & Co., 1975.

Broadbent, D. E. *Decision and stress.* New York: Academic Press, 1971.

Burns, B. DeLisle. *The uncertain nervous system.* London: Edward Arnold Publishers, 1968.

Buss, A. H., & Plomin, R. *A temperament theory of personality development.* New York: John Wiley, 1975.

Butzer, K. W. *Environment and archeology: An ecological approach to prehistory* (2nd ed.). Chicago: Aldine Press, 1971.

Calder, N. *The mind of man.* London: British Broadcasting Corporation, 1970.

Callot, E. *Histoire de la philosophie biologique par les textes.* Paris: Editions Doin, 1966.

Campbell, B. G. *Human evolution (2nd. ed.). Chicago: Aldine Press, 1974.*

Campbell, B. (Ed.). *Sexual selection and the descent of man, 1871–1971.* Chicago: Aldine Publishing Co., 1972.

Carpenter, C. R. (Ed.). *Behavioral regulators of behavior in primates.* Lewisburg: Bucknell University Press, 1973.

Chance, M. R. A., & Jolly, C. J. *Social groups of monkeys, apes and men.* London: Jonathan Cape, 1970.

Chiarelli, A. B. *Perspectives in primate biology.* New York: Plenum Press, 1974.

Chisholm, B. *Can people learn to learn? New York: Harper Brothers Publishers, 1958.*

Clark, J. D. *The prehistory of Africa.* New York: Praeger Publishers, 1970.

Clarke, E., & Dewhurst, K. *An illustrated history of brain function.* Oxford: Sandford Publications, 1972.

Cole, M., & Scribner, S. *Culture and thought.* New York: John Wiley & Sons, Inc., 1974.

Collins, R. *Conflict sociology*. New York: Academic Press, 1975.
Corning, W. C., & Balaban, M. *The mind: Biological approaches to its functions*. New York: Interscience Publishers, 1968.
Dahlberg, A. A. (Ed.). *Dental morphology and evolution*. Chicago: The University of Chicago Press, 1973.
Dansereau, P. *Biogeography: An ecological perspective*. New York: The Ronald Press Co., 1957.
Darley, F. L. (Ed.). *Brain mechanisms underlying speech and language*. New York: Grune and Stratton, 1967.
Day, M. H. *Guide to fossil man*. London: Cassell, 1965.
Day, M. H. (Ed.). *Human evolution*. London: Taylor & Francis, Ltd., 1973.
Deese, J. *The structure of associations in language and thought*. Baltimore: The Johns Hopkins University Press, 1965.
Dennett, D. C. *Content and consciousness*. London: Routledge & Kegan Paul, 1969.
De Vore, I. *Primate behavior*. New York: Holt, Rinehart, & Winston, 1965.
Dewsbury, D. A., & Rethlingshafer, D. A. *Comparative psychology*. New York: McGraw-Hill, 1973.
Dimond, S. J. *The double brain*. Edinburgh: Churchill Livingstone, 1972.
Dimond, S. J. *The social behaviour of animals*. London: B. T. Batsford, Ltd., 1970.
Dobhzhansky, T. G. *Genetics of the evolutionary process. New York: Columbia University Press, 1970.*
Eccles, J. C. *Brain and conscious experience*. New York: Springer-Verlag, 1966.
Ebling, F. J., & Heath, G. W. (Eds.). *The future of man*. London: Academic Press, 1972.
Escalona, S. K. *The roots of individuality*. Chicago: Aldine Publishing Co., 1968.
Essor, A. H. (Ed.). *Behavior and environment*. New York: Plenum Press, 1971.
Etkin, W. Social Behavior and the evolution of man's mental faculties. *American Naturalist, 1954,* **88,** *129–143.*
Etkin, W. Social behavioral factors in the emergence of man. *Human Biology*, 1963, *35*, 299–310.
Fair, C. M. *The physical foundations of the psyche*. Middletown: Wesleyan University Press, 1963.
Fletcher, R. *Human needs and social order*. London: Michael Joseph, 1965.
Folia Primatologica. *International Journal of Primatology*, 1951–1975, *Vols. 1–24.*
Freeman, K. *The pre Socratic philosophers (3rd. ed.). Oxford: Blackwell, 1953.*
Furth, H. G. *Piaget and Knowledge*. Englewood Cliffs, N.J.: Prentice-Hall, 1969.
Garn, S. M. (Ed.). *Culture and the direction of human evolution*. Detroit: Wayne State University Press, 1964.
Gavan, J. A. (Ed.). *The non-human primates and human evolution*. Detroit: Wayne University Press, 1955.
Genoves, S. T. Yearbook of Physical Anthropology, 1967. Cordoba (Mexico). *The American Association of Physical Anthropologists*, 1969, *15*.
Gersuni, G. V. (Ed.). *Sensory processes at the neuronal and behavioral levels*. New York: Academic Press, 1971.
Gibson, J. J. *The senses considered as perceptual systems*. Boston: Houghton Mifflin Co., 1966.
Giere, R. N., & Westfall, R. S. *Foundations of scientific method: The nineteenth century*. Bloomington, Indiana: Indiana University Press, 1973.
Gilbert, J. H. *Speech and cortical functioning*. New York: Academic Press, 1972.
Glaser, E. M. *The physiological basis of habituation*. Oxford: Oxford University Press, 1966.
Glick, T. F. *The comparative reception of Darwinism*. Austin: University of Texas Press, 1972.
Goslin, D. A. *Handbook of socialization theory and research*. Chicago: Rand, McNally & Co., 1969.

Greenberg, J. H. *Universals of language*. Cambridge: The M.I.T. Press, 1963.
Grene, M. *Approaches to a philosophical biology*. New York: Basic Books Inc., 1968.
Gurwitsch, A. *The field of consciousness*. Pittsburgh: Duquesne University Press, 1964.
Hafey, E. S. E. *The behaviour of domestic animals*. London: Bailliere, Tindall, & Cox, 1962.
Hawkes, J. P. *Prehistory: History of mankind - Cultural and scientific development*, Vol. 1, Part I *(UNESCO)*. New York: Mentor Books, 1965.
Hebb, D. O. *The organization of behavior*. New York: John Wiley, 1949.
Hecht, M. K., & Steere, W. C. (Eds.). *Essays in evolution and genetics in honor of Theodosius Dobzhansky*. New York: Appleton-Century-Crofts, 1970.
Helson, H. *Adaptation–Level theory*. New York: Harper & Row, 1964.
Herrick, C. J. *The evolution of human nature*. Austin: University of Texas Press, 1956.
Higgs, E. S. (Ed.). *Papers in economic prehistory*. Cambridge: University Press, 1972.
Hinde, R. A. *Animal behavior* (2nd ed.). New York: McGraw-Hill, 1970.
Hinde, R. A. *Biological bases of human social behavior*. New York: McGraw-Hill, 1974.
Hinde, R. A. (Ed.). *Non-verbal communication*. Cambridge: Cambridge University Press, 1972.
Hinde, R. A. *Social behavior and its development in subhuman primates*. Eugene: Oregon State System of Higher Education, 1972.
Horowitz, M. J. *Image formation and cognition*. New York: Appleton-Century-Crofts, 1970.
Hull, D. L. *Darwin and his critics*. Cambridge, Mass.: Harvard University Press, 1973.
Hull, D. L. *Philosophy of biological science*. Englewood Cliffs, N.J.: Prentice-Hall, 1974.
Huxley, J. S. *Evolution: The modern synthesis* (3rd ed.). London: Allen & Unwin, 1974.
Isaacson, R. L. (Ed.). *The neuropsychology of development*. New York: John Wiley, 1968.
Israel, J., & Tajfel, H. (Eds.). *The context of social psychology: A critical assessment*. New York: Academic Press, 1972.
Jacobson, M. *Developmental neurobiology*. New York: Holt, Rinehart & Winston, 1970.
Jarrard, L. E. *Cognitive processes of nonhuman primates*. New York: Academic Press, 1971.
Jay, P. (Ed.). *Primates*. New York: Holt, Rinehart & Winston, 1968.
Jenkins, F. A., Jr. *Primate locomotion*. New York: Academic Press, 1974.
Jerison, H. J. *Evolution of the brain and intelligence*. New York: Academic Press, 1973.
Jolly, C. J. (Ed.). *Early hominids of Africa*. New York: St. Martin's Press, 1978.
Jolly, C. J., & Plog, F. *Physical anthropology and archaeology* New York: Knopf, 1976.
Kahn, T. C. *An introduction to hominology: The study of the whole man* (2nd ed.). Springfield: Charles C Thomas, 1972.
Karczmar, A. G., & Eccles, J. C. (Eds.). *Brain and human behavior*. Berlin: Springer-Verlag, 1971.
Katz, R. L. *Empathy: Its nature and uses*. Glencoe, Ill.: The Free Press, 1963.
Kimble, D. P. (Ed.). *Experience and capacity*. New York: New York Academy of Science, 1968.
Kleinmutz, B. (Ed.). *Concepts and the structure of memory*. New York: John Wiley, 1967.
Klemm, W. R. *Science, the brain, and our future*. New York: The Bobbs-Merrill Co. (Pegasus), 1972.
Kluckhohn, C., & Murray, H. A. (Eds.). *Personality in nature society and culture* (3rd ed.). New York: Knopf, 1963.
Knigge, K. M., Scott, D. E., & Weindl, A. (Eds.). *Brain-endocrine interaction*. Basel: S. Karger, 1972.
Konorski, J. *Integrative activity of the brain*. Chicago: University of Chicago Press, 1967.
Krantz, G. Brain size and hunting ability in earliest man. *Current Anthropology*, 1968, *9*, 450–451.
Kraus, G. *Homo sapiens in decline*. Sandy, Bedfordshire: The New Diffusionist Press, 1973.

Kroeber, A. L. (Ed.). *Anthropology today: An encyclopedic inventory*. Chicago: University of Chicago Press, 1953.
Kroeber, A. L., & Kluckhohn, C. *Culture: A critical review of concepts and definitions*. New York: Random House, 1952.
Kuhn, T. S. *The structure of scientific revolutions* (2nd ed.). Chicago: University of Chicago Press, 1970.
Lasker, G. W. *Physical anthropology*. New York: Holt, Rinehart & Winston, 1973.
Laughlin, C. D. Jr., & D'Aquili, E. G. *Biogenetic structuralism*. New York: Columbia University Press, 1974.
Lewin, B. D. *The image and the past*. New York: International Universities Press, Inc., 1968.
Lewis, J., & Towers, B. *Naked ape or homo sapiens*. New York: Humanities Press, 1969.
Lilley, S. *Men, machines and history*. London: Cobbett Press, 1948.
Lunzer, E. A. *Contexts of education*, Vol. III. New York: American Elsevier Publishing Co., 1968.
Lunzer, E. A. *The regulation of behaviour*, Vol. 1. New York: American Elsevier Publishing Co., 1968.
Lunzer, E. A., & Morris, J. F. (Eds.). *Development in human learning*, Vol. II, New York: American Elsevier Publishing Co., 1968.
Luria, A. R. *Higher cortical functions in man*. New York: Basic Books, 1966.
Luria, A. R. Towards the problem of the historical nature of psychological processes. *International Journal of Psychology*, 1971, *6*, 259–272.
MacLeod, R. B., & Pick, H. L., Jr. *Perception: Essays in honor of James J. Gibson*. Ithaca: Cornell university Press, 1974.
Magoun, H. W. *The waking brain*. Springfield, Ill.: Charles C Thomas, 1963.
Maier, R. A., & Maier, B. M. *Comparative animal behavior* Belmont: Brooks/Cole, 1970.
Malefigt, A. de W. *Images of man*. New York: Knopf, 1974.
Malik, S. M. *The conquest of cosmophobia*. Worcester Park, G. B.: Roseneath Scientific Publications, 1972.
Manning, A. *An introduction to animal behaviour*. Toronto: MacMillan of Canada, 1972.
Maser, J. D. (Ed.). *Efferent organization and the integration of behavior*. New York: Academic Press, 1973.
Mayr, E. *Animal species and evolution*. Cambridge, Mass.: Harvard University Press, 1963.
McCulloch, W. S. *Embodiments of mind*. Cambridge, Mass.: The M.I.T. Press, 1965.
McGaugh, J. L. (Ed.). *Psychobiology*. New York: Academic Press, 1971.
Mead, M. *Continuities in cultural evolution*. New Haven: Yale University Press, 1970.
Mehrabian, A., & Russell, J. A. *An approach to environmental psychology*. Cambridge, Mass.: The M.I.T. Press, 1974.
Menzel, E. W., Jr. (Ed.). Precultural primate behavior. *Symposia of the Fourth International Congress of Primatology*, Portland, Ore., 1972, Vol. I. Basel: S. Karger, 1973.
Merg, L. *Animal languages*. London: Saxon House, 1971.
Michael, E. P., & Crook, J. H. *Comparative ecology and behaviour of primates*. London: Academic Press, 1973.
Milner, P. M. *Physiological psychology*. New York: Holt, Rinehart & Winston, 1970.
Mogenson, G. J., & Calaresy, E. R. (Eds.). *Neural integration of physiological mechanisms and behaviour*. Toronto: University of Toronto Press, 1975.
Monod, J. *Chance and necessity*. New York: Knopf, 1971.
Morgan, L. H. *Ancient society*. Calcutta: Bhanatic Library, 1958. (Originally published, 1877.)
Morton, J. (Ed.). *Biological and social factors in psycholinguistics*. Chicago: University of Illinois Press, 1970.

Munn, N. L. *The evolution of the human mind*. Boston: Houghton Mifflin Co., 1971.
Mussen, P. H., & Rosenzweig, M. R. (Eds.). *Annual Review of Psychology*, Vol. 24. Palo Alto: Annual Reviews, 1973.
Naroll, R., & Naroll, F. *Main currents in cultural anthropology*. New York: Appleton-Century-Crofts, 1973.
Neff, W. S. *Work and human behavior*. New York: Atherton Press, 1968.
Neubauer, P. B. *Children in collectives*. Springfield, Ill.: Charles C Thomas, 1965.
Nilsson, N. J. *Problem solving methods in artificial intelligence*. New York: McGraw-Hill, 1971.
Noback, C. R., & Demarest, R. J. *The nervous system: Introduction and review*. New York: McGraw-Hill, 1972.
Noback, C. R., & Montagna (Eds.). *The primate brain*, Vol. 1. New York: Appleton-Century-Crofts, 1970.
Norman, D. A. *Memory and attention*. New York: John Wiley, 1969.
Palmer, L. S. *Man's journey through time*. London: Hutchinson & Co., 1957.
Peeke, H. V. S., & Herz, M. J. (Eds.). *Habituation*, Vols. I, II. New York: Academic Press, 1973.
Penfield, W., & Roberts, J. *Speech and brain-mechanisms*. Princeton: Princeton University Press, 1959.
Pepper, S. C. *World hypotheses*. Berkeley: University of California Press, 1966.
Pieron, H. *Thought and the brain*. New York: Arno Press, 1973.
Piggott, S. (Ed.). *The dawn of civilization—The first world survey of human cultures in early times*. New York: McGraw-Hill, 1961.
Pilbeam, D. *The ascent of man*. New York: MacMillan, 1972.
Portmann, A. *Animals as social beings*. London: Hutchinson, 1961.
Pribram, K. *The languages of the brain*. Englewood Cliffs, N.J.: Prentice-Hall, 1971.
Reitman, W. *Cognition and thought*. New York: John Wiley, 1965.
Ribeiro, D. *The civilizational process*. Washington: Smithsonian Institution Press, 1968.
Restak, R. M. *Pre-meditated man*. New York: The Viking Press, 1975.
Reusch, B. *Evolution above the species level*. London: Methuen, 1959.
Robinson, J. T. *Early hominid posture and locomotion*. Chicago: University of Chicago Press, 1972.
Robinson, R. J. *Brain and early behavior*. London: Academic Press, 1969.
Roper, N. *Man's anatomy, physiology, health and environment*. London: Churchill Livingstone, 1973.
Rosenblueth, A. *Mind and brain*. Cambridge, Mass.: The M.I.T. Press, 1970.
Rosenzweig, M. R., & Porter, L. W. *Annual Review of Psychology*, Vol. 25. Palo Alto: Annual Reviews, 1973.
Roslansky, J. D. (Ed.). *The human mind*. Amsterdam: North-Holland Publishing Co., 1969.
Rowell, T. *The social behaviour of monkeys*. London: Penguin Books, 1972.
Ruse, M. *The philosophy of biology*. London: Hutchinson University Library, 1973.
Schaffer, H. R. (Ed.). *The origins of human social relations*. London: Academic Press, 1971.
Schmitt, F. O. (Ed.). *The neurosciences second study program*. New York: Rockefeller University Press, 1970.
Scott, J. P. *Animal behavior* (2nd ed.). Chicago: University of Chicago Press, 1972.
Sebeok, T. A. (Ed.). *Animal communication*. Bloomington: Indiana University Press, 1968.
Sebeok, T. A. (Ed.). *Approaches to animal communication*. The Hague: Mouton, 1969.
Sebeok, T. A. (Ed.). *Perspectives in zoosemiotics*. The Hague: Mouton, 1972.
Semenov, S. A. *Prehistoric technology*. (M. W. Thompson, trans.). New York: Barnes and Noble Inc., 1964. (Originally published; 1957.)
Sheehan, P. W. (Ed.). *The function and nature of imaging*. New York: Academic Press, 1972.

Simon, A., Herbart, C. C., & Straus, R. *The physiology of emotions*. Springfield: Charles C Thomas, 1960.
Simpson, G. G. *Biology and man*. New York: Harcourt, Brace & World, 1969.
Smith, A. *The human pedigree*. Philadelphia: J. B. Lippincott, 1975.
Smith, K. A. *Delayed sensory feedback and behavior*. Philadelphia: W. B. Saunders, 1962.
Smythies, J. R. (Ed.). *Brain and mind*. New York: The Humanities Press, 1965.
Sokolov, Y. N. *Perception and the conditioned reflex*. Pergamon Press, 1963.
Solso, R. L. (Ed.). *Theories in cognitive psychology: The Loyola Symposium*. New York: John Wiley (Halsted), 1974.
Sommerhoff, G. *Logic of the living brain*. London: John Wiley, 1974.
Stanley-Jones, D. *Kybernetics of mind and brain*. Springfield, Ill.: Charles C Thomas, 1970.
Stotland, E. *The psychology of hope*. San Francisco: Jossey-Bass, 1969.
Swartz, M. J., & Jordan, D. K. *Anthropology: Perspective on humanity*. New York: John Wiley, 1976.
Thass-Thienemann, T. *Symbolic behavior*. New York: Washington Square Press, 1968.
Thomas, W. L. (Ed.). *Man's role in changing the face of the earth*. Chicago: University of Chicago Press, 1956.
Triandis, H. C. Psychology and culture. *Annual Review of Psychology*, 1973, *24*, 355–378.
Turbane, C. M. *The myth of the metaphor* (rev. ed.). Columbia, S.C.: University of South Carolina Press, 1970.
Tuttle, R. (Ed.). *The functional and evolutionary biology of primates*. Chicago: Aldine Press, 1972.
Tylor, E. B. *Primitive culture* (2 vols.). New York: Harper Textbooks. 1958.
Ucko, P. J., & Rosenfeld, A. *Palaeolithic cave art*. London: Weidenfeld & Nicolson, 1967.
von Bonin, G. *The cerebral cortex*. Springfield, Ill.: Charles C Thomas, Publishers, 1960.
von Holst, E. *The behavioural physiology of animals and man*. Vols. I, II. London: Methuen, 1967.
von Uexkull, J. J. *Der sinn des leben*. Godesberg: H. Kupper, 1947.
Vygotsky, L. S. *Thought and language*. Cambridge, Mass.: The M.I.T. Press, 1962.
Waddington, C. H. *The evolution of an evolutionist*. Edinburgh: Edinburgh University Press, 1975.
Wallace, R. A. *The ecology and evolution of animal behavior*. Pacific Palisades: Goodyear Publishing Co., 1973.
Wallia, C. S. (Ed.). *Toward century 21*. New York: Basic Books, 1970.
Washburn, S. C. *Classification and human evolution*. Chicago: Aldine, 1963.
Wassermann, G. D. *Brains and reasoning*. London: MacMillan, 1974.
Wiener, N. *Cybernetics* (2nd ed.). Cambridge, Mass.: The M.I.T. Press, 1961.
Werner, H., & Kaplan, B. *Symbol formation*. New York: John Wiley, 1964.
Whiting, B. B., & Whiting, J. W. M. *Children of six cultures*. Cambridge, Mass.: Harvard University Press, 1975.
Wilson, E. O. *Sociobiology: The new synthesis*. Cambridge, Mass.: Harvard University Press, 1975.
Wolfensberger, W. *The principle of normalization in human services*. Toronto: National Institute on Mental Retardation, 1972.
Woodburne, L. S. *The neural basis of behavior*. Columbus, Ohio: C. E. Merrill, 1967.
Wooldridge, D. E. *The machinery of the brain*. New York: McGraw-Hill, 1963.
Woolf, H. (Ed.). *Quantification*. New York: The Bobbs-Merrill Co., 1961.
Wooley, Sir L. *The beginnings of civilization: History of mankind-cultural and scientific development*, Vol. 1, Part II. *(UNESCO)*. New York: Mentor Books, 1965.
Yagi, K., & Yoshida, S. *Neuroendocrine control*. New York: John Wiley, 1973.
Young, J. Z. *A model of the brain*. Oxford: Oxford University Press, 1964.

10

Richard Jung

NATURALISM, HUMANISM, AND THE THEORY OF ACTION

Naturalism and Humanism

Man: Fact—Construct—Artifact?

Since antiquity, two formulations of the basic nature of man have co-existed in most major cultures. One is the conception of man as one *fact* of nature—in no fundamental way outstanding among the myriad varied facts of the natural world. This conception, in recent times articulated within the framework of the historical account of big-bang cosmology and archaeological anthropology, has the theoretical underpinning of thermodynamics and Darwinian-Mendelian biology. Currently, its limits are being stretched by the attempts of some sociobiologists to reformulate hitherto sacrosanct notions about man.

The second formulation is of man as a special entity in the cosmos, where if not unique, he certainly is a member of an exclusive club and resides near, if not at, the apex of nonnatural excellence. This ontology gives us man as a *construct* possessing some particular, usually inner, properties such as consciousness, freedom of the will, responsibility, and various other special sensibilities, propensities, qualities, or faculties. This formulation is so pandemic in religions, theologies, and phi-

---

Richard Jung • Department of Sociology and Theoretical Psychology Center, University of Alberta, Edmonton, Alberta T6G 2H4, Canada.

losophies that it has been dubbed "the perennial philosophy." In the European tradition, the medieval formulations of Augustine and Aquinas exert a major influence on phenomenology, Heidegger, existentialism, and the Oxford philosophy of mind and action.

In modern times, a third conception of man is being articulated, perhaps in connection with such broad historical trends as the rationalization of production and administration. This is the view of man's nature as essentially an *artifact*. Man himself is seen as being fundamentally a product of the artificial symbolic and concrete environment that he has created—of his socialization, of the social control inherent in every social interaction, of the elaboration of social order (including laws, customs, and manners), and most fundamentally, of self-imposed subjugation of his activity to rules of conduct. These are rules not only of practical reason *(Zweckrationalitaet)* but also of belief, valuation, and expression. In this view man is, can only exist as, and actively strives to be an artifact of culture, that is of rules of intelligibility and warrantability of action. Contemporary utopian or apocalyptic anticipations—of genetically engineered and artificially conceived test-tube babies, raised in Skinner boxes on pharmacological and biochemical dietary regimes and on programmed instruction to qualify as specialized cyborgs in a telecommunicating technocratic state—are popular, though not entirely fictional, articulations of the third conception of the nature of man.

While adherents of these three views generally engage in polemics with each other, occasional attempts are made to incorporate elements of the other views into one's own. This makes it difficult to erect humanism on simple slogans, such as *Homo mensura res*, since a sleight of hand is required to deliver on the claim: *Ecce homo!*

The Controversy about Understanding and Explanation

I shall return to the differences between models of man later. In the present context, however, I would like to draw first on the distinction between naturalism and humanism as it arises out of the culture of the Enlightenment and, more specifically, as it was formulated during the conflict about the appropriate epistemology of the moral sciences *(Geisteswissenschaften)* in the late nineteenth and early twentieth centuries in Central Europe.

This debate, referred to variously as *der Methodenstreit* or *die Er-*

klaeren:Verstehen-Kontroverse, starts with reactions by German idealists (e.g., Schleiermacher, Droysen, Brentano, Scheler, and Dilthey) to inroads by Newtonian conceptions of science into the hitherto securely humanist disciplines of economics, history, psychology, and sociology. It is reflected in the controversy surrounding the birth of psychoanalysis and modern economics out of the Austrian school and the founding of modern psychology by Wundt and modern sociology by Vico, Durkheim, Marx, and Weber.

Far from resolved, the issue is still the primary concern of current authors, both in the German tradition (e.g., Betti, Gadamer, Habermas, Apel, Ricoeur) and in the Oxford tradition (from Wittgenstein to von Wright; from Ryle, Strawson, Anscombe, Kenny, Chisholm, and Winch to present-day speech act and functionalist philosophers). The issue is also prominent in the psychological and sociological writings of authors as diverse as Merleau-Ponty, Parsons, Lévi-Strauss, Piaget, Chomsky, Harré and Fodor. Unfortunately, even in its present form, most of the formulations reflect a fusion of ontologies of man (such as the three discussed above), which in my view need to be distinguished. To a significant extent, they are ontological statements about the nature of man, which in my view lie beyond the limits of scientific concern, rather than epistemological statements about the sources of man's curiosity concerning man and about possible methods of satisfying the different kinds of curiosity.

The Humanist Perspective

I shall now briefly outline my conception of what may constitute a "humanist perspective" in science, drawing the best I can on the various relevant traditions of thought, yet emphasizing an epistemological (and psychosociological) rather than an ontological (and philosophical) approach to the issue.

One source of man's curiosity about himself (and the rest of the world) is his own experience of himself. The central theme of this experience is *communication*—to himself, to others, and from others. The classical polarization of communication into *expression* and *understanding* gives rise to most of the concepts, problems, and methods associated with the humanist perspective. Among these are: meaning; accessibility of experience; subjectivity and intersubjectivity; autonomy and responsibility; givenness, thrownness, and alienation. A European academic tradition has developed around these concerns in theology, jurisprudence, history, and the arts, eventually giving birth to a methodology of understanding based on a theory of activity as an expression of meaning (hermeneutics) and to a philosophical approach to the conceptualization of experience and meaning (phenomenology and common-language philosophy).

It seems to me that the "humanist perspective" could be distinguished from the "naturalist perspective" by

1. The model of the ideal discipline (history, jurisprudence, literature, or art versus biology and physics);
2. The type of reduction (eidetic or phenomenological versus physiological);
3. The most advanced formulations from each perspective (economic decision theory or generative grammar versus genetics or thermodynamics of open systems);
4. The nature of curiosity, that is, the fundamental questions being asked about individual and aggregate phenomena. The difference results in divergent attempts to conceptualize: in the "naturalist" tradition as systems of energy; in the "humanistic" tradition as systems of meaning. The two perspectives emphasize different kinds of scientific entities: the naturalist realizes physiological and ecological systems; the humanist realizes psychological and sociological[1] systems.

As a mode of inquiry, the humanist approach to human studies has, over the last 50 years, developed into a fairly coherent and articulated method. The method starts with the attribution of meaning to human activity (Marx and Freud); meaningful activity—that is, action or conduct—is "formalized" as ideal types (Weber); and these are linked together into "formal" structures (Piaget, Lévi-Strauss, and Chomsky). This mode of inquiry appears to be epistemologically grounded in:

1. *Phenomenology,* in that the elements that enter into the configurations called "ideal types" must be elements of basic categories of human experience in order to serve as tools of understanding *(Verstehen)*
2. *Structural hermeneutics,* in that the explication of the structures linking the ideal types represents an advanced stage in the her-

[1] In this paper I will consistently use the term "sociological" in its broad sense, including economics, technology, institutions, ideology, and language.

meneutic process of interpretation (be it in Freud or Marx, Weber or Lévi-Strauss, Piaget or Chomsky) but falls short of theoretical explanation *(Erklaeren).*

Verstehen Is Not Enough

At this point, I would like to avoid semantic and ideological arguments. I acknowledge that "science" is not the only acceptable mode of social cognition; indeed, for some purposes other modes might be superior. Nor do I see it linked as closely with technology and the artifact view of man as many would. There are, of course, different conceptions as to what science is or ought to be. Personally, I think of science as a recently institutionalized human activity regulated by norms favoring systematic inquiries into domains of concrete phenomena, replicable interpretations of these phenomena within abstract conceptual systems, and theoretical explanation and deduction of generalizations about interpreted actual occurrences in the domain of inquiry.

Within this conception of science, only minimal logical or syntactic requirements are placed on conceptualization. There is ample room for special requirements arising from the humanist perspective. Not only phenomenological characterizations of human experience, such as intentionality, temporality, granularity, and reflexivity, but also common notions, such as purposiveness, sense of freedom or constraint, and so forth, can be easily accommodated. It is on the abstract level of conceptualization that phenomenology and language philosophy can make contributions to science. Similarly, hermeneutics is compatible with this conception of science and in fact helps to satisfy empiricist norms.

The stumbling block of "humanist science" is the problem of scientific explanation. I employ the term "explanation" in this context as it has been stabilized since the eighteenth century. This particular usage equates explanation, or theoretical explanation, with the subsumption of interpreted empirical generalizations under covering laws. The laws themselves are interpretations, to the same conceptual system as the empirical generalizations, of necessary relations in a formal, logical system.

This conception of scientific explanation, which I, for one, see as a sine qua non of any science, is clearly formulated by Kant (1785, p. 120), "Denn wir koennen nichts erklaeren, als was wir auf Gesetze zurueckfuehren koennen, deren Gegenstand in irgendeiner Erfahrung gegeben werden kann," as well as by Comte (1830, Leçon I, Section 2),

"L'explication des faits . . . n'est pas désormais que la liaison etablié entre les divers phénomènes particuliers et quelques faits généraux." However, the formal structure from which necessity is attributed to the explanandum need not be causal. The critical normative feature of scientific explanation is the logicality of deductive inference, rather than the ontological interpretation of the logical implications employed.

Yet even with this relaxation, structural hermeneutics does not provide an acceptable form, or equivalent, of scientific explanation. It is at best the humanist equivalent of naturalist modeling or simulation. A humanist scientific theory must have a formal, logical structure that is readily interpretable to a phenomenologically grounded conceptualization of hermeneutically reconstructed human activity.

One mode of scientific explanation seems particularly appropriate. It maps logically valid formulations on the subjective experiences of purposivity, autonomy, and constraint; it fits readily the phenomenological characterizations of experience discussed above; it formalizes the requirements of *aisthesis* (situational appreciation) and of the defeasibility of general (instrumental or expressive) propositions by context that are so dear to humanists' hearts. I shall characterize this mode of scientific explanation in the second part of the chapter.

Naturalistic, Humanistic, and Technical Metaphors

In my present view, the range of scientific curiosity about the activity of living systems can be exhaustively represented by four internally coherent, semantically exclusive, yet formally compatible and empirically complementary conceptual systems. Each of these systems encodes a different kind of curiosity into a distinct fundamental conceptual paradigm or metaphor.

The first well-articulated metaphor depicts the individual as an organism composed of input–output relations; the activity of the system is construed as its behavior. The second, equally articulated metaphor represents the individual as a mind with volition or intentions as its central content and with its activity interpreted as action.

While these two well-known metaphors reflect clearly the differences between the naturalist and humanist perspectives, as well as the differences between the ontologies of man as a fact and as a construct, two other as yet less articulated metaphors are of equal significance. The third paradigm conceives of the individual as a machine, whose content can best be thought of as dispositions and whose activity is interpreted as performance. The fourth, as yet least developed paradigm, envisions the individual as a semantic plexus wherein each nexus of meanings constitutes a rule, a convention, or a constraint which enables the interpretation of the activity of the system as conduct. Whereas differences between the third and fourth metaphor reflect the differences between the naturalist and humanist perspectives, both metaphors encode the key features of the ontology of man as an artifact.

Humanism and the Theory of Action

The theoretical program of the life sciences may well consist of the distinct realization of all the four conceptual systems and the formulation of their theoretical compatibility and empirical complementarity.

But further discussion of the metatheoretical problems in the science of life is beyond the scope of this chapter. In the second part of the chapter, I shall illustrate my approach to the integration of humanist curiosity with scientific method by focusing on the second metaphor and outlining the metatheoretical aspects of my attempts to contribute to the formulation of a theory of action.

The Unified Theory of Action

To construct a unified theory of action, I am using a method which I call *phenomenological systems analysis*. Phenomenology is used as a method of conceptualization, while systems analysis (not in the sense used by the "social systems analysts" or the "general systems analysts" but in the sense used by computer scientists and engineers) is used as a method of explanation.

The unified theory of action consists of three general theories. Each is concerned with a different fundamental problem, employs a different method for its solution, has its own special concepts, and invokes different systems of explanation. The three general theories are, however, unified by a common conceptual space, by a theory of structuring of action, and by a theory of aggregation of action.

One domain of inquiry, currently the primary concern of psychologists, microeconomists, and theoreticians of automata, is the *activity of individuals*, be they humans, animals, or machines. I call the method employed for its conceptualization *cybernetic phenomenology*. The explanatory system invoked is the logic of functional analysis (in the sense used in modern physics) and its elaborations in the calculus of variations and the various models of cybernetics. The proposed formalization of this domain is called the *general theory of action*.

Another domain of inquiry is the *activity of groups* of humans, other living entities, and machines. Groups are aggregate systems with all individuals and relations of interest identified. The subject is currently dealt with primarily in social psychology and theories of the firm, corporations, and games. The method employed for its conceptualization is *structural phenomenology*. The explanatory system invoked is primarily derived from set theory and its various elaborations and applications, such as graph theory, lattice theory, and matrix algebra. The proposed formalization of this domain is called the *general theory of interaction*.

A third domain of inquiry is the *activity of collectives*. Collectives are aggregate systems in which all individuals and/or relations of interest cannot be meaningfully identified, either because of the number of elements and relations or because of the heterogeneity that is of interest. The method employed for its conceptualization is called *stochastic phenomenology*. The explanatory system invoked is probability theory. Since this is a domain of inquiry largely abandoned by the present generation of sociologists, the models available are to be found primarily in macroeconomics, population genetics, and epidemiology. The proposed formalization of this domain is called the *general theory of transaction*.

The General Theory of Action

The general theory of action attempts to explain systems of actions, holding an individual actor constant as a point of reference and allowing situations to vary. While this statement is a technical abstraction, it reflects a naive curiosity about the activity of individuals (i.e., humans, other living entities, and machines).

Cybernetic Phenomenology

There are two radically different, yet complementary modes of analysis of any system. The identical element—a living or nonliving individual—can be equally appropriately analyzed either as a physiological system, through the application of concepts and principles of physics, chemistry, and biology, or as a psychological system, through the application of concepts and principles of psychology, economics, and sociology. Its complement—that is, environment—can be similarly analyzed either as an ecological system or as a system of situations, that is, a sociological system. The criterial difference between the two modes of analysis is whether the phenomena under study are conceived of as *systems of behavior* or as *systems of action*—that is, whether they are fundamentally construed as *systems of energy* or as *systems of meaning*.

The choice between the two modes of analysis does not require a particular belief about the nature of men or machines, but a particular kind of curiosity about their activity. In my case, it is not based on an ontological commitment but on an epistemological preference. Since my interest here is in the meaning of action and not in the thermodynamics of behavior, I am led by the above distinction as well as by other reasons to a choice of phenomenology as the method of conceptualization. The terms "actor," "action," and "situation" will, therefore, indicate that individuals, their environments, and their activity in these environments have been conceptualized phenomenologically.

The fundamental abstractions "actor," "action," and "situation" imply a choice of a particular mode of explanation with a long, illustrious, and troubled tradition in philosophy, psychology, and social science. This mode of explanation is focused on the presence or absence of regulation in the systems under study. Within this tradition, actions are simply those exchanges between individuals and their environments that are actually or hypothetically regulated. Actors (or situations) are those aspects of individuals (or environments) that are analyzed as sources of regulation or disturbance.

Actors, situations, and actions are terms for individuals, environments, and exchanges between them that have been conceptualized phenomenologically as systems of meanings and explained cybernetically as systems of regulation. This conception of action is compatible with two of Parsons's (Parsons & Shils, 1954, pp. 53–68) conceptions of action, which codify the basic terms of the classical tradition: action is interchangeably conceived by Parsons as the relation between the actor and the situation or as the distribution of energy, subject to specific constraints. My attempt to construct a general theory of action draws on the classical tradition of action analysis wherever possible. However, given the basic intent of such a conceptualization (i.e., the abstraction of the meaning of activity), I accept phenomenology as the only method of conceptualization appropriate in the construction of the theory. In the same vein, I adhere to the idea of constraints as the sole source of explanation and refuse to introduce any additional, incompatible, and empirically untenable explanatory ideas, such as purposiveness and goals, exemplified in a definition of action which pervades current theory, that is, actor seeks goals in situations.

Thus, the analysis radicalizes conceptualization of action by accepting phenomenology as its sole method. At the same time, it rejects prescientific, introspective, and romantic functionalism (with its teleological fallacy) as a method of explanation of action. Instead, it substitutes functional explanation based on variational principles (cf. Yourgrau & Mandelstam, 1955, Chapters 2, 3). This is a step that physics took 2000 years to take, from the formal structure of Hero's explanation of the activity of light rays as prescient and purposive to the logical structure of modern quantum, electromagnetic, and relativity theories. In social science, functional explanation has been applied only in decision (and game) theory.[2]

The formal structure of functional explanation is extremely simple. Given a set of boundary conditions (values of a set of independent variables), the activity of a functional system (a system of intervening variables) is internally constrained so that the value of an essential (dependent) variable is extremum. Extremum is a general term for either maximum or minimum values in a range or for constants. While the concept "extremum" permits, on the one hand, further formal elaboration of great explanatory power, it also imposes, on the other hand, a rigorous epistemological and methodological restriction. Functional explanation can be applied only if an essential variable with an extremum has been specified.

The general method of meaningful functional analysis of activity is also simple. First, discover an essential variable, the value of which in fact is extremum. Next, identify the necessary and sufficient set of variables that maintain the essential variable at an extremum. Third, discover through naturalistic observation, or by violation through laboratory experimentation, the set of necessary and sufficient boundary conditions under which the phenomenon occurs and without which it

[2] Because of the superiority of its formal structure, decision theory has been mistakenly upheld by some as the substantive (conceptual) basis of psychology. Similarly, game theory has been held as foundational for sociology.

disappears. Functional analysis is the foundation stone of cybernetics; the rest is a combination of functional chains through loops and the analysis of interaction between various sources of disturbance (variance).

The Fundamental Problem and Solution

The general theory of action conceptualizes activity of individuals in environments phenomenologically as *actions constrained by systems of meanings*. It constructs actors and situations as the sources of meanings and explains action cybernetically as the *mutual disturbance and regulation by a situation and an actor*. Thus conceived, the fundamental problem of the general theory of action becomes: How is action regulated by an actor and a situation? To solve the problem, the theory provides (1) conceptualization of boundary conditions that act as sources of disturbance, (2) specification of systems of intervening variables by formulating various processes into which ongoing activity can be meaningfully analyzed, (3) construction of a set of essential variables, and (4) postulation of a set of principles stating the propensities of the essential variables to assume extremum values. The principles regulate (which also means explain) the various processes.

The general theory of action posits that separate conceptualization and analysis of three special processes is necessary and sufficient for complete analysis of action. Each of the three processes expresses a different fundamental propensity of action. While embedded in the common conceptual and explanatory format of the general theory, the analysis of each process also requires special concepts, mechanisms, and principles. Thus, the actual analysis of action is accomplished by three special theories of action. The three special theories are (1) the *special theory of orientation* (Jung, 1965b), (2) the *special theory of motivation* (Jung, 1965a), and (3) the *special theory of decision*. The general theory provides the concepts, mechanisms, and principles necessary for the description and explanation of the interplay of the three special processes. It thus becomes the theory of integration or disintegration of action.

Each special theory is formalized by the employment of a different schema. The theory of orientation employs a schema derived from information theory, the theory of motivation, a schema derived from the theory of elasticity, and the theory of decision, a schema derived from the economic theory of decisions under risk. Each theory postulates a different principle regulating (i.e., explaining) the relevant process. The form of the principle is the same in all three special theories, as well as in the general theory, but its content differs with each theory.

The form of the principles derives from the logic of functional explanation described above: the value of an essential variable is maintained at extremum by a system of intervening variables only under a given set of boundary conditions. The extremum in each case is of the form: reduction of the maximum possible amount of *e*, with *e* being the value of the relevant essential variable.

The content (meaning, sense) of the principle varies with each theory and depends on the conceptualization of the respective process and the interpretation of the respective essential variable *e*. The essential variables of the three processes of orientation, motivation, and decision express the fundamental propensities of action, that is, to manage *uncertainty, tension,* and *risk*. The special principles of action are as follows: for the process of orientation, the reduction of the maximum possible amount of uncertainty; for the process of motivation, the reduction of the maximum possible amount of tension; and for the process of decision, the reduction of the maximum possible amount of risk.

The General Theory as a Theory of Integration and Disintegration of Action

The general theory of action is composed of the three special theories. Each describes an analytically distinguishable process of action, expresses a different fundamental propensity of action, and postulates a special principle regulating action. It is a fundamental postulate of the general theory that all three processes are not only sufficient but also necessary to regulate (i.e., to explain) action. This represents a radical departure from prevalent monistic thinking. The form of the principles is also decisively different from the form of current functional principles in sociology, economics, and psychology, where the values of the essential variables are not constrained to possible minima; instead, each action of the system is constrained to the maximum reduction of essential values. Life does not generally cease due to the fulfillment of its propensities but rather due to an inability to cope with disturbances that push the processes of action beyond systemic limits. Furthermore, the processes are postulated to be mutually independent within systemic limits—thus, the processes are as likely to be mutually antagonistic as they are to be mutually irrelevant or solidary. "The vital balance," as Meninger, Mayman, and Pruyser (1963, pp. 81, 88–89, 417) called it, is an important characteristic of life and a partial subject of the general theory of action. Yet, it is the *vital imbalance* that temporarily gives rise to the phenomenon called life.

The General Principle of Action

Having delegated most of the task of explaining regulation of action to the three special theories, the fundamental problem for the general theory of action becomes: What principle governs the interplay of the three special processes? Or, stated differently, under what conditions does action (i.e., meaningfully constrained activity) occur, and under what conditions chaos, meaningless activity, or death?

The salient features of the proposed solution are as follows. A constraint must be imposed on the independent operation of the three special processes. Their interplay is seen as a general process which manifests a propensity toward authenticity.[3] Stating the constraint in the format explained earlier, the general theory explains action as governed by a general principle of reduction of the maximum possible amount of inauthenticity. This principle governs the complex dynamic interplay of the three processes. When systemic limits on the independent operation of the three processes are exceeded, it imposes constraints which are reflected in experiences such as *guilt* or *anxiety* when *in*authenticity is increased and in relief when it is decreased. When the general principle operates, systemic limits are actually experienced.

Another way of stating the general principle of action is as a categorical imperative: above all, action must reduce as much as possible any discrepancy between the state of the individual as an organism and his definition as an actor.[4] Clearly, there are two simple ways of reducing such a discrepancy. The state of an individual as an organism can be changed to correspond to his definition as an actor, or his definition can

[3] The term "authenticity" is intended in its dictionary meaning and as used in phenomenology and existential philosophy. A cybernetic system (a regulator) is authentic (1) logically, if it equilibrates around the value set, (2) phenomenologically, if it experiences strain when dislodged from that value, and (3) existentially, if, when unable to reach the set value, it can reset (and thus maintain its coherence and functioning).

[4] Among the results of the process of orientation is precisely the continuing generation, evaluation, and acceptance or rejection of the two constructs: the state of an individual as an organism and his definition as an actor (cf. Jung, 1965b).

be changed to correspond to his state. The difference between the two ways is partly illustrated by the distinction between some mechanisms of adjustment, such as learning, and the mechanisms of defense; it is also relevant to socialization, deviance, and social control.

Summary

Cybernetic phenomenology is the method used to construct a general theory of action, one of three theories comprising a unified theory of action. General theory of action pertains to activity of individuals; general theory of interaction to activity of groups (systems with all individuals and relations identified); and general theory of transaction to activity of collectives (systems without meaningfully identified individuals and their relations). The three general theories are unified by a common conceptual space and by formal operations of structuring and aggregation. Each general theory, however, is concerned with a different fundamental problem and employs for its solution a different formalization schema and different key concepts.

The general theory of action draws on traditions of action analysis in psychology, sociology, economics, and philosophy. However, it radicalizes conceptualization by employing phenomenology, and explanation by employing cybernetics. Phenomenology describes action as a system of experienced meanings, while cybernetics accounts for regulatory features observed. Jointly, they permit the employment of a mode of functional analysis, commonplace in physics but unused in sociology. Instead of a teleological conception, action is seen as governed not by future goals but by past and present extremum constraints on essential variables that represent the fundamental propensities of action. Three such fundamental constraints are postulated, each giving rise to a special theory of action:

1. The special theory of orientation, governed by the principle of reduction of maximum possible amount of uncertainty
2. The special theory of decision, governed by the principle of the reduction of the maximum possible amount of risk
3. The special theory of motivation, governed by the principle of the reduction of the maximum possible amount of tension

Processes of orientation, decision, and motivation are mutually independent within systemic limits, thus accounting for the vital imbalance that is the distinguishing characteristic of the activity of living systems. The operation of systemic limits, and thus the integration of action, is accounted for in the general theory of action by the general principle of action: the reduction of the maximum possible amount of inauthenticity.

References

Comte, A. *Cours de philosophie positive*. Paris: Rouen frères (Bachelier), 1830.

Jung, R. Self-control in a sociological perspective: Introduction. In S. Z. Klausner (Ed.), *The quest for self-control: Classical philosophies and scientific research*. New York: Free Press, 1965. (a)

Jung, R. Systems of orientation. In M. Kochen (Ed.), *Some problems in information science*. New York: Scarecrow Press, 1965. (b)

Kant, I. *Grundlegung zur Metaphysik der Sitten*. Riga: J. F. Hartknoch, 1785.

Meninger, K., with Mayman, M., & Pruyser P. *The vital balance: The life process in mental health and illness*. New York: Viking, 1963.

Parsons, T., & Shils, E. A. Values, motives, and systems of action. In T. Parsons & E. A. Shils (Eds.), *Toward a general theory of action*. Cambridge, Mass.: Harvard University Press, 1954.

Yourgrau, W., & Mandelstam, S. *Variational principles in dynamics and quantum theory*. London: Pitman, 1955.

V

CRITICAL ANALYSIS

11

Herman Tennessen

THE VERY IDEA OF A "HUMANISTIC PSYCHOLOGY"

In what follows three not entirely independent points shall be argued: (1) The emergence of the very idea of a "humanistic psychology" can only be comprehended and justified when seen as a reaction against an image of scientific theory and praxis which may once well have been a dominant one but which is also one presently branded as archaic, antiquated, exploded—in point of fact, discarded and abandoned—not only by the avant-garde but virtually by the last few generations of almost all professional scientists, metascientists, methodologists, and philosophers of science. (2) The rejected image that vaguely comes to my mind is one that pictures the scientific endeavor (theory or praxis) as though it were a purely disintegrated, autonomous, autarchic, and entirely human-independent enterprise. (3) It is the occasional, unfortunate survival of exactly this image of science in the still pools of metatheoretical and general methodological deadwater which more than any other single factor represents a serious threat to all attempts at effective theorizing within contemporary psychological, behavioral, social, and other "soft" sciences in general.

To repeat, then, it is only in this peculiarly obsolete interpretation of "scientific" that it makes any sense at all to entertain the very idea of a "humanistic psychology" as opposed to a non- or antihumanistic

Herman Tennessen • Department of Philosophy and Theoretical Psychology Center, University of Alberta, Edmonton, Alberta T6G 2E9, Canada.

"scientific" psychology. The case for and against science today is a complex and bewildering one, and one that I shall carefully consider. However, there can scarcely be any doubt that were scientific enterprise today to be conceived as a threat to humanness or humanity it certainly could not be because it is bound to be considered autonomous, autarchic, or human-independent, let alone dehumanizing or impersonalizing. Contemporary images of the scientific enterprise all invariably stress the human roots of this most human undertaking—that science is man's most successful endeavor to figure out how things within and around him operate and whatever it is that might appear to be man's lot in the cosmos.

In one of my contributions to the XVth world Congress of Philosophy (September 17–22, 1973, Varna, Bulgaria) I began with the following rather trite observation:

> There is something peculiarly redundant in the very idea of *humanistic psychology*. Whenever a psychologist, *qua* psychologist, involves himself in whichever conceivable psychological enterprise, that enterprise is not only, needless to say, bound to be a human enterprise but, in point of fact, an enterprise more or less precisely and definitely conceptualised as a direct or indirect contribution to man's understanding of man, *viz.*, the all-human endeavour to figure out how things within man and around man operate—and what, after all, man's *lot* within the widest conceptual scheme may be. By the same token "non-humanistic psychology" is bound to designate nothing but a *contradictio in adjecto*. Its non-existence is a notational necessity. How anyone could ever come to believe that it might make sense to argue as though there actually *were* such a thing, has only psycho-patho-semantic interest. And the beguiling key conepts at work here, I shall suggest, are: "SCIENCE", "scientific", plus possibly: "objectivity", "theory-independent observations" or "percepts", "refutation", "autonomy", "autarchy", and related notions implicitly suggesting, *inter alia*, an image, a model of a theory/observation asymmetry, alleged to inexorably permeate all science—and metascience-theoretical activity." (Tennessen, 1974, p. 285)

There is no denying the historical importance of such an image or model. It constitutes an integral part of what I have elsewhere referred to as *"the old, disintegrated view of the scientific enterprise"* (Tennessen, 1970, p. 8). One can roughly distinguish six characteristics of the activity once considered "scientific" but which can presently at the best kindle a mild paleontological interest: (1) The sciences were, according to this view, totally autonomous, completely emancipated from anything that is related to man, society, philosophy, conceptual schemes, frames of reference, or total world views, let alone metaphysics, or philosophical systems. (2) The process of justification, testing, and validation of scientific theories, hypotheses, laws, and observational journals was considered a rational process to be carefully distinguished from the more erratic pragmatics and heuristics dealing with favorable conditions for discovery and invention of theories. (3) The sciences were, in a literal sense, accumulative, facts being added to facts and new, more comprehensive and accurate theories being substituted for old ones. Theories tended to grow less cognitively different, less mutually inconsistent, and more generally comprehensive. This led in the long run, one hazarded to speculate, to a unification of science. (4) One envisioned a parallel process of step-by-step approximation to the truth. (5) There were claims made to alleged "discoveries" that certain phenomena were physically, biologically, or otherwise "impossible," adding up to an *a priori* part of science. (6) On the other hand, "philosophical" reflections by man were viewed as a kind of reflection sui generis, using logical analysis and leaving empirical investigations to the so called "sciences."

The presurmised humanistic-scientific contraposition is fundamentally underbraced by those very same blunderous misconceptions of all scientific undertakings as have merely enjoyed historical curiousness at least during the last couple of decades (Butterfield, 1951). What I have in mind here is not just the steadily increasing number of well-argued apotropaic remonstrances against the incessant perpetration of the somewhat historically influential Vienna Circle's thought model, according to which it is relatively simple to distinguish such entities as, for example, perception/interpretation, fact/hypotheses, observation (protocol) sentences/theoretical sentences, and so forth (Tennessen, 1972). Nor am I simply concerned with that well-known area within the field of theories of theories where the last generations of metatheoreticians have reluctantly resigned vis à vis an overwhelming amount of readily available, pertinent testimonies—from theories of perception and cognition to *Grundlagenforschung*, history of science, and general-science methodology and general epistemology, all amounting to an unconditional renunciation of the extravagant fatuity of any attempt to retain *in vacuo* such notions as percepts, perceptions, sensa, observations, and facts ("that which is the case") *per se*, that is, as autonomous, self-contained entities, "things," or "objects," resting somewhere "out there" (as I say elsewhere, "patiently awaiting to be discovered by some brisk and assiduously enterprising scientist, for in turn to be employed as more or less crucial evidence for his hypothesis," Tennessen, 1972, p. 126). I am much more seriously concerned with the whole myth of *scientism* as a belief in some sort of scientific world view miraculously emanating from the main bulk of so called "scientific results." I see absolutely no reason why anything merely announced as "scientific results" should ever necessitate a change or even the slightest modification of man's orientation in life, his personal philosophy, or his general world view.

The quondam quite popular perpetrators of scientism would not have agreed, I suppose. They, it appears, seemed to have looked on science as a mighty, monstrous machinery that produced correct views and opinions *in abstracto,* as it were—completely independent of the integral part of this human endeavor's setting in individual, human *interests* and the motives and intentions of those who were to attend to it, oil it, serve it, improve it, spoil it, or neglect it (Habermas, 1966, 1970a, 1970b, 1971, 1974; Lobkowicz, Dallmayr, Lenhardt, Hill, & Nichols 1972). This vision was, needless to say, a disastrous delusion. It simply presented itself as nonsensically silly—for human beings and for their Weltanschauung purposes—to attempt a pursuit of science totally independent of the philosophic and general system-building enterprise. It soon transpired that only insofar as human beings are autonomous and articulate enough to have value priorities, action priorities, and ontological priorities can scientific results have a rational power of influencing, let alone drastically changing, their basic attitudes, their "philosophy," or their "world." Only under such circumstances do sentences expressing "results" of scientific research become sufficiently trenchant to touch, in a rational manner, on personal situations. We are forced to realize the necessity of a precise and consistent framework in order to make differentiated judgements—either appreciative or disclaiming—with regard to any phenomenon that appears to the consciousness. Let us, for instance, say that one of my learned friends alleges to have actually made one of those earth-shaking, thrilling "scientific" discoveries. He has "found" some startling "scientific fact" of what not. I can only engage in what would deserve to be called a "rational rencontre" with my friend, if I can meet his claim with a clear and distinct cognitive latticework, a grid, with a fabric, a texture fine enough to fix-in his so called "fact" and trace its possible impact on the whole structurer's putative foundations, as well as the effect it—according to the system—ought to have on man's currently most pressing priorities of any kind: action, intention, volition, cognition, perception, emotion, evaluation. Otherwise the effect would be an "irrational" or "mysterious" one in the sense that it would merely induce in me an uncontrolled disposition, a mood, like rainy or sunny weather would, or the faces of the moon (The Moon and You, 1968), or some mind-twisting drugs. I might adore his "discovery," his "fact," or I might detest it or neglect it; it does not matter. My reaction would only have psychopathological interest. And so would any hindsight rationalization I should be prepared to doctor up.

Thus, I have demonstrated the imperious necessity of human "worlds."

Quite another problem is this: How are world views possible? I certainly would not know where to start, were I given the task of constructing an all-embracing "world," in the sense of a precise and consistent, global, conceptual system. How could I even start attempting to justify my choice of a point of departure without already presupposing a framework to furnish me with the grounds for such a justification? To me, this initial but fundamental obstacle seems embarrassingly obvious and obstinate: in what I take to be the all-embracing sense of "world," which I strive to employ here, my "world" would necessarily embrace everything, comprising inter alia the only conceptual framework from which I can possibly draw the standards for evaluating anything. And this does not only include all and every appraisal of the validity or veridicality of my total view, or the "reality" of my "world," but also the simplest assessment of the meaningfulness or absurdity of this very question. I see, at the present, no way for me to arrive at an assessment of my world without presupposing a frame of reference entailed in and by that world of mine. Were I to employ a different frame of reference (acquired from where?) and apply it to my world, in what sense of "my world" would it then be my world to which it applied? Certainly not in the sense of my total view, my "system" or "synthesis"—which is, after all, the traditional philosophical world for a consistent, principally all-embracing total view, with its logic, ontology, epistemology, value system, and so on.

Only one thing can be said with some degree of certainty here: world views, whether "scientific" or not, never do automatically emerge from an abundant assemblage of so-called "scientific facts." There cannot, as it turns out, be any such thing as "a scientific world view," no established scientific knowledge in any sense of "knowledge" that can be found among the last generation of students of the scientific enterprise (among many others who have recently contributed, J. Agassi, H.

Butterfield, R. S. Cohen, J. B. Conant, A. C. Crombies, E. D. Dijksterhuis, B. Ellis, Paul K. Feyerabend, M. Jammer, A. Koyre, Tom S. Kuhn, Imre Lakatos, Arne Naess, Michael Polanyi, Richard Popkin, Sir Karl Popper, H. Tennessen, A. Wolf). Efforts toward a creative world orientation should consequently not be hampered by that narrow, disintegrated view of "science" or by "scientism" as indicated below. On the contrary, psychologists should be encouraged and enabled to utilize and participate in the humanly integrated science enterprise—but only provided they, as it were, "know who they are" to the extent of having at least provisionally articulated their basic priorities of evaluation and action. Because at a given time, in a definite human society, only one or a small number of views on a certain topic were considered scientifically "respectable," the "scientific" coercion would tend to induce conformity, spurious agreement, and other directedness. In short, "the old, disintegrated image of science" did, in fact, become impersonalizing and dehumanizing. It is a good thing that it is extinct.

On the other hand, the inability of any scientific enterprise per se to provide a world view should not make it less attractive to so-called "humanists," let alone "humanistic psychologists." Rather, it should be to the contrary. Many psychologists who turn their backs to scientific activity do so because of misunderstandings and misconceptions, like those mentioned above, as to what it really is and thereby lose an invaluable opportunity for participating in a most central *human* undertaking—indeed, one that in the long run may prove to be the sole collective and common enterprise for this remarkable species that man, after all, is. It is in this connection worth taking note of the fact that in the mid-twentieth century, a revolutionary movement was started which completely changed the image of science. With some simplification, one could, as I do, speak of this new image as an integrated image of science stressing the human side of a thoroughly human enterprise. And we find the rapidly expanding fields of history of science forming the main bridge between "humanistic" and "scientific" undertakings. These fields provide a particularly strong appeal to researchers who see themselves as representing a "humanistic" orientation. Even to professional "belletristic" writers, such as Arthur Koestler, the development of science has revealed itself as an exciting, exhilarating and colorful drama. The sciences, then, according to his new integrated image, are not, when articulated with care, autonomous; they constitute the most exactly formulated and interpersonally testable parts of existing, or more often potential, general views about man and the world.

Efforts to isolate what might properly have been called autonomous or pure science have failed and will continue to fail. Scientific revolutions, or more generally, any substantial, noteworthy change in scientific tradition, makes science (as represented by the small elite of creative scientists) shift loyalties within the area of human, total or near-total, world views.

History of philosophy, history of ideas, and contemporary philosophical movements furnish the most comprehensive examples and studies of such general views. Philosophers who have been trained as scientists are able to make broader frameworks of contemporary science more explicit and help to work out typologies of general world views with the ultimate aim of covering any possible, coherent, total view of man and his world.

The new and integrated view of "hard" ("scientific"?) and "soft" ("humanistic"?) sciences may therefore readily be seen to evoke a revival of the one, long dreaded, "metaphysical" but humanly significant concern with the so-called "total view" offering a global framework and hence in-principle-solutions to all conceivable problems which are not taken to be mere questions of details. If all sciences are seen as man's attempts at satisfying, at least in part, man's need for intersubjective and fairly precisely formulated general world views, the question seems inevitable: How can we ever get to know which of these total or near-total views is right, (the most) veridical, tenable, reliable, and confidence inspiring. Or, if you wish, which world is the real one? And how on earth would we know for certain? Those problems are dealt with in different papers (Tennessen, 1970, 1976, 1980). Their common aim, however, is to demonstrate the fatuous futility of the very idea of "scientific autarchy," a notion whose acceptance, as I see it, is in turn presupposed in the very idea of a "humanistic psychology."

References

Butterfield, H. *The origin of modern science*. London: Bell, 1951.
Habermas, J. Knowledge and interest. *Inquiry*, 1966, *9*, 285–301.
Habermas, J. On systematically distorted communication. *Inquiry*, 1970, *13*, 205–219. (a)

Habermas, J. Toward a theory of communicative competence. *Inquiry*, 1970, *13*, 360–376. (b)

Habermas, J. *Knowledge and human interest*. Boston: Beacon, 1971.

Habermas, J. *Theory and practice*. London: Heineman, 1974.

Lobkowicz, N., Dallmayr, F. R., Lenhardt, C. K., Hill, M. A., & Nichols, C. Review symposium on Habermas. *Philosophy of the Social Sciences*, 1972, *2*, 193–210.

Tennessen, H. *Which world is the real one, and how would we know?* Invited address to the American Psychological Association, Miami Beach, September, 1970.

Tennessen, H. On knowing what one knows not. In J. R. Royce & W. W. Rozeboom (Eds.), *The psychology of knowing*. New York: Gordon & Breach, 1972.

Tennessen, H. Against scientism and the chimeral humanistic/scientific dichotomy. *Porceedings of the XVth World Congress of Philosophy*. Sofia: Sofia Press Production Centre, 1974.

Tennessen, H. *Mysteries of mortal man*. Edmonton, Alb.: University of Alberta Bookstore, 1975.

Tennessen, H. Homo telluris: The conscious cosmic caddis fly. In J. L. Christian (Ed.), *Extra-terrestrial intelligence: The first encounter*. Buffalo, N.Y.: Prometheus Books, 1976.

Tennessen, H. *Problems of knowledge*. Assen: von Gorcum, 1980.

The moon and you. *This Week Magazine*, Baltimore, November 17, 1968.

12

Daniel E. Berlyne

HUMANISTIC PSYCHOLOGY AS A PROTEST MOVEMENT

The term "humanistic psychology" seems to stand not for a coherent, unified movement or theoretical position but rather for a heterogeneous, not very sharply delineated assortment of views. The main distinguishing feature that they have in common seems to be expression of dissatisfaction with much contemporary psychology, especially experimental psychology. Their intention is certainly to convey positive, life-affirming messages. But the fact remains that much of what exponents of the humanistic psychology currently write is negative in tone. It consists of criticisms aimed at alleged deficiencies in the work of many, if not most, other psychologists.

Humanistic psychologists make statements intended as contributions to psychological knowledge, as well as discussing the nature of psychological knowledge and how it should be sought. But this is not all that they do. They organize various forms of psychotherapy. They also publish a great deal of exhortatory and inspirational literature which is designed to help its readers live more satisfactory lives. It thus amounts to attempted psychotherapy of a mass audience. It resembles, at least in its aims, much of what religious leaders, moral philosophers, poets, and essayists have been writing over the centuries. Nevertheless, the ensuing discussion will be confined to epistemological issues raised

Daniel E. Berlyne • Late of the Department of Psychology, University of Toronto, Toronto, Ontario M5S 1A1, Canada.

by humanistic psychologists—that is, issues concerning psychological research.

Five lines of dissent can be discerned in the writings of humanistic psychologists. They appear to be protesting against (1) the application of scientific method to the study of human behavior, (2) the conception of science that is prevalent in contemporary psychology, (3) behaviorism, (4) neglect of some important characteristics of human beings, and (5) the current distribution of research effort among psychological topics. This fivefold division is admittedly a little arbitrary. All these five protests are interrelated, and individual humanistic psychologists give different degrees of emphasis to one or the other. Nevertheless, I will proceed to discuss these five protests in turn. I will suggest, for the sake of argument, that the first three of them have no merit whatever whereas the last two have some basis but are overstated.

The Application of Scientific Method of Human Behavior

The first protest is against use of scientific methods of inquiry in the study of human behavior. Such methods, it is felt, mean treating human beings "inhumanly" or as "objects."

Two main grounds are adduced for the objection. On the one hand, scientific inquiry means the employment, with reference to human beings, of research techniques, concepts, ways of thinking, and terminology that are used with reference to lower animals or even inanimate objects. This is felt to be offensive and degrading. It also prevents the investigator from recognizing ways in which human beings differ from nonhuman entities (which links up with the fourth protest, to be discussed later).

Secondly, scientific inquiry means adopting a dispassionate, objective stance. It means excluding the feelings of respect and sympathy that should be prominent in all human interaction. It means approaching research subjects either without emotion at all or with unseemly feelings of superiority. In Buber's (1947) terms, it means substitution of an "I–it" for an "I–thou" relationship.

Since we are dealing here with value judgments, it is possible to reject these views without being in a position to refute them. Much depends on whether the objectors veer toward a naturalistic or a non-naturalistic ethical position. Some of them offer what appear to be naturalistic, or even utilitarian, arguments. They assert that the scientific attitude encourages the treatment of human beings as instruments, the subordination of their interests to those of persons in authority or of some abstract notion of society, and the impoverishment of their lives through the stifling of their capacities.

It can hardly be denied that exploitation and debasement of mankind have been conspicuous since the advent of scientific psychology. A causal relation between the two is often hinted at or vigorously asserted. Some blame scientific psychology and the growth of science generally for the evils in question. Others see causality working in the opposite direction, which is no less derogatory to scientific psychology; they depict scientific psychology as something that could only have emerged in a reprehensible, degenerate social climate, of which it is an expression.

But there is little reason to believe that these evils have been more conspicuous recently than in previous ages. Massacres and enslavements have been widespread throughout history and in all geographical regions. If those responsible for them were any less effective than their modern counterparts (which is at least questionable), this was surely not because they lacked the will but because they did not have available to them gas chambers, atomic bombs, and other products of modern technology. There is little reason to believe that they would have had any compunction about using these aids if they had had access to them. We often hear the complaint that people nowadays represent no more than perforations in computer cards. It is doubtful whether things were any better when they represented hieroglyphs on papyruses. Furthermore, there is no reason to believe that the social evils of the twentieth century can be traced to scientific psychology. Those who can be blamed for perpetuating these evils do not seem to be particularly conversant with the findings of modern psychology. They have no need to be. Techniques that they have inherited from their predecessors of earlier centuries have proved effective enough.

On the other side, it is possible to point out that activities like engineering and medicine, which appear to have benefited human beings and to have spared them much suffering, are inseparable from scientific inquiries that treat human beings as objects, in the sense of bodies with particular physical and chemical characteristics and governed by the same physical and chemical laws as the rest of nature. And, since rational, objective analysis of human behavior began in the eighteenth century (although the introduction of controlled experimental and other empirical methods of investigation did not come until the late nineteenth century), there have been some noteworthy improvements in the way human beings treat one another, including the abolition of slavery and the introduction of humane methods for dealing with the insane, the criminal, and the poor.

Be that as it may, some writers render themselves impervious to this kind of consideration by maintaining that the scientific analysis of human life, regardless of its consequences, is intrinsically objectionable. They appear to favor some kind of intuitionist ethics. I have met people, for example, who maintain that they would oppose behavior therapy even if it could be shown to fulfill all its objectives with complete success and to be the only way of relieving certain distressing symptoms. It is, they hold, wrong to treat people that way in any circumstances. In previous centuries, there were like-minded people for whom it was more important to protect the soul against the dangers of heresy than to desist from torture and burning at the stake. In the early nineteenth century, there were comparable people who decried measures to relieve the pains of childbirth, attaching more importance to the fulfillment of God's will, to which they thought such measures contrary.

One can attempt to counter such attitudes with the help of the various forms of ethical debate reviewed by Stevenson (1944). But if the attitudes continue to be held steadfastly, there is no way of demonstrating that they are wrong. One can only contend that there is no good reason for believing that they are right and express one's own abhorrence of them.

Prevalent Conceptions of Science

The second protest is aimed at the conception of science that experimental and other empirical psychologists adopt and follow. It is objected either that this conception is too narrow or that it is inappropriate to the study of human behavior.

A simple semantic confusion seems, in large part, to underlie this line of objection. The word "science" has actually two distinct meanings. On the one hand, it has a narrow meaning referring to controlled empirical inquiry. In other words, it denotes, according to this narrower usage, the procedures and outcomes of experiments and other methods of investigation that confine themselves to statements about observable events and about statistical associations among them and to what can be inferred from such statements; it also denotes careful consideration of alternatives to the hypothesis favored by the investigator and research designs that incorporate controls for the obvious errors to which observations and conclusions drawn from observations are subject. But the word "science" also has a broader sense, referring to any form of systematic scholarship.

In the English language, usage has become confined almost entirely to the narrower sense, although traces of the broader sense are occasionally encountered. This narrower sense had established itself by the time the British Association for the Advancement of Science was founded in 1831. The *Oxford English Dictionary* has the following quotation from one W. G. Ward, writing in the *Dublin Review* in 1867: "We shall use the word 'science' in the sense which Englishmen so commonly give to it; as expressing physical and experimental science, to the exclusion of theological and metaphysical." In continental Europe, on the other hand, words like the French *science* and the German *Wissenschaft* (with their equivalents in other languages) often stand for what is called "science" in English but are commonly used in a much less restrictive sense. For example, it is quite usual in continental languages to call activities like history, philosophy, art criticism, and even theology "scientific." And most of the appeals for greater latitude in defining science that come to us from humanistic psychologists and others can be traced back, directly or indirectly, to some continental European influence, with the linguistic differences rarely recognized.

So, it cannot be maintained that the prevalent strict conception of "science" is too narrow and inappropriate. It is simply the only conception of science that is compatible with accepted English usage. The question still remains whether scientific investigation of human behavior, in this sense, should be supplemented or replaced by other kinds of research. But these other kinds of research, whatever their merits or demerits, cannot properly be called "science" by anybody writing in English. Some other term, such as "humanistic scholarship" or "speculative scholarship," must be applied to them. Here, the word "speculative" is, of course, not used in its pejorative sense but in its evaluatively neutral, somewhat technical sense.

The question at issue, freed from semantic red herrings, is whether there should be a kind of psychology that is not science but humanistic scholarship. In North American universities, it is customary to classify disciplines as "sciences" and "humanities" (the latter corresponding more or less to what in France are called "human sciences"). So, the question that is raised is whether psychology should be pursued as one of the humanities as well as, or instead of, being pursued as one of the sciences. This brings us back to a distinction between two kinds of research that was intensively discussed by German scholars in the nineteenth and early twentieth centuries (see Freund, 1973).

The distinction is ultimately attributable, like so much else, to Descartes's view of the human being as, to use Ryle's (1949) terms, a "machine" with a "ghost" in it. The human body was a mechanism governed by the same laws as animal bodies and inanimate objects. But a human being was also unique in possessing a mind or soul that could intervene in the functioning of the body and was quite different from the body in its characteristics and governing principles. Descartes's theory encouraged two divergent currents of thought with regard to methodological aspects of research into human behavior. On the one hand, his mechanistic conception of the body, especially with its anticipation of the later concept of the "reflex," prompted the extension to the human being of forms of inquiry that first proved their worth in physics and chemistry. It led eventually to the inclusion of neurophysiology, psychology, and other behavioral studies within the domain of science.

On the other hand, the uniqueness of the human mind and its role in the direction of behavior, as depicted by Descartes, suggested to many thinkers the need to attack the activities of human beings with quite different methods of inquiry from those that would do for other subject matter. The first to argue seriously along these lines was Vico (1725), although he was partly motivated by an objection to one aspect of Descartes's thought, namely his view of human nature as something fixed and unchanging. Vico suggested that the study of human society required a "new science" (the title of his main work). This must contrast with the kind of inquiry deemed suitable for other subject matter in such ways as making more use of imagination, being more tolerant of vagueness, and giving due weight to historical change and relativism. The historicist tradition launched by Vico, according to which human activities and their products can be understood only with reference to their historical settings, to their roles as elements in a process of development, became particularly popular in nineteenth-century Germany, especially with the powerful encouragement of Hegel's philosophy.

Another intellectual tradition of relevance is hermeneutics, the theory of interpretation (Apel, 1955; Radnitski, 1968; Rusterholz, 1973). Since classical antiquity, there has been a copious stream of literature on the various techniques through which meaning can be extracted from documents. Through the Middle Ages, these techniques were generally discussed with reference to the interpretation of the Holy Scriptures, Greek and Latin literary works, and legal texts. In the middle of the nineteenth century, Schleiermacher's (1838) treatment extended the scope of hermeneutics enormously, developing it as a collection of methods for the investigation of all kinds of texts and, in fact, all kinds of human artifacts and cultural products, even those that are nonlinguistic. There is currently an important school of epistemologists in continental Europe, the so-called "hermeneutic philosophers" (Apel, 1955; Radnitski, 1968), who are little known in English-speaking countries. Their writings are intended as serious challenges to positivistically inclined notions of how knowledge should be sought. They maintain that hermeneutic methods are the only proper methods for the "human sciences." The implication is that such disciplines as psychology and sociology should utilize the kinds of investigation on which disciplines concerned with documents, such as literary studies, history, law, and theology, depend. This is clearly an appeal for a psychology that is closer to the humanities than the sciences.

The historicist and hermeneutic currents gave rise to the distinction between two kinds of research that began to preoccupy German philosophers toward the end of the nineteenth century. Dilthey (1883) differentiated between *Naturwissenschaft* (natural science) and *Geisteswissenschaft*. The latter term means literally something like "mental science," but the questionable translation "moral science," introduced by John Stuart Mill, is sometimes used in English. Windelband (1894) contrasted "nomothetic" research and "idiographic" research. Rickert (1902) distinguished between natural science and *Kulturwissenschaft* (cultural science). These three pairs of words denoted more or less the same two kinds of intellectual activity, although the three philosophers mentioned introduced their own emphases. The dichotomy has been developed further in the twentieth century by Jaspers (1913), Spranger (1922), and contemporary hermeneutic philosophers.

It will be most convenient to use Windelband's terms. Nomothetic research corresponds to what is called "science" in English, whereas idiographic studies belong to what we have called "humanistic scholarship," although they are "science" in the continental sense.

Several polarities have been adduced to capture the contrasts between nomothetic and idiographic investigation. The one seeks generalizations pertaining to classes of objects or events, while the other aims to illuminate specific instances. It is often maintained that this distinction is meaningless on the ground that particular objects or events can only be understood by referring to classes of which they are members, to characteristics that they share with other objects or events, and by evoking general principles. But it can be pointed out likewise that investigations aimed at principles applicable to classes of objects or events cannot proceed without considering individual cases. There is surely a difference between research aimed primarily at what is generalizable and research aimed primarily at what is unique. To continue, the one aims at explanation, including explanation in terms of causal laws, while the other aims at understanding, including understanding of intentions and meaning. Many writers use the untranslated German word *"Verstehen"* to denote the special kind of understanding that is in question here (see Abel, 1948; Apel, 1955). The one isolates elements, factors, and variables, while the other relates elements to the wholes of which they are part and relates these wholes to their contexts. The one depends exclusively on observation and rational reflection, while the other draws heavily on imagination and emotion, bringing it close in many ways to art both in the sense of verbally incommunicable skill and in the sense of the kind of creativity that produces works of art. The one generates mainly quantitative statements, and the other, qualitative statements. The one keeps itself "value-free," that is, it holds itself aloof from evaluations other than judgments of truth and falsehood, while the other brings in values in at least two senses. It relates activities and products of human beings to their value systems, and it does not hesitate to make value judgments, not only with reference to what is good and bad or beautiful and ugly but also with reference to intrinsic value, that is, what is important or worthy of attention (see Berlyne, 1971, Chapter 6).

The idiographic method has been applied most extensively to the study of historical events, works of art, and social institutions. But it is also applicable to the personalities and specific acts of individual human beings. An idiographic investigator begins by interviewing and observing persons relevant to his investigation, becoming thoroughly immersed in documents and other artifacts produced by them and studying as many features as possible of the physical and social environment to which they have been exposed. All this enables him to recreate within his own mind and, through his writings, in the minds of his readers the conscious experiences of the actors in question. This is the "empathy" *(Einfühlung)* of Vischer and Lipps, the "reexperiencing" *(Nacherleben)* of Dilthey, and the "transferring oneself into the mental" *(sich hineinversetzen ins Seelische)* of Jaspers. From these recreated experiences, various conclusions are drawn, producing a sense of understanding the matter under discussion. The hallmark of validity is a "feeling of evidence" *(Evidenzerlebnis)* in the mind of the investigator and of his readers. The common human characteristics that they share with the human beings under study enables them to tell whether, subjected to comparable circumstances, they could have harbored such feelings, beliefs, values, and intentions and whether, harboring them, they would have acted, spoken, or written like that.

Before going any further, some possible misunderstandings must be cleared away. Although, as mentioned earlier, Descartes's psychophysical dualism was one of the remote sources of the nomothetic-idiographic distinction, the exponents of this distinction did not mean it to correspond altogether to the mind–matter distinction. In fact, with some exceptions, such as Rickert's contrast between natural and cultural sciences, the distinction was not one of subject matter at all but of method and aim. It was certainly felt that nomothetic science is particularly appropriate to inorganic matter and idiographic research to the interactions of human beings, but it was generally recognized that both kinds of research can be directed at the same phenomena. Some adverse remarks were certainly made about the alleged insufficiencies of a generalizing, nomothetic, experimental psychology, but it was not argued that there is no place at all for such a discipline. The point is essentially that experimental studies of human life, whether physiological or psychological, are limited in scope. They need to be supplemented, and perhaps eventually replaced, with a "descriptive and analytic psychology" (Dilthey, 1894) belonging to *Geisteswissenschaft*.

It is evident, therefore, that a nomothetic psychology and an idiographic psychology are both possible. Their objectives and hence their methods must be very different. The scope of each is vast but restricted. And as long as what each is trying to do has appeal for at least some people and neither can be shown conclusively to have socially harmful effects (although socially harmful effects have been ascribed to both by their detractors), who is to say that either of them is illegitimate? With the possible exception of overlapping areas of neighboring disciplines, such as neurophysiology, zoology, sociology, and anthropology, no other intellectual pursuit is attempting what empirical psychology aspires to accomplish. But idiographic psychology is open to the objection that its goals are precisely those that have been attained with impressive success by the great poets and novelists, not to mention composers and visual artists. Dilthey (1894) showed some impatience with the idea that literature could replace his "descriptive psychology," objecting that the psychological content of literary works is not usually set forth systematically. But it could be retorted that the extraction and exposition of the psychological content of literary works is the business of certain kinds of criticism. The goals of idiographic psychology are likewise close, if not identical, to those of some kinds of philosophy. It is, in fact, difficult to draw boundary lines to separate those forms of art, art criticism, philosophy, and idiographic psychology that achieve their convergent aims most effectively.

What is essential is to be clear about the distinct tasks of the two kinds of research, their limitations, and the sharp differences between them. What we choose to call them and, in particular, to which the word "science" should be applied is a secondary matter. There are, however, good reasons for complying with the conventions of the language one is using. And whatever meaning is given to it, "science" carries with it a burden of associations and attitudes. When we approach something labeled as a work of art, we expect it to convey the idiosyncratic beliefs and feelings of its creator, his "personal vision." We may admire, enjoy, and be deeply affected by the manner in which he transmits his message. We may well temporarily suspend disbelief in his message while under the spell of his work. But we know that, however meritorious the work, the message must ultimately be treated with skepticism or even suspicion and that we are more than likely to have good reasons for rejecting it. We can appreciate a poem or painting designed to glorify a baroque despotism while repudiating the political views that it expresses. And we do not feel bound to share the theological position of a Japanese sculptor, however effective we find his statue of the Amida Buddha. If, however, a work of idiographic psychology is presented as "science" rather than as "art", quite different attitudes are likely to be encouraged. The suggestion will be that the work makes, or at least intends, a contribution to established knowledge, and the validity of this suggestion needs to be examined in each case.

Psychological science and psychological humanistic scholarship are not mutually exclusive. But relations between them can create mischief in either of two conditions, neither of which is uncommon. One is the improper encroachment of one on the domain of the other. The second is any effort to pursue both simultaneously.

Empirical psychologists are in the wrong when they presume, in their professional capacities, to prescribe goals for society. They are, of course, within their rights when they recommend, on the basis of their findings, ways of arriving at goals on whose desirability there is general agreement. Similarly, they are wrong if they aspire to present a total picture of something within their area of interest, affording a sense of understanding it as a whole, with components clearly related to overall structure and essentials differentiated from minor features. Empirical science can estimate the relative importance of a particular variable, characteristic, or factor in a limited sense—that is, in terms of proportion of variance accounted for or amount of information generated but not in terms of relevance to the quality of human life or the overriding concerns of humanity.

On the other hand, speculative scholars are wrong when they make general assertions linking classes of events, causally or otherwise. This happens. Those who favor intuitive methods (including many who identify themselves as "humanistic psychologists") do not always confine themselves to the elucidation of specific instances. They often arrive at generalizations without going through the laborious techniques of data collection and statistical analysis that are customary among empirical psychologists, whom they tend to regard as a bunch of pedantic spoilsports. It is, interestingly enough, quite common to find anthropologists and sociologists who are extremely scrupulous and rigorous in making observations but who rely on little more than empathy in drawing general conclusions (for a good example, see Geertz, 1973). But there is unfortunately no substitute for the time-consuming and often tedious paraphernalia of controlled empirical research when it comes to arriving at explanatory laws and principles. The manifold sources of error with which observations and inferences from observations are fraught have been recognized for centuries. One need only mention the susceptibility of perception to illusion and biased selection, the well-documented tendency of human beings to misjudge the relative frequencies of particular kinds of events, or the usual confounding, in naturally occuring conditions, of several variables that could have some responsibility for observed effects.

When statements implying causal or other associations among classes of events are based on intuitive plausibility, however potent, or on the life experience of a scholar, however extensive, they cannot have the status of contributions to knowledge. As Max Weber (1922) recognized, they can have only the status of hypotheses that, valuable as they may be, remain to be verified. And their verification requires the controlled methods of science which are, by definition, the only methods that can distinguish what is probable enough to act on from what is unsubstantiated.

That the aims of nomothetic and idiographic research cannot profitably be pursued together has been hotly disputed by writers of Hegelian and Marxist inspiration, as well as by some recent spokesmen for humanistic psychology. It has been maintained that a science that aspires toward objectivity and refrains from evaluation is immoral, that to study human life as it is, without at the same time waxing indignant over its shortcomings and working toward its improvement, is to be guilty of complicity in the perpetuation of social evils. But this seems to be a misunderstanding of the essential point, which is not that reality should be examined without criticism but that ascertaining facts and deciding what to do about the facts should take place separately and successively. In fact, since they require different talents, they need not necessarily be done in succession by the same people. One also encounters, of course, the additional objection that to think one is seeking facts without bias is a delusion, that to aim to do so is to subscribe to, or at least unconsciously to further, certain undesirable theoretical positions. The point that facts and values are not separable is frequently encountered. It was put to me by Professor Howard Adelman of York University, who was good enough to comment on the initial version of this chapter, and versions of it appear in several contributions to this volume.

I am well aware that the notion of intersubjective "basic statements" has been severely criticized. It has often been objected that people with differing values, presuppositions, cultural backgrounds, linguistic habits, and so on may very well disagree on how an observable event should be described. These arguments seem generally to center around statements like "this is a table" or "this is blue." Such statements actually figure in Neurath's (1932) original discussion of "protocol sentences," which has given rise to so much controversy. But statements like these actually play little part in experimental science. There, observation statements commonly refer to occurrences in a number of alternative, clearly separated spatial or temporal locations. For example, a physicist notes which mark on a meter is closest to where the needle comes to rest or which light on a scintillation counter lights up. A psychologist might be concerned with whether somebody circles the word "yes" or "no" on a questionnaire or whether a rat enters the right or left goal box of a maze. Either might use as basic data which numerals appear in particular locations on a computer printout. There is, I submit, little evidence that people with different values, presuppositions, or ideological commitments are ever in serious disagreement about such spatiotemporal discriminations, provided that elementary precautions are taken to prevent indistinctness (e.g., making sure that the alternative spatial or temporal locations are sufficiently distant from one another).

It is true that sometimes (e.g., in the biological sciences) observables that differ quite markedly from spatiotemporal discriminations serve as basic data. For example, characteristics defining species of animals or symptoms defining diseases may very well be specified in other terms. In most cases, this seems to lead to a sufficient measure of agreement among observers. But when such characteristics or symptoms are not specified in a way that precludes serious disagreement over their presence or absence in particular cases, then biologists would, I imagine—and certainly should—reformulate them in relation to spatiotemporal discriminations, using measuring instruments if necessary. So, I suggest, should behavioral scientists.

I realize that science cannot content itself with simply recording spatiotemporal discriminations or other observables. It relates such data to higher-order concepts, it derives from them explanatory theories, uses them to predict future events, and so forth. There are fierce debates over how all this is done and how these products of science are related to observation statements. And it might very well be that which answer one gives to these questions depends on values of an extrascientific nature. The position presented here is meant to be neutral with respect to all these views. It is meant to be tolerant enough to count as "scientific" any statements that are inferred, with the help of specifiable rules of inference and subsidiary premises, from observation statements on which general agreement can be obtained.

The point is not that there is a sharp distinction between facts and values but rather that these are important differences between, on the one hand, inquiries aimed primarily at ascertaining facts, keeping out values that are extrinsic to those of pure science as far as possible, and, on the other hand, inquiries aimed primarily at evaluating facts and deciding what to do about them. The following analogy may be more apt than it will seem at first glance. No shirt can be completely clean. Microscopic examination will invariably reveal the presence of a substantial quantity of bacteria and foreign matter. And there is, of course, no clear cutoff point among the gradations that go from the least dirty shirt to the dirtiest. Nevertheless, there is a difference between somebody who tried to keep his shirts as clean as possible by changing them frequently and having them laundered regularly and somebody who wears the same shirt for months on end without ever having it washed. If shirt wearers were like some contemporary writers on social-science themes, they would use the fact that no shirt can be completely clean as an excuse to renounce any attempt at cleanliness or even deliberately to smear mud on their shirts. But I would suggest that this is indefensible.

The reasons that nomothetic and idiographic research cannot be carried on in conjunction with each other are essentially the same as the reasons that high-class sonnets cannot be composed while playing high-class football. These reasons are at least three in number. First, the decisions on which first-class football and first-class poetry depend are extremely demanding, and the limited channel capacity of the human nervous system precludes their simultaneous occurrence without mutual interference. Secondly, the constitutional endowments and kinds of training that the two activities require are rare enough to make their occurrence in the same individuals highly improbable. And thirdly, the processes and talents on which the two activities draw have a certain incompatibility. So likewise, nomothetic and idiographic psychology are so exacting and require such specialized, but different, talents and training that it is hard enough to do well either alone without hoping to fulfill the aims of both. And while imagination and emotional involvement certainly have their place in empirical science, they must be kept under tight rein there, whereas they must have wider scope in humanistic scholarship. The relatively detached and dispassionate approach of the empirical scientist is, as humanistic psychologists often rightly point out, inimical to anything beyond the circumscribed aims of the experimental and correlational study. On the other hand, the relatively untrammeled exercise of fantasy and intuition that are indispensable to the humanistic scholar can only encourage the kinds of error that the empirical scientist is constantly at pains to guard against.

Since the debate over the two kinds of research germinated toward the end of the nineteenth century, three developments have greatly complicated the issues that we are now discussing. The first concerns a form of hermeneutics called "allegoresis," originally recognized in the Middle Ages. This consisted of interpreting texts in conformity with, and in support of, a previously accepted theory. For example, the Old Testament, and occasionally even the works of pagan classical authors such as Virgil, were given symbolic meanings in line with the doctrines of the Church. In the twentieth century, modern techniques of communication and the ideals of free speech adopted in some parts of the world have engendered dozens of conflicting ideologies, political, religious, and psychotherapeutic. Each of them has its own views regarding human behavior, and each of them is apt to produce analyses of specific events, cultural products, and human actions in accordance with its own concepts and presuppositions. Each of these interpretations is likely to seem convincing to those who subscribe to the ideology in question. They are likely to reject as (to use a fashionable term) superficial those interpretations that bear the imprint of rival ideologies or of no ideology at all. As already noted, hermeneutic and idiographic studies use the "experience of evidence" as their touchstone of validity. The feeling of evidence is supposed to depend on the common human nature and experience of life that the investigator and his audience share with the human beings under study. But if a feeling of conviction depends not only on common humanity but also on whether or not somebody has been converted to a particular ideology, the utility of this touchstone as a means of distinguishing true understanding from misunderstanding becomes dubious.

Second, many contemporary brands of humanistic psychology and idiographic research (e.g., literary criticism, social philosophy) show the influence of psychoanalysis or other depth psychologies and, like them, interpret behavior with reference to unconscious mental processes. Idiographic psychology in the *Geisteswissenschaft* tradition depends, as we have seen, on the reliving or recreation of the conscious experiences that underlie the behavior of the human beings under investigation. But if their behavior is ascribed to mental events of which neither they nor those who would understand them can be aware, then reexperiencing, coupled with the experience of evidence, can hardly serve as a criterion of validity. This leaves us with the question of what criterion can serve in its place. Terms referring to unconscious processes can be used to denote intervening variables in nomothetic science, provided that the prerequisites of their legitimate employment in this capacity, such as avoidance of circular argument and precise and unambiguous coordination with terms descriptive of observable events, are fulfilled. But they rarely are.

The third complicating factor is the advent of phenomenology. This term was used in different senses by nineteenth-century philosophers such as Hegel and Peirce. But during the twentieth century, it has come to be reserved (except among physicists—cf. Crawford & Jennings, 1974) for the philosophical movement and techniques of inquiry introduced by Husserl (1900–1901) and for various derivatives of them. The phenomenological method is used by a number of prominent contemporary philosophical psychologists, especially in France. Husserl insisted vigorously that his phenomenological inquiries were "scientific" in the continental sense. And many participants of phenomenology have maintained that phenomenological studies, with their clarification of concepts and examination of the conscious experiences in which all knowledge originates, form a necessary preliminary to researches in empirical science. But phenomenology is certainly not empirical science, that is, "science" in the English sense. Like the exponents of *Geisteswissenschaft* and like the rationalist philosophers of the seventeenth and eighteenth centuries, it derives its conclusions from characteristics of thinking and consciousness that all careful inquirers will supposedly share and recognize. However, unlike the idiographic researcher, the phenomenologist does not concentrate on individual events, documents, or persons but aims at general principles, pertaining to classes or entities and to relations among classes of entities, through "intuition of essence" *(Wesenschau)*. So, it falls neither within the nomothetic nor within the idiographic category but in some way straddles both.

The potential role of the phenomenological method in psychology and the relations between phenomenology and other forms of inquiry call for lengthy and painstaking analysis. Here, there is room only for one or two comments. First, phenomenological inquiry necessitates highly sophisticated, specialized, and rigorous procedures. English-speaking psychologists, when they use the term, use it all too often as a euphemism to cover any kind of introspection. The work "introspection" has not recovered from the disrepute that it suffered with the demise of the introspective experimental psychology of Wundt and Titchener. But the term "phenomenology" is high-sounding and respectable enough to invite its improper use as a pretext to cover all kinds of naive, half-formed statements about consciousness and all kinds of untestable, or at least untested, intuitions. Secondly, although phenomenology, like empirical science, is concerned with generalizations and universals and devotes much of its attention to what is perceived through the sense organs, it does not aim to answer the same questions as empirical science. It does not aim to explain the occurrence of particular events and objects in particular spatiotemporal locations or to discover causal and other statistical associations. Its aim is essentially to describe. Consequently, there is no reason why there should be competition between a phenomenological psychology and an experimental, or more generally empirical, psychology.

All this brings us to the question of whether there is a third kind of psychology, namely, a philosophical psychology which is not scientific (in the strict sense) and yet, though it must be classed as humanistic scholarship, is distinct from idiographic psychology. Unlike idiographic psychology, its concern is with general statements about classes or entities, but, unlike scientific psychology, it is not concerned with statistical associations or causal explanations. It examines the language and concepts that are used with reference to behavior and mental processes. Nowadays, this kind of inquiry is usually carried on either with the methods of phenomenology or with those of post-Wittgensteinian ordinary-language analysis. In previous ages, it has relied on other methods. It is quite commonly spoken of as a form of psychology, and there seems to be little harm in this practice, provided that it is carefully differentiated from the other activities bearing this label that we have been discussing. Nevertheless, it seems to me better to regard it as a branch of philosophy, since it differs only in subject matter from other lines of philosophical inquiry.

We must touch on two remaining points in which misguided criticisms of empirical psychology have originated. One concerns the complaint that empirical psychology misses a great deal. For example, Chomsky (1971) states that if "scientific understanding of human behavior" were restricted to the "prediction of behavior from environmental conditions" it would be "inherently limited." As usual, he seasons this comment with piquant slurs like "uninteresting" and "trivial."

However, all scientific research is, by its very nature, "inherently limited," and in at least two ways. First, every branch of science must focus on a limited set of phenomena. Then, it can only aim to answer certain questions about these phenomena, namely, questions regarding properties, interdependences, interpredictabilities, and implications of observables. These are far from being the only kinds of questions about the phenomena that can reasonably be asked. But answers to them are worth having, limited as they are, both because the answers provide intellectual satisfaction for at least some people and because they furnish one kind of knowledge on which effective action must depend. An idiographic study, on the other hand, may likewise be limited with respect to subject matter; but it is not nearly so tightly restricted with respect to the questions it can ask and the kinds of information on which it can draw. On the contrary, everything—every fact, thought, feeling, evaluation—that has the slightest bearing on the subject matter or on its social and historical context must be welcomed as grist for the idiographic researcher, just as it is for the novelist.

Despite what has just been said about the scientist's need to focus his attention, one important aim of science has always been to seek links among dissimilar phenomena. The most conclusive way to do this is by "reduction," defined by Nagel (1961, p. 338) as "the explanation of a theory or a set of experimental laws established in one area of inquiry, by a theory usually though not invariably formulated for some other domain." The theory thus invoked, sometimes called the "reduction base," is invariably one embracing a wider set of phenomena than the area of research that it is called on to illuminate. So, although psychologists must have close relations with the social sciences, they do not usually seek reduction bases in sociology or anthropology because these sciences deal with the behavior of human beings within organized groups, which is only part of the animal and human behavior that the psychologist has to deal with. On the other hand, animal and human behavior have direct associations with some, though by no means all, physiological and vital processes, so that attempts at reduction in psychology usually look to physiology and especially to biology. Such attempts frequently produce hostile outcries. There are some (e.g., the contributors to a book edited by Koestler & Smythies, 1969) for whom "reductionism" is a sinister bugaboo. Like all bugaboos, it seems to be amorphous and nebulous; I myself have failed to find any clear definition of "reductionism" in the book under discussion. Nevertheless, there appear to be many contemporary psychological writers for whom anything stigmatized with this word is irretrievably discredited. In contrast, there are scientists (e.g., contributors to a book edited by Ayala & Dobzhansky, 1975) who scrupulously define various kinds of reductionism that are indispensable to the advancement of science. Certainly, most of the celebrated triumphs of science over the centuries have consisted of imaginative and successful reductions. The idiographic scholar with his quest for uniqueness, however, can do without them.

Behaviorism

The third protest is against behaviorism. This term has been applied at one time or another to a diversity of positions which are seldom differentiated, especially by their critics, as clearly as they should be. The original behaviorism consisted of a view of the task and methods proper to psychology. It was coupled with a comprehensive psychological theory, built up by Watson between his first pronouncement on the matter in 1913 and his withdrawal from scholarly publication toward the end of the 1930s. Several of Watson's contemporaries sympathized with his general orientation, both under his influence and independently of it, but nobody else seems to have accepted his theoretical system. Then, in the 1930s and 1940s, there grew up a variety of neobehaviorisms, which spent most of their time in dispute with one another but which nevertheless had some common characteristics that distinguished them from Watson's behaviorism. A second generation of neobehaviorists, differing in some important respects from the first generation (see Berlyne, 1968), is discernable since about 1950. The "radical behaviorism" of Skinner belongs to the neobehaviorist period. Skinner's views have features in common with Watsonian behaviorism and others in common with the bulk of the new behaviorists. But there are significant ways in which he is unlike either. Lastly, there is philosophical behaviorism, a view regarding the nature of the mind and of mind–body relations. Neobehaviorists have, by and large, steadfastly avoided having anything to say on these questions. Watson and other behavioristically minded psychologists have at times made statements suggestive of philosophical behaviorism, but the issues raised by these statements were far from central to their concerns.

The objections to behaviorism that have been voiced from time to time form a large and motley collection. They are not confined to exponents of nonscientific speculative psychologies but are found also among writers committed to empirical science. They are more often than not expounded with uncomplimentary insinuations regarding the mental capacity and the moral character of those who fail to recognize their cogency.

Anything like an adequate examination of the various lines of attack on behaviorism would require much more space than is available here. They all seem to me to stem from misconceptions, and some brief comments on the most bizarre but widespread of these misconceptions have been presented elsewhere (Berlyne, 1975).

Much of the trouble comes simply from the mistaken identification of behaviorism with the position either of Watson or of Skinner. It is often felt that to find flaws in the views expressed by either of these writers is to demolish behaviorism. But Watsonian behaviorism has had no adherents since at least 1930, and it is far too rarely realized that Skinner is in many ways an extremely atypical behaviorist.

Among the various meanings that have been foisted on the word "behaviorism," the one that was conferred on it at the time of its first public appearance must surely be granted precedence. This was in Watson's article in the 1913 *Psychological Review,* in which he stated, "Psychology as the behaviourist views it is a purely objective experimental branch of natural science. Its theoretical goal is prediction and control of behaviour" (p. 158). In other words, behaviorist psychology was distinguished from the outset simply by the way in which it defined its subject matter. Consequently, any criticism, however legitimate, of theories or statements produced by particular behaviorists do not constitute a refutation of behaviorism any more than to point to shortcomings in geological theories or in statements made by geologists is to refute geology.

There was a time, in the early days of experimental psychology, when psychologists considered their task to be the investigation of the mind and its contents, by which they meant conscious experiences. Watson and several of his contemporaries proposed the different conception of a psychology concerned with the study of behavior. Their influence, coinciding as it did with the eclipse of the older, introspective experimental psychology, encouraged a high proportion of later psychologists, including many who never thought of themselves as behaviorists, to accept and conform to this definition of their discipline.

In the last ten or twenty years, various writers have expressed dissatisfaction with the behaviorist demarcation of their subject matter and asserted that psychology should be regarded as the study of mental processes as well as, or instead of, behavior. Different reasons are given for the assertion, and different things are meant by "mental processes." For many neocognitivist and neostructuralist theorists, mental processes consist of internal events rigorously deduced from observable behavior. The subject is not necessarily aware of them, and yet they do not resemble the unconscious mental processes of the depth psychologists. They represent inferred, successively occurring decisions or choices among alternatives, involving generation, discarding, or recording of information as well as the storage of information and its retrieval from storage. They can be represented by mathematical or computer operations. Other contemporary psychologists, including many who use the humanistic label, favor, on the other hand, mentalistic concepts that are close to those used to discuss mental events and processes in everyday language, although some of them also recognize entities akin to the unconscious mental contents and forces of the Freudians and others.

The neomentalist view of psychology's responsibilities is in tune with the growing advocacy of realist philosophies of science by writers like Harré (1972) and Hesse (1974). These writers oppose the positivist conception of scientific theories as systems of statements that inform us directly, or indirectly, about sense data and relations among sense data. Instead, the realists contend that science should and does reveal structures of entities that underlie what can be observed but are not themselves observable. These, it is alleged, constitute the ultimate reality of the natural world, and observations of perceptible phenomena are important only to the extent that they provide clues to their nature. As far as psychology is concerned, the ultimate underlying reality consists, in this view, of structures of mental events.

We cannot do justice here to the carefully thought-out arguments adduced to support realist and superrealist philosophies of science. But it can be remarked that, since the beginnings of Western thought, there have been those who have attributed reality and importance only to what can be experienced through the senses. They have included the atomists and Epicureans of ancient Greece, the medieval nominalists, and the later empiricists. And there have been others who ascribe more importance and reality to unobservables that are presumed to underlie what the senses perceive. They include Parmenides and Plato, the medieval realists, and the later rationalists. After 2,000 years of debate, the disagreement between these two groups has not been resolved, and no resolution would appear to be imminent. We must thus assume that both of these contrasting tastes or convictions will continue to have their partisans.

There is no reason why psychologists catering to the corresponding preferences, consisting respectively of the investigation of behavior and of the search for mental processes to which the effects of behavior point, could not both be legitimate contributors to science. There are other examples of scientific disciplines that have overlapping subject matters and that treat the same phenomena from different ways dictated by different aims. Physiology and psychology form such a pair, as do anthropology and political science.

Nevertheless, psychologies inquiring into mental events in accordance with scientific canons are rarely advocated in a spirit of "live and let live." Their defense is more often than not accompanied by harsh attacks on psychologists who regard the study of behavior as their main business.

Both Watson and the great majority of neobehaviorists accepted the necessity for theories about behavior to make use of terms referring to inferred or hypothesized, but not directly observable, events going on inside the organism. Skinner has more than once expressed his abhorrence of terms that do not correspond to observable phenomena. But even he has made considerable use of them, from the "reflex reserve" of his early days (1938) to the "covert verbal responses" of the later period (1957).

The common tendency, mentioned above, to equate Skinner and behaviorism has promoted the erroneous impression that behaviorists must restrict themselves to terms descriptive of stimuli and responses. However, Tolman (1938) originated the concept of "intervening variable," which Hull (1943) developed further. It resembled the concepts of "hypothetical construct," "disposition," and "theoretical term" that have appeared in other writings on the philosophy of science, despite the subtle distinctions among these that have been proposed and fought over. In the heyday of neobehaviorist learning theory, it was accepted that intervening variables must be introduced with circumspection and, more particularly, that they must be kept to a minimum and rigorously related to the observable variables through which their values are deduced. Statements about intervening variables, it was believed, say things that could in principle be said in terms of observables alone but at the cost of greater, and often prohibitive, unwieldiness. This view anticipated the work of Craig (1953), who demonstrated that languages containing theoretical terms can be replaced by languages confining themselves to terms denoting observables but that this might require a theoretical system to have as many axioms as it has true statements.

Apart from various internal disputes and the standard protests of realists against positivistically inclined scientific activities, the non-Skinnerian neobehaviorists' way of using intervening variables has stirred up two kinds of objections. First, there are those (e.g., Locke, 1971) who aver that when behaviorists refer, through intervening variables or otherwise, to entities that are not behavior they are inconsistent with their professed occupation as specialists in the study of behavior. The prevalence of this criticism is rather astonishing. Aeronautical engineers have to examine, and talk about, atmospheric turbulence and metal fatigue, among other things. This does not mean that they believe that turbulence and metal fatigue are kinds of aircraft or flight or that they are untrue to their calling as specialists in the flight of aircraft.

Secondly, there are those who hold that terms descriptive of occurrences within the organism should be cultivated for their own sake and not simply tolerated as adjuncts in the pursuit of laws governing behavior. They hold, further, that scientists concerned with the mind should keep close to the terms in which mental events and processes are discussed in everyday conversation. This view is commonly supported with one or other of three kinds of argument. The first, which is related to the realist position in the philosophy of science, has been tersely expressed in Chomsky's (1968, p. 58) influential pronouncement that to define psychology as the science of behavior is like "defining natural science as the science of meter readings." Elsewhere (Berlyne, 1972, 1975), I have pointed out how inexact this analogy is. Behavior, unlike meter readings, existed long before there were scientists, and whereas meter readings hold no interest except as indices of other events, there are good reasons for paying attention to human behavior and the problems that it causes. Another frequently encountered version of the argument is found in Deese's (1972, p. 99) contention that "behavior is only the outward manifestation of what really counts." The point presumably is that what really matters is human conscious experience, how people think and feel and what they perceive. But what human beings experience is profoundly affected by how they and their fellowmen behave, just as it is profoundly affected by the weather. This fact surely strengthens, rather than removes, the justification for both an independent science of meteorology and an independent science of behavior.

A second kind of argument rests on the assumption, adopted by post-Wittgenstein ordinary-language philosophy, that everyday linguistic usage embodies a great deal of incontrovertible wisdom. Austin (1956, p. 8) has suggested (though with more cautions and qualifications than some who have echoed his view) that ordinary language, which is after all the product of centuries of experience and refinement, embodies the distinctions that human beings have found necessary. It may embody the distinctions that are useful for normal everyday discourse, but this does not mean that it has arrived at the distinctions that are important for the specialized purposes of science. To take just one example, users of ordinary language recognized for centuries, as many still do, a category of "fish" that includes starfish, crayfish, cuttlefish, jellyfish, shellfish, and whitefish. This category, which essentially distinguishes aquatic from nonaquatic animals, has some value for managers of aquaria and seafood restaurants, as well as for zoologists specializing in ecology. But for most scientific purposes, whales have much more in common with kangaroos than with sharks. Similarly, the concepts that ordinary language uses to discuss internal states and processes relevant to behavior need not be well adapted to the functions of a science of behavior. In any case, many of them are simply technical terms left in circulation by now outmoded philosophical and psychological theories.

The third line of argument, which is by no means rare, boils down to a blend of two classical fallacies, namely *circulus in demonstrando* and *argumentum ad hominem.* It is reasoned that behaviorist psychologies are inadequate because they do not make use of familiar mentalistic concepts and that familiar mentalistic concepts are necessary because psychologies that dispense with them are inadequate. This reasoning is usually liberally seasoned with characterizations of writings that do not conform to it as "trivial," "superficial," or "naive." Such epithets intimate that those who resort to them are disappointed by whatever they use them to describe. Since the beginning of history, the vast majority of intellectual endeavors have left the vast majority of the human race unthrilled. So the fact that some individuals are moved to express dissatisfaction in discourteous terms hardly constitutes evidence for or against an intended contribution to science.

Human Uniqueness

The fourth protest concerns what is perceived as a failure of scientific psychology to give due weight to those aspects of human nature that are both most important and unique to the human species. Human beings, it is pointed out, are aware of what is going on around them, of significant mental and physical processes going on within them, and of what they are doing. They build up images of themselves and of sections of the external world, actively seeking information to nourish these images, and their actions are determined by their perceptions.

These points are stressed not only by humanistic psychologists but also by many neocognitivist and neostructuralist psychologists identified with nomothetic, experimental science. Other human characteristics, however, receive emphasis from humanistic psychologists more than from others. They insist on the autonomy of the human being. His actions, they assert, depend on plans that he makes, on intentions that he forms, on his decisions and choices.

Excessive neglect of all these characteristics is felt to be reprehensible for two distinct reasons. First, it is felt to produce a grossly inaccurate, misleading, and incomplete account of how human beings function. Secondly, it is deemed apt to have undesirable political, social, and ethical consequences. It will, it is alleged, encourage us, or more especially people with power and authority, to treat human beings as objects to be exploited, ignoring or stultifying their higher potentialities.

In making these points, humanistic psychologists often disparage those whom they consider insufficiently sensitive to them, especially behaviorists and neobehaviorists, as exponents of "push-button" or "slot machine" theories of human behavior. This is, however, an exaggeration and a misunderstanding. It is true that Watson (1925) defined as the goal of behavioristic psychology "to be able, given the stimulus, to predict the response—or, seeing the reaction taking place to state what the stimulus is that has called out the reaction" (p. 11). And Skinner has certainly emphatically insisted on attributing responses to external stimuli rather than to invisible internal events. Nevertheless, even a cursory perusal of the writings of these two figures will remove any impression that they really believe in a one-and-one correspondence between stimulus conditions and responses. Other neobehaviorists, particularly Tolman, Hull, Hebb, and those influenced by them, have fully acknowledged that behavior depends not only on the external stimulus situation of the moment but on variables descriptive of the organism's state (including its motivational state) and on various covert events: "pure-stimulus acts," "cue-producing responses," "mediators," motives, expectancies, and even images.

On the other hand, in their zeal to defend what they see as the cause of human dignity and rationality, humanistic psychologists all too often advocate an uncritical, simple-minded (I have avoided the terms "naive" and "superficial"!) blend of psychophysical interactionism, voluntarism, and vitalism. Far from attempting to refute the various criticisms that have been directed at this kind of position over the centuries, they tend to write as if they have never heard of them.

Humanistic psychologists often claim that the uniquely human functions on which they place so much weight are not amenable to empirical investigation because they are internal. They are consequently entitled to immunity from the rigors of empirical psychology. But one cannot have it both ways. Science is a cooperative human enterprise. If we are to study psychological processes in people other than ourselves at all, then statements about these processes must correspond, in the sense of being logically equivalent or equipollent, to statements about observable behavior. This avoids embroilment in the age-old and evidently interminable debates over such questions as whether statements about internal processes mean the same as, or are translatable into, statements about behavior and whether mental events are identifiable with behavioral events. The statements about behavior can, of course, be quite complicated compound statements, involving implications, disjunctions, and conjunctions. The behavioral events to which they refer can belong to quite different points in time from the internal events in question. In other words, people in whom particular psychological processes are said to occur must at some time act, speak, or write in a way that is in some respect different from how they would act, speak, or write if these processes were absent. In that case, these processes can and should be studied through their carefully specified observable correlates. If there are no such correlates, then the person possessing the internal psychological processes under discussion can build up his own private science about them. But nobody else can know about them, investigate them, or do anything about them. They can play no part in the social activity called "science."

There are certainly times when human behavior is based on deliberate relatively autonomous decisions, based in their turn on deliberate, conscious weighing of alternatives and of relevant information. And for scientific purposes, such behavior can, with the help of references to signs and symbols (Berlyne, 1965, 1975), be handled in terms of what can be observed and without commitment to free will or to psychophysical dualism. But it is equally true that human beings often behave in an unreflective, automatic, irrational manner. Those who focus on the one possibility to the exclusion of the other are in the wrong, as are those who fail to recognize the scientifically and morally important distinctions between the two. Most of us feel that it is ethically, socially, and politically preferable to influence the behavior of others through rational conviction, with the help of accurate, pertinent information and valid logical arguments, than in other ways which exploit human weaknesses. This distinction, which has been developed a little further elsewhere (Berlyne, 1975), resembles Argyris's (1975) distinction between "Model-1" methods of producing social change through some form of direct manipulation and "Model-2" methods of working through "valid information, free and informed choice, and internal commitment." On the other hand, there are times when the rational persuasion of Model-2 methods is not practicable, such as when values are to be imparted to children or when antisocial values, defective reasoning powers, or unfortunate learned responses turn adults into social menaces. Psychologies that soft-pedal the dangerous, primitive, irrational side of human nature are surely as irresponsible as those that overemphasize them.

It is, however, fully possible, without departing from the constraints of science, to recognize the profound contrast between rational, uniquely human forms of behavior and the involuntary, unpremeditated forms of behavior that bring human beings nearer to other animal species. Two developments can contribute to a balanced view of this sort.

First, there are currents in twentieth-century psychology that differentiate between behavior governed by internal symbols and behavior that is evoked or emitted independently of them. They offer criteria by which the intervention of symbolic processes can be detected through properties of observable behavior. They indicate ways in which symbolic processes are likely to have grown out of simpler, more elementary functions, showing behavior governed by symbols to possess similarities with other forms of behavior as well as important differences. Theoretical treatments working in these directions include those of the semiotic movement, developed by American philosophers from Peirce (1897/1940) to Morris (1946). The conception of symbolic processes produced by this movement merged smoothly with the one adopted by the Hullian current in neobehaviorism (Berlyne, 1965; Dollard & Miller, 1950; Hull, 1930; Mowrer, 1960; Osgood, 1952). The Hullian tradition of due attention to motivational problems, converging with the influence of Hebb (1949), has further given rise to theoretical and experimental work on motivational aspects of symbol-manipulating activities, including science, philosophy, mathematics, and art (see Berlyne, 1963, 1965, 1971). Then, there is Piaget's theory (1947/1950, 1945/1951) with its distinction between the forms of behavior that originate during the sensorimotor stage and the forms of behavior that are dependent on symbols, and especially on operational thinking, that appear later. Finally, a great deal of Soviet psychology shows the joint influence of Pavlov's distinction between responses dependent on the first and second signal systems (e.g., Ivanov-Smolenski, 1963; Koltsova, 1963) and of Vygotski's distinction between behavior that is and is not regulated by "inner speech" (e.g., Luria, 1961; Zaporozhets, 1960).

The second development is the accumulation, during the last decade, of evidence supporting multilevel conceptions of behavior. This has come mainly from studies of phylogenetic development (see especially the review by Razran, 1971; also Bitterman, 1975; Voronin, 1971/1973) and studies of the modifications that occur in turn in the activity of different brain structures in the course of learning (Olds, 1973). But supportive evidence comes also from studies of ontogenetic development (see Thompson, 1968; White, 1965). The upshot of this evidence is that human beings possess a number of superimposed levels of behavior, dependent on structures belonging to different levels in the brain. These levels of behavior depend partly on inherited, unlearned neural connections and partly on different forms of learning that appear successively in the course of evolution and in the course of child development. These forms of learning obey different principles in some respects and similar principles in others. Symbolic functions associated with voluntary and rational control over behavior are peculiar to the highest level of behavior, which, although it has its rudimentary forerunners in the higher infrahuman mammals, is unique to the human species and results from the unique characteristics of the human neocortex, particularly the frontal lobes (Luria, 1973; Pribram, 1971). The use of covert symbolic responses to represent inaccessible objects and events makes it possible for these entities to influence action despite their absence from the external environment of the moment. They permit human beings to acquire and use knowledge, that is, information stored in symbolic structures (see Berlyne, 1960, Chapter 10). They enable problems to be solved by thinking (Berlyne, 1965). By permitting anticipatory representation of consequences of future actions, they can direct behavior toward the fulfillment of "expectations," "goals," "intentions," and "purposes." And when they are used to represent both possible alternative courses of action and their likely outcomes, we can appropriately speak of a piece of behavior as resulting from a "choice" or a "decision."

Distribution of Research Effort

The fifth protest of humanistic psychologists is against the current distribution of time and effort among research topics, which certainly bears no resemblance to the distribution of relative importance among topics, no matter by what criteria, theoretical or practical, importance is judged. In particular, humanistic psychologists object, quite rightly, that questions whose answers are needed to guide people in the conduct of their lives and to remedy pressing social ills are neglected or completely ignored.

The reasons that empirical psychologists defer the study of complex psychological processes, which have deep human interest, are often misunderstood. For example, Giorgi (1970, pp. 64–65) complains that a phenomenon "is merely avoided until someone comes along with a technique for measuring it. This, of course, explains why so many peculiarly human phenomena—like crying, laughing, friendship, love—have not as yet made psychological textbooks in depth; they have not as yet been rigorously measured." He goes on, "for academic psychology *measurement precedes existence.*"

Now, there is actually a substantial empirical literature on each of the four phenomena that Giorgi cites, and measuring techniques have been devised without too much difficulty for each of them. But the amount of dependable knowledge that has so far been gained about these topics does not yet warrant their substitution for more traditional topics in elementary textbooks. The point surely is not that scientific psychology disdains anything that is not measurable. It is rather that it cannot accept something within its purview unless it is detectable to an external observer, that is, until the external indices of its occurrence have been specified with adequate precision. As long as one can reliably distinguish situations where a phenomenon can be said to occur from situations where it is absent, one can attach distinct labels, numerical or nonnumerical, to the two kinds of situations. Some would regard this as the most primitive form of measurement, the construction of a nominal scale. Others would withhold the term "measurement" until additional conditions, notably the axioms of measure theory, have been met. But this semantic question is a minor one.

One principle that scientific inquiry must observe was formulated by Descartes in his *Discourse on Method:* "to conduct my thoughts in such order that, by commencing with the simplest objects and the easiest to know, I might ascend little by little and, as it were, step by step, to the knowledge of the more complex." The chemistry of organic compounds must be of particular concern to us, since we consist of them, ingest them, and secrete them. But organic chemistry could not advance far until much time had been spent on the elements and on the simplest inorganic compounds. The specialist in human heredity must reckon with 46 chromosomes and numerous complications, making it difficult to separate what is heritable from what is acquired. But a great deal of patient work has had to be done with the *Drosophila melanogaster,* which has four chromosomes, and with the *Escherichia coli* bacterium, which has one, before much headway could be made in human genetics. Psychological scientists must similarly reconcile themselves to prolonged concentration on the simplest and most tractable phenomena before they can hope to have much to say about the phenomena that excite the laymen's interest most readily.

Nevertheless, empirical psychologists are excessively timid about approaching complex human processes and elaborating research methods appropriate to them. This is largely due to mundane factors inherent in the organization of contemporary scientific institutions, especially in North America where the greater part by far of current psychological research takes place. There are always pressures pushing a graduate student's interests closer to those of his thesis supervisor. These are intensified by confusion between work done as a research assistant, paid out of a grant intended to support a specified project that has been proposed by the supervisor, and work for which a student must assume responsibility as a means to research training, the development of research interests, and the establishment of research competence. Once he has entered the postdoctoral scientific community, habit and inertia tend to keep him working in familiar areas, for which productive methodologies are well entrenched. And the increasingly ferocious competition for appointments, research funds, and journal space inevitably discourages innovative departures from beaten tracks, such as will take some time to yield statistically or theoretically significant results and run an appreciable risk of never doing so.

The progressive concentration of research on a limited number of fragmented areas, sealed off from one another and fortuitously selected, should disquiet empirical psychologists. They should look for some means of remedying this unhealthy state of affairs, and the strictures of humanistic psychologists, and of laymen influenced by them, may provide salutary fillips in this direction.

References

Abel, T. The operation called *Verstehen*. *American Journal of Sociology*, 1948, *54*, 211–218.

Apel, K. O. Der Verstehen (eine Problemgeschichte als Begriffsgeschichte). *Archiv fur Begriffsgeschichte*, 1955, *1*, 142–149.

Argyris, C. Dangers in applying results of social psychology. *American Psychologist*, 1975, *30*, 469–495.

Austin, J. L. A plea for excuses. *Proceedings of the Aristotelian Society*, 1956, *57*, 1–30.

Ayala, F. J., & Dobzhansky, T. *Studies in the philosophy of biology: Reduction and related problems*. Berkeley: University of California Press, 1975.

Berlyne, D. E. *Conflict, arousal and curiosity*. New York: McGraw-Hill, 1960.

Berlyne, D. E. Motivational problems raised by exploratory and epistemic behavior. In S. Koch (Ed.), *Psychology—A study of a science* (Vol. 5). New York: McGraw-Hill, 1963.

Berlyne, D. E. *Structure and direction in thinking*. New York: Wiley, 1965.

Berlyne, D. E. Behavior theory as personality theory. In E. F. Borgatta & W. W. Lambert (Eds.), *Handbook of personality theory and research*. Chicago: Rand McNally, 1968.

Berlyne, D. E. *Aesthetics and psychobiology*. New York: Appleton, Century, Crofts, 1971.

Berlyne, D. E. Invited commentary: B. F. Skinner's Beyond Freedom and Dignity. *Journal of Behavior Therapy and Experimental Psychiatry*, 1972, *3*, 261–263.

Berlyne, D. E. Behaviourism? Cognitive theory? Humanistic psychology?—To Hull with them all! *Canadian Psychological Review*, 1975, *16*, 69–80.

Bitterman, M. E. The comparative analysis of learning. *Science*, 1975, *188*, 699–710.

Buber, M. *Between man and man*. London: Routledge & Kegan Paul, 1947.

Chomsky, N. *Language and mind*. New York: Harcourt, Brace, 1968.

Chomsky, N. The case against B. F. Skinner. *New York Review of Books*, December 30 1971, *17*(11).

Craig, W. On axiomatization within a system. *Journal of Symbolic Logic*, 1953, *18*, 30–32.

Crawford, R. L., & Jennings, R. (Eds.). *Phenomenology of particles at high energies*. London, New York: Academic Press, 1974.

Deese, J. *Psychology as science and art*. New York: Harcourt, Brace, 1972.
Dilthey, W. *Einleitung in die Geisteswissenschaften*. Leipzig: Duncker & Humblot, 1883.
Dilthey, W. Ideen uber eine beschreibende und zergliedernde Psychologie. *Sitzungsberichte der Berliner Akademie der Wissenschaften*, 1894, 1309–1407.
Dollard, J., & Miller, N. E. *Personality and psychotherapy*. New York: McGraw-Hill, 1950.
Freund, J. *Les theories des sciences humaines*. Paris: Presses Universitaires de France, 1973.
Geertz, C. *The interpretation of culture*. New York: Basic Books, 1973.
Giorgi, A. *Psychology as a human science*. New York: Harper & Row, 1970.
Harré, R. *The philosophies of science*. London: Oxford University Press, 1972.
Hebb, D. O. *The organization of behavior*. New York: Saunders, 1949.
Hesse, M. B. *The structure of scientific inference*. London: Macmillan, 1974.
Hull, C. L. Knowledge and purpose as habit mechanisms. *Psychological Review*, 1930, *37*, 511–525.
Hull, C. L. The problem of intervening variables in molar behavior theory. *Psychological Review*, 1943, *50*, 273–291.
Husserl, E. *Logische Untersuchungen*. Halle: Niemeyer, 1900–1901.
Ivanov-Smolenski, A. G. *Opyt obektivnogo izucheniia raboty; vzaimodeistviia signal'nykh sistem golovnogo mozga* [An attempt to study the work and interaction of the signal systems of the brain]. Moscow: Medgiz, 1963.
Jaspers, K. *Allgmeine Psychopathologie*. Berlin: Springer, 1913.
Koestler, A., & Smythies, J. K. *Beyond reductionism: New perspectives in the life sciences*. London: Hutchinson, 1969.
Koltsova, M. V. *O formirovanii vysshei nervnoi deiatel'nosti rebenka* [On the formation of the higher nervous activity of the child]. Moscow: Medgiz, 1963.
Locke, E. A. Is "behavior therapy" behavioristic? *Psychological Bulletin*, 1971, *76*, 318–327.
Luria, A. R. *The role of speech in the regulation of normal and abnormal behavior*. New York: Liveright, 1961.
Luria, A. R. *The working brain*. Harmondsworth: Penguin, 1973.
Morris, C. *Signs, language and behavior*. New York: Prentice-Hall, 1946.
Mowrer, O. H. *Learning theory and the symbolic processes*. New York: Wiley, 1960.
Nagel, E. *The structure of science*. New York: Harcourt, Brace, & World, 1961.
Neurath, O. Protokollsatze. *Erkenntnis*, 1932, *3*, 204–214.
Olds, J. Brain mechanisms of reinforcement learning. In D. E. Berlyne & K. B. Madsen (Eds.), *Pleasure, reward, preference*. New York: Academic Press, 1973.
Osgood, C. E. The nature and measurement of meaning. *Psychological Bulletin*, 1952, *49*, 197–237.
Peirce, C. S. Logic as semiotic: The theory of signs. In J. Buchler (Ed.), *Philosophical writings of Peirce*. London: Routledge & Kegan Paul, 1940. (Originally published, 1897.)
Piaget, J. *La psychologie de l'intelligence*. Paris: Colin, 1947. [*The psychology of intelligence*.] (M. Piercy & D. E. Berlyne, trans.). London: Routledge & Kegan Paul, 1950.
Piaget, J. *La formation du symbole chez l'enfant*. Neuchachatel: Delachaux & Niestle, 1945. [*Play, dreams and imitation in childhood*.] (C. Cattegno & F. M. Hodgson, trans.). New York: Norton, 1951.
Pribram, K. *Languages of the brain*. Englewood Cliffs, N. J.: Prentice-Hall, 1971.
Radnitski, G. *Contemporary schools of metascience*. Göteborg: Akademiforlaget, 1968.
Razran, G. *Mind in evolution*. Boston: Houghton Mifflin, 1971.
Rickert, H. *Die Grenzen der naturwissenschaftlichen. Begriffsbildung*. Tübingen: Mohr, 1902.
Rusterholz, P. Hermeneutik. In H. L. Arnold & V. Sinemus (Eds.), *Grundzüge der Literatur und Sprachwissenschaft* (Vol. 1). Literaturwissenschaft Munich: dtv, 1973.
Ryle, G. *The concept of mind*. London: Hutchinson, 1949.

Schleiermacher, F. Hermeneutik. In *Sammtliche Werke* (Vol. 3). Berlin: Reue, 1838.

Skinner, B. F. *The behavior of organisms*. New York: Appleton-Century-Crofts, 1938.

Skinner, B. F. *Verbal behavior*. New York: Appleton-Century-Crofts, 1957.

Spranger, E. *Der gegenwärtie Stand der Geisteswissenschaften und die Schule*. Leipzig: Teuber, 1922.

Stevenson, C. C. *Ethics and language*. New Haven: Yale University Press, 1944.

Thompson, W. R. Development and the biophysical bases of personality. In E. F. Borgatta & W. W. Lambert (Eds.), *Handbook of personality theory and research*. Chicago: Rand McNally, 1968.

Tolman, E. C. The determiners of behavior at a choice point. *Psychological Review*, 1938, *45*, 1–41.

Vico, G. B. *Principj di scienza nouva*. Naples, 1725.

Voronin, L. G. Stages in the evolution of higher nervous activity. *Soviet Psychology and Psychiatry*. 1973, *11*, 93–112. [Originally published in G. B. Voronin (Ed.), *Analiz assotsiativnoy deiatel'nosti golovnogo mozga* (No. 1). Moscow: Moscow University Press, 1972.]

Watson, J. B. Psychology as the behaviorist views it. *Psychological Review*, 1913, *20*, 158–177.

Watson, J. B. *Behaviorism*. New York: People's Institute, 1925.

Weber, M. *Wirtschaft und Gesellschaft*. Tubingen: Mohr, 1922.

White, S. H. Evidence for a hierarchical arrangement of learning processes. In L. P. Lipsitt & C. C. Spiker (Eds.), *Advances in child development and behavior* (Vol. 2). New York: Academic Press, 1965.

Windelband, W. *Geschichte und Naturwissenschaft*. Strassburg: University of Strassburg, 1894.

Zaporozhets, A. V. *Razvitie proizvol'nykh dvizhenii* [The development of voluntary movements]. Moscow: Academy of Pedagogical Sciences, 1960.

13

Floyd W. Matson

EPILOGUE

"Humanistic psychology" is a term which, after two decades of persistent invocation, still has a dramatic resonance. While its denotative meaning is, if anything, even less clear today than in 1960 (as the present volume strongly attests), its connotations are vivid, rich, and evocative. For most nonprofessionals, I suspect, the term conjures up a movement rather more social than psychological, springing from the youthful counterculture of the late 1960s and descending into the "me generation" and "culture of narcissism" of the 1970s. In this popular misconstruction of the term, humanistic psychology is the intellectual and moral armor of the Human Potential Movement. Its emphasis is insistently on the self—self-expression, self-actualization, self-gratification—and its credo is graphically conveyed by the notorious proclamation of the late Fritz Perls which adorned the walls of a generation of the self-absorbed: "I do my thing and you do your thing. I am not in this world to live up to your expectations and you are not in this world to live up to mine. You are you and I am I. And if by chance we find each other it's beautiful."

If that prayer to Narcissus describes the prevailing public image of humanistic psychology today, there is another and very different image which antedates it by at least a decade and which has run a parallel if quieter course through the intervening years. This is the composite portrait developed by a number of academic and practicing psycholo-

Floyd W. Matson • Department of American Studies, University of Hawaii at Manoa, Honolulu, Hawaii 96822.

gists in the United States who regarded themselves as dissenters from the twin orthodoxies then regnant in their discipline—namely, behaviorism in academic psychology and Freudianism in therapeutic psychology. It is this latter stream of thought and impulse, commonly known as the "third force," with which the present volume was mainly and appropriately concerned.

There is no need here for another rehearsal of the career and genealogy of the third force, which has been amply if selectively discussed by Giorgi, Graumann, and Weckowicz in the first part of this volume. But there are a few salient features of the movement which, I believe, have not received adequate recognition in these proceedings—due mainly to the inherent limitations of edited volumes—and which are important to a fully balanced appraisal of the origins, purposes, and significance of humanistic psychology.

The first of these has to do with the United States–American background, the particular cultural matrix, of the movement. Without minimizing the various streams of influence from Europe, it is reasonable to regard humanistic psychology in its third-force version as a characteristically American phenomenon—no less American, ironically, than its bête noir, behaviorism. Indeed, the persistent struggle between these two polarized standpoints might be interpreted as an expression of the peculiarly American dialectic in which realism and idealism have contended, from generation to generation, on the battlefields of social thought. In this perspective, the issue is simply that of mind versus matter: which is the prime mover in the affairs of men?

However, that scenario presents some difficulties. For one thing, despite its obvious idealist component, American humanistic psychology has its primary source in pragmatism, the very essence of the realist tradition. The psychological correlate of pragmatism, at the turn of the century and after, was functionalism—a school of thought and research which soon split into two disparate wings, those of Watsonian behaviorism and McDougall's purposivism. (To be sure, there were occasional attempts to synthesize the opposites or at least to blur the distinctions, as in Tolman's "purposive behaviorism" and G. H. Mead's mind-centered "social behaviorism;" but such efforts at reconciliation were seen to be more semantic than synthetic.) Pragmatism might appear to nourish the behaviorist school because of its emphasis on action ("behavior") as distinct from contemplation; but the action it affirmed was not that of the environment on man (as in the Skinnerian postulate) but of man on his environment. Dewey in particular was unremitting in his attention to the volitional, coordinated, and intentional character of the act—all the way from his early critique of the mechanistic reflex arc concept, in the 1890s, to his final thoughts on transactionalism more than half a century later. It is not accidental that Dewey preferred to speak of human conduct where others saw only behavior; his favored term conveyed, as it was meant to do, an element of responsibility, of organization, and of conscious purpose which was altogether missing in the ism of "behavior."

This pragmatic view of character and conduct was, of course, singularly American in its assumptive framework. It expressed the Yankee "will to believe" in the national myths of opportunity, individualism, and human freedom; in a land of beckoning frontiers, in an age of enterprise and invention, it was above all a psychology of coping, of doing and creating, striving and achieving. There was in it no hint of fatalism or resignation, of determinism either cosmic or cultural; there was only possibility, potentiality, and adaptability. The instrumental philosophy and functional psychology of Dewey and his school would have been immediately understandable to Thoreau and Whitman, and barely less so to Franklin and Jefferson.

The pertinent contribution of the pragmatists, then, was a distinctive psychology of the self—regarded as the active and resourceful center of personal experience—which provided the grounding for the later formulations of those American theorists of personality and motivation who constituted the first wave of humanistic psychology in the 1950s, notably Gordon W. Allport, Gardner Murphy, Abraham H. Maslow, George A. Kelly, Henry A. Murray, and Hadley Cantril, all of whom, except Kelly, became founding sponsors of the (American) Association for Humanistic Psychology. In such forms as Allport's personalism, Kelly's psychology of personal constructs, and Maslow's theory of self-actualization (anticipated by Kurt Goldstein, another AHP founder), this fundamental notion of the active self, with its attention to consciousness and cognition, flexibility and purpose, came to represent what might be termed the highest common denominator among the diverse expressions of American humanistic psychology.

But, a crucial point for the present discussion, in this interpretation the self is not only active but *interactive*. It is not a closed system but what Charles W. Morris has called an "open self." Again, it was Dewey who set the tone by his demonstration of the social and communicative character of all human action; there is a clear unwavering line from his initial emphasis on interaction to the transactional theory of Cantril and others in the 1950s. In the intervening decades, two major reinforcements of this "sociable" dimension appeared from theorists working different territories but sharing the same pragmatic tradition: the philosopher G. H. Mead, with his immensely influential system of symbolic interactionism, and the psychiatrist H. S. Sullivan, with his psychology of interpersonal relations. It is important to recognize the centrality of this orientation in the evolution of humanistic psychology because of the widespread belief (shared by Graumann, this volume, p. 13) that the movement has been preoccupied with the subjective experience of the solitary individual somehow sealed off, like the windowless monads of Leibniz, from all human connection. As suggested above, that may be the impression given by the self-indulgent subcultures of narcissism (with their derivative subliterature hailing the "new selfishness" and bearing titles such as *Looking Out for Number One* and *Winning Through Intimidation*); but these are pop therapies which derive their inspiration not from academic psychology, humanistic or otherwise, but from an older American folk myth of self-improvement and self-help which runs from Samuel Smiles through Dale Carnegie to Dr. Joyce Brothers and Werner Erhard.

Having sketched briefly a few of the characteristics of humanistic psychology which give it a singularly American visage, it should also be acknowledged that the movement has been continuously invigorated by infusions of European thought. To be sure, the transatlantic commerce has often seemed one-sided; if it is true (as Graumann and others maintain) that the American movement has made no significant impact on European psychology, it is plainly not the case that continental thought and research has left the Americans unaffected. Without European antecedents and precedents, it is doubtful that any of the American versions of psychological humanism could have developed at all. Just as Watsonian behaviorism presupposed the reflexology of Pavlov and Bechterev, so Allport's theory of personality depended on the personalism of William Stern, while Maslow's conceptual framework was shaped by a number of European mentors including Goldstein, Lewin, and Wertheimer, not to mention Freud. (It might plausibly be argued that Maslow was the preeminent exemplar of what John Seeley has termed the "Americanization of the unconscious.")

Mention of the father of psychoanalysis leads us to a stream of

European influence on the development of humanistic psychology which has been relatively underestimated, or at least understated, by contributors to the present volume. In their valuable assessments of continental "humanisms," attention has been concentrated mainly on the metapsychologies of phenomenology and existentialism. Granting the importance of these magisterial structures of thought, it is probable that their combined impact on humanistic psychology has been considerably less profound than that of the successive generations of psychoanalytic theorists—beginning with the members of the original "Vienna circle" and continuing through the revisionist writings of the neo-Freudian schools. This is not the place for a full accounting of the substantial debt owed to those followers of Freud who ceased to follow; but it may be in order to review briefly certain of the contributions which psychoanalysis has made to present-day humanistic psychology.

There was, to begin with, always something stalwartly affirmative and hopeful about the therapeutic enterprise conceived by Freud, as distinct from the psychogenetic determinism and reductionism of his formal theory. Where the academic psychologists of his time (and ours) generally dismissed the mind as an illusion or epiphenomenon and limited themselves to the observation of behavior, the new "depth" psychologist regarded the mind as independently real and (as ego) potentially responsible and so dared to probe the terra incognita of inner experience. Moreover, the analyst did not work alone; the patient was also a participant in the search for clues and the struggle for understanding. The dialogue of therapy rested fundamentally on the rationalist faith that, to borrow a phrase I have used elsewhere, men may know the truth (about themselves) and the truth will set them free.

In retrospect it seems that this therapeutic premise was more deeply apprehended by various of Freud's colleagues than by the master himself. While his own speculations became increasingly pessimistic as well as deterministic (especially with the introduction of the concept of instinctual aggression), others were moving in the opposite direction—so conspicuously so that, in the cases of no less than five major disciples (Adler, Jung, Stekel, Rank, and Ferenczi), the result was a succession of open breaks with Freud. These "deviationists," for all their differences with one another, shared a common dissatisfaction with the mechanistic reductionism of Freudian theory as well as a more affirmative regard for the capacities, purposes, and simple dignity of the person, both in therapy and in life. Adler has often been regarded as the true father (or forefather) of humanistic psychology by virtue of his emphasis on such aspects of personality as uniqueness (embodied in the concept of life-style), wholeness, purpose or will, and consciousness. It is not by coincidence that Adler's foremost disciple in America, Heinz L. Ansbacher, is listed among the founding sponsors of the Association for Humanistic Psychology.

This is not the place for a full accounting of the numerous contributions of the ex-Freudians of the first psychoanalytic generation to the pool of ideas and values which was to shape humanistic psychology; but there was one article of faith, to which they were all were committed, which has particular relevance. This was the perception of the therapeutic interview not in terms of the conventional power relationship of omnipotent doctor and sick patient but as a dialogical encounter (what Tillich was to call a "loving contest") between partners mutually engaged in the search for understanding. Psychotherapy, according to Adler, "is an exercise in cooperation and a test of cooperation. We can succeed only if we are genuinely interested in the other. We must be able to see with his eyes and listen with his ears." Jung was even more insistent on the reciprocity and virtual equality of the relationship and came to regard it as a model for interpersonal relations in the everyday world. This sense of the therapeutic dialogue, with its implicit respect for the client and its demand for sympathetic engagement rather than objective detachment on the part of the therapist, was further elaborated by Rank in his specialized concept of "relationship," which began as a technique of treatment and developed into a dialectical theory of human nature and conduct. It was Rank's "democratization" of therapy, as it might be called—severely delimiting the authority of the therapist while maximizing the client's powers of self-determination—which provided a clear precedent for the client-centered and nondirective approaches to counseling later made famous by Carl R. Rogers, one of the key figures in the development of humanistic psychology.

As is well known, the second generation of psychoanalytic thinkers, the so-called neo-Freudians of the 1930s and 1940s, greatly broadened this relational or interpersonal component to include culture and society as a whole. At the hands of Fromm and Horney in particular, psychoanalytic thought entered the domain of social psychology and represented a new form of philosophical anthropology. Here was no privatized vision of an encapsulated and feral self, living out a Robinson Crusoe existence in splendid isolation from human society; rather it was an image of the person as firmly situated (to use Graumann's term, p. 15, this volume) in a matrix of affiliations and associations. But to be situated in society was not to be mired in it; the neo-Freudians were not cultural determinists. Man, as Fromm insisted, is the creator as well as the creature of his culture; he is not only a part of society but apart from it, "forced to be free" by a human nature that has attained self-consciousness and strives toward self-realization. In their stress on the potentially autonomous self, as well as on the wholeness and uniqueness of individual personality, the post-Freudian revisionists working and writing in America since the mid-1930s exerted a direct and immediate influence on the humanizing trends in psychology during the 1940s and 1950s; and it is instructive to recall that Fromm was himself among the founding sponsors of AHP. (Another of the founders, incidentally, was the sociologist David Riesman, whose landmark study of social character in America, *The Lonely Crowd,* depended for its psychological underpinnings on the work of Fromm.)

It should be apparent from even this brief review of two parallel seedbeds of contemporary humanistic psychology—the American pragmatic tradition and the European psychoanalytic tradition—that the movement cannot be categorized simply as an expression of sensual and self-infatuated hedonism or as a sui generis phenomenon of the turbulent 1960s, a rebellious orphan lacking legitimate parentage. The latter image of a rebellion without much cause (implicit in Berlyne's treatment in this volume, pp. 261–293, "Humanistic Psychology as a Protest Movement") conveys the impression of a cult of irrationalists hostile to science and reason, intent on smashing the idols of the laboratory like so many latterday Luddites. There is, no doubt, a germ of truth in this caricature; humanistic psychology is indeed a movement, both of thought and praxis (therapeutic if not cultural), and its voluminous literature is replete with manifestoes, declarations, and rhetorical catchphrases such as the "third force." In this regard, of course, humanistic psychology resembles nothing so much as the behaviorist movement in its Watsonian heyday—unless it is the psychoanalytic movement in its Freudian insurgency.

But it would be a serious error to suppose that the major expositors of humanistic psychology are opposed to "science" when in fact they have been prominently and persistently engaged in an ambitious attempt to construct (or reconstruct) a psychological science appropriate to its subject matter. This is true not only of Maslow (whose *Psychology of*

Science was based on the scientific philosophy of Michael Polanyi) but also of Murphy, Rogers, Kelly, Murray, Cantril, Charlotte Buhler, Allport, May, Schachtel, Jourard, Maurer, and Bugental, among others. What they have protested against, it should be clear, is not science but scientism—that is, the dogmatic adherence to a rigid and rusting definition, derived from seventeenth-century physics, of what science is and ever must be. Tennessen, in his lively and irreverent contribution to the present volume (pp. 253–260), has put the case unequivocally from the standpoint of a sophisticated philosopher of science: it is not only humanistic psychologists but a vast body of theoretical physicists, speculative biologists, historians of science, and scientific philosophers who have repudiated what Tennessen (p. 254) calls "the old, disintegrated view of the scientific enterprise." For those psychologists who still remain wedded to that antique model (many of them neobehaviorists, like Berlyne), the "very idea" of humanistic psychology must appear utterly unscientific if not antiscientific; but it should be noted that by their own standard, as Sigmund Koch has persuasively demonstrated, the entire field of human psychology (as distinct from animal psychology or "robot psychology") is very likely disqualified from admission into the tight fraternity of true sciences. At best, it is to be relegated to the second-class status of a "soft science," sincere and interesting but imprecise and unobjective, like its fuzzy-minded brethren of the social studies (sociology, anthropology, politics, history, and the rest). Perhaps this is as it should be; but it ought to be recognized that, if this judgment is to represent the consensual wisdom of the field, humanistic psychology is no worse off nor farther out than any of its counterparts.

It is not only the meaning of "science" that is at issue in this volume; it is the meaning of "humanism" as well. Some of the contributors (notably Graumann and Giorgi), in search of genealogical authentication, have sifted through the assortment of humanisms, humanologies, humanistics, and humanities that have accumulated over the millennia since Protagoras built his prototype on the premise that "man is the measure of all things." That may still be the best statement of the case, although it would seem to exclude all forms of religious humanism except the one called the "religion of humanism" (which Julian Huxley publicized as "religion without revelation"). If man is the measure, as Joseph Wood Krutch suggested a generation ago, then it is risky to take the measure of man, that is, to appraise him by a "higher" standard or to alter his dimensions to fit an external pattern. That is why the issue of experimentation on persons, of "human guinea pigs," remains alive in the behavioral sciences. For, whatever else it may be, any humanism worthy of the name must surely begin with respect for the humanness, the inherent dignity, of its subject matter; if it believes human nature to be at bottom wicked, corrupt, or empty, it may indeed be successful in its experiments and efficient in its engineering (it may turn some men into machines and others into vegetables), but it should not be permitted to masquerade as a humanism. Nor will it do to accept the plea of "humane" intentions as verification of a claim to humanism; as Giorgi has observed, in effect, everyone can cop that plea. Machiavelli only wanted the unification of Italy, after all, surely a good intention at the time; and the Grand Inquisitor sought only the happiness of his flock in silencing all that mischievous talk of freedom. Similarly, the road to *Walden Two* is paved with the good intentions of its founder.

All psychologists, like all scientists and all poets, are in fact committed to one or another set of "good intentions," that is, of values. Not all, however, are comfortable with this disposition, which is often regarded as a frailty and a bias that should be thoroughly suppressed (how embarrassing to be informed, in a whisper, that one's bias is showing). Those adherents to the venerable creed variously known as value neutrality, value freedom, or total objectivity would do well to ponder the probable consequences for humanity were they ever in actuality to attain their goal (i.e., to be perfectly free of values and valuation). Something like that eventuality was envisioned a generation ago by the founder of cybernetics, Norbert Wiener, who made us aware of the apocalypse that would almost certainly result from placing our destinies in the mechanical arms of a pure intelligence devoid of sympathy for human aims. The urgent message contained in his book of prophecy, *The Human Use of Human Beings,* was that of a visionary scientist who was also, unmistakably, a humanist.

Humanistic psychologists have had the temerity to flout the sacred myth of value neutrality by openly declaring their value commitment instead of denying or decrying it. In brief, they value humanity—both the original nature of being human and the potentiality of becoming "more human." There is a definite element of trust, and therefore of risk, in this evaluation; human nature is seen as a quality to be nurtured, released, and allowed to grow rather than as a thing to be constrained or reconditioned. To treat ordinary humans, young or old, with such inordinate respect is admittedly an act of faith; for if the humanists of psychology are mistaken, they may be liberating a race of monsters. Such was the fear, you will recall, which was felt by nearly all conventional psychologists when Pinel took it on himself to carry out the ideals of 1789 by unchaining the lunatics of the asylum at Bicetre. History has already passed judgment on the unprecedented action of this famed practitioner of humanistic psychiatry; it is the hope of some of us, at least, that future historians will have the opportunity of judging the widespread practice and broadly felt effects of humanistic psychology.

AUTHOR INDEX

Italics indicate pages on which full references appear.

SUBJECT INDEX